WALTER WINK

WALTER WINK

COLLECTED READINGS

HENRY FRENCH, EDITOR

Fortress Press
Minneapolis

WALTER WINK
Collected Readings

Copyright © 2013 Fortress Press. All rights reserved. Except for brief quotations in critical articles or reviews, no part of this book may be reproduced in any manner without prior written permission from the publisher. Visit http://www.augsburgfortress.org/copyrights/contact.asp or write to Permissions, Augsburg Fortress, Box 1209, Minneapolis, MN 55440.

Unless otherwise noted, Scripture quotations are from the New Revised Standard Version Bible, copyright © 1989 by the Division of Christian Education of the National Council of Churches of Christ in the USA, and are used with permission.

The essay "Write What You See" is reprinted by permission, Polebridge Press, Willamette University, 900 State Street, Salem, Oregon 97301.

Cover design: Tory Herman

Cover image: Texture painting with paints © iStockphoto / Artem Povarov

Library of Congress Cataloging-in-Publication Data is available

Print ISBN 978-0-8006-9987-1

eBook ISBN 978-1-4514-6518-1

The paper used in this publication meets the minimum requirements of American National Standard for Information Sciences—Permanence of Paper for Printed Library Materials, ANSI Z329.48-1984.

Manufactured in the U.S.A.

This book was produced using PressBooks.com, and PDF rendering was done by PrinceXML.

CONTENTS

Foreword	vii
Marcus Borg	
Editor's Introduction	xi
Bibliography of Works Cited	xvii
Abbreviations	xix
An Autobiographical Essay: "Write What You See"	xxi

Part I. The Bible in Human Transformation

1.	The Bankruptcy of Biblical Paradigm	3
2.	Toward a New Paradigm for Bible Study	11

Part II. Naming the Powers

3.	Introduction	31
4.	Interpreting the Myth	35

Part III. Unmasking the Powers

5.	Introduction	63
6.	Satan	71
7.	The Gods	107

Part IV. Engaging the Powers

8.	Introduction	133
9.	The Myth of the Domination System	145
10.	The Nature of the Domination System	167
11.	Jesus' Third Way: Nonviolent Engagement	191
12.	The Acid Test: Loving Enemies	215

Part V. The Human Being

13.	Introduction	235

14. The Human Being in the Quest for the Historical Jesus	239
15. Jesus and the Human Being	251
16. The Human Being	301
Bibliography	305
Index	307

Foreword

Marcus Borg

I am pleased that this book of readings from Walter Wink's work is being published, for both personal and more than personal reasons. He was a close friend, beginning almost thirty years ago when we met at a professional meeting of Jesus scholars. Because of our friendship, I will refer to him as Walter in the rest of this foreword.

The more than personal reason is that he was one of the foremost American New Testament scholars of the last forty years. His many books and articles not only reflect thorough historical and interdisciplinary research but are filled with passionate applications to our lives today. The title of one of his earliest books, *The Bible in Human Transformation,* expresses the conviction that animated his vocation: the Bible has transforming power for individuals, communities and the world.

Walter's passion for the transforming power of the Bible flowed into his life. He lived much of what he wrote about. He never succumbed to the scholarly temptation to become a curator of a museum of ancient texts. More than most of his academic colleagues in the study of Christian origins, including me, he lived his life as a Christian intellectual who moved from thought to *praxis*. In workshops around the world, he trained people about *praxis*—practical means for changing the world. He engaged in perilous practice himself, including entering South Africa illegally during the decades of apartheid in order to encourage and equip black South Africans in the methods and goals of nonviolent resistance to oppression—methods and goals grounded in Walter's perception of God as revealed in Jesus.

Though I met him only in the 1980s, I had known about him since the fall of 1969 when I was in the first year of my doctoral program at Oxford. I had just embarked on three years of reading everything I could about the historical Jesus. I began with Jesus' relationship with John the Baptizer, his mentor. I read everything I could find on him, including Walter's 1968 book on John the Baptist. I was impressed. Indeed, I regarded him as the world's leading authority on John. Little did I know that he was only about thirty when he wrote the book, just a few years older than I was. But he was a "big name" for me "way back" in 1969.

In the decades since, my respect and admiration for Walter and his work continued to grow. Indeed, he was one of the two or three colleagues in New Testament scholarship from whom I have learned the most. In my life as an itinerant lecturer, I recommend his books wherever I go (and that's now almost two million miles).

My personal favorites are *Engaging the Powers* and his small book, *Jesus and Nonviolence*. I used both in courses that I taught for many years in a public university. Students loved them—and found them provocative, as Walter's books always are.

Not only have I learned much from him, so has the discipline of New Testament scholarship as a whole. Several of his major themes have become widely shared by mainstream scholars. Without trying to be comprehensive, I mention the following notions that have now become part of the "accepted wisdom" of many scholars of the New Testament and early Christianity:

- **The concept and language of "domination systems."** More than anybody else in New Testament studies, Walter has given us language for the most typical form of political and economic organization in the ancient world, and its importance for understanding Jesus, early Christianity, and, by extension, the Bible as a whole. And he makes it clear that domination systems continue in the modern and postmodern world.
- **The claim that Jesus advocated "nonviolent *resistance*."** Jesus resisted the domination system of his time and did so through nonviolent protest and advocacy: protest against oppression and advocacy of a domination-free order brought about through nonviolence. In Walter's exegesis of the familiar sayings in the Sermon on the Mount about loving enemies, turning the other cheek, going the second mile, and giving up your shirt as well as your cloak, he argues that these are counsels to and examples of active nonviolent resistance. Moreover, he takes the argument for nonviolence beyond the first century by describing the many times that it has succeeded as a significant means of social change in human history. Thus he counters the common notion that a commitment to nonviolence is unrealistic and argues that it is practical, wise, and right.
- **His work on "the principalities and powers."** This is connected to his emphasis on domination systems, of course. But it deserves separate mention as another of his distinctive contributions. Indeed, he wrote a trilogy on "the powers" as a crucial element in the early Christian understanding of the world. He then wrote a fourth book

on "the powers" in which he summarized in one volume his understanding of "the powers that be." He not only highlighted this theme in the New Testament, but helped to make us aware that "systemic evil" is bigger than any of us as individuals. Whatever we think ontologically of "the powers," they are real. Walter, more than any other New Testament scholar of our generation, helped us to see this.

It has been a privilege to write this foreword. Walter was a brilliant New Testament scholar, a valued colleague, a passionate Christian, and a dear friend. I commend to you not only this reader, but everything he wrote.

Marcus Borg

Editor's Introduction

Walter Wink died on May 10, 2012, at the age of 76, leaving behind a legacy of progressive Christian thought and practice that powerfully integrated social justice concerns and biblical scholarship. Throughout his long and productive career, Wink wore many hats, all of them well—a biblical scholar who made significant contributions to the discipline and brought interdisciplinary skills to the study of the Bible; a prolific writer of books, essays, and articles that speak to the inquiring ordinary man or woman as well as to practitioners and scholars; an activist for peace and nonviolent but aggressive resistance to evil who "walked the talk" and placed himself at risk in Latin America and South Africa; a pastor with a pastor's heart; a champion of gay rights; and a much in demand speaker and workshop leader with his wife, June Keener Wink.

Walter Wink's life and work demonstrate the reciprocal relationship between one's biography and one's bibliography. Indeed, one of his chief critiques of many of his colleagues in the guild of biblical scholars was the pervasive "false consciousness" of objectivism that separates "theory from practice, mind from body, reason from emotion, knowledge from experience."[1]

The ideology of objectivism encouraged and enabled a false perception of distance between life and work that blinded scholars to the impact that biography necessarily has on bibliography. As Wink noted in the first chapter of *The Human Being:*

> "Objective view" is itself an oxymoron; every view is subjective, from a particular angle of vision. We always encounter the biblical text with interests. We always have a stake in our reading of it. We always have angles of vision, which can be helpful or harmful in interpreting texts.[2]

In *The Bible in Human Transformation*, a devastating critique of the way the historical critical study of Scripture was being carried out—a critique that eventuated in his not receiving tenure at Union Theological Seminary—Wink asked two sharply pointed questions:

> Is anything but intellectualism possible when our questions do not arise primarily out of the struggle with concrete problems of life and society, from the blistering exposure to trial and error, from the

need for wisdom in the ambiguous mash of events? Can historical criticism, practiced in the academy, ensnared in an objectivist ideology, ever do more than simply refer the data of the text *away from an encounter with experience* and back to its own uncontrolled premises?[3]

It is not hard to understand why, when the time for a tenure vote came, Wink's fellow biblical faculty at Union voted it down. In spite of the cost, throughout his career Wink demonstrated great courage in continuing to stand for objectivity in research while standing against the ideology of objectivism that, in his estimation, stultified the practice of biblical scholarship in the academy. At the same time, he insisted on recognition of the roles "emotions, will, interests, and bias" play in the life—and thus the work—of scholars, while warning against equally stultifying subjectivism.

Wink's concern to integrate experience and reason began in his college years. In an autobiographical piece, "Write What You See" (the title itself points to such integration), Wink traces his journey from a childhood steeped in Methodist perfectionism under the influence of a liberal Methodist pastor in Dallas, Texas to an "atheist phase" during college. In the summer of his sophomore year, Wink went to Oregon to work in a lumber mill. For a month or so he wrestled with the idea of God. Finally, his internal struggle led him to once again affirm the reality of God, but it was belief in a God with no content. In his own words: "I said the word 'God,' and something resonated as true, but I had abandoned my childhood faith and had not arrived at anything else."[4]

Before the summer was over, Wink, at the invitation of another roomer at his boarding house, attended a Pentecostal church where he experienced "the gift of the Holy Spirit." It was a deeply powerful, profound, transformational experience, the reality of which could not be denied.

After his return to college, however, Wink discovered that this not-to-be-gainsaid experience "threatened to split [him] in half, between reason and experience."[5] He could not tolerate the intellectual aridity and theological rigidity of Pentecostal fundamentalism, but neither could he repudiate his religious experience to satisfy his intellect. He found himself, still a student, with a complex but ultimately stimulating task, one that defines the arc of his career: "I was faced with the arduous task of trying to integrate this concussive experience with the rest of my life, and to figure out how to think about it in the context of science, history, politics, psychology, and theology."[6] The interplay between reason and religious experience is a bright thread that runs throughout Wink's corpus.

Another major theme that runs throughout Wink's work, and can be traced to this foundational religious experience, is his defense of the "intention of the text." The disinterested study of the Bible made no sense to Wink. It is a violation of the intention of the text, which is to further personal and social transformation.

His first book (after his doctoral dissertation was published in 1968), was *The Bible in Human Transformation*, published in 1973 (the title points to where he was headed). In this controversial study, Wink stated clearly that correcting "the failure of the old paradigm [of historical critical study of the Bible] to interpret Scripture so as to enable personal and social transformation today" was the task he was setting himself.[7] In his last major book, *The Human Being*, he continued the theme he had first addressed some 30 years earlier: "Historical study, while indispensable, is incapable of providing the kind of insights that can make the Bible come alive with the power to facilitate transformation—which is *the manifest intention* behind its writing and preservation in the first place."[8]

When Wink encountered a text exegetically, he was neither disinterested nor dispassionate. He allowed himself to be examined by the text he examined, questioned by what he was questioning, interrogated by a text that could not ultimately be domesticated. In this, as he saw it, he was yielding himself to the humanizing purposes of God. "No doubt a part of me wants to whittle Jesus down to my size so that I can avoid painful, even costly change. But another part of me is exhilarated by the possibility of becoming more human. *So I listen in order to be transformed.*"[9] Wink's use of the word "listen" with reference to the text is significant. From the beginning to the end of his career, "in the text [he] hope[d] to encounter an alien speech which is finally the self-disclosure of God."[10]

In my opinion, Wink's most important work is *The Human Being* where, in a way never before attempted or accomplished, he provided a masterful interpretation of the biblical son-of-the-man sayings. However, most fans of Wink's work would probably list the Powers trilogy—especially the last volume, *Engaging the Powers* —as his most significant contribution. It has certainly had an international impact and is an invaluable resource for reflecting on the nature of structural/systemic evil and domination systems in the light of biblical categories.

The genesis of the Powers trilogy again illustrates the close relationship between biography and bibliography in Wink's scholarship. As he explains in the preface to the first volume (*Naming the Powers*), Wink, accompanied by his wife June, spent a sabbatical semester in 1982 in Latin America, largely in

Chile. He had gone to experience life under Chile's military dictatorship, to get a firsthand look at the country's horrendous civil rights abuses, and to see how the churches were responding to the "everyday crush of oppression."

It was a traumatic experience; weeks of hearing the stories of the families of the "disappeared," of speaking with those who had been tortured by the government, of witnessing the poverty, hunger, and hopelessness concomitant to dictatorship left its mark on Wink. He became ill and disheartened and angry at both the oppressors and the oppressed. In his own words:

> The evils we encountered were so monolithic, so massively supported by our own government, in some cases so anchored in a long history of tyranny, that it scarcely seemed that anything could make a difference.[11]

He had experienced firsthand what he would spend much of his remaining career reflecting upon, researching and writing about—the "principalities and powers" that express the inner spirituality of the domination systems that throughout human history have bedeviled the lives of the many to the advantage of the few. Wink brought the questions—religious/spiritual, political, economic, social, psychological, philosophical—that emerged from his horrific Latin American experience to Scripture, seeking categories of interpretation and understanding that would lead to praxis. His masterful study of "power" in all its expressions in the Scriptures and in contemporary life was the result.

In the first volume of the Powers trilogy, Wink lays the groundwork by identifying all of the biblical terms for "power," exegeting them within their context, and then offering an interpretation of "the Powers" as the inner spiritual aspect of material reality in general, and structures and systems in particular. In so doing, he returns to the church biblical language capable of critically addressing the nuances of power and its expressions in the contemporary world.

In the second volume (*Unmasking the Powers*), Wink looks in depth at seven of the Powers mentioned in Scripture and identified in the first volume. Wink's intention in "unmasking" the Powers is to make visible in the contemporary context realities that materialistic reductionism has banished from view:

> . . . a reassessment of these Powers—angels, demons, gods, elements, the devil—allows us to reclaim, name, and comprehend types of experiences that materialism renders mute and inexpressible. We have the experiences but miss their meaning. Unable to name our experiences of these intermediate powers of existence, we are simply

constrained by them compulsively. They are never more powerful than when they are unconscious. Their capacity to bless us are thwarted, their capacity to possess us augmented. Unmasking these Powers can mean for us initiation into a dimension of reality "not known, because not looked for," in T. S. Eliot's words.[12]

Wink has given us language with which to understand and express experiences that a materialistic worldview would rather not talk about.

In the third volume (*Engaging the Powers*), Wink brings the conversation into the contemporary world with a profound discussion of the role of violence in general, and the "myth of redemptive violence" in particular, in modern life. In previous volumes he had argued persuasively that the Powers were the "hidden interiority" or spiritual aspect of material reality. In this volume he examines their more visible institutionalized, structural, systemic forms. However, as the title suggests, he does it with an eye toward praxis, toward engagement that aggressively but nonviolently resists the structures of domination.

His sabbatical experience in Chile had led Wink to believe that nonviolent but aggressive resistance was the only way to resist and overcome the institutionalized, systemic evil that he had witnessed firsthand. In 1986, this conviction took him to South Africa on sabbatical leave; the result was a small but immensely influential book titled *Violence and Nonviolence in South Africa*. This little book was later reworked both into a chapter in *Engaging the Powers* and into a standalone volume (*Jesus and Nonviolence: A Third Way*, 2003). During a subsequent—and unauthorized—visit to South Africa in 1988, Wink moved about doing workshops on peace and nonviolence until he was expelled by the South African government. Once again we see the foundational place of experience in Wink's scholarship and his ongoing concern for personal and social transformation through encounters with texts that interrogate and challenge.

This book contains a sampling of Walter Wink's work published by Fortress Press. Like the tantalizing variety of chocolates in a Whitman's Sampler, these selections from Wink's corpus are meant to whet your appetite for more. At the end of this volume you will find a complete bibliography of Wink's books. For a complete bibliography of articles, essays and chapters written by Wink, I refer you to *Enigmas and Powers: Engaging the Work of Walter Wink in Classroom, Church, and World*, ed. D. Sieple and Frederick W. Wieddmann (Eugene, OR: Wipf and Stock, 2008). This excellent book, written by friends and colleagues of Dr. Wink on the occasion of his retirement in 2005 from Auburn Theological Seminary in New York, offers cross-disciplinary insights into and appreciation for his body of work and his life. As always, and as it should be, Walter Wink combined bibliography and biography in a powerful way.

Notes

1. Walter Wink, *The Bible in Human Transformation* (Minneapolis: Fortress Press, 2010), 5.
2. Walter Wink, *The Human Being: Jesus and the Enigma of the Son of the Man* (Minneapolis: Fortress Press, 2002), 7.
3. Wink, *The Bible in Human Transformation*, 5 (emphasis added).
4. Walter Wink, "Write What You See," *The Fourth R*, 1994 (http://www.westarinstitute.org/resources/the-fourth-r/write-what-you-see/).
5. Ibid.
6. Ibid.
7. Wink, *The Bible in Human Transformation*, 47.
8. Wink, *The Human Being*, 12 (emphasis added).
9. Ibid., 16 (emphasis added).
10. Wink, *The Bible in Human Transformation*, 56.
11. Walter Wink, *Naming the Powers: The Language of Power in the New Testament* (Philadelphia: Fortress Press, 1984), ix.
12. Walter Wink, *Unmasking the Powers: The Invisible Forces that Determine Human Existence* (Philadelphia: Fortress Press, 1986), 7.

Bibliography of Works Cited

The Bible in Human Transformation: Toward a New Paradigm of Biblical Study. Philadelphia: Fortress Press, 1973.

The Powers Trilogy:

Naming the Powers: The Language of Power in the New Testament. Philadelphia: Fortress Press, 1984.

Unmasking the Powers: The Invisible Forces That Determine Human Existence. Philadelphia: Fortress Press, 1986.

Engaging the Powers: Discernment and Resistance in a World of Domination. Minneapolis: Fortress Press, 1992.

"Write What You See," *The Fourth R*, 1994. (http://www.westarinstitute.org/resources/the-fourth-r/write-what-you-see/).

The Human Being: Jesus and the Enigma of the Son of the Man. Minneapolis: Fortress Press, 2002.

Abbreviations

ANRW *Aufstieg und Niedergang der römischen Welt: Geschichte und Kultur Roms im Spiegel der neueren Forschung.* Edited by H. Temporini and W. Haase. Berlin, 1972–

B.C.E. Before the Common Era

C.E. Common Era

CW Carl G. Jung, Collected Works, Bollingen Series XX (Princeton: Princeton Univ. Press, 1954–78)

De gig. De gigantibus (On Giants)

IDB *The Interpreter's Dictionary of the Bible.* Edited by G. A. Buttrick. 4 vols. Nashville, 1962.

JB Jerusalem Bible

LXX The Septuagint

NEB New English Bible

NHL The Nag Hammadi Library, ed. James M. Robinson, rev. ed. (San Francisco: Harper & Row, 1988)

NRSV New Revised Standard Version

REB Revised English Bible

RSV Revised Standard Version

TDNT Theological Dictionary of the New Testament, ed. G. Kittel and G. Friedrich, trans. and ed. G. W. Bromiley, 10 vols. (Grand Rapids: Eerdmans, 1964–74)

TEV Today's English Version of the Bible (The Good News Bible)

* An asterisk indicates that the translation of the preceding passage of Scripture is my own.

An Autobiographical Essay: "Write What You See"

The title of this short autobiographical piece, written in 1994, elucidates a key insight informing Walter Wink's work—spiritual blindness impedes biblical scholarship; spiritual experience, spiritual awareness or "sight," opens the scholar to the transformative impulse of the text. In this piece, Wink traces the major movements in his spiritual development that led him to ground his scholarship in experience. From a childhood steeped in Methodist perfectionism and the ethics of the Sermon on the Mount, he moved into an atheist phase in college and, as a budding intellectual, adopted reason as his God. After some struggle, he returned to the conviction that God existed, but the notion of God had no real content for him. In the summer of his sophomore year that all changed when Wink had a powerful, transforming Pentecostal experience in which he received "the gift of the Holy Spirit." The power of that experience created for Wink a temporary conflict between reason and experience. The conflict was resolved when he rejected Pentecostal fundamentalism and began the life-long task of integrating his spiritual experience with his scholarship. It will not be hard for the careful reader of Wink's work to trace the continuing and positive influence of his Pentecostal experience on his biblical scholarship. After five years in parish ministry, Wink returned to Union Theological Seminary to teach and soon discovered that the "community of accountability" for biblical scholars had shifted from the church to the academic guild with the result that most biblical scholarship was irrelevant to the ongoing and contextualized transformation of faith communities and individual people of faith. He took it as his task to challenge that trend, insisting that (1) biblical scholarship be responsive to the real issues that faith communities and ordinary people of faith contend with, and that (2) the results of biblical scholarship be presented in such a way as to be accessible to those people.

Source: Wink 1994: "Write What You See". Reprinted by permission, Polebridge Press, Willamette University, 900 State Street, Salem, Oregon 97301.

My first vivid encounter with Jesus took place in the fourth grade, when I was expelled from Sunday school for rowdiness. My parents punished me by making me skip Sunday dinner and stay in my room. For my comfort, my mother handed me the Revised Standard Version of the New Testament, which had just been published. I began at the beginning, with the "begats," which the RSV rendered," was the father of." The farther I read the more fascinated I became. Here is the most important book in the world, I thought, and yet it doesn't make any sense. Why begin a book with this long list of ancestors? Thus was my curiosity about Scripture piqued. The pastor of my Methodist church in Dallas, from my first awareness until I entered college, was Marshall T. Steel, a graduate of Union Theological Seminary in New York, a Harnack liberal who preached only on the gospels, and a highly diplomatic and cautious advocate of the United Nations and racial integration in an atmosphere that was extremely conservative. My whole theology was the "Fatherhood of God and the Brotherhood of Man." I was never abused by threats of hellfire and damnation. I was untouched by fundamentalist strictures. I never heard the Pauline message; I was totally unfamiliar with the terms grace and justification. I was a Methodist perfectionist, steeped in the Sermon on the Mount, convinced that my only hope was to achieve the perfection demanded of me by Scripture and church and parent.

In my sophomore year of college I underwent an atheist phase (though I knew that the God whom I no longer believed in was still calling me to the ministry). One Sunday in church I heard a reading of Matt 6:25-34. "Consider the lilies of the fields . . . Seek first [God's] kingdom and [God's] righteousness, and all these things shall be yours as well." Suddenly it struck me: this passage—this promise—can be put to empirical, scientific test. Rather than simply doubt God's existence, I will make a trial of it. I will commit the coming summer to behaving as if it were true. Then I will know whether there is a God or not.

That summer I went off to Oregon to work in a lumber mill. Without any friends, thrown back on my own collapsed spiritual resources, I found myself one afternoon in a forest of virgin Douglas fir. At their feet were rhododendrons fifteen feet tall, in full flower. Previously, such a sight would have filled me with adoration of God, for the beauty of nature had always been my most immediate avenue to God. But now I felt totally alienated from what I beheld. If there was no God, there was no one to thank for the glories of nature, no way to commune with God through nature, no Other that met me in the things that have been made.

I tried reading my pocket RSV New Testament. For some reason I turned to Acts. The more I read, the more alienated I felt. The Holy Spirit poured out on the disciples, healings—none of it seemed possible. Either the whole thing was a lie, or at least most of it, or else my world was a lie, or at least part of it. As a college "intellectual" I had made reason my God. I was unaware that I had accepted the materialistic worldview while still holding on to the biblical worldview.

My doubts were, in fact, the consequence of trying to embrace two antithetical worldviews simultaneously.

After a month of wrestling in my soul, I came to the conclusion that there had to be a God. But there was no content. I said the word "God," and something resonated as true, but I had abandoned my childhood faith and had not arrived at anything else.

About this time I received a letter from a friend mentioning a five-day spiritual retreat near Portland. It was sponsored by the Camps Farthest Out, a pietistic prayer movement headed by such leaders as Glenn Clark and Frank Laubach. The leader of this retreat was Roland Brown, whose willingness to take time to talk with me and to pray for me was for me an incarnating of the love of God. In the closing worship, Matthew 5:25-34 was again read, and I reaffirmed my empirical experiment. The summer was half gone.

A woman asked me what I intended to do next. I had lost my job at the sawmill due to an industry-wide strike, and had been a migrant fruit picker for the previous weeks, sleeping in the town dump in Eugene and a barn in Salem while picking strawberries and cherries. I said I didn't know, but thought I'd head back to Salem. She said she owned a sawmill not on strike (so typical: a Christian with a non-union shop), and if there was a place, I had a job. But she couldn't find out till Monday. She and her companion offered to drop me off in Salem, though it was out of the way.

As we entered Salem, she asked if I'd mind if they stopped to see an old friend, the head of the Chamber of Commerce. She asked him if anybody was hiring, and he said, "Well, Carl Hoge is having a sale at his furniture store; maybe he could use a hand." Just then the doorbell rang, and in walked—Carl Hoge. Yes, he needed someone to restock furniture and be janitor. I had a job.

"Now, where will you stay?" the woman asked. I mentioned that someone visiting the retreat had offered to put me up at his place. The women demurred; they insisted that I let them put me up in a hotel. But it seemed logical to stay at my friend's home, so I had them drop me there, even though it was 9:30 p.m. and no one was at home. After an hour's wait, my friend and his father arrived—from the funeral home. My friend's mother had died just that day, and there I was, in the right place at the wrong time.

Next day I determined to listen more closely to the guidance I seemed to be getting. I set out with the rental ads in hand to find a room. In an uncanny way, it seemed almost as if the houses were speaking to me: "It's all right to stay here"; "No! Not here"; "Possibly." Suddenly I saw a house with a sign on the porch: "Rooms." Something said, "This is it!" A man was watering the lawn. I went up to him and said, "I have to stay here." He was sorry but the house was full. "That's impossible!" I blurted out. "Could you go look? Maybe someone moved out overnight." Well, he said, he could look, but he was pretty sure.

Just then his wife came out on the porch. I hailed her, saying I had to stay there. She said there was nothing—unless I were to sleep on a cot on the basement landing. I took it. She hung a bedspread for privacy, and gave me a lawn chair by the furnace. That would be my home for the next six weeks.

Next morning the landlady came walking down the basement stairs as I sat in the lawn chair. Without even turning her head toward me, she announced, "God has sent you here to receive the gift of the Holy Spirit." That's all she said. Within five days I had.

This was in 1954, several years before the earliest beginnings of the "charismatic movement." I knew nothing about the Holy Spirit, only what I had read in that virgin forest in Acts. One of the roomers, though in great pain in a body cast, took me to the Pentecostal church five blocks away. What happened next is set down in a letter I wrote immediately after the event in July 1954:

> Imagine me in a room full of people all singing choruses—simple sincere songs about us and Christ. The people all have their eyes shut, singing in prayer, some clapping, some reaching their arms up, yearning with all their hearts to have more of Jesus. Over on the side is a piano, a bass fiddle, and accordion. As we stood singing suddenly my fingers began to burn, tingle as if they'd gone to sleep. But they weren't! Circulation was unhindered. This burning spread to my arms. I wanted to lift my arms to Him, but pride held me back, and now pride chained my arms to my sides. Not thwarted, the tingling ecstasy spread to my knees, my feet, my back. It was as if some power had shot me through with electricity. I couldn't stand it! It was like nothing I'd ever felt before. I was crushed to my seat, mystified, confused—and still the echo of the tingling remained. I knew that something Real, something more powerful than dynamite had been playing over me.
>
> Then the minister rose and said, "Let's worship the Lord." On all sides people started singing, saying "Praise the Lord," "Hallelujah," "Thank you Jesus," making up the strangest experiences I've ever

witnessed happened. People began prophesying and speaking in tongues.

The most important thing is what happened after the service. At the close we'd risen again to worship the Lord, and the power of God was so strong in that group that it cascaded from heart to heart like pounding surf. Again that strange, overpowering tingling. I was crushed to my seat. I was dimly aware that the service was over, that those who desired to could stay and pray, but I couldn't move. I was knotted by conflict. One minister said, "Somehow I feel that there is someone in this room tonight whom God has something special for." As I was still under the surge of this electrical tension one of the preachers came up to me, took my hand and asked me if I was ready to serve the Lord no matter where it led me. When I murmured yes, he led me to the platform. Then the three ministers stood around me as I knelt, praising God and speaking in tongues and raising the most glorious din you've ever heard. Suddenly all my fears, pride, doubt, all my holdouts slipped away. It was just God and I, and the praising was a barrier to keep all else out.

Now the Power pulsing through my blood, my nerves, increases. My feet burn, tingle, as do my hands. Suddenly my legs are touched by heat. It spreads. [This is all the physical reaction. Actually this is dimly remembered, as my central consciousness was with Jesus in Paradise. That's all I sought. The rest—just happened to me.] I remember the glorious release as, kneeling, I stretched my hands to God. Then I remember being on my feet. Then I felt myself falling backwards as I stretched deeper and deeper into the burning light, as all my flesh throbbed with the wind of His passing. They caught me, but I didn't care. I was in Jesus' hand. I went down perfectly relaxed and lay there.

Then the power increased yet more. Now single spots were touched—my neck at the throat, my back, my tongue, my head, and always my hands, my feet . . . . A preacher said, "Praise Him, open your mouth." And suddenly I found myself singing, stronger, stronger still, making up melodies in complete release, complete abandon, complete love. Then I spoke a little in tongues, but fear held me back. I didn't believe in it, you see. I sang, and sang, and praised God. Then I was swept with such joy that I began laughing where I lay. Still I tingled. Then the waves subsided . . .

My landlady suggested that a fast might be a good complement to the experience, so I undertook a seven-day water-only fast. A powerful image came to me during that fast: a nail was being driven into an anvil. Such a thing is impossible, of course—unless the anvil is superheated. That is what was happening to me in the fast. Since then I have never been able to doubt the reality of God. During the "death of God" fad, I felt I should at least try to doubt God's presence, but I couldn't even muster a mild skepticism.

When I returned to Southern Methodist University and tried to share this experience with my friends, all but two thought I had flipped out. Yet I had never felt so sane. In some ways, however, the experience threatened to split me in half, between reason and experience. I found very quickly that I couldn't stomach Pentecostal fundamentalism. I had, after great struggle, offered my intellect to God, and had the very clear sense that God had handed it back, with the injunction to use it for God rather than my own ego. Those instructions said nothing about making a sacrifice of my intellect. So now, with very little help from church or seminary, and from only a few friends, I was faced with the arduous task of trying to integrate this concussive experience with the rest of my life, and to figure out how to think about it in the context of science, history, politics, psychology, and theology. That journey has been long and exhilarating, and I am grateful God found a way to make it even more complex.

For many years I shared that experience with no one else. Even now I feel a twinge of embarrassment at my nineteen-year-old exuberance. But that experience has colored everything I do as a biblical scholar. Historical research depends on analogy to understand the past. If we have limited analogues—if for some reason our life experience is truncated, or too narrow, or filled with anxiety about overstepping the permissible, then our capacity to understand the past will suffer as a result. A person raised in a rationalistic, scholastic religion, a religion circumscribed by deadly fears of heresy and dogmatically confined to an oppressive orthodoxy, is not going to be able to enter empathetically into the spontaneity and boundary-shattering milieu of the early church. As a result of my own experience, I have no trouble believing in the plausibility of some events that to some of my fellow scholars simply seem impossible.

Spiritual healing, for example, was part of the Camp Farthest Out and the Pentecostal experience. So when I became a pastor of a church in Texas, I inaugurated a healing service. Ministerial colleagues that I shared this with thought I was crazy. (This was 1964, before spiritual healing had made a comeback through the efforts of Agnes Sanford and the charismatic movement.) The Friday before our first healing service I received a call from a woman in our church who had just been told by her doctor that she had a tumor in her uterus the size of an orange. I cheerfully told her that would be nothing for God to heal, and to show up Sunday night. (I have never done that since!) Being of a literal cast of mind, she believed me. We laid on hands and prayed, and the next week she went back to her doctor. "I have the biopsy report here on my desk," he said, "but first let's have a look at you." Then, "Who's been messing with you!?" "Why?" she asked. "It's gone. Your tumor's gone!"

Because of that, and many similar experiences with spiritual healing, I have no difficulty believing that Jesus actually healed people, and not just of psychosomatic diseases. Other scholars, who have never experienced such healing, either in themselves or others, may find themselves totally rejecting the historicity of the healing stories. They might even defend their understanding of reality by deciding that the story I just told is untrue. This judgment, however, would be made not on historical grounds, but on the basis of their worldview, which is materialism. Historical discussion is often made to bear the weight of what are essentially differences of worldview, which cannot in principle be settled by historical method. Worldviews are constituted by what one believes about the nature of reality, and therefore by what one conceives to be possible. People with an attenuated sense of what is possible will bring that conviction to the Bible and diminish it by the poverty of their own experience. Consequently, one of the best preparations for historical work on the Bible is continually to expand the horizons of our experience, especially our experience of spiritual reality.

In that blue-collar parish near Houston I quickly learned that my inability to explain some aspect of faith or theology to my congregants was not the fault of their lack of intelligence or schooling, but of my not understanding it well enough. This learning has had enormous impact on my writing, not just in striving for clarity, but in overcoming the conceit of technical vocabulary and esoteric references that plague the academic field. I have come to the point now where I will write only what the average intelligent person can read, no matter what the subject or occasion (even if it is a gathering of scholars). This has resulted in the rejection of articles by the *Journal of Biblical Literature* and the *Journal of the American Academy of Religion* because my work is too "chatty" or "popular." But I refuse to abandon as my readership that vast and hungry throng of non-specialists who wonder why scholars only talk to each other and won't include them in the conversation. I can only admire Bob Funk's development of the Jesus Seminar Associates and his continually prodding the Fellows to speak and write in a way that includes them.

After five very educative years in the parish I returned to teach at Union Seminary in 1967. These were the years of the student revolution, the Black economic development crisis, and the Black Panther bail fund, all of which brought Union into incredibly exciting and vitriolic turmoil. New forms of governance were sought that were more democratic and participatory. It was a time of heightened consciousness about racism and patriarchalism. Through all of this I was attempting, with only small success, to relate the Bible to the upheaval we were undergoing. It had become clear to me in the parish that most biblical scholarship was irrelevant to the lived concerns of everyday people. The vast majority of scholars were now interested only in answering questions they were asking each other. The community of accountability among biblical scholars had ceased to be the church and had become the academic guild of professional scholars. Now, back in an academia under siege, I sensed all the more powerfully the impotence of the detached, objective approach to Scripture for dealing with the real issues of life.

I began searching for a better way to do biblical work, one that would place the relevance of the text for contemporary life not at the end of the endeavor, but include it from the outset. I began exploring the various technologies of the "human potential movement," finding much that was helpful to me personally and professionally in a general framework of narcissism and naïveté about the depth of human evil. But the real help came when I discovered the Guild for Psychological Studies in San Francisco. Led by a remarkably creative thinker, Elizabeth Boyden Howes, the Guild focuses through seminars on the life and teaching of Jesus, aided by a Socratic, questioning approach and the depth psychology of Carl Jung. I had already been in Jungian analysis and had used the Socratic approach, though not in seminary, so I found the Guild a perfect match.

More important, however, was what began to happen to me. I began to sense that I had to do something about the poverty of my own self. Otherwise, I would be unable to proceed closer to the mystery in Scripture, but would simply continue to circle its perimeter, accumulating ever more information without myself being changed by the encounter.

I am beginning to understand that no scholar can construct a picture of Jesus beyond the level of spiritual awareness that she or he has attained. No reconstruction outstrips its reconstructor. We cannot explain truths we have not yet understood. We cannot present insights that we have not yet fathomed. Our picture of Jesus reflects, not only Jesus, but the person portraying Jesus, and if we are spiritual infants or adolescents, there are whole realms of human reality that will simply escape us. In Revelation 1:19, the seer John is ordered, "Now write what you see." The problem lies precisely there, in sight: we can only describe what we see, and if we haven't seen it, we may miss the revelation entirely. It is my spiritual blindness that is the greatest impediment to my scholarship.

One of the early exercises in the first seminar I attended at the Guild in 1971 was to take the story of the Healing of the Paralytic in Mark 2:1-12 and internalize it by making in clay my own inner paralytic. I had a PhD and a prestigious academic appointment; I "had" no paralytic. Life was careening along just fine, I thought. But to be a good sport I tried it. Shutting my eyes as they suggested, I let my hands have their way. After a period of time had passed, I looked to see what my hands had done. They had made a beautiful bird—with a broken wing! I am no artist, and was simply astonished that my hands had done this. More significant still, I suddenly knew precisely what that broken-winged bird was in me: an atrophied feeling function. Thus began the task of recovering my capacity to feel that was to last, in earnest, for the next eight years.

I immediately adapted what I was learning to my classes at Union. The students loved it, but my colleagues were a bit put off by the notion of graduate students working in clay and pastels like Sunday school kids. Nor did they appreciate it when we bellowed the Lord's Prayer at the top of our lungs (in order to do justice to the imperative force of each of its petitions). When I published *The Bible in Human Transformation* (Philadelphia: Fortress Press, 1973), with its infamous opening line, "Historical biblical criticism is bankrupt," my fellow biblical faculty greeted it politely, with demurrers, but largely simply waited for my tenure to come up. When it did, they voted it down.

Since that book had also incensed large numbers of other biblical scholars, I found myself virtually blacklisted. Bob Lynn of the Union faculty was also overseeing the operation of a small continuing education and research center in the Union buildings, Auburn Theological Seminary, and took me on half time. The other half was assumed by Hartford Seminary, which had closed shop as a degree-granting institution and was engaged in a project to improve church ministry. Thus began my new career as a peripatetic leader of continuing education events.

In time, my wife June and I began to do workshops together, using not only clay and pastels, mime and role playing, but also her own unique blend of meditation and movement. Now I am doing what I wanted from the time of my experience in Oregon: to lead people in an encounter with Scripture that can be transformative. God had also been providentially at work in my being refused tenure.

My concern with Bible study method was only the pedagogical side of my life in that period, however. On the scholarly front, William Stringfellow's *Free in Obedience* (New York: Seabury, 1964) had provided me a vision of how the biblical category of principalities and powers could serve as the basis for a social ethic based on the New Testament. The received wisdom till then was that the New Testament is only concerned with personal ethics; if one is interested in a social ethic, one must turn to the Exodus or the prophets. Work on the Powers series, first conceived as a single volume, grew into three, and occupied 28 years. The titles in the Powers trilogy are *Naming the Powers*, *Unmasking the Powers*, and *Engaging the Powers*. A related volume, *Cracking the Gnostic Code*, rounds out the understanding of the Powers in the early centuries of our era.

As a part of my preparation for writing about the Powers, June and I decided to spend a sabbatical semester in Chile in 1982, so that we might experience what it is like to live under a military dictatorship. I became increasingly convinced that nonviolence was the only way to overcome the domination of the Powers without creating new forms of domination. I decided to test this hunch in South Africa, where we spent part of a sabbatical in 1986. On our return I wrote a little book, *Violence and Nonviolence in South Africa* (Philadelphia: New Society Publishers, 1987), which urged the churches of South Africa to become more involved in nonviolent direct action against the apartheid regime. With the financial help of the Fellowship of Reconciliation, our little church in the Berkshires of Massachusetts individually addressed 3,200 copies to the black and white English-speaking clergy of South Africa. Later, the South African Roman Catholic Church sent out another 800.

The book infuriated some: how dare a white American male tell those who are already suffering to suffer more, voluntarily and deliberately. Even more anger came from those committed to a violent solution. But the book had its intended effect. Someone from the outside had to say what few inside could say without losing credibility. The book redefined nonviolence (which was heard there, thanks to the white missionaries, as nonresistance and passivity) in an active, militant sense, and did so by appeal to Jesus' own teaching. Within a year the debate had completely reversed itself (my book was only one of the factors) and the head of the South African Council of Churches, Frank Chikane, was calling on the churches to engage in active nonviolence.

In 1988 I was invited to return to South Africa to do workshops on nonviolence. When the government refused to issue a visa, the person who invited me, Rob Robertson, suggested that I try to enter illegally. First Richard Deats and I led a workshop in Lesotho (which I could enter without a visa), where we sang each day as our theme song "Thine is the glory, risen, conquering Son." Then Rob and I headed for the South African border. As we entered the border post, the soldier in charge was whistling—"Thine is the glory"! It was like a biblical story: the eyes of the soldiers were blinded (by an out-of-season torrential rain that darkened the border post), they couldn't see well enough to read, so they asked me to read my passport for them. They never even looked for the visa! Those two weeks were the only other time in my life besides Oregon that I experienced the moment-by-moment guidance of God in such complete abundance. I was never apprehended; I went cheerfully about doing workshops on nonviolence until time to leave, when we "turned me in" and I was expelled from the country.

My growing interest in nonviolence led to an appointment as a Peace Fellow for the year 1989–90 at the United States Institute of Peace in Washington. Without that year I don't know when I would ever have finished *Engaging the Powers* (a book that won three awards as "Best Religious Book of 1993.") During that year June and I also led workshops on nonviolence in Northern Ireland, East Germany, Iona in Scotland, and in London. I also made a solo trip to do the same in South Korea.

My preoccupation all these years has been to facilitate personal and social transformation through Scripture and art, movement and meditation. Now I am trying to turn full circle, back to the Jesus who has transfixed my attention all these years. I am slowly cranking up on a project on Jesus and the Son of Man. I participate with an uneasy conscience in the Jesus Seminar discussions about a database for the Jesus traditions. The discussions are so exciting and informative, the participants so brilliant and fun to be with, that I find it easy to set aside my objections to the kitschy (though decision-forcing) business of voting our preferences with beads.

My greatest hesitation about the Jesus Seminar is the idea that it is possible to build, from the bottom up, a perspective-free, objective database. Such a neutral, "pictureless" standpoint is impossible. Every analysis is value-laden. We cannot help projecting onto the texts our own unconscious needs and desires for transformation or confirmation, to say nothing of our socio-political location and biases. We need to take seriously the implications of the Heisenberg principle: that the observer is always a part of the field being observed, and disturbs that field by the very act of observation. In terms of the interpretive task, this means that there can be no question of an objective view of Jesus "as he really was." "Objective view" is itself an oxymoron; every view is subjective, from a particular angle of vision. We always encounter the biblical text with interests. We always have a stake in our reading of it. We always have angles of vision, which can be helpful or harmful in interpreting texts. Every description of Jesus is a form of advocacy, whether positive or negative. All lives of Jesus are a kind of apologetics.

Thus liberals will tend to construct a liberal Jesus, conservatives a conservative Jesus, pietists a pietistic Jesus, radicals a radical Jesus, and atheists an unattractive Jesus. Scholars who believe Jesus was like a cynic philosopher will tend to reject as non-historical any data that suggests otherwise. When the cynic school prevailed, for example, in the voting at the Jesus Seminar, the apocalypticists quit coming; this further skewed the vote. The Seminar is denied the fresh perspective that liberationists and feminists might bring since there are almost no women or non-Caucasians in the group. So the picture that is emerging of Jesus is remarkably like that of a tweedy professor interested in studying Scripture.

I have abandoned the quest for the historical Jesus, conceived as an objective, value-free endeavor. Instead, I am in quest of the originative impulse released by Jesus, and will value traditions regardless of their source, so long as they are faithful to that originative impulse. So I intend to ignore the Seminar's database and voting tabulations when I begin to write on the Son of Man.

What I will value, however, are the remarkable collection of papers on individual pericopes that we have all churned out, and the invaluable friendships that have developed in the course of our work together. Despite my hesitations, the Jesus Seminar has been the most rewarding experience I have ever had with my colleagues in the biblical field, and I am grateful to Bob Funk for convening us.

PART I

The Bible in Human Transformation

1

The Bankruptcy of Biblical Paradigm

The infamous opening line of this slim volume—"Historical biblical criticism is bankrupt"—defines the arc of Walter Wink's scholarly career. Faced with a scholarly discipline that was no longer commensurate with, or even cognizant of, its primary purpose—the spiritual transformation of individuals and communities—Wink courageously named the elephant in the room and set himself the task of both delineating and demonstrating an alternative approach to biblical studies. Wink notes that the writers of the New Testament were writing "from faith to faith" with the intention of eliciting or strengthening faith. He then argues that modern historical critical study of the Bible has abandoned the intention of the scriptural texts by adopting a false stance of "objective neutrality" over against those texts. This professed "objective standpoint" from which historical critical scholars approach New Testament texts, Wink asserts, masks the scholars' unavoidable but unquestioned subjectivity while negating the intention of the texts to address questions of faith arising out of the realities of life as it is lived. It also allows the biblical scholar to avoid being examined by the texts he or she examines, thereby subverting the intention of those texts to examine the examiner, to question the questioner, to interrogate the interrogator. Wink notes that the discipline's legitimate concern for objectivity has devolved into the ideology of objectivism and thus ignores to its own peril the role of subjectivity—emotions, will, interests, or bias—in the encounter with the text. This, together with a certain "technologism" that elevates technique over text, thereby limiting the scope of questions that can be asked and answered, leads to a discipline that, in Wink's view, has "outlived its usefulness as presently practiced." This did not make him popular with the guild of biblical scholars.

Source: Wink 1973: Chapter 1

Historical biblical criticism is bankrupt.

I use "bankrupt" in the exact sense of the term. A business which goes bankrupt is not valueless, nor incapable of producing useful products. It still has an inventory of expensive parts, a large capital outlay, a team of trained personnel, a certain reputation, and usually, until the day bankruptcy is declared, a façade which appeared to most to be relatively healthy. The one thing wrong—and the only thing—is that it is no longer able to accomplish its avowed purpose for existence: to make money.

It is in this precise sense that one can speak of the historical critical method generally, and of its application to biblical studies in particular, as bankrupt. Biblical criticism has produced an inventory of thousands of studies on every question which has seemed amenable to its methods, with a host of additional possibilities still before it. It has a method which has proven itself in earlier historical periods to be capable of remarkable achievements. It has in its employ hundreds of competent, trained technicians. Biblical criticism is not bankrupt because it has run out of things to say or new ground to explore. It is bankrupt solely because it is incapable of achieving what most of its practitioners considered its purpose to be: so to interpret the Scriptures that the past becomes alive and illumines our present with new possibilities for personal and social transformation.

How did biblical criticism become insolvent? Here are at least a few of the reasons.

1. The method as practiced was incommensurate with the intention of the texts.

The writers of the New Testament bore witness to events which had led them to faith. They wrote "from faith to faith," to evoke or augment faith in their readers. Ostensibly, historical criticism is not hostile to these intentions, but should serve to make the same decision for faith or unfaith accessible across the gulf of centuries to readers today. In actual practice, however, this seldom happens, and for good reason. For the very essence of scientific and historical inquiry in modern times has been the suspension of evaluative judgments and participational involvement in the "object" of research. Such detached neutrality in matters of faith is not neutrality at all, but already a decision against responding. At the outset, questions of truth and meaning have been excluded, since they can only be answered participatively, in terms of a lived response. Insofar as they are retained at all, "truth" is reduced to facticity, and the text's "meaning" is rendered by a paraphrase.

Such "objective neutrality" thus requires a sacrifice of the very questions the Bible seeks to answer. But if our questions do not anticipate a certain type of answer, how can we hope to receive it? If our methodology is not designed to reveal meaning, the possibility that meaning might emerge is blocked in advance, through the manner in which the problem is stated. Having initially turned to the text seeking insights about living, we find ourselves ineluctably drawn by our method further and further from the place where the text might speak.

This detached, value-neutral, ahistorical point of view is, of course, an illusion. For all empirical work can be carried out only on the basis of certain meta-empirical, ontological, and metaphysical judgments, and the expectations and hypotheses which follow from them. "He who makes no decisions has no questions to raise and is not even able to formulate a tentative hypothesis which enables him to set a problem and to search history for its answer."[1]

Historical criticism did operate, although covertly, on the basis of such meta-empirical underpinnings: a faith in reason and progress and an ontology of naïve realism. In the context of belief in progress, historical method became the means to delineate the development of ideas and institutions toward that historical apex modern times. It is clear in all this that the "objective standpoint" is none other than the historically conditioned place where we happen to be standing, and possesses no neutrality or detachment at all.

We will see later that the historical critical method had a vested interest in undermining the Bible's authority, that it operated as a background ideology for the demystification of religious tradition, that it required functional atheism for its practice, and that its attempted mastery of the object was operationally analogous to the myth of Satan and the legend of Faust. For the time being the point is solely that the fiction of "detachment" made vital relatedness to the content of the text impossible. By detaching the text from the stream of my existence, biblical criticism has hurled it into the abyss of an objectified past. Such a past is an infinite regress. No amount of devoted study can bring it back.

The biblical writers themselves never treated their own past in such a manner. Their past was a continual accosting, a question flung in their paths, a challenge, and a confrontation. But because the scholar has removed himself from view, no shadow from the past can fall across his path. He has insulated himself from the Bible's own concerns. He examines the Bible, but he himself is not examined—except by his colleagues in the guild! This disregard of the voices of the past, this systematic stopping of the ears and restraint of the will do not constitute objectivity but are instead the negation of the manifest intent of the subject matter.

The historical critical method has reduced the Bible to a dead letter. Our obeisance to technique has left the Bible sterile and ourselves empty. The further we have advanced in analysis the more the goal has receded from our sight, so that today many of us might well say with Nietzsche, "Ich habe meine Gründe vergessen"—I have forgotten why I ever began.²

2. The ideology of objectivism drew historical criticism into a false consciousness.

Objectivism as used here refers to the academic ideal of detached observation of phenomena without interference by emotions, will, interests, or bias. It can be spoken of as an ideology because it does not correspond to reality and is incapable of realization. The error of objectivism as an ideology lies in its intellectualism, its blindness to the irrational or unconscious, and its separation of theory from practice. Its falsehood lies in the systematic repression of its error.

Objectivism is intellectualistic. Intellectualism, says Mannheim, is "a mode of thought which either does not see the elements in life and in thought which are based on will, interest, emotion, and Weltanschauung—or, if it does recognize their existence, treats them as though they were equivalent to the intellect and believes that they may be mastered by and subordinated to reason."³ Intellectualism is characterized by a complete separation of theory from practice, of intellect from emotion, and finds emotionally determined thinking intolerable. When it encounters a mode of thinking which is necessarily set in an irrational context, as political or religious thought always is, the attempt is made so to construe the phenomena that the evaluative elements will appear separable from a residue of pure theory. Left obscured is the question of whether in fact the emotional is so intertwined with the rational as to involve even the categorical structure itself, thus making the sought-for isolation of the evaluative elements de facto impossible.⁴

Here the problem of the academy becomes unavoidable, with its endemic separation of theory from practice, mind from body, reason from emotion, knowledge from experience. Is anything but intellectualism possible when our questions do not arise primarily out of the struggle with concrete problems of life and society, from the blistering exposure to trial and error, from the need for wisdom in the ambiguous mash of events? Can historical criticism, practiced in the academy, ensnared in an objectivist ideology, ever do more than simply refer the data of the text away from an encounter with experience and back to its own uncontrolled premises?

In such a context biblical study is rendered innocuous from the start. Here we are trained to think in a framework which strives to negate every evaluation, every trace of mundane meaning, every proclivity toward a view of the whole. The result is a hermeneutic with whose categories not even the simplest life-process can be thought through. The outcome of biblical studies in the academy is a trained incapacity to deal with the real problems of actual living persons in their daily lives.

Objectivism is not simply in error, however. It is a false consciousness. Error is unintentional. Falsehood knows but has sought to forget its own face. Objectivism is a false consciousness because evidence of its error is systematically repressed. It pretends detachment when in fact the scholar is attached to an institution with a high stake in the socialization of students and the preservation of society, and when he himself has a high stake in advancement in that institution by publication of his researches. It pretends to be unbiased when in fact the methodology carries with it a heavy rationalistic weight which by inner necessity tends toward the reduction of irrational, subjective, or emotional data to insignificance or invisibility. It pretends to search for "assured results," "objective knowledge," when in fact the method presumes radical epistemological doubt, which by definition devours each new spawn of "assured results" as a guppy swallows her children. It pretends to suspend evaluations, which is simply impossible, since research proceeds on the basis of questions asked and a ranked priority in their asking. But such judgments presuppose a system of values and an ontology of meanings which not only give weight to the questions but make it possible to ask them at all. Even the choice of syntax and vocabulary is a political act that defines and circumscribes the way "facts" are to be experienced—indeed, in a sense even creates the facts that can be studied.[5] And finally, objectivism pretends to be neutral when in fact the scholar, like everyone else, has racial, sexual, and class interests to which he is largely blind and which are unconsciously reflected in his work. (Why, for example, do German scholars persist in using the offensive term "Spätjudentum," as if Judaism ceased to exist with the rise of Christianity? Why are there so few women and Black biblical scholars in this country? Why has hermeneutical scholarship so long ignored the rich tradition of Black preaching?)

On the American scene the problem has been exacerbated by the struggle to gain standing for departments of religious studies in secular universities previously closed to all religious instruction. In order to dissociate religious studies from denominational and dogmatic stigmatization, it seemed necessary to assert the scientific character of the discipline. The descriptive approach became the magic key to academic respectability. This has in actual practice meant objectivism with a vengeance, and accounts at least in part for the virtual abandonment recently (regardless of theoretical leanings, which were often of the best sort) of the beachhead which Bultmann had established.

Objectivity is much to be desired. But objectivity must be separated off from the ideology of objectivism and given new footing. A new type of objectivity is attainable, not through the exclusion of evaluations, but through the critical awareness and proper use of them. Lest this be construed as counsel simply to try harder under the old presuppositions, let us be clear that what is demanded in the face of bankruptcy is not a pep talk to the sales force but new management. If all historical knowledge is relational knowledge, and can only be formulated with reference to the position of the observer, we are faced with the task of developing a radically different model for the role of the interpreter vis-à-vis the text.

3. Biblical studies increasingly fell prey to a form of technologism which regards as legitimate only those questions which its methods can answer.

Technique is absolutely essential in any field of inquiry. But technique is essentially value-blind. It depends for its functioning on orders given outside its area of competence. It is all the more crucial then that the technique employed be commensurate with its object, for techniques can only produce those results for which they are created. I have already argued above that the historical method as practiced has not been adequately commensurate with the biblical texts. In this case the carrying over of methods from the natural sciences has led to a situation where we no longer ask what we would like to know and what will be of decisive significance for the next step in personal or social development. Rather, we attempt to deal only with those complexes of facts which are amenable to historical method. We ask only those questions which the method can answer. We internalize the method's questions and permit a self-censorship of the questions intrinsic to our lives. Puffy with pretensions to "pure scholarship," this blinkered approach fails to be scholarly enough, precisely because it refuses to examine so much that is essential to understanding the intention of the text and our interest in reading it.

Preoccupation with technique leads to a self-perpetuating reductionist spiral. Existing technique determines the direction of further inquiry, including the developing of additional techniques, which themselves presuppose the previous techniques, ad infinitum. In this process there is no room for an examination of premises, nor is there any capacity to question the appropriateness of the techniques employed for answering the questions which the text might pose.

Technologism need not be disastrous, whether in oil production or in biblical criticism. But it must be subordinated—always, in every field, without exception—to an adequate hermeneutic. Yet, in spite of remarkable strides in hermeneutical thought, biblical technologism reigns unchecked. The horse rides the horseman and the goal is not reached.

4. Biblical criticism became cut off from any community for whose life its results might be significant.

Historical biblical research, as long as it was situated in an antithetical position to orthodoxy, was the Wehrmacht of the liberal church. During this period its relationship to the vital centers of an entire community's life was crucial. Gradually, as success became assured, a shift took place. The community of reference and accountability became, not the liberal church, but the guild of biblical scholars. The guild, however, is not a community but a collective. It is simply a peer group on the model of any other professional guild, subject to the same virtues (preservation of high standards, rewards in terms of prestige to those deemed most worthy, centralization and dissemination of information, etc.) and vices (development of an "expert" ethos, invention of a technical esoteric language, repression of innovation, conformity to peer-group values) which characterize all other professional groups.

This removal of scholarship from a vital community had consequences disastrous for both. For the community it was disastrous because its own self-consciousness as a people under the Word was largely deprived of critical and constructive contributions. For scholarship it was disastrous because the questions asked of the texts were seldom ones on which human lives hinged, but those most likely to win a hearing from the guild. Historical criticism sought to free itself from the community in order to pursue its work untrammeled by censorship and interference. With that hard-won freedom it also won isolation from any conceivable significance. For since truth is not absolute, but only approximate and relational, its relevance can only emerge in the particularity of a given community's struggles for integrity and freedom.

Here the crisis in biblical studies links up with the crisis in the churches generally, since they themselves have become problematic as the locus of Christian community. For many liberal Protestant scholars in America, the most urgent question has become that of finding a context in which their interpretations of the Bible might have significance—or, stated more fundamentally, a context which would give that interpretation significance. Here, as at every other point, the crisis in biblical scholarship is seen as an epiphenomenon of a far more comprehensive crisis in the culture itself. . . .

To say that biblical criticism has now . . . become bankrupt is simply to summarize the entire discussion to this point. It was based on an inadequate method, married to a false objectivism, subjected to uncontrolled technologism, separated from a vital community, and has outlived its usefulness as presently practiced. Whether or not it has any future at all depends on its adaptability to a radically altered situation.

Notes

1. Karl Mannheim, Ideology and Utopia, trans. Louis Wirth and Edward Shils (New York: Harcourt, Brace & World, 1936), 89.
2. Ibid., 20.
3. Ibid., 122.
4. Ibid., 123.
5. R. D. Laing, The Politics of Experience (New York: Pantheon Books, 1967), 62.

2

Toward a New Paradigm for Bible Study

After critiquing historical biblical criticism as "bankrupt" in chapter 1 of The Bible in Human Transformation, *Wink proceeds in chapter 3 to offer a new paradigm for biblical study. He develops a "dialectical hermeneutic" which, in its movement from "fusion" to "distance" to "communion," allows for a reciprocal engagement between reader and text within which the personal transformation of the reader becomes possible. Such transformation is the original, but lost, interest in studying the text in the first place. Wink insists that his critique of biblical criticism is not that it doesn't work, but that it has gotten "stuck" in the second dialectical moment—the negation that creates necessary "distance" from both text and context but that also shields the scholar from the intention of the text to question the one who questions it. Rather than remaining safely stuck in the resulting subject-object dichotomy, Wink argues that the scholar must risk displacing the subject-object dichotomy with a subject-object relationship (communion) through, using Paul Ricoeur's phrase, an "archaeology of the subject" by the object. When subject and object are allowed the integrity to question each other, transformation becomes possible. In order to demonstrate how the movement from fusion to communion works practically, Wink describes a group study of the parallel Gospel stories of the healing of the paralytic. In the process, he returns to a place where biblical criticism, frozen in "alienated distance" from the text, cannot go—that place where the text can be experienced as the "self-disclosure of God."*

Source: Wink 1973: Excerpted from Chapter 3

By way of one such attempt at a new paradigm for biblical studies, I propose a dialectical hermeneutic whose dynamic moments might be schematically outlined as follows:

1. Fusion
N¹ Negation of fusion through suspicion of the object

2. Distance
N² Negation of the negation through suspicion of the subject

3. Communion

This dialectic would apply both to the exegesis of texts and to the history of interpretation as a whole.[1]

Between the naïveté of uncritical fusion with the horizon of one's own heritage and the sundering of that unity by the distance of objectification lies a moment of negativity which can be variously described as suspicion, alienation, doubt, detachment, temptation, or death. And between this alienated distance and the birth of communion lies a negation of the negation, a recoil of suspicion against the suspector, an analysis of the analyzer. This second negation opens the way to an interaction between reader and text that can make possible our own personal and social development today.

1. Fusion

In the beginning is the stream of tradition in which we live and move. At least for Western culture, however secular, there can be no reading of the Bible which is not already predisposed by a certain way of seeing, by key ideational preconceptions and preliminary intentions (why we read this text and not another) which are themselves a function of the influence of the biblical tradition. The tradition is our world, prior to all "objectivity," all conceptualizing, prior also to our own subjectivity.[2] It is so encompassing, so close as to escape notice. We see right through it; yet we can see nothing without it, since it provides the grid of meanings by which we filter the manifold of experience. It is our horizon. The idea of "the past" is already an objectification. But at the level of fusion, the past is the present of the heritage as the matrix in which we perceive our existence. Tradition furnishes us with our conceptions, it hides itself in our language, it provides the "available believable" which sets the parameters of belief, and it provides an orientation for the process of reasoning.

N¹: Negating the Fusion

First fusion, then confusion. A suspicion is planted. A doubt festers. One dares to question the tradition, to think the unthinkable. This is the first negativity, the achievement of distance from the heritage by means of its objectification. . .

Negation is here an essential objectification and hence distancing of oneself from prevailing cultural and intrapsychic images and preunderstandings, and consequently a dialectical moment of necessary alienation on the way to freedom and truth. Negation requires an initial suspension of prevailing understandings—"a flight from knowledge that is to be cured by knowledge. . . ."3

The Bible, wrenched from its matrix in ecclesiastical tradition, is thus objectified by critical scholarship. It was, to be sure, written by persons, but it can no longer be treated as an immediate Thou, since it has passed into the world of objects by virtue of the act of writing. It is the objectification of the thoughts, experiences, emotions, and visions of persons, but an object nonetheless. As such it has rights which the scholar attempts to champion, both apart from the tradition which enshrined it, and apart from his own enmeshment with it or bias against it. A special askesis is laid upon the analyst. He must seek to disentangle his and his culture's history from the text before him. He must attempt to withdraw his projections, overcome his defenses, achieve sympathetic penetration of the text in its otherness, and restore genuine distance through interpretation. It is this "otherness" in its fascination and mystery which requires protection against subjectivism, propagandistic exploitation, projected self-understandings, and all the other ways we generally fail to hear and see the other in its otherness.

Consequently, though objectivism has been exposed as a false consciousness, objectivity cannot be surrendered as a goal. It is more than just a special word for honesty, for what is at stake is an elementary respect for the other and its rights.

So the scholar distances the Bible from the church, from the history of theology, from creed and dogma, and seeks to hear it on its own terms. In this search he is sometimes aided by his tools, the "criticisms." They were well named: for source, form, and historical criticism not only prepared the ground for interpretation; they also provided the initial negativity required for distantiation. The knowing which knows it knows not is not immediately possible with a text ingested from childhood or perceived as an alien cultural superego. The "criticisms" serve the function then of decomposing the "picture" of Jesus and the early church delivered by Christendom. It is only after the negation of the ecclesiastical and intrapsychic images of Jesus and primitive

Christianity that we ourselves are thrown into the open space where genuine questioning, and hence freedom and truth, becomes possible. . . .

The judgment on biblical criticism is not, then, that it doesn't work, but that it has "got stuck" in the second moment of the dialectic of understanding. It has become fixed and immobile in the antithesis, rigidified in a necessary but alienated distance, and captive in its very victory. Unable to extricate itself from its own diabolical descent, objectivism must itself be negated to be transcended.

N^2: Negating the Negation

One always wanted to respect fully the distance of the interpreter from the text, but for the same reason one wanted also to overcome it.[4]

There can be for us no retreat from analysis, no flinching from the knife of criticism. However future ages may judge us, it has become our destiny to follow this way to its end. But that end is dialectical, not linear. Criticism rounds upon the critic. There is a further work of destruction, but this time a destruction of what destroys, a deconstruction of the assurances of modern man. There is another kind of suspicion, but this time a suspicion lodged against ourselves, against those who suspect what is suspected.[5]

Do not forget that, as Marx once said, the educator himself has to be educated; in modern jargon, the brain of the brainwasher has itself been washed. The historian, before he begins to write history, is the product of history. . . . It is not merely the events that are in flux. The historian himself is in flux.[6]

This requires that we put ourselves at a distance as a first step in overcoming the alienated distance of objectivism.

"To object": this is the counterattack of the object against the manipulative self-assertion of the subject. The object by objection can, for its dialectical moment of ascendency, subject the subject long enough to listen. This restores the true meaning of "object": objectum, something thrown in the way (from jacere, to throw, and ob, before). It becomes Gegenstand, not Objekt; that which stands over against us as resistance, opposition, and tension, as opposed to the passive recipient of a scrutinizing, active subject.

The greatness of Freud, says Bakan, lay not simply in his astounding facility for maximizing distance with respect to modes of thought in which minimal distance prevailed initially—things like dreams, slips of speech, or jokes. Rather, it was his enormous courage in the willingness to make, not just his own and his patients' dreams, but his responses to them, the subject of investigation. The result was a public psychoanalysis, one which relieved his own depression and opened the way to a new kind of therapy.[7]

What Freud achieved, biblical criticism has, on the whole, failed to do, remaining frozen in a distance that provides not a perspective for relating, but rather remoteness from view. We have failed not only to penetrate the object in communion with it; we have failed to be in communion with our own selves and to allow penetration of ourselves by the object. If objectification is the necessary flight from union wherein the subject renders itself invisible to analysis and hence invulnerable in respect to the object, then it is precisely at the point of subject-vulnerability that a way forward can be forged. . . .

Interpretation must now pass through a second negativity: the loss of our own emotional predisposition not to be unsettled, our easy acquiescence to contemporary questions, languages, and perspectives. We must pass through a fiery river of social and self-analysis in order to make possible what Ricoeur calls "an archaeology of the subject."[8] This archaeology is aided by two approaches: a sociology-of-knowledge analysis of the cultural role of biblical criticism and a psychoanalytically informed critique of the way we read the text. . . .

It is necessary then to struggle against our own forgetfulness of the question in the text, that is, to struggle against our own alienation from what operates in the question. This too, says Ricoeur, is a destruction, a deconstruction of the assurances of the destroyer. There is, he argues, a profound unity between destroying and interpreting; any modern hermeneutic must be a struggle against idols, and consequently it is destructive. In the language of the three great "masters of suspicion," it must be a critique of ideologies (Marx), a critique of all flights and evasions into otherworldliness or illusion (Nietzsche), a struggle against repression (Freud). "For what we wish is to hear through this destruction a more original and primal word, i.e., to let a language speak which though addressed to us we no longer hear."[9]

This more primal hearing cannot, however, be achieved by means of demythologizing alone. For there is a certain arrogance in making our world view normative for a demythologizing of the ancient world view. We have to struggle against the presuppositions of our own culture, against the assurances of modern man himself, in order to regain that "interval of interrogation" of which Ricoeur speaks, wherein the primal question can once again address us as the question of our own being. This limits demythologizing to the task of differentiating the etiological from the symbolic functions of myth. By exposing the scientific pretentions of the myth, demythologizing liberates its symbolic function. This permits a "second naïveté," a postcritical equivalent to precritical fusion, a return to the powerful immediacy of symbols—but all this on the basis of distance, on the basis of criticism and "demythologization."[10]

This recovery of the symbolic function requires that the thinking subject be "humiliated": that he abdicate his superior vantage point, given in the very semantics of the subject-object dichotomy. The image of Faust yields to that of Narcissus, confounded by his own reflection. It is the thinking-feeling subject, the cogito, and not just the object, the religious symbol, which must now undergo deeper exploration, in order that it can become open to the reality expressed in symbols. For this, Ricoeur proposes psychoanalytic psychology as an "antiphenomenology," the purpose of which is to conduct an archaeology of the subject as a means of reflection on symbols.

And because the activity of interpretation bears a reciprocal relation to the subject's personal history, the symbol gives rise not only to thought but to becoming, to individualism, to the metamorphosis of personality.

> The interpreter as he moves from symbolism to rationality will find that he must make another movement, back into the shadows of his ego and history, for he discovers that his being is mirrored in the reality of life and history and simultaneously created by him in the moment of comprehension.[11]

Let me illustrate how such an "archaeology of the subject" might look when carried out in reference to the story of the healing of the paralytic (Matt. 9:1-8; Mark 2:1-12; Luke 5:17-26). The procedure I am about to detail is one actually developed and in use by Dr. Elizabeth Howes and the Guild for Psychological Studies in San Francisco. The material reproduced is a conflation of several different seminars on the same text, drawn both from those in which I participated at the Guild for Psychological Studies and from my own classes. It is offered as a concrete example of at least one way in which the dialectical hermeneutic under discussion is being practically implemented.

Suppose a group of us is in a circle examining the story of the paralytic in a Gospel synopsis, using as our modus operandi a consistently maintained Socratic dialogue. Our leader guides us into the text by means of a carefully conceived series of questions, based on his or her own previous exegesis of the text.

First we analyze the passage, noting the differences and seeking to account for them.[12]

Matt. 9:1-8	Mark 2:1-12	Luke 5:17-26
¹ And getting into a boat he crossed over and came to his own city. ² And behold, they brought to him a paralytic, lying on his bed; and when Jesus saw their faith he said to the paralytic, "Take heart, my son; your sins are forgiven." ³ And behold, some of the scribes said to themselves, "This man is blaspheming." ⁴ But Jesus, knowing their thoughts, said, "Why do you think evil in your hearts? ⁵ For which is easier, to	¹ And when he returned to Capernaum after some days, it was reported that he was at home. ² And many were gathered together, so that there was no longer room for them, not even about the door; and he was preaching the word to them. ³ And they came, bringing to him a paralytic carried by four men. ⁴ And when they could not get near him because of the crowd, they removed the roof above him; and when they had made an opening, they let down the pallet on which the paralytic lay. ⁵ And then Jesus saw their faith, he	¹⁷ On one of those days, as he was teaching, there were Pharisees and teachers of the law sitting by, who had come from every village of Galilee and Judea and from Jerusalem; and the power of the Lord was with him to heal.¹⁸ And behold, men were bringing on a bed a man who was paralyzed, and they sought to bring him in and lay him before Jesus; ¹⁹ but finding no way to bring him in, because of the crowd, they went up to the roof and let him down with his bed through the tiles into the midst before Jesus. ²⁰ And when he saw their faith he said, "Man, your sins are forgiven you."²¹ And the scribes and the Pharisees began to question, saying,

say, 'Your sins are forgiven,' or to say, 'Rise and walk'? [6] But that you may know that the Son of man has authority on earth to forgive sins"—he then said to the paralytic—

"Rise, take up your bed and go home." [7] And he rose and went home. [8] When the crowds saw it, they were afraid, and they glorified God, who had given such authority to men.

said to the paralytic, "My son, your sins are forgiven."

[6] Now some of the scribes were sitting there, questioning in their hearts,

[7] "Why does this man speak thus? It is blasphemy! Who can forgive sins but God alone?"

[8] And immediately Jesus, perceiving in his spirit that they thus questioned within themselves, said to them, "Why do you question thus in your hearts? [9] Which is easier, to say to the paralytic, 'Your sins are forgiven,' or to say, 'Rise, take up your pallet and walk'? [10] But that you may know that the Son of man has authority on earth to forgive sins"—he said to the paralytic—[11] "I say to you, rise, take up your pallet and go home." [12] And he rose, and immediately

"Who is this that speaks blasphemies? Who can forgive sins but God only?"[22] When Jesus perceived their questionings, he answered them, "Why do you question in your hearts?

[23]Which is easier, to say, 'Your sins are forgiven you,' or to say, 'Rise and walk? [24]But that you may know that the Son of man has authority on earth to forgive sins"—he said to the man who was paralyzed—"I say to you, rise, take up your bed and go home." [25] And immediately he rose before them, and took up that on which he lay, and went home, glorifying God. [26]

| | took up the pallet and went out before them all; so that they were all amazed and glorified God, saying, "We never saw anything like this!" | And amazement seized them all, and they glorified God and were filled with awe, saying, "We have seen strange things today." |

The initial line of questioning might run like this:

Q.—How does Matthew's account differ from that in Mark? In Luke? How would you account for the absence in Matthew of reference to the four men, the tearing out of the roof, and the lowering of the paralytic? Why does Matthew not explain the charge of blasphemy? How does the ending of Matthew's account differ from the other accounts, and why? Which appears to be the earlier source?

Q.—What is the form of this narrative? What happens when you remove Mark 2:6-10? Would the scribes have responded the way "all" are said to do in verse 12 of Mark? How do you account for the presence of two discrete forms of the oral tradition (a healing story and a conflict story) in a single narrative? Has the church fused these, or are they expressions of a complex event? What light is thrown on this question by the distant cousin of this account in John 5:1ff.? Or by the similar complex forms in Mark 3:1-6; Luke 13:10-17; 14:1-6?

This line of critical questioning can of course go on indefinitely, to issues of context (the relation of Mark 2:1-12 to the conflict block, 2:1—3:6 and its prehistory), redaction, historicity, and so on. The leader must decide how far to pursue each line of questioning in terms of the available time, his own assessment of the value of the yield in terms of his careful preparation of the text, and the nature of the group's objectives. The issue is not whether we do justice to each question we can conceive of asking, but which questions require the greatest weight in the light of the specific exegetical task.

Rather than blending the Gospels into an undifferentiated harmony, we are able by means of this critical foray to see the actual differences between them. Our results are, however, less than conclusive. Is this account the fusion of a miracle story with a conflict story? If so, which if either is historical? Or is it, like three other healing-conflict stories and its distant parallel in John, a mixed form, reflecting perhaps a complex event? I am no longer confident that we can decide definitely either way. In situations like this, when the critical conclusions are ambiguous (as is so often the case), scholars tend to become dogmatic in order to defend the critical method. As a result, evidence is sometimes presented with more assurance than is warranted; what begins as a possibility becomes in the next paragraph a probability and ends as indisputable fact.

It just may be, however, that the critical procedure is more important than its results. By means of it we have achieved distance. It has undermined residual or manifest views of plenary inspiration, literalism, and bibliolatry, and has set the conditions for a pre-Christological and non-sanctimonious reading of the life of Jesus. In doing so we have brought to the fore the literary problems. It is not always necessary to solve them before going further. It may not even be necessary to dwell at any great length on critical prolegomena. In each pericope the problems of the text itself, and not the critical method, should determine the manner in which techniques are employed.

Now we seek to enter more deeply into the story, each person proceeding on the basis of those critical conclusions which commend themselves as most cogent. (It is a dogmatic fallacy to demand a consensus where matters of probability are concerned.) Working through the account once more, we now try by means of historical imagination to revivify the scene so far as we are able, with historical and literary data serving as continual checks on speculation.[13] This intermediate step enables us to ask what Jesus or the church understood to be the relationship between healing and forgiveness, what was meant by "the Son of Man," or what is presupposed in the pericope about the nature of God. Such factual questioning avoids premature self-reflection unchallenged by what is most alien or unexpected in the text.

This second line of questioning might include questions such as these:

Q.—Try now to picture this scene as it is described in Mark. For what purpose do the four friends bring the paralytic to Jesus? What do they do when they can't reach Jesus? What did Jesus "see" which he identifies as "faith"? What evidence is there as to the attitude of the paralytic himself? Why does Jesus speak of forgiveness? Does Jesus forgive him? How do the scribes hear him? What is meant by "which is easier"? Who is the Son of Man?

Once again, a third time, we take a fresh look at the text. Only this time the distance collapses upon us in an interrogation of the subject. It becomes necessary to ask how the text resonates in us. The insight that revolutionized the analysis of dreams—that the characters in the dream represent psychic phenomena within the dreamer—has a certain applicability to the analysis of other texts as well. For even if, unlike a dream, I did not produce the story in the text, its capacity for evocation depends on its resonance with psychic and sociological realities within or impinging upon me. It is therefore legitimate to introject the characters in the Gospel story as probes into one's own self-understanding.

A third line of questioning might proceed then as follows:

Q.—Who is the "paralytic" in you? That is to say, with what aspect of ourselves does this character resonate, if any? (long pause)

A.—It is the way I've been overacademized. The way I reduce everything to an intellectual exercise.

—It's the suppressed power I have as a woman, which is only allowed expression as bitchiness. Women weren't—aren't—supposed to have strength.

—It's the loss of my whole feeling side, my incapacity as a man to know how I feel about things that happen.

—My "paralytic" is a decade of semi-childhood lost. I don't know how to find it again.

—It's my inability to speak up in groups like this.

Q.—Now, who is the "scribe" in you?

A.—It's the part of me which is always judging me, making me feel unworthy.

—My "scribe" is my intellectualism. My theologian. My skeptic.

—The "scribe" in me is saying it doesn't like what you're doing in this discussion.

—It's the part of me that can think well of myself only by repressing all knowledge of the injured, imperfect, or evil parts of me. So it hates me for having a paralytic, and does everything in its power to keep it down.

Q.—But why doesn't the "scribe" want the "paralytic" healed—both in you and in the story?

A.—Because he can't admit that this too is a part of him. He wants too badly to think well of himself.

—That's why I'm so self-righteous around people who represent this part of me. I see in them what I can't admit is in me and then try to cut them down.

Q.—So what is the relationship between the "scribe" and the "paralytic"?

A.—Well, the paralytic is as bad off as the scribe, since he's internalized the scribe's judgments of him as being accurate. Isn't that why Jesus has to begin by forgiving his sin? The man accepts for himself the current notion that sickness is the result of sin.

—And if this is psychosomatic paralysis, he may be right. At least Jesus treats him as if his guilt is real.

—I think the paralytic wanted to be sick. I mean, if Jesus thinks he needs forgiveness, possibly the guy did do something that has led him to seek punishment unconsciously. And what better way than to be immobilized, incapable of sinning again! So Jesus has to go right to the heart of the matter and see if the man is ready to let his punishment go.

—Yeah, he's playing God, like, he judges and pronounces sentence on himself: You dirty sinner, I'm going to paralyze you for that!

Q.—Okay, this is speculative, but speculation based on what's given in the text and what is known of certain kinds of functional paralysis today. But how are the "paralytic" and "scribe" related?

A.—The paralytic needs the scribe to condemn him. The scribe needs the paralytic to feel superior to.

—So every "scribe" has his "paralytic," and every "paralytic" has his "scribe"!

Q.—Now, who are these four helpers? What resources are available to bring us to the healing value? What would it be like to marshal your paralytic and helpers to move to the healing source? That, after all, is what the story's about, isn't it?

A.—Do you mean inner or outer?

Q.—How would you answer that?

A.—I'd say both.

—I just wonder if I have four friends who would do this for me.

—In any case we don't heal ourselves. This isn't "self-actualization," but participation in a process which leads to healing.

—I'm getting really angry about the way this discussion is going. I feel as if we've just fallen back into the old trap of talking about it as if it were just a matter of understanding and straightening ourselves out, of self-therapy, or even group therapy. I've been down that road, and that's not where I'm at. For me the issue is forgiveness. Does forgiveness really happen, and do we know what it means actually to be forgiven? I mean, are we just going to sit around parading our hang-ups, or does God have something to do with all this? (long pause)

—Yes, why does Jesus use the "divine passive" ("Your sins are forgiven" as equivalent to "God forgives your sins")? Is he saying that God forgives his sin, or simply, look buddy, forget your guilt-trip, it's all over, like the whole sin thing is a big hang-up and Jesus doesn't buy it?

—I think that's a modernization. I think Jesus took sin seriously, but God more seriously still.

—Jesus was fighting for this cat's life. He's saying, right, you sinned, but here's a new start. The power that gave you life says, "Start over, you're all right, I love you. Now take off."

—Let me see if I can say what I'm feeling. The scribes think Jesus is claiming to forgive sins. Jesus may or may not be claiming that power—there's a tension between "Your sins are forgiven" and "The Son of Man has authority on earth to forgive sins"—but he is clearly asserting the man's forgiveness. The church certainly believed Jesus was forgiving his sins—at least in Matthew's conclusion: "They glorified God, who had given such authority to men." Could you say it this way: The healing power had its locus in Jesus. But it also had its locus in the paralytic. And Jesus could evoke that power in the man. And this same power continued to have its locus in the church.

—You're talking about the Holy Spirit.

Q.—Could you say that without using "Holy Spirit"?

A.—(After some discussion the group agreed on the following as the content of the phrase "Holy Spirit"): Jesus evoked the life-transformative process in the paralytic.

—That's why he had to come to Jesus. Someone has to spark it in you. If we could do it for ourselves, we would.

—But the man also had to do something. He not only had to come, but to trust Jesus when he was told to take up his bed and walk.

—Is that what is meant by the Son of Man here? Is that merely a title of Jesus, or does it refer to an immanent principle of eschatological wholeness in each of us? Is God transcendent God immanent in the Son of Man?

(The period ends. Each participant is given a bag of clay and asked to model their "paralytic" or their "scribe" in the light of the day's discussion and bring it to the next seminar.)

In this example we still employed the critical tools (source, form, redaction, historical criticism). Have we then contradicted what was said at the beginning about the bankruptcy of biblical criticism? Not at all. For these "tools" are now under new management. After every scientific revolution, as Kuhn points out, while the researcher still uses much of the language and methods he used before, he does so to different ends and within a different gestalt.[14] It is most certainly not a question of serially adding to the old techniques and tools new ones, such as sociology and psychology. That can take place under the old paradigm (and has!) without so much as touching the problem of objectivism. The issue from the outset has not been the need for new and better tools, but the solution of the fundamental anomaly of the field: the failure of the old paradigm so to interpret Scripture as to enable personal and social transformation today. The techniques and the "agentic" manner of thought employed by the historical critical method were themselves functions of the kinds of questions asked and the presuppositions shared under the old paradigm.

Theory and practice are therefore not so simply disentwined. In a certain sense the historical critical paradigm has been, like Paul's notion of the Law, our pedagogue till now. A new paradigm means both the supercession and the fulfillment of the old. It is necessary to assert this, on the one hand, against those who would incorporate the new within the old and, on the other, against any historical critical Marcionites who, out of justifiable frustration or simple sloth, are ready to throw over the old altogether. When we take up previous methods into a new totality we are not then "beginning with the Spirit and ending with the flesh." After all, it was precisely those who said that Christ was the end of the Law who ransacked the Old Testament like a treasure trove! So let me repeat: the new paradigm is a theory and a practice, indeed, a theory about a practice. As such it is constitutive of the entire ethos connected with that practice. To change a paradigm is thus to change theory, practice, and ethos. That the scholarship of the future will continue to need critical tools is indisputable; but which and how and in what measure—that is a genuinely open question.

It should be clear from the example that exegesis has been transposed into a holistic context in which questions of technique have been subordinated to the overarching purpose of enabling transformation. It should be equally clear, however, that such self-exploratory analysis is not subjectivism or intrapsychic reductionism, for the understanding of ourselves which the text evokes makes possible a far more profound understanding of what the text itself actually says. . . .

Everything said earlier about the bankruptcy of biblical scholarship can now be summarized in a single phrase: it "got stuck" in the Faustian moment of alienated distance. The consequence of this separation was objectivism: the subject-object dichotomy. The restoration of communion and genuine dialogue between interpreter and text depends on the practical resolution of the subject-object problem. . . .

It has been the argument of this book that one cannot get beyond the subject-object dichotomy except by going through it. In this sense the attempt to eliminate the subject-object dichotomy by an unmediated existential encounter is hopeless. That dichotomy is not only unavoidable; it is necessary, in order to fight free from the stream of life which carries us. But it can and must be transcended in a dialectical sense, not by its obliteration, to be sure, but by its transformation. The subject-object dichotomy gives way, by means of the archaeology of the subject, to a subject-object relationship. Alienated distance is bridged so as to become relational distance, in which the integrity of each party is preserved by the reciprocity of dialogue. Subjects and objects remain, each as object of the other, each as subject to the other. Together they become copartners in the quest of life. Having begun (fusion) as the object of a subject (the heritage), I revolt (distance) and establish myself as a subject with an object (the text), only to find myself in the end (communion) as both the subject and object of the text and the subject and object of my own self-reflection.

Thus there is achieved a communion of horizons, in which the encounter between the horizon of the transmitted text lights up one's own horizon and leads to self-disclosure and self-understanding, while at the same time one's own horizon lights up lost elements of the text and brings them forward with new relevance for life today. In this encounter some elements of one's own horizon are negated and others affirmed; some elements in the horizon of the text recede and others come forward.[15] Both text and interpreter have been called into question in terms of the answer they have given to the questionableness of existence, which has been given precise form by the text and by our interest in the text. Interpretation is then no longer a question of accepting or rejecting what is said in the text, but of self and social exploration in terms of the question which the text, possibly even in an inadequate or antiquated way, has nevertheless been indispensable in helping us to recover. That is why all knowledge is inevitably linked to the self-formative process of the knowing subject. "In this sense, then, every true hermeneutical experience is a new creation, a new disclosure of being; it stands in a firm relationship to the present, and historically could not have happened before."[16]

Such a conclusion does not imply subjectivism, either as manifested in a will to power over the object or as a projection into the object. On the contrary, it makes possible a genuine objectivity, wherein an interpretation is only able to grasp its object and penetrate it in a relation in which the interpreter reflects on the object and himself at the same time as moments of an objective structure that likewise encompasses both and makes them possible.[17]

Paradoxically, we are more certain of the unfathomable depth in ourselves, once it has been revealed to us in experience, both that it is and what it is, than we are of our own consciousness. And we know that the wholeness which we all at heart seek is not under our conscious control (though we must cooperate with it), but lies beyond us as a process to which we can only offer ourselves. This process gives itself to be known by us; it comes before us as subject in the relation of object. It meets us in the great myths and religious texts, preeminently in the figure of Jesus of Nazareth, and shows a knowledge of us which we ourselves lack. As knower I know that in the knowledge gained of the object I am first of all known. There is here an unveiling through the object that discloses to me a depth beyond my reckoning, a depth through which I begin to be released from egocentric stratagems and reunited with all creation.

If the subject-object relationship dialectically supplants the subject-object dichotomy, and in doing so establishes a communion of horizons, then there is worked a transformation of our life-relation to the text. The interests which motivated our reading, and the applications we hoped to secure, move from the fringe of consciousness to which they were exiled by objectivism, and occupy a place of honor in the full light of critical awareness. . . .

For too many of us too much of the time, our emancipatory interest in the text, which originally led us to seek in it the insights that evoke transformation, has been bribed by more superficial interests such as advancement, publication, or fame. These intervening interests are purely "agentic," however, and lack any practical relationship to the truth of the text. In fact, the question of truth is beside the point, for a publication need not be true to bring about public recognition; in some cases quite the contrary. Knowledge is thus separated from experience, theory from practice, reason from the interest in reason, scholar from life-context.

If, on the other hand, our interest is recentered around the depth-concerns of our existence—if, for example, we define our interest as the search for personal and social transformation in the light of the teaching of Jesus—then we already presuppose a process which makes transformation possible. And to seek the question which renders my own existence questionable is to assume that my not yet being what I am is encompassed by the possibility of becoming what I am but am not. When we "let the text speak," therefore, we do not value equally everything it has to say, but fashion an order of ranked priorities in terms of the resonances it establishes with our own unknown but higher potentialities. We know of this unknown through our or the text's unanswered questions. Therefore we do not listen just for what pleases us. Indeed, we learn to watch for what displeases us, what is most alien to us, since our interest is explicitly in being altered. It is because we do not know who we are that we need the text. For the insights which it makes possible are the means by which, in Ricoeur's words, we advance toward our being.

Apart from the initial conviction that knowledge is consummated in communion, the dialectic of interpretation does not climax in transcendence but only reversal, in an infinite series of reversals: the antithesis simply becomes a new thesis, which is displaced by a new antithesis, ad infinitum. We would not have entertained the first negativity had we not believed that our betrayal of the heritage would lead to higher truth. Why would we have busied ourselves with the very text which the heritage enshrines, unless we believed it taught another truth which the heritage had lost?

So we listen to the text. But with whose voice does it speak? It is a text still, not a person. It has no voice of its own. "Letting the text speak" is, after all, only a figure of speech. Whose voice? Bultmann's? Marx's? Jung's? Calvin's? Billy Graham's? The text is mute! So apart from the prior assumption, from the very outset, that something speaks through the text which called the text and myself into being, the text is cast into a swamp of total relativism, and interpretation is reduced to ventriloquy.

So I repeat: in the text I hope to encounter an alien speech which is finally the self-disclosure of God. That is the ultimate ground of the attempt at objectivity. For if I scramble the message, if I impose on the text my own subjectivity, I close off to myself my own transformation, including whatever social consequences hang thereon.

Notes

1. By "dialectical" I mean specifically a triadic movement from thesis to antithesis to synthesis. This establishes the schema of fusion, distance, and communion in a dynamic relationship which is tipped off balance forward so as to impel each successive step. For purposes of descriptive clarity such a model is justified. In actual practice, however, work is always more random, more hit-and-miss, trial and error. Historically, dialectic refers to many different forms of argumentation, from dialogue (Socrates, Plato) to disputation (the Scholastics) to a triadic universal process (Hegel). In reference to Hegel's use of dialectic, one should perhaps add that there should be no attempt to read a dialectical movement onto the physical universe, or to install it as a special logic. Nor does the thesis "produce" its antithesis; only our critical attitude does that, and its failure means that no antithesis is forthcoming. Similarly, "struggle" between thesis and antithesis does not "produce" a synthesis. The struggle is one of human beings, and they must produce new ideas. And the synthesis is not just a compromise; it usually contains new ideas which cannot be reduced to earlier stages of the development. Cf. Karl C. Popper, Conjectures and Refutations (New York: Basic Books, 1965), pp. 314ff. By dialectic we mean, following Bernard Lonergan, "a combination of the concrete, the dynamic and the contradictory." Insight (New York: Philosophical Library, 1957), 217; cf. also 421.

2. Richard E. Palmer, Hermeneutics (Evanston: Northwestern University Press, 1969), 132–33.

3. Lonergan, Insight, 200.

4. Ernst Fuchs, "Response to the American Discussion," in The New Hermeneutic, ed. James M. Robinson and John B. Cobb Jr. (New York: Harper & Row, 1964), 238.

5. Paul Ricoeur, "The Language of Faith"; this and another article to be cited, "The Critique of Religion," were translated by Bradley DeFord in the Union Seminary Quarterly Review, Spring 1973.

6. Edward H. Carr, What Is History? (New York: Knopf, 1961), 44 and 51.

7. David Bakan, Sigmund Freud and the Jewish Mystical Tradition. (Princeton, N.J.: D. Van Nostrand Co.), 232 and 251.

8. Paul Ricoeur, Freud and Philosophy, trans. Denis Savage (New Haven, Conn.: Yale University Press, 1970), 419ff.

9. Ricoeur, "Language of Faith"; cf. also The Symbolism of Evil, trans. Emerson Buchanan (Boston: Beacon Press, 1969), 349: "Beyond the desert of criticism, we wish to be called again."

10. Cf. Ricoeur's Symbolism of Evil, part 2.

11. Charles H. Long, "Archaism and Hermeneutics," in The History of Religions, ed. Joseph M. Kitigawa (Chicago: University of Chicago Press, 1967), 86–87; cited by Peter Homans, "Psychology and Hermeneutics: Jung's Contribution," Zygon 4 (1969): 351ff.

12. The text is taken from Gospel Parallels, ed. B. H. Throckmorton (New York: Thomas Nelson & Sons, 1949).

13. This procedure is comparable to the amplification method used in dream analysis, but with contributions from all participants. Cf. Elizabeth Boyden Howes, "Analytic Psychology and the Synoptic Gospels," Intersection and Beyond (1971), 152; available from the Guild for Psychological Studies, 2230 Divisadero Street, San Francisco, California 94115.

14. T. S. Kuhn, The Structure of Scientific Revolutions, 2nd ed. (Chicago: University of Chicago Press, 1970), 120–35.

15. Palmer, Hermeneutics, 244.

16. Ibid.

17. Jürgen Habermas, Knowledge and Human Interests, trans. J. J. Shapiro (Boston: Beacon Press, 1971), 181.

PART II

Naming the Powers

3

Introduction

This book, the first in what has come to be known as the Powers trilogy, was written by Walter Wink following a four-month experience living "under military dictatorship" in several different Latin American countries. He had gone to Latin America to see firsthand the human rights abuses and poverty that afflicted so many. The trip was research; the research was overwhelming. He returned to the United States ill and in despair over the monumental evil he had encountered—evil that his own country largely supported. While recovering from his experience, Wink read a book about principalities and powers in the New Testament. He disagreed with this book, but it drove him to do his own research in the hope that understanding New Testament conceptions of power might open up understanding of the structural and spiritual powers behind the horrors he had witnessed in Latin America. Wink argues against the modern mind's imposition of materialistic categories of interpretation on biblical notions of power, thereby masking the spiritual aspect of the exercise of power. In Wink's words: "I will argue that the "principalities and powers" are the inner and outer aspects of any given manifestation of power. As the inner aspect they are the spirituality of institutions.... As the outer aspect, they are ... all the tangible manifestations that power takes."

Source: Wink 1984: Excerpted from the Introduction

Power in Its Mythological Context

The reader of this work will search in vain for a definition of power. It is one of those words that everyone understands perfectly well until asked to define it. Sociologists and political scientists generally complain that no one (prior to their writing) has ever provided an adequate definition, but the definitions they offer are in turn rejected by others. This is all quibbling. The dictionary definitions of power will do quite well, as long as the word is not pressed to answer for the myth with which it presently keeps company.

Our use of the term "power" is laden with assumptions drawn from the contemporary materialistic worldview. Whereas the ancients always understood power as the confluence of both spiritual and material factors, we tend to see it as primarily material. We do not think in terms of spirits, ghosts, demons, or gods as the effective agents of powerful effects in the world. When the typewriter jams, I do not suspect a jinni of having jimmied with it, though I sometimes *behave* as if I did, nor do I lay on hands and pray for it, though I confess to having friends who do. No, most of us, if we are truly "modern," look for nonspiritual, material causes. What happens then when we moderns examine the biblical understanding of the Powers? Will we not tend to assume that what the ancients called "Powers" were merely little-understood manifestations of material power: the laws of physical power, institutionalized forms of corporate power, psychological forms of power, perhaps even various forms of psychic power? And whatever residue we cannot force into our material categories, we will tend to regard as "superstition." The ancients could not help it if they did not understand the physical laws of the universe uncovered by our science. They could deal with these invisible, unknown forces only by personifying them and treating them as if they were conscious, willing beings.

There is a fine irony here. We moderns cannot bring ourselves by any feat of will or imagination to believe in the real existence of these mythological entities that traditionally have been lumped under the general category "principalities and powers." We naturally assume that the ancients conceived of them and believed in them the same way we conceive of and disbelieve them. We think they thought of the Powers quite literally as a variety of invisible demonic beings flapping around in the sky, occasionally targeting some luckless mortal with their malignant payload of disease, lust, possession, or death. This view of their view finds its way into even the best modern translations of the Bible, where words like "spiritual" and "spirits" are constantly being added to the text gratuitously in order to make it clear that spiritual, not material, or material/spiritual, entities are involved. When we read the ancient accounts of encounters with these Powers, we can only regard them as hallucinations, since they have no real physical referent. Hence we *cannot* take seriously their own descriptions of these encounters—as long as our very categories of thought are dictated by the myth of materialism.

In short, our eyes and minds are themselves captive to a way of seeing and thinking that can only regard such entities as mere fantasies conjured up by the prevailing belief system. It is as impossible for most of us to believe in the real existence of demonic or angelic powers as it is to believe in dragons, or elves, or a flat world. For us the intermediate realm—what Henry Corbin has called the "imaginal" realm—is virtually unknown. We simply do not have categories for thinking of such Powers as real yet unsubstantial, as actual spirits having no existence apart from their concretions in the world of things. We play a double trick on ourselves, first personifying spiritual entities that are in fact not "persons," and then dismissing the creations of our own personifying as improbable, nonempirical, unscientific superstitions.

Thus a gulf has been fixed between the biblical writers and us. We use the same words but project them into a wholly different world of meanings. What they meant by power and what we mean are incommensurate. If our goal is to understand the New Testament's conception of the Powers, we cannot do so simply by applying our own modern sociological categories of power. We must instead attend carefully to the unique vocabulary and conceptions of the first century and try to grasp what the people of that time might have meant by power, within the linguistic field of their own worldview and mythic systems.

It is a virtue to disbelieve what does not exist. It is dangerous to disbelieve what exists outside our current limited categories. The three volumes comprising this study are themselves the record of my own pilgrimage away from a rather naive assurance that the "principalities and powers" mentioned in the New Testament could be "demythologized," that is, rendered without remainder into the categories of modern sociology, depth psychology, and general systems theory. The Powers, I thought, could be understood as institutions, social systems, and political structures. They would provide a means for developing a Christian social ethic from within the language of the New Testament.

Much of that proved true. But always there was this remainder, something that would not reduce to physical structures, something invisible, immaterial, spiritual, and very, very real. Perhaps knowing briefly where I came out in the concluding section of this volume would help the reader. I will argue that the "principalities and powers" are the inner and outer aspects of any given manifestation of power. As the inner aspect they are the spirituality of institutions, the "within" of corporate structures and systems, the inner essence of outer organizations of power. As the outer aspect they are political systems, appointed officials, the "chair" of an organization, laws—in short, all the tangible manifestations which power takes. Every Power tends to have a visible pole, an outer form—be it a church, a nation, or an economy—and an invisible pole, an inner spirit or driving force that animates, legitimates, and regulates its physical manifestation in the world. Neither pole is the cause of the other. Both come into existence together and cease to exist together. When a particular Power becomes idolatrous, placing itself above God's purposes for the good of the whole, then that Power becomes demonic. The church's task is to unmask this idolatry and recall the Powers to their created purposes in the world—"so that the Sovereignties and Powers should learn only now, through the Church, how comprehensive God's wisdom really is" (Eph. 3:10, JB).

This hypothesis, it seems to me, makes sense of the fluid way the New Testament writers and their contemporaries spoke of the Powers, now as if they were *these* centurions or *that* priestly hierarchy, and then, with no warning, as if they were some kind of spiritual entities in the heavenly places. In order to try to distinguish the material from the spiritual pole I will refer to the latter as the "spiritual aspect of the Powers." By that means I hope to make it clear that the Powers generally are only encountered as corporealized in some form. The implications of this view for healing the split between one-sided materialism and one-sided spiritualism are, I believe, extremely far-reaching. But I leave that for Part Three and the subsequent volumes. Enough has been said, at least, to provide the reader with a way to test the data to see if they do, in fact, support the hypothesis. . . .

To aid in the analysis of the data, let me propose a series of preliminary observations as guidelines.

> 1. The language of power pervades the whole New Testament. . . .
> 2. The language of power in the New Testament is imprecise, liquid, interchangeable and unsystematic. . . .
> 3. Despite all this imprecision and interchangeability, clear patterns of usage emerge. . . .
> 4. Because these terms are to a degree interchangeable one or a pair or a series can be made to represent them all. . . .
> 5. These Powers are both heavenly and earthly, divine and human, spiritual and political, invisible and structural. . . .
> 6. These Powers are also both good and evil. . . .

The six observations above will prove indispensable for evaluating the mass of data that must now be examined in order to establish how the Powers were regarded in the first-century world and in the New Testament in particular.

4

Interpreting the Myth

After examining the uses of the many terms of power in the New Testament and other sources in Part One of Naming the Powers *and then dealing with exegetical issues in Part Two, Wink turns in Part Three to the task of interpreting the meaning of biblical notions of power in their original context and for our context. Wink does not—as the ancients did—view the Powers as having a "separate, spiritual existence"; they are, rather, the "inner essence," the "inner aspect" or the "spiritual aspect" of concrete manifestations of power in institutions or individuals or groups of individuals. Clearly Wink resists the modern tendency to reduce reality to the material. He argues that reality is bipolar—those poles being matter and spirit—and he insists on the inseparability of the material pole from the spiritual pole. These institutions and movements, individuals and groups that variously manifest social and cultural, political and economic or military power, sometimes for good, often for ill, must in the quest for justice be addressed not only in terms of their materiality but also in terms of their spirituality. In the struggle against injustice, then, it is not enough to struggle only to change oppressive material systems and structures; it is also necessary to struggle for the conversion (liberation) of people from the spiritualities of those systems and structures that oppress them. As Wink puts it: "Evangelism is always a form of social action," and "social action is always evangelism, if carried out in full awareness of Christ's sovereignty over the Powers."*

Source: Wink 1984: Excerpted from Chapter 5

We ended Part Two having found ourselves in a cul de sac of interpretation. Ephesians 3:10 spoke of the church's task as proclaiming the manifold wisdom of God to the principalities and powers in the *heavenly* places. We were unable to find anything in the first-century background capable of making that intelligible within the limits of the modern worldview. But perhaps that point of unintelligibility was reached for some readers even earlier, when, for example, Christ was declared to have already put the Powers under his feet, or when God was said to have led them captive in Christ's triumphal procession, or when the Powers were affirmed as having been created in and through and for Christ. For the mythic dimension—the atemporal, cosmic, supernatural aspect of the story—was not inserted in the final text we dealt with, as if we had held back the worst for last. It has accompanied us from the outset, permeating every statement made about the Powers. We found, in short, that the mythic is not the residue left over and discardable after everything meaningful has been explained. It is the very framework of the entire notion of the Powers, the means by which they have been brought to language. For that reason a simply reductionistic explanation of the Powers is closed to us. They cannot be treated as "nothing but" the personification of human institutional and cultural arrangements, since these institutions and cultural arrangements are just as much the creation of the Powers as their creators. Reductionistic explanations are inadequate because they omit the one essential most unique to the New Testament understanding of power: its spiritual dimension.

There is a certain irony in the fact that liberation theologians have, in the main, followed the reductionist path and treated the Powers as *just* institutions and systems, with little attempt to comprehend their spiritual dimension or take seriously their mythic form.

The Powers Are the Inner Aspect of Material Reality

What might we learn if we listened to the ancient myth on its own terms and tried to decipher, by an act of interpretive divination, what is moving within it? The ancients regarded the spiritual Powers as nonmaterial, invisible, heavenly entities with specific characteristics or qualities. These Powers are the good creations of a good God, but all of them have "fallen," becoming more or less evil in intent, and may even be set on the destruction of humanity. They were called angels, gods, spirits, demons, devils. This view was carried by the momentum of Jewish apocalyptic thought right into the New Testament, but Paul has already taken key steps toward "demythologizing" or at least depersonalizing it by means of the categories of sin, law, the flesh, and death. I suggest we follow Paul's lead in this, and attempt to reinterpret the mythic language of the Powers. By this I do not mean to abolish the New Testament myth but to transpose it into a new key. Or, put another way, the goal is not "demythologizing" if by that is meant removal of the mythic dimension, but rather juxtaposing the ancient myth with the emerging postmodern (mythic) worldview and asking how they might mutually illuminate each other.

What I propose is viewing the spiritual Powers not as separate heavenly or ethereal entities but as *the inner aspect of material or tangible manifestations of power.* I suggest that the "angels of nature" are the patterning of physical things—rocks, trees, plants, the whole God-glorifying, dancing, visible universe; that the "'principalities and powers" are the inner or spiritual essence, or gestalt, of an institution or state or system; that the "demons" are the psychic or spiritual power emanated by organizations or individuals or subaspects of individuals whose energies are bent on overpowering others; that "gods" are the very real archetypal or ideological structures that determine or govern reality and its mirror, the human brain; that the mysterious "elements of the universe" (*stoicheia tou kosmou*) are the invariances (formerly called "laws") which, though often idolized by humans, conserve the self-consistency of each level of reality in its harmonious interrelationship with every other level and the Whole; and that "Satan" is the actual power that congeals around collective idolatry, injustice, or inhumanity, a power that increases or decreases according to the degree of collective refusal to choose higher values. The second volume of this work will devote a section to each of these Powers. It is hoped that my cryptic remarks here will carry readers through the remainder of this volume and ready them for the next, where these themes will be given thorough and practical amplification.

These "Powers" do not, then, on this hypothesis, have a separate, spiritual existence. *We encounter them primarily in reference to the material or "earthly" reality of which they are the innermost essence.* The spiritual aspect of the Powers is not simply a "personification" of institutional qualities that would exist whether they were personified or not. On the contrary, the spirituality of an institution exists as a real aspect of the institution even when it is not perceived as such.

Let me illustrate. A "mob spirit" does not hover in the sky waiting to leap down on unruly crowds at a soccer match. It is the actual spirit constellated when the crowd reaches a certain critical flashpoint of excitement and frustration. It comes into existence in that moment, causes people to act in ways of which they would never have dreamed themselves capable, and then ceases to exist the moment the crowd disperses. Or take a high school football team. Its team spirit is high during the season, then cools at the season's close, although it continues to persist to a degree in history (memories) and hope (the coming season). The spirit of a nation endures beyond its actual rule, in the lasting effects of its policies, its contributions to culture, its additions to the sheer weight of human suffering. And the spirits of things that just last and last, like rocks and trees, would appear to be eternal, but they too are inseparable from their material or physical concretions.

None of these "spiritual" realities has an existence independent of its material counterpart. None persists through time without embodiment in cellulose or in a culture or a regime or a corporation or a megalomaniac. An ideology does not just float in the air; it is always the nexus of legitimations and rationales for some actual entity, be it union or management, a social change group or the structure it hopes to change. As the inner aspect of material reality, the spiritual Powers are everywhere around us. Their presence is real and it is inescapable. The issue is not whether we "believe" in them but whether we can learn to identify our actual, everyday encounters with them—what Paul called "discerning the spirits."

If the "spiritual" Powers are the inside or essence of physical or social entities or systems or structures, then the long and inconclusive debate over whether the Powers are human or divine can now be ended. Like most such debates, its very inconclusiveness was evidence that each party held a portion of the truth which it could not in all justice relinquish and that the issue could be resolved only in a higher synthesis encompassing the truth of both. This theory appears to do just that. It understands the spiritual and physical aspects of the Powers to be inseparable but distinguishable components of a single phenomenon—power in its concretions in this world. The writers of the New Testament, as other writers of the period, could thus refer to now the spiritual (or inner) aspect, now the physical (or outer) aspect, depending on which aspect was more apparent or significant in the moment. If pressed, Paul would probably have readily conceded that spiritual forces did lie behind the Roman Empire. But when he wrote Rom. 13:1, he apparently was, *at that moment,* focusing on just those human authorities whom he describes later in the paragraph as wielding the sword and collecting taxes. In 1 Cor. 2:6-8, when Paul mentions the rulers of this age, his language can appear so ambiguous because he is probably thinking simultaneously of both human *and* demonic agents of Jesus' death. No doubt, however, some of his original readers, to say nothing of centuries of interpreters since, would tend to think he meant either human or divine powers, depending on their own bent. Elsewhere Paul could use the very same terms to speak of what seem to be primarily spiritual powers (Rom. 8:38-39), without needing to provide any explanation for the shift. And if in other contexts the writers heap expressions on expressions to indicate the full compass and sweep of power, earthly and heavenly, they use the very same words to accomplish that purpose. . . .

The very demons themselves, so long regarded as baleful spirits in the air, are pictured by the Gospels as abhorring decorporealization. When Jesus orders the "Legion" of demons out of the Gerasene demoniac, they plead to be allowed to possess a nearby herd of swine (Mark 5:12). The historicity of the conception is guaranteed regardless of the historicity of the event. The unclean spirit can find no rest without a physical body in which to reside (Luke 11:24-26). The sense is clear: demons can become manifest only through concretion in material reality. They are, in short, the name given that real but invisible spirit of destructiveness and fragmentation that rends persons, communities, and nations.

In light of our analysis, the expression "the Powers" should no longer be reserved for the special category of spiritual forces, but should rather be used generically for all manifestations of power, seen under the dual aspect of their physical or institutional concretion on the one hand, and their inner essence or spirituality on the other. Popular speech, often more accurate in unconscious matters than it is given credit for being, has quite properly referred to the whole range of phenomena as "The Powers That Be."

Even to say, as Cullmann did, that the Powers are *both* earthly *and* heavenly is, on this reading, still too imprecise. "Both" suggests two different sets of agents, some human or institutional, others divine or demonic. What we are arguing is that *the Powers are simultaneously the outer and inner aspects of one and the same indivisible concretion of power.* "Spiritual" here means the inner dimension of the material, the "within" of things, the subjectivity of objective entities in the world.

Instead of the old dualism of matter and spirit, we can now regard matter and spirit as united in one indivisible reality, distinguishable in two discrete but interrelated manifestations. Nothing less than insistence on this unity makes sense of the unexplained ambiguity in the usage of the New Testament language of power. Nothing less can account for the authors' apparent expectation that readers will understand exactly what is meant despite the great fluidity and imprecision of usage.

This ambiguity is intrinsic to a degree in every manifestation of power. For example, before us we have the chairperson of a political committee. Which is really the Power here—the person, or the role? Not the person—she can be replaced with another and the job will go on being done. Not the role either—for some use it to great benefit and others irresponsibly. Is it then the person-in-the-role? But then what authorizes her to act? Is it then the authority invested in her by the constituting charter of the group? But what gives the charter its binding character? Where is power finally to be located, unless we see it as the total interaction of all these aspects, visible and invisible? And how is power to be brought to heel, unless it is addressed on its own terrain—unless, that is, we address not only the physical manifestations of the group but also its "spirit" or "angel"? This is certainly the way the "one like a son of man" goes about attempting to reform the churches in Revelation 1–3. . . .

Franz Hinkelammert has recently formulated a similar analysis in order to clarify theologically the meaning of Marx's theory of "fetishism."[1] He distinguishes between the *material institutions* that organize modern society and the *spirit* of these institutions. Political economics makes manifest the anatomy of the institutions, and the theory of fetishism analyzes the institutionalized spirituality of modern society. The "fetish" is the spirit of the institutions, Hinkelammert writes, and this spirit is every bit as important as the physical aspects of institutions. If someone violates this spirit, though he keeps all the laws and precepts of the system, the system will condemn him to death. Conversely, if someone submits to this spirituality, he will be able to live in spite of violating all its laws and flouting all its institutions.

This makes sense of the way hardened thieves and criminals in communist prisons are made trusties, while decent people being held as political prisoners are subjected to every conceivable indignity.[2] In the logic of Hinkelammert's analysis, the thieves, although they break all the rules, accept the spirit of the system, in some ways actually exemplifying it, whereas the "politicals," though fully law-abiding and in most cases innocent of any real infraction of the law, question the spirit of the system and so are regarded as the worst criminals of all.

This analysis also explains why it is impossible to discover in the Gospels an "adequate" cause for Jesus' execution. Every such attempt has presupposed that he must have done something punishable by death. But he did not. That is the whole point. He was innocent and yet executed. But the Powers did not err. He had rejected their spirituality; he had shaken the invisible foundations by a series of provocative acts. He was therefore a living terror to the order of things. He *had* to be removed.

The spirituality of institutions does not drop from heaven, however. It only arises, Hinkelammert argues, within a definite social organization. In Marx's view, the single most important determinant of the spirit of institutions is the means of production. The spirit of life or death in a society is not a function, then, of the good will or bad will of individuals, but the consequence of a determinate institutionalized spirituality in a determinate material organization of relations between people. The capitalist system, for example, is able to produce and reproduce not only surplus value and social classes but also its own symbolic universe, its own spirituality, its own religion.

Fetishism, says Hinkelammert, is the personification of capital and the "thingification" of persons. The "invisible hand" is regarded as a benign providence to which people surrender their decisions over their own life or death. An invisible mercantile mechanism thus becomes the arbiter of human destiny, producing results in apparent independence of the human beings who comprise the system it governs. It is the tendency to deify the mechanism and reduce human agents to mere things that creates the peculiar demonism of modern capitalist economics.

It would have been helpful if Hinkelammert had extended his analysis to the peculiar demonism of communist regimes as well. In terms of our hypothesis, perhaps we could say that the dialectic in Marx is between "fetishized" structures and the proletariat, who in becoming aware of their own history and determination by these structures, revolt and establish the dictatorship of the proletariat until all bourgeois tendencies have been overcome. But since in Marx's utopia there will be no institutions, Marxism provides little guidance to a Poland, for example where the institutional structures of the state are unable to contain the positive spirit of the actual proletariat and hence must crush Solidarity. There are, in effect, no recognized sources of positive authority in institutional structures; hence the sheer need and desire for power becomes a new fetish in the absence of any positive legitimation of present interim institutions.

In the Bible, by contrast, the dialectic is between different possible spiritualities within a given institution (reform) or between different institutions (revolution), and none is granted privileged status. All, even the prophets who oppose the kings, are under the judgment of God. And in the New Jerusalem there will still be a role for institutions ("the nations," Rev. 21:24-26; 22:2).

Hinkelammert's analysis can be broadened to fit every human institution. Every organization is made up of human beings who make its decisions and are responsible for its success or failure, but these institutions tend to have a suprahuman quality. Although created and staffed by humans, decisions are not made so much by people as for them, out of the logic of institutional life itself. And because the institution usually antedates and outlasts its employees, it develops and imposes a set of traditions, expectations, beliefs, and values on everyone in its employ. Usually unspoken, unacknowledged, and even unknown, this invisible, transcendent network of determinants constrains behavior far more rigidly than any printed set of rules could ever do. It governs dress, social class, life-expectations, even choice of marriage partner (or abstention). This institutional momentum through time perpetuates a self-image, a corporate personality, and an institutional spirit which the more discerning are able to grasp as a totality and weigh for its relative sickness or health.

We must learn to break the habit of taking a merely visible part for the whole. No one, comments Hinkelammert, has ever seen a company, a school, a state, or a system of ownership. What they have seen are the physical elements of such institutions, that is to say, the building in which the school or business functions, or the people who are its operatives. The *institution*, however, is the totality of its activities and as such is a mostly invisible object.[3] When we confuse what the eye beholds with the totality, we commit the same reductionist fallacy as those Colossians who mistook the basic elements (*stoicheia*) of things for the ultimate reality (Col. 2:8, 20). The consequence of such confusion is always slavery to the unseen power behind the visible elements: the spirituality of the institution or state or stone.

If, then, the church must now make known the manifold wisdom of God to the principalities and powers in the heavenlies, it cannot be content with addressing the material aspect of an institution alone. It must speak to the spiritual reality of the institution as well. The early church understood this quite clearly. When the Roman archons (magistrates) ordered the early Christians to worship the imperial spirit or *genius,* they refused, kneeling instead and offering prayers on the emperor's behalf to God. This seemingly innocuous act was far more exasperating and revolutionary than outright rebellion would have been. Rebellion simply acknowledges the absoluteness and ultimacy of the emperor's power, and attempts to seize it. Prayer denies that ultimacy altogether by acknowledging a higher power. Rebellion would have focused solely on the physical institution and its current incumbents and attempted to displace them by an act of superior force. But prayer challenged the very spirituality of the empire itself and called the empire's "angel," as it were, before the judgment seat of God.

Such sedition could not go unpunished. With rebels the solution was simple. No one challenged the state's right to execute rebels. They had bought into the power-game on the empire's terms and lost, and the rules of the game required their liquidation. The rebels themselves knew this before they started. *But what happens when a state executes those who are praying for it?* When Christians knelt in the Colosseum to pray as lions bore down on them, something sullied the audience's thirst for revenge. Even in death these Christians were not only challenging the ultimacy of the emperor and the "spirit" of empire but also demonstrating the emperor's powerlessness to impose his will even by death. The final sanction had been publicly robbed of its power. Even as the lions lapped the blood of the saints, Caesar was stripped of his arms and led captive in Christ's triumphal procession. His authority was shown to be only penultimate after all. And even those who wished most to deny such a thing were forced, by the very punishment they chose to inflict, to behold its truth. It was a contest of all the brute force of Rome against a small sect that merely prayed. Who could have predicted that the tiny sect would win?

This is not to suggest that in most circumstances prayer is enough, but in that situation it was the most radical response imaginable. Then, "Jesus is Lord" shook the foundations of an empire; in the "free" world today, "Jesus is Lord" bumper stickers mainly occasion yawns. Cars adorned with them are not stopped at police roadblocks or firebombed by paramilitary saboteurs. The only people scandalized by the phrase are those who regard its language as sexist. But there are countries where "Jesus, friend of the poor" can get you killed. Fidelity to the gospel lies not in repeating its slogans but in plunging the prevailing idolatries into its corrosive acids. We must learn to address the spirituality of institutions, as well as their visible manifestations, with the ultimate claim of the Ultimate Human.

The failure of the gnostics to maintain the material pole of this task constituted their great apostasy. As a result of their almost pathological hatred of matter, they spiritualized the Powers altogether. Without a base in materiality, the Powers lost all mooring on the earth. Boundless speculations about heavenly hierarchies replaced careful strategizing about real power in the one and only real world. The Powers vaporized into guardians at the gates of the successive spheres of heaven, whom the soul encountered only after death in its attempt to ascend to God. They no longer represented the inner, spiritual reality of actual earthly entities. Therefore life on earth could, correspondingly, be depoliticized. As Pagels points out, gnostics were notoriously loath to suffer persecution.[4] The created world in its physical and spiritual dimensions was abandoned for a split reality to be experienced serially, the material episode to be despised in order that the later, heavenly episode might be secured. Here is how the gnostic *Apocalypse of Paul* speaks of divine punishment for sinners: "The soul that had been cast down [went] to"—hell? eternal fires? No!—"[a] body which had been prepared [for it]" *(NHL*21:19ff.). Reincarnation in a physical body on the earthly plane is hell!

Severed from materiality, the Powers in gnosticism were identified with planetary forces. But the real psychodynamic was one of projection. The gnostics were the earliest psychologists, comments Victor White. They explored the inner world by the indirect means of the language of myth, projecting their interior phantasms out on the screen of the heavens and dressing them out in a pretentious allegorizing philosophy. Their radical introspection led them to reject the material world and to be caught finally in the abyss of the archetypes of the collective unconscious.[5] The gifts they might have brought to the world at large were vitiated by their understandable inability to make this unconscious process conscious. But they were not even drawn to do so, because their ideology had already rejected the structure of this world for a pseudoreality in the beyond.

The orthodox church, for its part, rigidly cleaved to materiality but soon found itself the darling of Constantine. Called on to legitimate the empire, the church abandoned much of its social critique. The Powers were soon divorced from political affairs and made airy spirits who preyed only on individuals. The state was thus freed of one of the most powerful brakes against idolatry, although prophetic voices never ceased to be raised now and again anyway.

These deviations from the New Testament view of the Powers were the result not simply of wrong thinking but of powerful political pressures. Any time the church has chosen to address the spirituality of institutions in their concrete embodiments, persecution has resulted. Far from a show of gratitude at being recalled to the will of God, the Powers explode in a frenzy of rage and retaliation. This brings to focus another curious aspect of the myth.

The Powers Are Ignorant of God's Plan

None of the archons of this age understands "the *hidden* wisdom of God," "for if they had, they would not have crucified the Lord of glory" (1 Cor. 2:7, 8). Not even angels are omniscient. They are told only what they must know in order to deliver the revelation necessary for a specific moment. They are seldom personified, can be spoken of interchangeably with God, and vanish when the message is received. They are as much "message" as messengers, "informations" as informers.

The hymn that bursts from the lips of the dictating author of 1 Tim. 3:16 stresses the revelation that angels themselves received when Christ, after his resurrection, was "seen by angels" and "believed in the cosmos."[6] We saw the same motif of the ignorance of the archons elaborated in the *Ascension of Isaiah.* Apparently it was important that the angels see Christ vindicated. What is the mythic point common to all these texts, with their insistence that Christ was previously unknown to the angels? How is it possible for them to be ignorant of their very own principle of systemicity (Col. 1:17, *synestēken,* the etymological root of our word "system"), the one in whom all things "hold together," "cohere," "find their harmonious unity"? How is it that they are ignorant of that in and through and for which they exist (Col. 1:16)? We must lay aside all systematic and logical objections and simply let the myth speak for itself. What it seems to claim is that the universe itself is blind to its own principle of cohesion. It operates cohesively, but without the parts perceiving that fact. Put in a more modern mode, the universe is late in arriving at awareness of itself as a unity, and this awareness has come into the world for the first time with humanity. We can actually date the moment of its dawning in the axiological period of the great prophets of Israel, the philosophers of Greece, and Buddha and Lao-tzu in the East.[7] It was then that the historically unprecedented sense of the unity of all things first was effectively articulated, although it was probably intuitively sensed far earlier. On the strength of that apprehension, both Israel's conception of Yahweh's universal sovereignty and Greek science and philosophy became possible.

With Christ Jesus a new dimension was added, however. The just man is killed. The embodiment of God's will is executed by God's servants. The incarnation of the orderly principles of the universe is crucified by the guardians of order. The very nucleus of spiritual power in the universe is destroyed by the spiritual powers. The parts do not or cannot know the effect of their acts on the whole, and some, less innocently, by their worship of their own selfish short-term interests, have become detrimental to the good of the whole. The angels did not know the Lord of glory, nor did the captains and jailers and chief priests and governors. The cosmic process of reconciliation could not begin until they "saw" him.

This is why Phil. 2:9-11, Col. 2:15, and Eph. 1:19-23 are so adamant in stressing that Christ is *already* seated at God's right hand, has *already* unmasked the Powers, has *already* put these Powers under his feet and has already had bestowed on him the name that IS above every name—even though empirical evidence for such claims seems totally nonexistent. For if the crucified Jesus is "Lord"—if the marred and disfigured form of the one truly human being who ever lived has become the criterion and norm of ultimate truth, life, and reality—then we and every power in heaven and on earth and under the earth are forever after utterly without excuse. We can no longer act in ignorance of the Whole or pretend to be oblivious to the value of the Human over every proximate goal. We can no longer act as if the world is not a single system converging on the One in and through and for whom it exists. We are, indeed, free to pretend not to know, and even to deceive ourselves into believing that our own values and goals are ultimate. But it will only be "bad faith," in Sartre's terms, and we will have to learn the truth very precisely in order to conceal it the more carefully. And this suppression will force us to become the more violent and brutal against all we love, in order to mask our remembered deception from ourselves. We can ravage the ecology, suppress the poor, murder protesters, adulterate the gospel, shake our fists defiantly at

God, and declare the world a mechanism and human beings machines. But the System of the systems remains the ultimate arbiter, and we can no more secede from its jurisdiction than we can stop breathing air. The judgment comes again, and again, and finally. *For the angels have seen.* And the gospel has been preached to the nations.

The Powers did not know, but they know now. Even many modern secular states bear a legacy of titles that remind them, against even their own dominant ideologies, Whose they are, and why. These states continue to name the various branches of government the civil *service,* the military *service,* the *ministry* of justice, the *ministry* of education, revealing in these very titles the tacit recognition that they exist only on behalf of the Human revealed as the criterion and basis of all governmental action. When such agencies make themselves ends in themselves, or subject human needs to departmental efficiency or budgetary convenience, they do so, consciously or not, in violation of their vocation. "Are they not all ministering spirits sent forth to serve, for the sake of those who are to obtain salvation?" (Heb. 1:14). Did not Paul himself say that the person who is in authority "is God's servant for your good" (Rom. 13:4)?

Even tyrants understand this, perhaps better than most. The adage that runs "Mussolini made the trains run on time" bears witness to the fact that even dictators must manage to win the consent of the governed by providing sufficient services to buy their allegiance. And even the most aggressive nations feel obliged to justify military interventions by placing the loftiest of idealist excuses before the bar of world opinion. One U.S. delegate to the Baptist World Alliance Congress in Berlin in 1934 described his experience of Nazism:

> It was a great relief to be in a country where salacious sex literature cannot be sold; where putrid motion pictures and gangster films cannot be shown. The new Germany has burned great masses of corrupting books and magazines along with its bonfires of Jewish and communistic libraries.

Surely, so the reasoning went, a leader who does not smoke or drink, who wants women to be modest, and who is against pornography cannot be all bad![8] Evil, as always, is parasitic of the good and must masquerade as good in order to remain in office.

The church's task, then, in making known the manifold wisdom of God now to the principalities and powers in the heavenly places, does not involve the arduous and hopeless effort of bringing the Powers to a place they have never been, or to a recognition they have never shared. It involves simply reminding the Powers Whose they are, a knowledge already encoded in their charters, titles, traditions, insignia, and money. Even in the case of communist regimes, the task is the same: to recall them to the One whose humanity itself is the best promise of a new humanity in the age to come, and to convert them to the humanism which lies at the base of their own ideology.

"The Powers did not know": seen from the perspective provided by our hypothesis, evangelism and social action are the inner and outer approaches to the same phenomenon of power. I have already described the subversive character of the early church's refusal to worship the imperial genius and its recourse instead to prayer. Many modern Christians have unfortunately understood injustice in simply materialistic terms and have not recognized the need to "convert" people from the spirituality that binds them to a particular material expression of power. It is not enough merely to change social structures. People are not simply determined by the material forces that impinge on them. They are also the victims of the very spirituality that the material means of production and socialization have fostered, even as these material means are themselves *the* spin-off of a particular spirituality. In a new structure people will continue to behave on the basis of the old spirituality, as they have to varying degrees in every communist regime, unless not only the structures but also their own psyches are reorganized.

Evangelism is *always* a form of social action. It is an indispensable component of any new "world." Unfortunately, Christian evangelism has all too often been wedded to a politics of the status quo and merely serves to relieve distress by displacing hope to an afterlife and ignoring the causes of oppression. The repugnance with which most liberal Christians regard evangelism betrays their own failure to discern that all liberation involves conversion. Whenever evangelism is carried out in full awareness of the Powers, whether in confronting those in power or liberating those crushed by it, proclaiming the sovereignty of Christ is by that very act a critique of injustice and idolatry. And as the churches of South Korea and Brazil and Chile and around the world have learned, such evangelism will inevitably spark persecution. In sum, structural change is not enough; the heart and soul must also be freed, forgiven, energized, given focus, reunited with their Source.

The converse is equally true: social action is always evangelism, if carried out in full awareness of Christ's sovereignty over the Powers. Jesus did not just forgive sinners, he gave them a new world. And for those who could not go back to what or where they had been, he created a new structure—his vagabond, sexually mixed, scandalous band of followers who shared what they had in common. Too often our social action has been as devoid of spirituality as our evangelism has been politically innocuous. Too often we have told the Powers that they were wrong but not Whose they are. Too much of the time we have drawn on secular models of social change without drawing as well on our own rich fund of symbolism and imagery, liturgy, and story. Many dismissed the hymns and gospel songs, the eucharists and prayers of a Martin Luther King, Jr., or Cesar Chavez as merely shrewd accommodations to the subcultures with which they worked. Such critics did not perceive that these were essential forms of struggle in themselves, that the enemy is not always self-evident, that engaging a Power on its own terms guarantees that the victor, whichever it is, will perpetuate the same terms. They did not address themselves to the transcendent One who alone could work changes which do not themselves bear the seeds of new evils.

How would it change the shape of social struggle if we understood that we wrestle not just against flesh and blood but also against principalities, against powers, against the world rulers of this present darkness, against the spiritual hosts of wickedness in the heavenlies? What are the practical implications of putting on the whole armor of God and praying at all times in the Spirit (Eph. 6:10-20)? How would it change the nature of our wrestling if we did so in the context of continuous Bible study and singing and worship? For those still working their way out from under the weight of an oppressively pious upbringing, that probably does not resound as good news, but it is. It is the way increasing numbers of others have learned they must live, in order to keep on struggling against the Beast without being made bestial.

For the struggle is both physical and spiritual, and for the long haul we need waybread that can replenish hope. We have perhaps forgotten how to use our tradition this way, but our sisters and brothers in the black churches or in the Latin American base communities, and many in the disarmament movement, have known this all along or are relearning it fast. That tradition bears within it, neglected but recoverable, a whole vocabulary about the Powers, and models for their confrontation, and wisdom concerning their stratagems. The myth does not provide final explanations, but it preserves a *structure* by which evil in all its depth can be discerned and held up to consciousness. It mobilizes awareness and catalyzes action. It calls us to a recognition of our own complicity and determination by the Powers and offers us liberation. It is not merely a human creation, but a revelation of the nature of ultimate reality, humanly mediated. Like DNA, the story is a chain of symbols in exquisitely condensed form, providing the culturally encoded information required for social and psychic survival and transformation. Like a holograph, it provides an authentic "picture" of the invisible nature of ultimate reality, discernible even in its most minute parts. There is, put simply, nothing else quite like it, and we neglect it to our peril.

Heaven Is the Transcendent "Within" of Material Reality

To this point I have suggested that the Powers can be interpreted as the visible and invisible aspects of real social, structural, and material entities in the world. I suggested further that the writers of the New Testament could refer to either the visible or the invisible aspects of the Powers, or even both together, as the context required. It is most difficult for us, given our modern materialistic worldview, to comprehend the invisible aspect. It was with this very issue that Eph. 3:10 confronted us: what does it mean to communicate the manifold wisdom of God to the principalities and powers in the *heavenly* places? It is a question children always ask and parents assiduously avoid: what do we mean by "heaven"?

Popular culture has tended to regard heaven (if it has any regard for it at all) as a transcendent, otherworldly sphere qualitatively distinct from human life, to which the dead go if they have been good. What if we were instead to conceive of it as the realm of "withinness," the metaphorical "place" in which the spirituality of everything is "located," as it were? "Heaven," in religions all around the world, is precisely that—the habitat of angels, spirits, cherubim, and seraphim, but also of demons and the devil and all the Powers "in the heavenly places." Heaven is simply where they "reside."

But heaven is a great deal more as well. It is where God is enthroned and thus is the source of the transformative possibilities that God presents to every actual entity. In the language of process theology, God envisions all possibilities and is forever presenting every created thing with the particular relevant possibilities that can maximize the total situation in which it exists, both for itself and for the larger unity of which it is a part. To paraphrase Whitehead, "Heaven" is the "home of the possibles," not simply in the abstract sense that our potentialities have been planted in us like seeds and that it is up to us to make them sprout. Quite the contrary, our own given potentiality, like that of the acorn, is always merely to repeat the past, to go on being and doing what we have always been and done before. The heavenly possibilities are presented to us as a lure challenging us to go beyond our conditioning and habits, our collusion in oppressing or being oppressed, our inertia, fear, and neuroses. God offers the heavenly possibilities for creative novelty, and we can accept wholly, or accept in part, or reject completely and simply go on repeating our past.

When we do realize a transformative possibility, we quite rightly speak of the experience of ecstasy that accompanies that realization as "heavenly." We have a sense of enhanced realness, of becoming more than we knew we could become. There is a rightness about it that resonates throughout the universe and unites us with the larger purposes of God. Thus when Jesus healed or cast out demons or preached to the poor, he could declare that in that instant the "Reign of heaven" had come on them. When justice is done, we experience a sense of heaven. When a person's individual interests coincide with the interest of the Whole, there is an epiphany of heaven. When we die to our egocentricity and abandon ourselves to God, what opens to receive us is heaven.

"But God, who is rich in mercy, out of the great love with which he loved us, even when we were dead through our trespasses, made us alive together with Christ . . . and raised us up with him, and made us sit with him in the heavenly places in Christ Jesus" (Eph. 2:4-6).

Heaven is also the negation of possibles. We should conceive possibles no longer as a static set of immutable scenarios drawn up before the world began but as an infinite number of possible worlds dynamically emerging from the internal decisions and interactions of the present world. And because these possibles confront us with an "if . . . then" that is fateful and often irreversible, the possible also confronts us as judgment for lost opportunity, squandered gifts, or rejected love. Hence heaven is where John sees "thrones, and seated on them were those to whom judgment was committed" (Rev. 20:4).

"Heaven" here cannot be conceived of as "up there" in such a way that it is out of relationship with the earth, for believers are already, while alive, established in it. It was precisely this problem that created the impasse in the interpretation of Eph. 3:10. If the church now must make known God's manifold wisdom to the principalities and powers in the heavenlies, the heavenlies must somehow be accessible to the church. Insofar as "heaven" encompasses the entire universe, it is certainly not limited to the earth, but it interpenetrates all things, is present in all things, bearing the secret of the potential and inwardness and unfolding of all things. Thus, according to the *Gospel of Thomas,* when Jesus' disciples ask him when the kingdom will come, he responds, "It will not come by waiting for it. It will not be a matter of saying 'Here it is' or 'There it is.' Rather, the kingdom of the Father is spread out upon the earth, and men do not see it" *(NHL,* sec. 113). It was said just as well by a seventh-grader in a recent confirmation class: "Heaven is wherever God is acknowledged."

The ancients sought to express the ubiquitous quality of heaven by piling up numbers in astronomical proportions to indicate the infinity of the hosts of angels (Rev. 5:11, 13; 19:1, 6). Yahweh was the Lord of the universe, but even more often and specifically, "Lord of hosts," "Lord of Spirits," "Lord of the Powers" as if the real test of lordship is the capacity to control the transcendent realm of determining forces that exercise the real day-to-day governance of every aspect of life on earth. The ancients perceived that there was an angel for everything, down to the last blade of grass. This notion, laughed to scorn for the past few centuries, now appears to have been, symbolically, precisely correct: every blade of grass, every rock crystal, acorn, and ovum has its "messenger" *(angelos)* from God to instruct it in its growth, however we name it (DNA, the "laws" of crystalline formation, etc.).

Such a view of heaven finds it to be "nearer than breathing, closer than hand or foot," yet still transcendent. But its transcendence is not a transcendence of *matter;* that is the bias of the old worldview, infected by Neoplatonic aversion to the material universe. "Heaven" in our hypothesis has a transcendence of an altogether different kind; it is the transcendence of the "worldly" way of viewing reality, of the alienated order of existence, of egocentric ways of living, of idolatry of the part in defiance of the Whole, of the unrealized present by the consummation to come. It is transcendent by virtue of inwardness, invisibility, and futurity, not by remoteness and distance. One must, in traditional terms, be "saved" in order to perceive it, not just be better informed. It cannot just be known about; it must be *known.*

Mystics have traditionally used the language of projection to attempt to describe the ineffable quality of their experience of this dimension of existence. They have spoken of it as "another world," "the beyond," "the spiritual realm," meaning by that a quality of consciousness not reducible to anything perceivable by normal sensory awareness or by thought. In their desperation to awaken those who are content with the world of appearances they sometimes spoke of their being captives held by jailors in the prison of the body. They sometimes (usually under the spell of Neoplatonism) detested the material world, heaping it with derision. They perceived it to be the cause of blindness rather than simply the occasion of it. They blamed the *means* by which people deadened their higher senses rather than the cause, which was a delusion of the spirit.

Recent studies in neurophysiology[9] have reminded us, however, that every human experience is bodily, even so-called "out of body" experiences, insofar as such experiences (quite apart from their interpretation) necessarily involve the brain in order for the subject to be aware of them at all. Thinking and brain activity are simply two sides of a single indivisible process. Neither can be reduced to the other (though some philosophers have fruitlessly treated ideas as the sole reality and some scientists have reduced thought to brain activity). Even archetypes have electromagnetic patterning in the brain. There is, in fact, nothing that affects us psychologically that does not have some corresponding configuration in the brain. Everything spiritual has its concomitant incarnation in the body—even spiritual theories which advocate denial of the body. Kundalini yoga quite rightly insisted that spiritual mastery consists not of transcending the body but of lifting the instinctual energies from "lower" to "higher" centers along the spine (the "chakras"). "Higher" here is used paradoxically, however. It does not mean an increase in instinctual energies but rather their transmutation into more subtle forms, much as an electrical transformer takes the high voltage from the power line and reduces it to an amount usable in the home.

If heaven is not some other reality but the inner essence of present reality in its fullest potentiality, then the mystical "ascent" is not out of the body and into a wholly incorporeal spiritual realm, but *into the body's very own essence as the temple of the Holy Spirit within us.* What seems to be qualitatively different from normal bodily experience is indeed qualitatively different, but not because it escapes the body. On the contrary, it appears to be so different precisely because the inner essence of bodily existence has for once been actually apprehended. The beatific vision does not involve renunciation of the stuff of our humanity, but the recognition that our human stuff can itself become translucent, incandescent with the fire of the divine which indwells us. Perhaps that is why the Sufis called the Holy Spirit the "Angel of Humanity."

It is precisely the Jews' insistence on the inseparability of soul and body that led them to affirm the resurrection of the whole person, spirit, soul, and body. Popular Christianity long since abandoned that for belief in the immortality of the soul, that is, of a bodiless continuation in the pure realm of spirit. Against this view Paul had already coined the notion of a "spiritual body" (1 Cor. 15:35-57). Just what this paradoxical formulation means is not nearly so important as *that* it is asserted. We cannot conceive it, but it serves to hold the myth open into eternity and prevents its collapsing into a dualism of spirit versus matter. However incomprehensible it is in literal terms, it is the necessary symbolic affirmation that life is always life in a body, that spirit cannot exist apart from its concretion in form, that the victory of life over death includes the transformed vehicle by means of which, and solely by means of which, we have known what it means to be alive. All the rest is trust.

So how did Christianity become almost solely preoccupied with getting into heaven after death? One can find very little trace of that concern in the Bible. The Old Testament, for its part, knows almost nothing of eternal life.

The idea was late in developing in Judaism. The New Testament itself jostles between the poles of eternity seen as a present experience on the one hand and as a future hope on the other. Ephesians and the Fourth Gospel stress the former, Paul the latter, but all maintain a tension between the "already" and the "not yet" of Christian existence. Paul is far more dubious than they of the adequacy of our foretastes of heaven in this life; he longs to be "at home with the Lord" (2 Cor. 5:8; Phil. 1:23). The Spirit is a down payment, to be sure, but no guarantee against floggings, shipwreck, hunger, or loneliness (2 Cor. 11:23-29). In fact, preoccupation with heavenly existence can become a diversion from the costliness of obedience in the concrete sociopolitical world. The heaven awaited by the faithful is not a "place" in the sky, but a redeemed reality in which even the physical universe will be "freed from the shackles of mortality and enter upon the liberty and splendor of the children of God" (Rom. 8:21, NEB). The soul does not escape the body to return to the ideal realm on high, but is granted a transformed bodily existence when Christ returns to earth at the consummation (Phil. 3:20-21).

Christianity cannot live without the longing for "heaven," for that longing is in part a longing for the realization of the transcendent possibilities of human life *on earth*. It is the sense of these heavenly possibilities that accounts for the restlessness of creation, what Paul called its "eager longing" to be "set free from its bondage to decay" (Rom. 8:19, 21). For heaven is not simply the "within" of all present reality; it is also the womb of the future, that toward which God entices us by offering us in each moment new ways of becoming more real, more vital, more united with that which tends toward the good of the whole. And yet the realization of heavenly possibilities on earth cannot bring complete heavenly peace, since each realization brings with it a new challenge for creative novelty. In that sense, heaven is the negation of all our attempts to build surrogate "heavens" on earth at the expense of the poor and oppressed. It is the sublime subverter of our tendencies to be seduced from further transformations by the pleasure of those already achieved. And finally, heaven is the treasury of every sacrifice and contribution made in time, whereby God receives the world and all our actions in such a way as to try to salvage whatever good can be gained from it, with a tender care "that nothing be lost."[10]

I do not wish to leave the impression, however, that the spiritual is just an epiphenomenon, like Galileo's "secondary qualities," as if the material were primary. The material and spiritual poles of reality are inseparable. They come into existence together and cease to exist together. Neither is the "cause" of the other. Historically, the church has tended to stress the spiritual to the neglect of a genuinely positive respect for the material. In reaction, recent centuries in the West have witnessed a compensatory and equally one-sided emphasis on the material, often in utter disregard for and even denial of the spiritual. Developmentally, in Western societies we tend to lose a sense of the spiritual and be captivated by the material side of reality, and only after often excruciating personal struggle are we "reborn" into the other dimension of the one and only real world.

The New Testament's vision of the Reign of God, however, is of a transformed reality that involves both a new heaven (spirituality) and a new earth (materiality). If classical Christianity emphasized the former, Marxism and secular humanism have emphasized the latter. This new metaphor attempts to synthesize the valid elements of both. Marx's real intent, after all, was not to make people materialistic, if by that we mean preoccupied with consumption and themselves. Nor was he set on reducing reality to mere matter and replacing freedom with an iron determinism. His materialism was dialectical; he was attempting to explain how people *are* reduced to mere things and made the slaves of machines and masters, in order to uncover the laws by which they might secure their freedom.[11] If, as proposed here, we join Teilhard de Chardin in locating spirit at the very heart of matter—if we see it as the "within" of actual people, institutions, the state, nature—then the establishment of the material basis for the full and free development of people must be an indispensable aspect of our vision of God's Reign. Acts of justice cannot then simply be an optional movement at the fringe, but the very stuff of existence before God. "Suppose a brother or a sister is in rags with not enough food for the day, and one of you says, 'Good luck to you, keep yourselves warm, and have plenty to eat,' but does nothing to supply their bodily needs, what is the good of that? So with faith. If it does not lead to action, it is in itself a lifeless thing" (James 2:15-17, NEB).

But this formulation leaves me a bit uneasy. I can hear another voice rising up in me, saying: "All this demystifying is just another form of mystification. Here the poor person stands before you in her need and you do not declare immediate solidarity with her and make her cause yours. You want instead to pursue a quixotic and mystical assault on some alleged spiritual Power that 'holds' her in subjection. Anyone with eyes can see that she is held in subjection by the capitalist economic system, and all this talk of 'Powers' merely serves to remove your neighbor from before your eyes and interpose something more 'interesting.' You are still caught in the legacy of idealism. You really believe ideas are more real than bloated bellies. You would rather discuss your thoughts than deal with concrete injustice. So you interpose a realm of Powers that you can go on talking about, maybe even praying about, as a way of avoiding your neighbor."

That cuts straight to the bone. How can I deny the truth of that? And—suppose a whole new generation of scholars were to become absorbed in exploiting this new field (already dubbed "exousiology" by Berkhof), with no actual opposition to real structures of injustice or contact with those who are most oppressed. If the theology of the future must win its right to speak by being a continual reflection on praxis, on the actual struggle of humanity for authentic being, then we must be careful to keep the ring of that voice clear in our ears. At the same time, however, one still must ask how the neighbor became oppressed and is kept that way. How has she *internalized* that spirit of oppression and granted legitimacy to the very Powers that oppress her? How can all the "flaming darts of the evil one" that have carried their poisonous secretions into her very bloodstream be pulled out, one by one, and the toxins filtered out? How can she be freed to authentic struggle, unless the very ideas and images that have been planted in her are torn out by the very roots, through the vision of a counterreality capable of improving her lot?

But now I can hear an objection from the other side. Is it *our* responsibility to help her? Isn't it God's task to deliver the captives? Christians all over the globe have raised that very objection, convinced that on biblical and dogmatic grounds the church is *forbidden* to become engaged in struggles against systemic injustice. The issue must be met head-on, because those who argue this way have at least one leg on very firm ground. Just a sample of passages shows that their concern is not simply for proof-texting but for a proper regard for the sovereignty of God. "Stand still and see this great thing, which the Lord will do before your eyes" (1 Sam. 12:16). "A king is not saved by his great army; a warrior is not delivered by his great strength. The war horse is a vain hope for victory, and by its great might it cannot save" (Ps. 33:16). "Power belongs to God" (Ps. 62:11; see also Isa. 30:15; Zech. 4:6). In the face of such texts, quietism and docile trust would seem to be the order of the day.

Yet nowhere in the Bible do we see anyone standing still. All the human agents of God's will are working, not only hard but with almost superhuman effort. Moses' care for his people exhausts him to distraction, and Jesus' movements through Galilee resemble a blitzkrieg. Why then the curious *passivity* that the Bible seems to enjoin in the struggle against the Powers? Perhaps our distinction between outer and inner might cast a feeble light on this baffling paradox of human action and heavenly grace. We are told, on the one hand, "Work out your own salvation with fear and trembling" (Phil. 2:12), because it is our responsibility to change the outer arrangements by which power is structured in the world. We can reform or revamp the organization, elect better leaders, win equal rights for or as the disadvantaged, or even engage in revolution. But we cannot affect the inner, spiritual dimension of institutions directly. Blacks could not simply settle for winning the right to sit at the front of the bus; they needed to lay siege to the very citadel of racism itself, the hearts of members of the white majority. But how were they to *storm* hearts? For we have no unmediated access to the "within" of a system, or institution, or even another person, for their "withins" are a function not of our acts alone but of all the history and traditions, beliefs and experiences that make up their reality at any given moment. That is where faith and prayer come in. We intercede before the Sovereign of the Powers to rectify this institution's or person's balance, to align its spirituality with the good of the whole, to convert it and transform it. That is something we cannot bring about no matter how much outer change we achieve, but it is precisely the outer changes we make that challenge, lure, and goad the oppressor toward inner change. Hence the Philippians passage continues, "for God is at work within you, both to will and to work for his good pleasure" (2:13).

Yes, *stand still,* if you want to carry the battle to the very heart of the matter, if you want fundamental change—still, at the still point of the turning world, where all is action without motion, where God inaugurates the great sea-change that runs deep under countervailing waves to turn the tide.

And yet we are also to struggle, equipped with the whole panoply of God's armor, "and *having done all,* to stand" (Eph. 6:13). We are to work with determined persistence at the outer, and to trust God to change the inner. We may be over familiar with this paradox, so frequently stated in Scripture (e.g., Phil. 2:12-13; Gal. 2:20; Mark 8:35); perhaps we can hear it afresh in Henry Corbin's remark on a verse from the Koran: "'It is not you who cast the dart when you cast it, but Allah casts it' (8:17). And yet, yes, it is you who cast it; and yet, no, it is not you who cast it."[12]

The issue, then, is not social struggle versus inner change, but their orchestration together so that both occur simultaneously. The transformation of society and persons can begin at either end. The early church began from the pole of steadfastness in prayer and the refusal of idolatry, manifesting that *hypomonē* which the Book of Revelation regards as the highest Christian virtue. It is usually somewhat limply rendered "patient endurance," but it is in fact closer to "absolute intransigence," "unbending determination," "an iron will," "the capacity to endure persecution, torture, and death without yielding one's faith." It is one of the fundamental attributes of nonviolent resistance.

But that same transformation can begin at the pole of social struggle and work an inner change along the way. Many people entered the civil rights movement because they were concerned with justice for blacks, and in the course of involvement in nonviolent direct action discovered an even greater change taking place in themselves. When F. D. Dawson III and I drove from Texas to Selma, Alabama, to join the thousands of clergy who had converged to support the black struggle for voting rights there, we were accosted at the edge of town by a man in a pickup who chased us all over town honking his horn and shouting obscenities and threats. His truck was equipped with a gun rack; we were afraid he might be armed. We were terrified. When we finally got away from him, we were as pale as ghosts. We were not ready to die. After two hours of training in nonviolent action the next day, we joined the marchers moving down the main street, fully prepared to die. Perhaps our presence among so many aided their struggle in a minuscule way, but their struggle aided us enormously. We had gone to champion social justice; in the process we were forced to deal with the very personal question of the cost of discipleship. There is no more effective way of undergoing the spiritual discipline of dying to one's ego than to position oneself directly in the path of the possibility of actual death—say, on the tracks of a train loaded with nuclear warheads or before the prow of a Trident sub. Social involvement of that kind can do wonders for the soul—if the leadership understands the essential unity of body and spirit and addresses them both.

This unity must be kept paramount in addressing the Powers. It is easy enough to set oneself against the visible evil of a Power. But we never have control over that inner dimension of reality which we are calling the spiritual dimension of power. The outer signs, symbols, personnel, buildings, and structures of a Power can be manipulated, opposed, altered, but we never know if our intervention will in fact affect the essential spirit of the entity and bring genuine change. The students who struck Columbia University in 1968 succeeded in winning significant aspects of their program, but the university's "angel" was not itself changed in any substantial way, and the moment student pressures eased, reaction set in.

Change is possible, but only if the spirit as well as the forms of Power are touched. And that spirit can only be spiritually discerned and spiritually encountered. This is what made Martin Luther King, Jr. a figure of world-historic proportions. With only the powerless at his side, he formulated actions that would provoke and make visible the institutional violence of racism. By absorbing that violence in their own bodies, they exposed the legalized system as immoral, stripped it of legitimacy, and forced unprecedented numbers of people to choose between their racism and their Christianity. He resolutely refused to treat racism as a political issue only; he insisted that it be seen also as a moral and spiritual sickness. He did not attack the soul of America, but appealed to its most profound depths. His confrontational tactics were attempts to address that soul. He called a nation to repent, and significant numbers did. In the process the spirit of the nation itself began to change. His assassination, and the abandonment of the moral basis of the struggle for one of black power versus white power, allowed the worst elements of the ugly racist spirit to reassert themselves, this time with blacks no longer the vanguard of reconciliation and conversion, but openly espousing a counterracism of their own. Those who continued to insist on loving the enemy and working interracially were buried under the flood of poisons now unleashed from both sides. Blacks and whites not only ceased to work together, but even stopped speaking. The adoption of the methods of the oppressor had finally turned all parties into oppressors, and it was now only a matter of finding someone weak enough to oppress. (Black power advocates generally targeted meek white liberals unable to deny their residual racism and unwilling or unable to counter being dumped on.) Once the moral grounds of struggle had been yielded, it was merely a matter of which side had more power. In a contest of that sort, it did not require a Solomon to predict which side would win. The revival and new respectability of the Ku Klux Klan, the collapse of the political coalition of blacks and whites, the abandonment or abatement of efforts for equal rights in employment and housing—all that was predictable the moment the spiritual basis of the struggle shifted from love to resentment, from nonviolence to the rhetoric of violence, from moral force to the force of anger. Impatient with the pace of a struggle that sought not only legal equality but the conversion of the very heart of the nation from racism, black power attempted the quick fix of structural change by a frontal assault on white power. Its epitaph can be formulated as an axiom: the direct use of power against a Power will inevitably be to the advantage of The Powers That Be.

This is a mistake, however, that has been repeated in one struggle after another. The Weather Underground correctly criticized the U.S. government for its barbaric violence in Vietnam and then mirrored the very barbarism it condemned by adopting violence as its means. Whenever we let the terms of struggle be dictated by the Power that we oppose, we are certain to become as evil. Nothing about this insight is new. It is written for anyone to read in Rev. 17:15-18. There the Beast on whom the Harlot (Roma) sits turns against her and shifts his allegiance to the ten enemy kings. These will hate the harlot and burn her up with fire. The Beast can shift loyalties precisely because he knows that the means employed to overthrow the Harlot will make the kings every bit as much the children of hell as she.

That is why we must not engage the Powers without rigorous examination of our own inner evil, which we often project on our opponents. We must ask how we are like the very Power we oppose, and attempt to open these parts of ourselves to divine transformation. We must attempt to stop the spiral of violence both within ourselves and in our tactics vis-à-vis the Powers. We must discern the spirituality that we oppose and be careful not to grant it victory within ourselves. And we must settle it within ourselves, once and for all and then over and over again, that we will not celebrate any victory feast that does not include a setting for our enemy.

In short, we must develop a fine-tuned sensitivity to what the ancients called "the war in heaven." It is the unseen clash of values and ideologies, of the spirituality of institutions and the will of God, of demonic factionalism and heavenly possibilities. The unique calling of the church in social change lies in making clear the dual nature of our task. We wrestle on two planes, the earthly and the heavenly—what I have called the outer and inner aspects of reality. The ancients, in terms far more picturesque, spoke of this as the coincidence of what is above with what is below.

Notes

1. Franz Hinkelammert, *Las Armas Ideológicas de la Muerte*, 2d ed. (San José, Costa Rica: Departamento Ecuménico de Investigaciones, Apado. 339, San Pedro Montes de Oca, 1981). Translated into English as *The Ideological Weapons of Death: A Theological Critique of Capitalism* (Maryknoll, NY: Orbis, 1986).

2. See, e.g., Aleksandr Solzhenitsyn, *The Gulag Archipelago,* 3 vols. (New York: Harper & Row, 1973–78).

3. Hinkelammert, *Las Armas Ideológicas,* 8–9.

4. Elaine Pagels, *The Gnostic Gospels* (New York: Random House, 1979), 84ff. The gnostic "Two Books of Jeu" ascribed this saying to Jesus: "Blessed is he who has crucified the world, and has not allowed the world to crucify him" *(NT Apoc.*1:261).

5. Victor White, *God and the Unconscious* (Cleveland: World Publishing Co., 1952), 225.

6. Author's translation.

7. Karl Jaspers, *The Origin and Goal of History* (London: Routledge & Kegan Paul, 1953).

8. William Loyd Allen, "How Baptists Assessed Hitler," *Christian Century* 99 (September 1–8, 1982): 890–91. The quotation is of the Rev. John W. Bradbury in the *Watchman-Examiner,* September 13, 1934.

9. See, e.g., Eugene d'Aquili and Charles Laughlin, Jr., "The Biopsychological Determinants of Religious Ritual Behavior," *Zygon* 10 (1975): 32–58.

10. Alfred North Whitehead, *Process and Reality,* corrected ed. by David R. Griffin and Donald W. Shelburne (New York: Free Press, 1978), 346. See also p. 351.

11. Nancy Bancroft, "Materialism and the Christian Left: Rethinking Christian Use of Marx," *JES* 20 (1983): 43–66.

12. Henry Corbin, *Creative Imagination in the Sūfism of Ibn 'Arabī* (Princeton: Princeton University Press, 1969), 214.

PART III

Unmasking the Powers

5

Introduction

*In the first volume of the Powers trilogy—*Naming the Powers*—Walter Wink set out to identify biblical terms for "power," exegete them within their context, and then make the case that these terms point to the inner or spiritual aspects of concrete manifestations of power in human experience both then and now. He thus sought to recapture a language and interpretive categories for human experience that modern reductionistic materialism had lost. In this volume of the trilogy, Wink continues to argue against the presuppositions of a materialistic worldview. Such a worldview sees the "principalities and powers" of the biblical texts and religious experience as, at best, mere personifications for institutions and systems and the powerful who populate them. At worst, they are "archaic relics of a superstitious past," not to be spoken of except with derision. But as Wink points out, the psychology of a culture can be discerned by examining what that culture endlessly talks about and what it refuses to talk about. It takes little serious examination to determine that our culture endlessly talks about, practices, and sanctions violence, but adamantly refuses to speak of—and thus give voice to—the spiritual essence of those "principalities and powers" that either promote and sanction violence or seek to subvert or subdue violence. Wink sees the "myth" of materialism collapsing all around us, resulting in a spiritual hunger experienced by many. He has set himself in this volume the task of revitalizing a "powerful counter-myth" capable of accommodating the genuine achievements of the materialistic, scientific worldview while ridding us of its unconstructive reductionism.*

Source: Wink 1986: Excerpted from the Introduction

One of the best ways to discern the weakness of a social system is to discover what it excludes from conversation. From its inception Christianity has not found it easy to speak about sex. Worse yet, it could not acknowledge, even privately, the continued existence of inner darkness in the *redeemed*. Because Gnosticism attempted, often in bizarre forms, to face sex and the inner shadow, it was declared heretical and driven underground, where it ironically became symbolic of the very repressed contents that it had attempted to lift up into the light. Gnosticism became Christianity's shadow.

Nineteenth-century science could not deal with the "secondary qualities" of objects—color, taste, smell, texture—or the emotions of people, which were merely subjective and not a part of the objective, analyzable world. In reaction to this arbitrary exclusion of soul from the universe, the Romantic movement attempted to redress the balance, only to lend, by its failure, an even greater sense of legitimacy to the ideology it opposed.

What does late twentieth-century Western society exclude from conversation? Certainly not sex; at least in more "sophisticated" circles accounts of sexual exploits scarcely raise an eyebrow. But if you want to bring all talk to a halt in shocked embarrassment, every eye riveted on you, try mentioning angels, or demons, or the devil. You will be quickly appraised for signs of pathological violence and then quietly shunned.

Angels, spirits, principalities, powers, gods, Satan—these, along with all other spiritual realities, are the unmentionables of our culture. The dominant materialistic worldview has absolutely no place for them. These archaic relics of a superstitious past are unspeakable because modern secularism simply has no categories, no vocabulary, no presuppositions by which to discern what it was in the actual experiences of people that brought these words to speech. And it has massive resistance even to thinking about these phenomena, having fought so long and hard to rid itself of every vestige of transcendence.

Why then trouble secular materialism by "the return of the repressed," these "spiritual hosts . . . in the heavenly places," and all their ilk, both good and evil? There are several compelling reasons. The first is that materialism itself is terminally ill, and, let us hope, in process of replacement by a worldview capable of honoring the lasting values of modern science without succumbing to its reductionism. In that emergent worldview, spirituality will be perceived as the interiority of material, organic, and social entities, as I have suggested in volume 1 of The Powers (*Naming the Powers*).

Having repressed the spiritual so long, however, we no longer have ready access to it. The wells of the spirit have run dry. We can scarcely rediscover in a few generations what it has taken the race millennia to learn by costly trial and error. So we find ourselves returning to the ancient traditions, searching for wisdom wherever it may be found. We do not capitulate to the past and its superstitions, but bring all the gifts our race has acquired along the way as aids in recovering the lost language of our souls.

A second reason for approaching these old symbols with new respect is that true individuation seems to take place only when thought, feeling and behavior are integrated around a central myth-system at the core of the self.[1] To a degree far beyond current recognition, the myth of materialism has served as such an integrating agent for modern society, but it has been an integration bought at the cost of what is most human, most aesthetic, and most meaningful in life. Alternative myth-systems are not easily come by, however. Western civilization has in all its centuries known as few as seven.[2] With the collapse of materialism, many people sense an acute spiritual hunger and are reaching out, at times blindly and in every direction, for adequate sustenance. Often, however, they react not only against materialism itself but against the Judeo-Christian myth that seems to have proven so ineffective in stemming materialism's advance. Some look to the East, not recognizing that the contents of their own unconsciouses are still to a great extent conditioned by the biblical myth. Even when insights of exquisite worth are discovered in Eastern thought, it is not possible to integrate them fully until they have found a niche in one's core myth, or until one's core myth has been altered to accommodate them. Since virtually all religions in all cultures have spoken of angels, spirits, and demons, the traditional religions are in some sense all natural allies against materialism and can mutually enrich each other. But mere spiritual nomadism—that aimless wanderlust that characterizes so much of the current ferment—will scarcely prove any more effective against entrenched, senescent materialism than Romanticism before it. Only the revitalization of a powerful countermyth, capable of incorporating the valid aspects of materialism while jettisoning the rest, will be capable of securing the "new age" that so many neoromanticists are heralding.

There is at least one more reason for dusting off these old terms and asking what they may have designated in the actual lives of real people. Teilhard de Chardin[3] has eloquently evoked the picture of human evolution as no longer physical but social, no longer the product of random events but increasingly the consequence of choice and invention. Humanity has gradually begun to become aware of itself as an entity. Two world wars, in all their horror, illustrate this infolding of humanity upon itself, this shrinking of the world through communication, economic and military dependency, scientific cooperation and even tourism. What our century has thus far survived to witness is the staggering speedup of this socialization process. But this global totalization has been going on for several thousands of years. We see a sharp increase in critical consciousness in classical Greece, and simultaneously in Israel, India, and China. We observe the spread of Greek culture and its intersection with Israel and the

East through Alexander the Great and his successors, and then the pervasive establishment and institutionalization of this culture under the Pax Romana.

Hellenization: the term has hitherto referred to the imposition of Greek culture, the collapse of the Greek city-states and their replacement by a cosmopolis, and the breakdown of traditional religions and their incorporation in religious forms and cults capable of universal vision. It is time that we also see Hellenization as a large groundswell in the rising tide of human destiny, when for the first time—in the West at least—this infolding process, due to sufficient density of population and a sufficiently universal vision of humanity, *began to be perceived*. And it was perceived the way artists and seers always perceive the dark new shapes of things—through the language of symbol. They spoke of angels, of demons, of principalities and powers, of gods and elements of the universe, of spirits and Satan. This was not simply a hangover from an even more remote antiquity. Much of this language was new, and what was not new was altered. It was the amorphous, vague but descriptively accurate language of a new awareness, the awareness of powers operative *among and between people:* not transcendent like God, but higher than humans. "Intermediate beings" they seemed, and the names for them mattered little, *so long as one knew they were there.*

That rough and ready phenomenology of the infolding social dimension of reality served well for almost two millennia. Its survival and even revival today (in fundamentalism, Satan cults, tongue-speaking, visions, exorcism, and renewed belief in the devil) is testimony to both its descriptive effectiveness and its profound symbolic power. If the modern age saw fit to renounce such categories of experience, it was because they were thought to be insufficiently precise, and because their residual symbolic power was experienced not as helpful but as a tyranny. Between the use of the Satan image to excuse irresponsibility and its use to terrify people into compliance to sectarian mores, there was little left to commend it. But the modern world threw out the reality with the words, and now finds itself without an adequate vocabulary for powers even more real today than two thousand years ago, due to the ever-tightening compression of the human infolding. *Without a vocabulary—* yes, we have no single language for speaking of the total phenomenon the ancients knew as "the Powers"; but also, *too many vocabularies—* the languages of quite unrelated disciplines each vie in a Babel of technical, esoteric tongues to account for their own discrete sectors of reality. It would be my hope that as more comprehensive languages are developed for describing these intermediate powers which so largely determine personal and social existence, we will recover a degree of respect for the monumental spiritual achievement of our forebears—an achievement that we have not yet overtaken. With a proper humility, perhaps we can more soberly ask ourselves what it was that came to expression in these archaic terms, and what we might be able to learn from them today.

In *Naming the Powers* I developed the thesis that undergirds all three volumes of this work: that the New Testament's "principalities and powers" is a generic category referring to the determining forces of physical, psychic, and social existence. These powers usually consist of an outer manifestation and an inner spirituality or interiority. Power must become incarnate, institutionalized or systemic in order to be effective. It has a dual aspect, possessing both an outer, visible form (constitutions, judges, police, leaders, office complexes), and an inner, invisible spirit that provides it legitimacy, compliance, credibility, and clout.

In the ancient world people discerned and described the interiority of things by the only means available to them: symbolic projection. They were able to monitor the actual impact of the spirituality of an institution like the Roman Empire or the priesthood by throwing it up against the screen of the cosmos in the form of visual images in which the interiority of the social entity was perceived as a personal entity: an angel, demon, or devil. For many this approach still works, but at the cost of considerable mystification. The material or institutional sources of distress often escape notice while the actual spirituality is split off and fought as a separate demonic agency "in the air." Some analysts of this phenomenon have tended to debunk the spiritual as a smokescreen masking the real material determinants: the economic system, the state apparatus, the power elite. This was no doubt often the case. But a proper understanding of the dynamic of symbolic projection leads to quite a different conclusion: every economic system, state apparatus, and power elite *does* have an intrinsic spirituality, an inner essence, a collective culture or ethos, which cannot be directly deciphered from its outer manifestations (they, in fact, may be deliberate attempts to deceive people through propaganda, image making, and advertising). The corporate spirits of IBM and Gulf Western are palpably real and strikingly different, as are the national spirits of the United States and Canada, or the congregational spirits ("angels") of every individual church. What the ancients called "spirits" or "angels" or "demons" were actual entities, only they were not hovering in the air. They were incarnate in cellulose, or cement, or skin and bones, or an empire, or its mercenary armies.

In the present volume we will be focusing on just seven of the Powers mentioned in Scripture. Their selection out of all the others dealt with in *Naming the Powers* is partly arbitrary: they happen to be ones about which I felt I had something to say. But they are also representative, and open the way to comprehending the rest. Nor are they the end of the story. For while the Powers dealt with in this volume—Satan, demons, angels of churches, angels of nations, gods, elements, angels of nature—are instances of the hidden interiority of reality, volume 3 (*Engaging the Powers*) will provide an occasion to look at some of their more visible, institutionalized forms. The list of possible candidates for examination there is virtually endless: economics, militarism, propaganda, education, language, ideologies, rules, roles, values, the legal system, politics, sports, religion, families—all of social reality falls under the category of the Powers.

We will begin in this volume with the more immediate personal experience of evil (the devil, demons) and gradually bring into focus the issue of worldview or cosmology. It is not my intent to defend the biblical worldview, for it is in many ways beyond being salvaged, limited as it was by the science, philosophy, and religion of its age. This very relativity of the biblical cosmology to its historical epoch led many theologians earlier in our century to discount cosmology as unimportant altogether, a husk to be stripped from the kernel and cast aside. We can now see, however, that such an approach simply meant acquiescing without a struggle to the worldview of modern materialism. That uncritical capitulation is the cause in large part of the split that runs through so many religious people today, who want to hold two utterly incompatible things together: belief in God as the Creator of the world and Sovereign of the Powers, and belief in the materialistic myth of modern science, which systematically excludes God from reality.

Cosmology is not gospel. It is not the core proclamation, not the revealed truth of human existence. But cosmology certainly determines how that message can be spoken and how heard. It is not the Word made flesh, it is its cradle. But it is a very important cradle. It is not a matter of indifference that the New Testament proclamation was couched in the language, thought-forms and concepts of the Greco-Roman world, even as it poured new and finally shattering contents into them. At one level, Christian evangelists sought only to convert people, but at another, they sought to claim an epoch, to take captive an entire culture, to mediate a new way of seeing the world. They accomplished these objectives so thoroughly that the question of cosmology could be dropped from the theological agenda for fifteen hundred years. *The gospel had become its own cosmology.* With the rise of the worldview of scientific materialism, however, that cosmology became first problematic, then dubious, and finally unintelligible. And because the gospel had become indistinguishable from the cosmology in which it was couched, it faced compounded difficulties in addressing the whole life of modern people meaningfully.

What increasing numbers of people are now realizing, both inside and outside organized religion, is that Christianity's lack of credibility is not a consequence of the inadequacy of its intrinsic message, but of the fact that its intrinsic message cannot—simply, categorically, cannot—be communicated meaningfully within a materialistic cosmology. Some, sensing the irresolvable contradiction, have simply abandoned religion. Others have dismissed modern science altogether—a sacrifice of the intellect made all the sadder by the fact that modern science need not have, and never should have, wedded itself to the mechanistic images and materialistic philosophy of Democritus in the first place. Still others have attempted a desperate compromise, in blind faith that two things that seem so true, science and religion, must be finally reconcilable, even if it is not yet evident how.

This book attempts to go beyond these alternatives. It is not simply a commentary on New Testament cosmology, though that is inevitably our starting point, but an attempt to contribute toward a new, postmaterialist cosmology, drawing on biblical resources. I will not argue that all of the Powers featured in this volume are equally weighted in Scripture. Satan holds a prominent place in most of the books of the New Testament, but demons are more frequently encountered in the Synoptic Gospels, and gods, elements, and the angels of nature, nations, and the churches make only infrequent appearances. It is not my purpose to argue that they were central aspects of the gospel. What I wish to argue, however, is that recovery of these concepts and *a sense of the experiences that they named* can play a crucial role in eroding the soil from beneath the foundations of materialism. At the same time they can provide a language for naming these experiences in the new worldview that is emerging. Just as the materialist paradigm cannot tolerate the mere *possibility* of ESP, clairvoyance, psychokinesis, or spiritual healing, even when scientific evidence is piled up in their favor, so it cannot account for the kinds of spiritual experiences identified by the traditional terminology of Satan, demons, gods, and angels. It is precisely their incompatibility with the dominant scientific mind-set, their incomprehensibility within its rubrics that makes these biblical categories so important today. They are a scandal, a stone of stumbling, a bone in the throat of modernity. They represent a worst-case test of its capacity to give an accounting of the whole compass of human experience. Properly understood, they expose the soft underbelly of a philosophical system which has attempted to banish God from the earth; and not God only, but all spirits from the earth; and not spirits only, but our own spirits as well.

More intimately, a reassessment of these Powers—angels, demons, gods, elements, the devil—allows us to reclaim, name, and comprehend types of experiences that materialism renders mute and inexpressible. We have the experiences but miss their meaning. Unable to name our experiences of these intermediate powers of existence, we are simply constrained by them compulsively. They are never more powerful than when they are unconscious. Their capacities to bless us are thwarted, their capacities to possess us augmented. Unmasking these Powers can mean for us initiation into a dimension of reality "not known, because not looked for," in T. S. Eliot's words. In the new world of quantum physics and the new sciences of life and consciousness, these antiquated, repudiated, and neglected Powers can open new awareness of the richly textured plentitude of life, its abysses as well as its ecstasies. The goal of such unmasking is to enable people to see how they have been determined, and to free them to choose, insofar as they have genuine choice, what they will be determined by in the future.

We are living through a watershed period intellectually, a vast sea-change in the metaphors with which we describe and make our home in the world. This work is but one of many that are questioning the adequacy of *the* materialist metaphor and groping for its replacement. As is so often the case with things that are new and thus have no history of failures, there is in many of these attempts a naive utopianism, as if all that is faulty is the old metaphor and not me. Such approaches lack seriousness about the intractability of evil, and believe that education, or meditation, or a new worldview, or an ecological attitude, or the application of science to human values, is all that it will take to bring in a time of peace and plenty. Once again, the deep wisdom of the past must figure in the emergence of the new, or else we will be consigned to repeat or even augment the evils of the past.

Notes

1. I am using myth here in the best sense, as the privileged narrative by which a community has come to understand and relate to what it holds to be the ultimate meaning of reality. "Myth" as it is used in these volumes has nothing of the old sense of falsehood, unreality, or specious fabrication.

2. Paul Ricoeur finds only four fundamental mythic structures that have played a vital role in Western life (*The Symbolism of Evil* [New York: Harper & Brothers, 1957]), Morton Kelsey identifies seven (*Myth, History and Faith* [New York: Paulist Press, 1974]).

3. Pierre Teilhard de Chardin, *The Future of Man* (New York: Harper & Row, 1964), 271ff.

6

Satan

After noting that the concept of Satan commands little belief and less respect in the modern world with its materialistic worldview, Walter Wink begins his study of Satan in Scripture and in the world with the curious but demonstrable assertion that, in his three Old Testament appearances and in many of his New Testament appearances as well, Satan functions as a "servant of the living God." In the Old Testament, Satan functions in three capacities: (1) as one who executes God's wrath against the sinful, (2) as the "accuser or prosecuting attorney" in the heavenly court, and (3) as an agent provocateur. In each of these functions, Satan exhibits great zeal for divine justice but, as Wink points out, "excessive zeal for justice always becomes satanic." Although in the New Testament and in subsequent Christian thought Satan was transformed from the Servant of God into the Enemy of God, Wink identifies nine New Testament texts where the case can be made that Satan still functions on God's behalf—which must be on behalf of humankind as well. Wink concludes that the apparent contradiction between Satan as God's Servant and Satan as the Evil One can be resolved by placing these notions at the opposite poles of a continuum. The moral choices that humans make locate their experience of Satan on that continuum in varying degrees of evil and servanthood. As a spiritual reality manifest in tangible expressions of power, Satan's function veers toward evil when humans make uncreative rather than creative choices. As Wink wisely asserts, "Whether one 'believes' in Satan ... is not nearly as important as that one recognizes the satanic function as part and parcel of every decision."

Source: Wink 1986: Excerpted from Chapter 1

Nothing commends Satan to the modern mind. It is bad enough that Satan is spirit, when our worldview has banned spirit from discourse and belief. But worse, he is evil, and our culture resolutely refuses to believe in the real existence of evil, preferring to regard it as a kind of systems breakdown that can be fixed with enough tinkering. Worse yet, Satan is not a very good intellectual idea. Once theology lost its character as reflection on the experience of *knowing* God, and became a second-level exercise in *knowing about*, the experiential ground of theology began to erode away. "Although mythologically true," Morton Kelsey writes,

> the devil is intellectually indefensible, and once it was realized that the conception of the powers of evil was "only" a representation of peoples' experience, no matter how accurate, the devil began to fade. . . . With only sense experience and reason to go on, and with no rational place for an evil first cause, enlightened people simply dropped the devil from consideration. With direct psychic experience no longer admissible as evidence of his reality, the devil was as good as dead.[1]

Nor is this picture essentially altered by polls that show belief in Satan to be sharply on the increase. As we shall see later, such belief is most frequently a component of neurotic religion, and the remarkably subtle character of Satan is collapsed into a two-dimensional bogeyman that has only vague similarities with the biblical devil. The Satan image, even where it lingers on, has been whittled down to the stature of a personal being whose sole obsessions would seem to be with sexual promiscuity, adolescent rebellion, crime, passion, and greed. While not themselves trivial, these preoccupations altogether obscure the massive satanic evils that plunge and drive our times like a trawler before an angry sea. When television evangelists could try to terrorize us with Satan and then speak favorably of South African apartheid, we should have sensed something wrong. When the large evil went undetected, when the symbol no longer attracted to the fact, when evil ran roughshod through corporate boardrooms and even churches, unnoticed and unnamed, while "Satan" was relegated to superego reinforcement and moralistic scare tactics then we should have caught the stench—not of brimstone, but of putrefaction. Not that we had progressed beyond evil. On the contrary, *the evil of our time had become so gigantic that it had virtually outstripped the symbol and become autonomous, unrepresentable, beyond comprehension.*

We had killed Satan. For those who never mourned his passing, who even met it with relief, I offer this awkward and perhaps unwelcome parody, pilfered (satanically) from any number of poets:

> Killed Satan!
> Hardly the words are out

before we notice the sky has darkened,
not into perpetual night,
but into unending grey.

Satan dead!
and we scarcely even missed him,
that old tempter with whom we toyed
and lost, enjoying the thrill of transgressing
something that could be transgressed.
Now, without Satan,
Where's the thrill?

So Satan is gone!
And now how will we recognize evil
before it has us already in its maw?
How will we know we have crossed the boundary
beyond human return,
without Him there to say,
"Oh, come on across."

Every point gives vertigo,
we reel, dizzy and sick,
every spot on earth a mount of temptation,
without a tempter, without bounds,
with no stakes left, nor obedience,
nothing but survival into that grey,
never-ending, dawnless day.

While the symbol may have fallen on hard times, the reality to which it gave expression has become all the more virulent. Satan did not begin life as an idea, but an experience. The issue is not whether one "believes" in Satan, but whether or not one is able to identify in the actual events of life that dimension of experience the ancients called "Satan." Nor is the metaphysical question, Does Satan really exist? of any real urgency, unless the question is asked in the context of an actual encounter with Something or Someone that leads one to posit Satan's existence.

Without a means of symbolization, however, evil cannot come to conscious awareness and thus be consciously resisted. Like an undiagnosed disease it rages through society, and we are helpless to produce a cure. *Evil must be symbolized precisely because it cannot be thought.* [2] Is there any way we can resymbolize evil? Thought cannot resuscitate Satan, but only committed persons consciously making choices for God, as we will see. But thought can perhaps roll away the stone. Then perhaps, if we can live through that dark interval between Satan's death and resurrection, we may yet see Satan functioning again—as a servant of the living God!

Satan as a Servant of God

We are not accustomed to thinking of Satan as God's servant. But when Satan makes his late appearance in the Old Testament, that is precisely what he is. The faith of early Israel actually had no place for Satan. God alone was Lord, and thus whatever happened, for good or ill, was ascribed to God. "I kill and I make alive," says the Lord, "I wound and I heal."

So it was not inconsistent to believe that Yahweh might call Moses to deliver Israel from Egypt and then, on the way, attempt to murder him. The text, much neglected by preachers, is Exod. 4:24-26a. "On the journey, when, Moses had halted for the night, Yahweh came to meet him and tried to kill him. At once Zipporah, taking up a flint, cut off her son's foreskin and with it she touched the genitals of Moses. 'Truly you are a bridegroom of blood to me!' she said. And Yahweh let him live" (JB). Perhaps Moses had fallen critically ill, or had been almost killed by and attack or fall or avalanche, or had somatized his terror at the enormity of his task. In any case, the attack was ascribed, not to natural causes, but to God.

The God who led Israel out of Egypt, however, was a God of justice. How then could God demand justice, be just, and still cause evil? Had not Abraham challenged God with the question, "Shall not the Judge of the earth do right?" (Gen. 18:25)? This problem was the terrible price Israel had been forced to pay for its belief that Yahweh was the primary cause of all that happens. Morally, the cost was unbearable. Gradually Yahweh became differentiated into a "light" and a "dark" side, both integral to the Godhead, with Yahweh transcending both as the unity that encompasses multiplicity.[3] The bright side came to be represented by the angels, the dark by Satan and his demons.

Yet this process of differentiation was completed so late that Satan makes only three appearances in the Old Testament. In 2 Sam. 24:1 Yahweh in anger against Israel had incited David to carry out a census (the basis of taxation and military conscription). But in Chronicles, a postcaptivity revision of Samuel and Kings, this same passage is changed to read, *"Satan* stood up against Israel, and incited David to number Israel" (1 Chron. 21:1). The Adversary has assumed the function of executor of God's wrath. Satan is an *agent provocateur* who plants oppressive ideas in a mortal's mind. He does not represent disorder, chaos, or rebellion here, but rather the imposition of a suffocating bureaucratic order (the census). Satan furthers God's will by visiting wrath on disobedient mortals, and in so doing carries out the will of God.

In Zech. 3:1-5 we find "the satan" in the role of accuser or prosecuting attorney.

> Then he showed me Joshua the high priest standing before the angel of the Lord, and Satan (*ha satan*) standing at his right hand to accuse him. And the Lord said to Satan, "The Lord rebuke you, O Satan! The Lord who has chosen Jerusalem rebuke you! Is not this a brand plucked from the fire?" Now Joshua was standing before the angel, clothed with filthy garments. And the angel said to those who were standing before him, "Remove the filthy garments from him." And to him he said "Behold, I have taken your iniquity away from you, and I will clothe you with rich apparel." And I said, "Let them put a clean turban on his head." So they put a clean turban on his head and clothed him with garments; and the angel of the Lord was standing by.

The scene is set in the heavenly council, with the accuser at the right of the accused, Joshua.[4] The high priest, representing the whole people of Israel, is dressed in filthy garments, symbolic of the sins that Israel's prophets had identified as the cause of Israel's exile in Babylon. The vision is dated around 520 b.c.e.; this means that upward of three generations of Jews had lived with the belief that they had gone into captivity in 585 as punishment for their infidelity to Yahweh. Joshua bears all that collective guilt. The Adversary merely reiterates what the accusing conscience of the people has been affirming all along. The guilt is real, and it is deserved. Only God's undeserved grace causes the case to be quashed.

Satan is clearly not demonic here. If anything, Satan echoes what everyone knows to be the attitude of *God* toward Israel, prior to God's unexpected reversal of the judgment. Satan merely repeats what the prophets had been saying all along! Nevertheless God intervenes. Israel is a "brand plucked from the fire"; it will be consumed by guilt and succumb to hopelessness unless it experiences forgiveness soon. Satan is thus not merely a mythological character invented out of whole cloth; the "adversary" is that actual inner or collective voice of condemnation that any sensitive person hears tirelessly repeating accusations of guilt or inferiority. And indeed, there is often a degree of truth in the charges.

But Satan's demand for strict justice, untempered by mercy, can crush the spirit of a person or a people. This "voice" is a phenomenological fact; its mythic conceptualization makes it possible to isolate it, lift it to consciousness, and ask whether it is indeed the voice of God.

The final Old Testament reference to Satan is in the prologue to Job. "Now there was a day when the sons of God (*bene elohim*) came to present themselves before the Lord, and Satan (*ha satan*) also came among them." Here again, Satan is not a fallen angel but a fully credentialed member of the heavenly court. "The Lord said to Satan, 'Whence have you come?' Satan answered the Lord, 'From going to and fro on the earth, and from walking up and down on it.'" His role is somewhat like that of a district attorney, zealously seeking out lawbreakers to bring before the bar of divine justice. "And the Lord said to Satan, 'Have you considered my servant Job, that there is none like him on the earth, a blameless and upright man, who fears God and turns away from evil?'" Satan has indeed considered him well: "Then Satan answered the Lord, 'Does Job fear God for naught? Hast thou not put a hedge about him and his house and all that he has, on every side? Thou hast blessed the work of his hands, and his possessions have increased in the land. But put forth thy hand now, and touch all that he has, and he will curse thee to thy face.' And the Lord said to Satan, 'Behold, all that he has is in your power; only upon himself do not put forth your hand.' Satan went forth from the presence of the Lord" (Job 1:6-12).

This is more than simply prosecution, however. It is entrapment. Not content merely to uncover injustice, Satan is here, as in 1 Chron. 21:1, an *agent provocateur*, actively striving to coax people into crimes for which they can then be punished. Excessive zeal for justice always becomes satanic. All Job's oxen, asses, camels, sheep, and servants are slain; then finally all his sons and daughters. Yet Job holds piously to his faith (1:21).

When next they meet, God chides Satan for his failure: Job "'still holds fast his integrity, although you moved me against him, to destroy him without cause'" (2:3). What kind of God is this that trifles with the lives and flesh of human beings in order to win a bet? This God is too bent on sheer power to mark the sufferings of mere people. The author seems to be deliberately lifting up the God of a degenerated Deuteronomic theology to ridicule. That God (represented by Job's three "comforters"), who rewards the wealthy landed aristocrats with riches and long lives and curses the poor, is the butt of a merciless lampoon that issues from the outraged sensibilities of a writer who has acutely observed how the oppressed and infirm suffer undeserved evil at the hands of the powerful and rich. Those God has not blessed, who have no such vast herds and spacious houses, but barely subsist on the land, must relish seeing this rich man stripped of his props and reduced to their level. And they must have chuckled with delight at the storyteller's artful repetition in 2:1-3, where God behaves like a forgetful potentate unable to recall the job description of his own appointee!

Job's Satan, in short, while no friend of Job's, is in fact humanity's best friend, who lures God into a contest that will end by stripping God of the projections of the oppressors. Satan has already persuaded God to act arbitrarily ("to destroy him without cause"). Now Satan compounds the murder of Job's children with the torture of Job's own body: "'Put forth thy hand now, and touch his bone and his flesh, and he will curse thee to thy face.' And the Lord said to Satan, 'Behold, he is your power; only spare his life.'" (2:5-6).

In all this, Satan manifests no power independent of God. Even when Satan slays, it is not Satan who does so, but God who slays through Satan ("the fire *of God*," 1:6; God alone is supreme; Satan is fully integrated into the godhead in a wholly nondualistic fashion. Satan is not evil, or demonic, or fallen, or God's enemy. This adversary is merely a faithful, if overzealous servant of God entrusted with quality control and testing. Satan, in fact prompts God and humanity (in the person of Job) to explore the problem of evil and righteousness at a depth never before plumbed—and seldom since.

These three passages exhaust the references to Satan in the Old Testament and even in these Satan is more a function ("the adversary") than a personality. It is only in the period between the testaments, and even more in the period of the New Testament and early church, that Satan gains recognition. Soon he will become known as the Enemy of God, the Father of Lies, the Black One, the Arch-Fiend, and assume the stature of a virtual rival to God. We will come to all that. But first we must do justice to those passages in the New Testament where Satan continues to function as a servant of God. So accustomed are most of us to thinking of Satan as purely evil that we tend to read this interpretation into passages where there is nothing of the kind. If we suspend that bias, the evidence points toward a strikingly different picture.

Luke 22:31-34. Jesus is speaking: "'Simon, Simon, behold, Satan demanded to have you [plural], that he might sift you [plural] like wheat, but I have prayed for you [singular] that your [singular] faith may not fail; and when you have turned again, strengthen your brethren.' And he said to him, 'Lord, I am ready to go with you to prison and to death. He said, 'I tell you, Peter, the cock will not crow this day, until you three times deny that you know me.'" Satan is God's sifter, the left hand of God, whose task it is to strain out the impurities in the disciples' commitment to God. Had Peter been fully conscious of his frailty and flightiness, he would never have responded with such bravado. Had he been able to say, "Yes, Lord, I am weak and impulsive; pray for me to stand through this trial," perhaps such sifting would not have been necessary. But it is clear that nothing Jesus has been able to do has weaned him or the rest from egocentricity. Satan has made a legitimate request; they deserve to be put to the test. *Jesus has to grant Satan's request.* He does not pray that they be delivered from the test, but only that their faith may not fail through it. *Satan is depicted here as able to accomplish something that Jesus had himself been unable to achieve during his ministry.* If we refuse to face our own evil, and take refuge, like Peter, in claims to righteousness, our own evil comes up to meet us in the events triggered by our very unconsciousness. Satan is not then a mere idea invented to "explain" the problem of evil, but is rather the distillate precipitated by the actual existential experience of being sifted. When God cannot reach us through our conscious commitment, sometimes there is no other way to get our attention than to use the momentum of our unconsciousness to slam us up against the wall. Heavenly jujitsu practiced by God's "enforcer," this meat-fisted, soul-sifting Satan—servant of the living God!

1 Corinthians 5:1-5. A man in the Corinthian church is sleeping with his stepmother. Paul writes:

> Let him who has done this be removed from among you.
> For though absent in body I am present in spirit, and as if present, I have already pronounced judgment in the name of the Lord Jesus on the man who has done such a thing. When you are assembled, and my spirit is present, with the power of our Lord Jesus, you are to deliver this man to Satan for the destruction of the flesh, that his spirit may be saved in the day of the Lord Jesus.

This reads uncomfortably like a text from the Spanish Inquisition. Is the man to be ritually murdered? The language is extreme, but apparently Paul only means that they should excommunicate him (5:2, 13), thus forcing him to choose between his sexual preoccupation and his faith in Christ. Destruction of the "flesh" would then refer, not to his body, but as is usual in Paul, to the whole life-orientation that his actions betray him to be mired in, body, soul, and spirit: a world reduced to the limits of sensual gratification. Satan is to work him over through the choice forced upon him by the act of ceremonial exclusion (and possibly shunning), "that his spirit might be *saved*"—at least on Christ's return, but possibly, through Satan's good offices, rather immediately.

Apparently the man did repent, for 2 Cor. 2:5-11 seems to relate the outcome of the punishment. Ironically, however, the very congregation that had tolerated his sin as an expression of Christian freedom from the law now refuses to forgive him and receive him back. And the same Paul who chastised them with the full force of his spiritual authority now must plead with the congregation to forgive and comfort him lest he be overwhelmed by excessive sorrow. Such self-righteous, judgmental behavior manifests the very qualities we saw associated with Satan in Zech. 3:1-5. Their new-found zeal for justice is as overweening and one-sided as their previous indifference. Paul wants to "keep Satan from gaining the advantage over" them (2 Cor. 2:11), an advantage that would be won, not through their tolerance of sin, but by their refusal to forgive!

Satan's role here is remarkably fluid. Satan is again God's holy sifter. Using the momentum of the man's sin, Satan casts him into the annealing fire of a solitude in which he is given precisely what he thought he wanted—and absolutely nothing else besides. But the choice could have gone either way. Had he chosen for the woman and against the church, Satan would have appeared to have been the instrument of his damnation.

Again, if the church had refused to tender its forgiveness to the man, Satan would have caught them in a charade of self-righteousness, thus "gaining the advantage over us" (2 Cor. 2:11). By refusing to forgive, the church plays the role of Satan in Zechariah 3, reiterating an accusation that God is prepared to drop. Satan is thus not an independent operative, but rather *the inner and actual spirit of the congregation itself when it falls into the accusatory mode*. So Satan cannot be described here as "good" or "evil." It is *our choices* that cause him to crystallize as the one or the other.

And most astonishing of all, Paul does not say that Satan enticed this man to sin; rather, Satan is the means of his deliverance! This understanding of Satan has little in common with the irremediably evil Satan of popular Christian thought.

1 Timothy 1:20. The writer of 1Timothy says (in the name of Paul) that he has delivered the heretics Hymenaeus and Alexander "to Satan that they may learn not to blaspheme." Apparently the writer does not mean that he has damned them to hell for eternal punishment. He really seems to expect them to learn to stop blaspheming and return to the fold. Once we acknowledge that Satan is a devoted servant of God, the meaning is transparent: these men, like the fellow in 1 Corinthians 5, are to be excommunicated in order to force them to recover a sense of "conscience" (1:19) and abandon their libertine ways.

Matthew 4:1-11 (Luke 4:1-13). Jesus has just left his baptism where he has heard God declare him his beloved son. The dovelike Spirit that came upon him there now leads him out into the wilderness "to be tempted by the devil." What kind of collusion is this? Why, if he needs testing, does the Spirit not provide it? Why place him in ultimate jeopardy by throwing him into the hands of Satan? It makes no sense at all—if Satan is evil personified. But if he is the heavenly sifter, the setter of choice, then we have a different story altogether.

"And the tempter came and said to him, 'If you are the Son of God, command these stones to become loaves of bread.'" What is so wrong about that? Later he will feed the five thousand. The fast of forty days has ended (*"afterward* he was hungry," v. 2); now he must eat or die. If he could demonstrate such to meet the basic needs of the masses, surely he could generate an instant following. Moses had cried to God and God had sent manna to the people of Israel; how much more ready should God be to perform mighty works on behalf of Jesus? People would recognize him as the New Moses, the prophet of the end time, the deliverer of Israel, and flock to his banner.

Jesus refuses. Is it because such acts violate the nature of the "Father" revealed to him at his baptism? Or is it because of that sticky *"if* you are the Son of God" with its taunt to prove his sonship by a miracle?—an act that could only prove his mistrust. For whatever reason, he turns the temptation aside by means of Deut. 8:3. He will not live by bread alone, but "by every word that proceeds from the mouth of God." He will live by what God says, and God had said at his baptism, "Thou art my beloved son."

Nothing exposes one to temptation more dangerously than a successful rebuff of temptation. Satan seizes upon the very answer as the next temptation. You mean to live by every word that proceeds from the mouth of God? Very well, then here is one such word. *"It is written,* 'He will give his angels charge of you,' and 'on their hands they will bear you up, lest you strike your foot against a stone'" (Ps. 91:11-12). Put God to the test. Trust God's promises. "If you are the son of God, throw yourself down" from the pinnacle of the temple in Jerusalem. Surely the courtyard will be teeming with people. They will instantly recognize in such an amazing rescue God's stamp of approval on the Chosen One of God.

What could be appealing to Jesus in such a suicidal fantasy? He is being tempted to prove himself invulnerable, indestructible, a superhuman being immune to the threat of death. Having just forsworn the shortcut of feeding the masses, what guarantee has he that God will protect his life on the more difficult path of making disciples? He has received an immense calling; what will become of his mission if he is prematurely killed? Will God intervene to guarantee his survival until he has accomplished his task?

This temptation takes place at the temple, where Malachi had prophesied that the Lord would suddenly appear to cleanse it of pollution and purify the priesthood (Mal. 3:1-4). Is he perhaps called to be the Priestly Messiah who would restore true worship in Israel?

Jesus again refuses. "Again it is written, 'You shall not tempt the Lord your God.'" To live by what one has heard from God does not mean biblical prooftexting. It means listening to what God says to us about the specific life-tasks to which we are called. The word of God must be found and heard among all of the welter of voices of Scripture, tradition, creed, doctrine, experience, science, intuition, the community; but God's word is none of these alone, or perhaps even all of them together. Jesus is being nudged by God toward a new unprecedented thing, for which no models existed. No one else could have helped advise him. Scripture itself seemed loaded in the opposite direction—toward messianic models of power, might and empire. The dominant image was—but let Satan say it:

> Again, the devil took him to a very high mountain, and showed him all the kingdoms of the world and the glory of them; and he said to him, "All these I will give you, if you will fall down and worship me." (Matt. 4:8-9)

Satan is offering him the kingdom of David, grown to the proportions of world empire. Scripture was rife with this hope. Israel seethed with longing for some form of its fulfillment. Jesus could not but have internalized that desire: freedom from Roman oppression, restoration of God's nation, the vindication of Yahweh's honor. This is no bald seduction. What is Satan tempting him with here and in each of these "temptations," if not *what everyone knew to be the will of God?* Mosaic Prophet, Priestly Messiah, Davidic King—these were the images of redemption which everyone believed God had given them in scripture. (And in no time at all they would be the titles given Jesus by the church: Prophet, Priest, and King.) What irony: everyone in Israel knew the will of God for redemption—except Jesus. He was straining with every nerve to hear what it was *as if he alone did not know it.*

And Satan's function in all this? He is no archfiend seducing Jesus with offers of love, wealth, and carnal pleasures. Satan's task is far more subtle. He presents Jesus with well-attested scriptural expectations which everyone assumed were God's chosen means of redeeming Israel. Satan throws up to Jesus the collective Messianic hopes, and by so doing brings them for the first time to consciousness as options to be chosen rather than as a fate to be accepted. Tested against his own sense of calling, they did not fit. Jesus could perceive them to be "yesterday's will of God," not what was proceeding out of the mouth of God.

Satan offers him, in short, not outright evils but the highest goods known to Israel. That is when the satanic is most difficult to discern—when it offers us the good instead of the best. That does not mean Satan is benign. By no means! We have so moralized him that we fail to see that the most satanic temptation of all is the temptation to become someone other than ourselves. When people try to "be good Christians"—what is that but Satan's crowning victory? For "being a good Christian" is always collectively defined by some denomination or strong religious personality or creed. One does not need to "live by every word that proceeds from the mouth of God" in order to be a "good Christian"; one need only be pliant, docile, and obedient. Is it not easier to "let Jesus do it all for us" or imitate Christ, rather than embark on the risky, vulnerable, hazardous journey of seeking to find God's will in all its mundane specificity for our own lives? That harder way will certainly entail mistakes and failures, false starts, and sin masquerading as innovation. Perhaps the collective way is better—but what am I doing, my friends? With whose voice am I speaking?

So Satan again appears to be a strange servant of the living God. When Jesus is depicted as leaving the wilderness and moving "with a sure, fierce love towards Galilee," [5] he does so not so much knowing who he is and what he will do, as who he is not and what he will not do. The rest will emerge through interruptions (most of the stories in the Gospels are accounts of interruptions), through listening, through being true to the baptismal voice as the entelechy of his being. As Rivkah Scharf Kluger puts it, "The human will becomes conscious through its collision with the divine will, by coming up against the adversary. Thus, behind the deadly threat of the divine opposition there is also hidden a positive, purposeful aspect; the adversary, as such, is at the same time the creator of individual consciousness." [6] In short, the conscious devil is useful; the unconscious devil is perilous.

John B. Cobb, Jr., has defined the eternal Logos (the divine Word) as the lure that attracts us to "that specific actualization which is the best outcome for the given situation."[7] Held up against the divine Logos, Satan here would represent the lesser lures and promptings that appear alongside the lure of the highest. Some of these lures are flagrantly evil; most are not intrinsically evil but merely trivial, less than best: a diversion, a waste. In another situation or for another person they might in fact represent the "will of God"—the persuasive call to creative transformation. But here, now, with this person or event, they would mean a diminishing of the potential for creative novelty in the world, a regression to collective tendencies, a settling for an old novelty that has exhausted its creative strength—in short, *yesterday's will of God.*

Satan, our adversary, is the one who puts the question at the leading edge of possibility—right at the place where the creative potentiality can be suffocated. The issue then is what we bring to the encounter. If we relate to choice unconsciously, it can become for us "evil" (even if our choice is, as so often for Christians, to be "harmless"). But if we bring consciousness to choice, along with commitment to doing God's will in the situation, Satan serves us and God by bringing to consciousness those unconscious roles and expectations that prompt so much regressively habitual action. Related to properly, Satan can be the centrifuge by means of which what is not essential to selfhood or society is precipitated out. Satan is not gentle; if we relate to him unconsciously we can be destroyed. Satan plays for the highest stakes of all, but for those who bring the light of the image of God to the struggle for choice, Satan is "Lucifer," light-bearer—a very brilliant servant of God.

Am I belaboring the point? I shall labor even more, to rectify two millennia in which Satan has been so persistently maligned. Satan served Paul personally, caught as Paul was in his own proclivities for boasting, as the next text shows.

2 Corinthians 12:1-10. "And to keep me from being too elated by the abundance of revelations, a thorn was given me in the flesh, a messenger of Satan, to harass me." Three times he asked God to remove it; the third time God spoke: "'My grace is sufficient for you, for my power is made perfect in weakness.'" Did Paul *need* a disability in order to combat a pride too powerful for him to master? We cannot even begin to guess what his "thorn" was; what is clear is that what might have been merely a satanic affliction is made, by Paul's faithfulness in confronting it, a means by which his own chronic tendencies to inflation were continually kept in check. How kind of Satan to assist—as he is always ready to do—when we cannot consciously let some part of our egos die!

1 Corinthians 7:5. Some couples in the church at Corinth are abstaining from sex. Paul responds: "Do not refuse one another except perhaps by agreement for a season, that you may devote yourselves to prayer; but then come together again, lest Satan tempt you through lack of self-control." Satan operates like a thermostat: when a husband and wife have abstained from sex for the sake of prayer for too long, temptations arise, signaling that piety has become foolishness, and that conjugal relations should be resumed, "lest Satan tempt you through lack of self-control." It is worth noting, as Trevor Ling points out, that Satan is depicted here as having to wait until we present him with an opportunity, and that *not sexuality but an abnormal abstinence from it* provides the satanic occasion.[8] The image of a thermostat is especially pertinent, because Satan seems to operate at both extremes, and acts as a negative constraint prepared to exploit both our ascetic silliness and our libertine excesses.

Ephesians 4:26-27. "Be angry but do not sin; do not let the sun go down on your anger, and give no opportunity to the devil." Note this: the anger is not caused by the devil. The author regards it as absolutely essential, even going so far as to *command* his hearers to express it: "Be angry." But one must then deal with it, and not let it sink into the unconscious, where it can connect up with all sorts of autonomous complexes and balloon into a murderous wrath. We work with our anger consciously, or else the devil works with it. There is no escape from anger, either way. How sharply this contrasts with the belief of so many people that anger *itself* is satanic, rather than how we deal with it.

James 4:7. "Submit yourselves therefore to God. Resist the devil and he will flee from you." This is not the devil of popular fantasy, that enemy of our race. This devil knows his place! St. Ignatius Loyola understood this with clinical precision. "It is the nature of our enemy to become powerless, lose courage, and take to flight as soon as a person who is following the spiritual life stands courageously against his temptations and does exactly the opposite of what he suggests. On the contrary, if a person begins to take flight and lose courage while fighting temptation, no wild beast is more fierce than the enemy of our human nature as he pursues his evil intention with ever increasing malice."[9] In short, *we* elicit Satan's demonic aspect by our refusal to face the regressive alternative he poses.

Jude 1:8-9 (2 Peter 2:10-11). In light of all this, we should not revile Satan. "But when the archangel Michael, contending with the devil, disputed about the body of Moses, he did not presume to pronounce a reviling judgment upon him but said, 'The Lord rebuke you'" (see Zech. 3:2). Some lost legend lies behind this, alluded to in the *Assumption of Moses:* When God sent Michael to bury the body of Moses, the devil laid claim to it on the ground that Moses had murdered the Egyptian. Here again Satan is characterized by an excessive zeal for strict, merciless justice. Michael calls on God to rebuke Satan, not because Satan is evil but because he is a legalist.

Nevertheless, Michael shows respect, unlike the "revilers" in Jude's church, for Satan has a thankless job which should not be made more miserable by vilification. Or as the writer of Ecclesiasticus put it with deep psychological insight, "When the ungodly curseth Satan, he curseth his own soul" (21:27). For it is not Satan's fault when we refuse to learn from the dark side of God about the dark side of ourselves.

Do not unfairly revile Satan. When one rabbi preached that Satan acts only from the highest motives, the Talmud relates, Satan came and kissed his feet in gratitude (*T. B. Baba Batra* 15b-16a)! When one has the task of God's enforcer, prosecutor, sifter, *agent provocateur,* tester, catalyst of consciousness, advocate of strict justice, and guardian of the status quo, though one be ever so faithful a servant of the living God, one gets little appreciation.

This aspect of Satan as God's servant is stated with wonderful simplicity in the following dialogue between Sidney Harris and his daughter:

> My little nine-year-old girl said to me, "Daddy, there's something peculiar about the whole story of God and the devil and hell. It just doesn't hold together." "Oh," I said, "and why doesn't it hold together?" "Well," she continued, "God is supposed to love good people, and the devil is supposed to favor bad people. Right? The good people go to God, but the bad people go to hell, where the devil punishes them forever. Isn't that the story?" When I agreed that it was, she continued, "It doesn't make sense. In that case, the devil couldn't be the enemy of God. I mean, if the devil really was on the side of the bad people, he wouldn't punish them in hell, would he? He'd treat them nicely and be kind to them for coming over to his side. He'd give them candy and presents and not burn them up." "You've got a point," I said. "So how do you work it out?" She thought for a moment, and then she asserted, on the side of God, "It seems to me that if the whole story is true, then the devil is secretly on the side of God, and is just pretending to be wicked. He works for God as a kind of secret agent, testing people to find out who's good or bad, but not really fighting against God." "That's remarkable!" I exclaimed. "Do you think there's any proof?" "Well," she concluded, "here's another thing. If God is really all-powerful, no devil would have a chance against him. So if a devil really exists, it must be because he's secretly in cahoots with God!"[10]

But there is another side to Satan, one more familiar to most of us, and far more chilling. How did Satan pass from being God's servant—to God's enemy?

Satan as the Evil One

Already we have seen Satan in his role of *agent provocateur* (1 Chron. 21:1; Job 1-2; Matt. 4:1-11 par.). A curious feature of such agents all through history is the way they tend to overstep their mandate. Recall in this connection the activities of the FBI in instigating murders that it ostensibly existed to prevent. Viola Liuzza was gunned down during the civil rights struggle by an undercover FBI informer, and anti-Vietnam war groups were infiltrated and incited to violence by FBI operatives. The FBI even deceived a succession of U.S. Presidents by withholding data on the John F. Kennedy assassination and setting illegal wiretaps in an attempt to blackmail Martin Luther King, Jr. The FBI director, J. Edgar Hoover, also appears to have acted against his own chief executives by keeping blackmail files on presidents in order to prevent them from firing or retiring him. Add to this revelations about the clandestine activities of the CIA, and we find ourselves possessed of a secret and virtually autonomous government within the government which threatens the very basis of our democratic system.

The comparison is particularly apt, for Satan also seems to have evolved from a trustworthy intelligence-gatherer into a virtually autonomous and invisible suzerain within a world ruled by God. The original model for the figure of Satan may actually have been the oriental spy, who in the absence of a state police apparatus served as a "mobile inspector," the "eyes and ears" of the king.[11] The prologue of Job had already portrayed Satan as capable of causing sickness, catastrophes, pillage, and death. It would not take the popular imagination long to turn this free operative into "the god of this world" (2 Cor. 4:4).

Another element in Satan's transformation from a servant of God into the epitome of evil was the need for a more adequate explanation of the origin of evil. The story of the fall of Adam and Eve simply could not account for *undeserved* evil, such as that rained on Job. Nor could the figure of Satan as God's tester render noneducative or nonredemptive sufferings intelligible. The sheer massiveness of evil in the world pointed to a more malevolent source than the isolated infidelities of puny human beings. The ancient allusion to a "fall" of the angels through their intercourse with women (Gen. 6:1-4) provided the seedbed of a whole new species of ideas about evil that proliferated wildly and finally narrowed to that of Satan and his fallen angelic hosts.

These elements: the overzealous *agent provocateur*, the fall of the angels, and the later, postbiblical myth of Satan's fall, have formed the backdrop for Christian understandings of Satan. They have been augmented by other New Testament passages so familiar that they scarcely need elaboration. Satan is called "the devil" (a *false* accuser, slanderer, calumniator), "the evil one," "the ruler of this world," "the prince of the power of the air," "Belial," "Beelzebul," "the god of this world," "the Destroyer," "a murderer from the beginning," and "the enemy."

These are titles virtually unknown to Pharisaic Judaism.[12] According to this strain of New Testament imagery, Satan is the chief of the demons, who prevents shallow people from hearing the gospel. He binds people in prison or under disease, hinders Paul in his journeys, provokes lies, attempts to destroy the church, and enters into Judas in order to lead him to betray Jesus. He is the father of unbelieving Jews. All pagans are under Satan's power; their worship of idols is really worship of Satan. God will (or has) cast Satan out of heaven and will chain him in the bottomless pit and later burn him in unquenchable fire. Jesus encountered these aspects of Satan in the collective messianic expectations, in the possession of demoniacs, in the defection of Judas, as a regressive pull against consciousness, as a dynamic agency that seized upon the personalities even of the disciples, and as a will to destroy God's emergent purpose.

It would be difficult to develop a systematic picture from all this. Some of it is plainly repugnant: there is a straight line from John 8:44 (you Jews "are of your father the devil") to the persecutions and pogroms directed at Jews by Christians; and the scorn with which "pagan" religion is regarded in these passages will haunt us into the future.

There is a terrible splitness in these images of Satan as evil. Satan appears to have virtually no relationship with God, serves no redemptive function, even negatively, and strains the outer limits of the notion that there is but one ultimate, benevolent Reality in the world. But there is also something existentially accurate here. For Satan's fall did in fact take place, not in time or in the universe, but in the human psyche. Satan's fall was an archetypal movement of momentous proportions, and it did indeed happen every bit as much as the Peloponnesian War, but it happened in the collective symbolization of evil. "The whole world is given over to the evil one" (1 John 5:19, au. trans.): Satan has become the world's corporate personality, the symbolic repository of the entire complex of evil existing in the present order. Satan has assumed the aspect of a suprapersonal, nonphysical, spiritual agency, the collective shadow, the sum total of all the individual darkness, evil, unredeemed anger, and fear of the whole race, and all the echoes and reverberations still vibrating down through time from those who have chosen evil before us.

The image of Satan is the archetypal representation of the collective weight of human fallenness, which constrains us toward evil without our even being aware of it. It is a field of negative forces which envelops us long before we learn to think or to speak, and fills us with racial, sexual, and role stereotypes as if they were indubitable reality itself. Satan is "the god of this world" (2 Cor. 4:4) because we human beings have made him god as a consequence of willfully seeking our own good without reference to any higher good, thus aligning our own narcissistic anxiety with the spirit of malignant narcissism itself. But since narcissism is antithetical to the needs of a harmonious and ecological universe, Satan has become, by our practice of constantly giving over the world to him, the principle of our own self-destruction.

When in Luke 4:6 Satan declares that he can give Jesus all the kingdoms of the world and their glory, he is not lying; "for it has been delivered to me, and I give it to whom I will." God *permits* Satan such power, but has not handed it over to him; *we have delivered it,* as a consequence of all the consciously or unconsciously evil choices we have individually and collectively made against the long-range good of the whole. Satan thus becomes the symbol of the spirit of an entire society alienated from God, the great system of mutual support in evil, the spirit of persistent self-deification blown large, the image of unredeemed humanity's collective life.[13]

All this runs the risk of personifying Satan, however, and personification was the subtle poison by which Satan's theological assassins did him in. Personification is too rationalistic to deal with archetypal realities. It merely uses the word "Satan" as a shorthand sign for a cluster of ideas—ideas that could fare quite well without the name.

If Satan has any reality at all, it is not as a sign or an idea or even an explanation, but as a profound *experience* of numinous, uncanny power in the psychic and historic lives of real people. *Satan is the real interiority of a society that idolatrously pursues its own enhancement as the highest good.* Satan is the spirituality of an epoch, the peculiar constellation of alienation, greed, inhumanity, oppression, and entropy that characterizes a specific period of history as a consequence of human decisions to tolerate and even further such a state of affairs.

We are not dealing here with the literal "person" of popular Christian fantasy, who materializes in human form as a seducer and fiend. The Satan of the Bible is more akin to an archetypal reality, a visionary or imaginal presence or event experienced within. But it is more than inner, because the social sedimentation of human choices for evil has formed a veritable layer of sludge that spans the world. Satan is both an outer and an inner reality.

It is not then a question of whether we "believe" in Satan or not, but of how the archetypal and/or social reality of evil is currently manifesting itself in persons and in society. Perhaps we should distinguish between the *archetypal images of Satan* that are served up in actual encounters with primordial evil (what M. Scott Peck calls the extraordinarily willful spirit of "malignant narcissism"[14]), and the *theological use of the term* "Satan" for speaking about such experiences and reflecting on their meaning. "Belief" in Satan serves only to provide a grid that one can superimpose on the actual experiential phenomenon in order to comprehend it, and even then the wrong kind of belief in Satan may do more harm than good, since it is usually so one-sided.

But the phenomenon itself is there, named or unnamed. We wake up screaming, terrified by an image in a dream. We watch our feet walking straight into acts which we consciously know risk everything we most value over the long haul. We encounter a landlord who deliberately attempts to blow up an apartment building full of tenants by opening a gas main in order to end their rent strike. Or we hear of a teenager trying to get off drugs whose "friends" spike her candy with a fatal dose. Here the issue is not whether there is a metaphysical entity called Satan, but how we are to make sense of our actual experiences of evil. In that sense, Satan is an archetypal image of the universal human experience of evil, and is capable of an infinite variety of representations. The archetype itself is unfathomable; the primordial power of evil is as much more than our images of it as God is more than our images of God.

If some literal-minded person were to pick up the jargon of Transactional Analysis and conclude that there "really is" a being designated by the term "the negative parent," that would probably parallel what has happened to Satan: the name given to the personal reality that functions as an accuser, slanderer, inner critic, was granted metaphysical status as an actual being. This worked fine as long as the metaphysical entity was still experienced as an aspect of the process of living. Once the experiential dimension was lost, however, Satan became a "being" in whom one was free to believe or disbelieve, quite apart from the phenomenology of everyday life. That is why in this study I am relatively uninterested in the metaphysical question, Is there a Satan? If we do not encounter the experience that came to be named "Satan," we really have no further need for the word.

Beliefs about Satan are matters of debate. The experience of Satan is a brute and terrifying fact. A couple very dear to us lost their ten-year-old son to cancer after a heroic and utterly devastating nine-month fight. Some time after the death they went to the beach to try to restore themselves from the ordeal. One night, on the ninth floor of the hotel, the husband had this dream: He was standing by a great bog. He knew it was his own inner evil, and that he couldn't run from it, so he just jumped in. With that he woke up. As he lay there at two in the morning, a voice said to him, "Why don't you go to the balcony and jump?" My friend said no, thinking he must still be dreaming. But the voice insisted. "Go ahead, you won't hurt yourself. You'll land in the trees; they'll break your fall." He got up, went to the bathroom, dashed water on his face, trying to break out. He went back and sat on the edge of the bed. The voice assailed him again. "You can jump to the swimming pool." No, I'd never make it, and anyway, the nearest part is the shallow end. "But if you jumped you would see your son." At that moment a vision of his dead son seemed to hang in the room. For the first time the idea of jumping became appealing. He resisted, and the voice began to scream: "Jump! Jump! Jump!" relentlessly. Then it got very quiet. "Why don't you just go out and sit on the balcony?" This went on for more than two hours. Finally, he woke his wife and asked her to hold him. The moment she did, the assault ceased.

No doubt such an experience is susceptible to a variety of explanations. The satanic voice could be interpreted as the "voice" of a part of this man that felt defeated and despairing after the long and futile struggle for his child's life. Or it could be considered an external malevolent power attempting to exploit a father's grief as a way of destroying him. The problem is that this question cannot in principle be settled, and from a phenomenological point of view need not be. Whether Satan be located inside or outside, what matters is that the experience actually happened and could have led to suicide. What this man experienced as "Satan" was an actual force of evil craving annihilation, however it be conceived, and is far more pervasive in human experience than most people are aware.

Where does this life-quenching power come from? Why does it desire murder (the devil is "a murderer from the beginning," John 8:44)? Why does it seek to suck us down into feelings of worthlessness and despair ("Beliar," one of Satan's names, is a corruption of *Belial,* "worthless," 2 Cor. 6:15)? To this day I know next to nothing about the devil, despite all that I have heard and read. Yet I am familiar with the voice of that "slanderer." It is the voice that whispers to us, just when we most need to marshal all our abilities in order to perform an important task, "You're no good, and you never will be any good." "You're not smart enough, you'll never succeed in this job." "You deserved this, you had it coming, this is what you get." "You're ugly, fat (or skinny), and unlovable." Do you recognize that voice? It is the voice that railed at Joshua, smearing him with Israel's guilt in Zech. 3:1-5. No doubt it gains leverage from every flaw, every grain of remorse, every impossible perfectionist demand and unachievable ego ideal we lay upon ourselves, and flays us with them. These are all aspects of the unreality we have embraced, and by our own connivance in illusion we give life to "the real spirit of unreality"[15] and deserve to be worked over by it until we dare to face the truth. Satan could well prove to be God's servant in such a role. But this does not explain the sheer destructiveness, the wanton hatefulness of this "voice." It wants to persuade us that we ought to die—not in order to overcome the illusions of the ego or to liberate us from perfectionism, but simply to exterminate us. The fact that in some this voice is raucous and shrill, and in others scarcely even heard, indicates that the structure of the individual personality or the extremity of the circumstances has a great deal to do with its effectiveness. But does that mean that Satan is a product of our neuroses, or does Satan gain entry by means of them?

This "spirit of worthlessness" tells lies, and is the father of lies (John 8:44), because in God's sight we are precious, beautiful, beloved, of infinite worth, and gifted with untapped potentialities of almost infinite reach. We ourselves are totally responsible for whether we listen to this spirit or not. Once we know—really know personally, existentially—of God's inexhaustible love for us, then this voice only continues to have whatever power we choose to give it.

And yet, where does all this resistance in us come from? Where do we get this ineffable magnetic attraction toward non-being, toward human diminution, toward being a fraction of ourselves? Whence this imploding black hole in moral space, sucking up life and energy and giving back no light whatever? Freud himself finally posited a *Thanatos* (death) instinct to account for it; it would have been as scientific to have called it Satan.

I am oppressively aware of the hazards involved in labeling things satanic; yet there are some evils too horrendous to be labeled otherwise. And naming something correctly can sometimes help us see it in the right light. When we label the nuclear arms race satanic, for example, we realize that the struggle is not between the administrations in Washington and Moscow, but that both are on the same side.

Whether we call it death or evil, Satan or the satanic, there seems to be some irreducible power which cannot finally be humanized, cured, or integrated, but only held at bay. And it is never more diabolical than when it has become linked in a pact with human beings. "We are driven to conclude that the Devil too would incarnate in and through man."[16] There is a concentration of evil in a directional pull counter to the will of God. And however intolerable it is when encountered personally, its manifestations are most disastrous when they are social.

There is something sad in the moralistic tirades of fundamentalist preachers terrifying the credulous with pictures of Satan lurking in the shadows, coaxing individuals to violate rules which are often enough satanic themselves and deserve to be broken, while all the time ignoring the mark of the cloven hoof in economic or political arrangements that suck the life out of *whole generations* of people. The media have made a sensation out of a few rare cases of possession of pubescent youth, with no comprehension whatever of Satan's grip on our entire civilization. Why should Satan reveal himself more often in individual cases, when he can, from invisibility, preside over an entire global culture that spreads out over the whole surface of the planet like a cancer: a civilization that systematically erodes traditional religions, that treats people as robots for producing and serving things, that denies not only the spiritual but even the poetic, the artistic, the inner, that propagates belief in the ultimate power of money, and that organizes an economic system exploitative of most of the peoples of the world and anchored in a permanent war economy?

Liberal Christianity has so reacted against the misuse of the Satan-image in fundamentalist circles that it has tended to throw out the notion altogether. The absence of any really profound means of imaging radical evil has left us at the mercy of a shallow religious rationalism that is naive, optimistic, and self-deceiving. We need not return to medieval superstition in order to appreciate the power of the Satan-image, *not* as an explanation of evil—for Satan explains nothing—but as a way of keeping its irreducible malignancy before our eyes.

How are we to evaluate, for example, the proposal first conceived by J. D. Bernal in 1929 and renewed by D. E. Wooldbridge,[17] that the brain of a living human being be removed and rehoused in a short cylindrical container that not only would keep it alive but whose apparatus the brain itself could direct? This being would be a completely effective mentally directed person "mechanized for science rather than for aesthetic purposes." Through such technology Bernal looked forward to a time when the masses would be kept in a "perfect docility under the appearance of perfect freedom."[18] There is no indication that he himself planned to submit to the operation; he would be needed to direct all these automatons in the proper actions.

How can scientists of such stature even conceive of such things? Because, says Wooldbridge, he and his kind are "strongly attracted by the idea of a lawful universe," in which "all we can observe or feel is caused by the operation of a set of inviolable physical laws upon a single set of material particles." We must, he argues, abandon even the small vestige of claim to human uniqueness left to us by the discoveries of Galileo and Darwin, and know ourselves to be nothing but machines. This is the price we must pay, he says, "for a world view in which all human experience is lawful and orderly."[19]

Wooldbridge seems to feel no twinge of regret at having become dehumanized, and even fewer compunctions over surgically dismembering some living person's brain. (The experiment has already been successfully performed on animals.) As the physicist Walter Heitler warns, "When once we have got to the stage of seeing in man merely a complex machine, what does it matter if we destroy him?"[20]

No doubt the vast majority of scientists simply passed this off as absurd. But it is worse than absurd. Bertrand Russell was able to name it rather precisely. He called this kind of misuse of science devil-worship. Noting that we seek knowledge of an object either because we love it or desire power over it, Russell observed in 1949 that in the development of science the power impulse has increasingly prevailed over the love impulse. As physics has developed, it has deprived us step by step of what we thought we knew concerning the intimate nature of the physical world. "Colour and sound, light and shade, form and texture . . . have been transferred from the beloved to the lover, and the beloved has become a skeleton of rattling bones, cold and dreadful." Thus, reasoned Russell, "disappointed as the lover of nature, the man of science is becoming its tyrant." More and more, science has "substituted power-knowledge for love knowledge and as this substitution becomes completed science tends more and more to become sadistic."

Russell was therefore apprehensive about the desirability of a society controlled by science. He thought it probable that its sadistic impulses would in time justify more torture of animals and humans by surgeons, biochemists, and experimental psychologists. "As time goes on," he warned, "the amount of added knowledge required to justify a given amount of pain will diminish." In short, *"the power conferred by science as a technique is only obtainable by something analogous to the worship of Satan, that is to say, by the renunciation of love."* [21]

It is not my intention to single out science as satanic. I am profoundly grateful for many of its discoveries, and not a little awed by its competence. My choice of Bernal and Wooldridge as examples is largely arbitrary; we could easily have focused instead on human or animal torture, or the pesticide or tobacco industries, or the nuclear arms race.

Indeed, a nuclear holocaust would beggar every other evil imaginable. How could Satan benefit from such a catastrophe? Whitehead once described evil as "the brute motive force of fragmentary purpose, disregarding the eternal vision."[22] As the principle of fragmentation, Satan can never achieve the totalization of evil it desires; there is a contradiction built into the very nature of evil that prevents it from ever gaining complete ascendancy. The whole is too harmonious in its foundations and fabric, and evil must always be conceding too much to the good, since it must mimic the good and pass itself off as desirable in order to win adherents. But a nuclear holocaust—that is as close as we could come to totalizing fragmentation.

"We"? Did I say "we"? When we tear away the mask from Satan, do we then find—ourselves? Have we, after all, breathed life into this image and kept it alive by our continually stoking the fires of Armageddon? Does that mean then that there is a retrogressive pull in us that fears the creative possibilities of self-transcendence, and which would finally blow everything up to avoid *that* pain? Is it our own willful refusal of abundant life that has turned Satan from a servant into a monster? Was this our counterattack on God, whereby we seduced God's seducer and won him to our side? Must Satan then after all be redeemed, freed, delivered—not from his own overweening pride, but from *ours?*

Satan as Chameleon

Satan has been called a snake. Better he had been called a chameleon. For Satan is never quite the same from moment to moment, but changes his colors according to circumstances. How Satan appears to us will then be at least in part a function of how *we* have responded to the choices set before us. If we drift with the collective roles and expectations, or yield to regressively instinctual behavior, or are caught in egocentric strategies for self-aggrandizement without reference to the whole, or actually opt for what we know to be wrong, we augment Satan's power as a force for evil. We reinforce the sheer bulk of collective unconsciousness and shadow that presses down on events, and help to set off a train of consequences that can only wreak evil on ourselves and others. If, however, we respond to choice with a conscious commitment to creative transformation, if we use the encounter with the voice of the shadows as an occasion for self-discovery and pruning, if we are willing to risk the uncertain path of seeking God's will and to allow our egos to undergo the mortification necessary to allow the greater self to emerge, then Satan appears as God's Servant, and even our mistakes and wrong choices can become the catalysts of our transformation (Rom. 8:28).

All that is true on the individual level. But the history of evil does not begin with us. We enter a world already organized for evil. The satanic is already crystallized in the institutional values and arrangements in which we find ourselves. The victims of the bombings of Hiroshima and Hamburg and the Plain of Jars were not fully responsible for the evil they suffered. Africans seized by slavers or forced into townships were not faced with a choice between the good and the better, but between death-in-life and death. There are evils that God can redeem; Solzhenitsyn goes so far as to assert that no great literature can exist apart from suffering.[23] But there are events of torture, psychosis, suicide, and violence for which there is not apparent redemption this side of the grave. There are experiences, to be sure, when we encounter Satan as sifter. But there are others in which we come face to face with an evil so raw, so malevolent, so unredeemable, that Jesus could only counsel us to pray to be delivered from the encounter. But this then raises the question: How can these two poles be held together within one godhead, without splitting it into an absolute dualism?

Earlier we saw that Israelite religion originally had no place for Satan. God alone was the source of everything, good or ill. As Yahweh was ethicalized, good and evil were differentiated within the godhead, and Satan became the prosecuting attorney in the heavenly council. This idea seems wholly incompatible with the later notion of Satan as God's Enemy, who possesses no apparent redeeming functions whatever. Yet it was only this latter tributary that emptied into mainstream Christianity. Diagrammed, the development would look something like this:

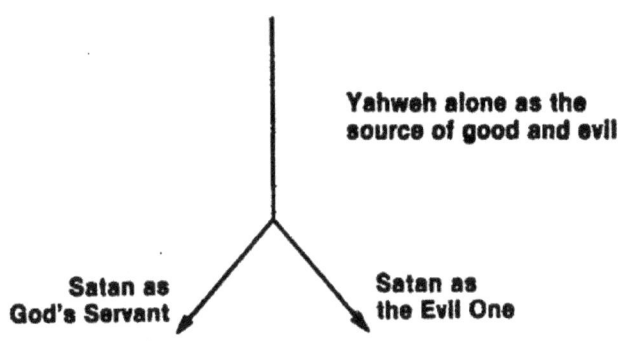

It would be tempting to conclude that what we find here are two competing and mutually exclusive interpretations of Satan, and to opt for one or the other on the basis of personal theological preference. But that easy solution is denied us by the fact that the early church seems to have seen some inner connection between the contrary views, for both representations of Satan appear in the same document or from the hand of the same author.

Servant	*Evil One*
Luke 22:31	Luke 10:18; 13:16; Acts 5:3; 13:10; 26:18
Matt. 4:1-11 par.	Matt. 12:24-29 par.
1 Cor. 5:1-5; 7:5 (Paul)	1 Thess. 2:18; 2 Cor. 11:14-15 (Paul)[68]

This duality is nowhere more vivid than in Luke's version of the temptation narrative, where Satan simultaneously claims (with sufficient empirical justification) to have authority over all the nations, and yet serves, in the very act of revealing this fact, to bring Jesus to awareness of other alternatives (Luke 4:1-13). Perhaps then we should think of a continuum:

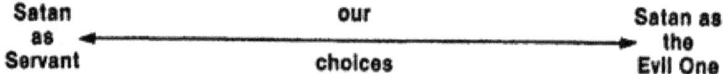

and of our responses to the satanic occasion as the determining factor in how Satan is constellated. When we combine this continuum with the following schema of historical development, the apparent contradiction would appear to be resolved.

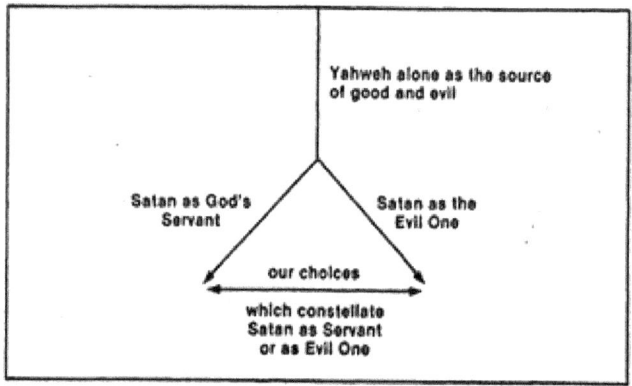

This would help to account for Satan's incredible pliability ("and no wonder, for even Satan disguises himself as an angel of light," 2 Cor. 11:14). He can be described by one writer as "the suspended superego," the seducer into sin (the psychologist David Bakan[24]), and by another as the polar opposite: the harsh superego, the voice of condemnation, the rigorous legalist who lashes and flails us with laws which, in some cases, should never have been decreed (Norman O. Brown[25]). No doubt both are right. One moment the devil lures us to boundlessness, the next to moralistic rigidity. We all know him as licentious; he can also be a pursed-lipped prude. In Bishop Bossuet's words, he follows the current of our inclinations and presses us and overthrows us on the side to which he sees we are leaning.[26]

The difficulty then lies precisely in discerning God's will in a field where Satan appears prepared to suit up for either team. But precisely that is his service:

Satan prevents our presuming, on the basis of theology, Scripture, tradition, custom, reason, science, instinct, or intuition, that we can know the will of God, apart from listening acutely for every word that proceeds from the mouth of God. Hence the shock of those who had prophesied and cast out demons and done stunning miracles, all in Christ's name, when he turns to them and declares, "'I never knew you; depart from me, you evildoers'" (Matt. 7:22-23). They were doing what "everybody knows" is the will of God. But they had not consulted God. They had substituted activity for a relationship.

Perhaps God intended something quite different for them, and they had never stopped to listen.[27] That is why we must never attempt to straitjacket Satan in rigid doctrinal categories. Satan is not a fixed, unnuanced figure. The tendency of some Christians to regard Satan as unambiguously evil breeds a paranoid view of reality. It justifies the demonizing of opponents. It prevents our loving our enemies. It legitimates violence against those whom we regard as irredeemably evil. It conceals from us our own shadow and our ambivalence toward evil. The rejection of Satan altogether by others has scarcely worked better. It induces blindness to the radicality of evil, trivializes the struggle for conscious choice, and drives the satanic underground, converting the unconscious into a cesspool of erupting nightmares.

Perhaps in the final analysis Satan is not even a "personality" at all, but rather a function in the divine process, a dialectical movement in God's purpose which becomes evil only when humanity breaks off the dialectic by refusing creative choice. Whether one "believes" in Satan is thus not nearly as important as that one recognizes the satanic function as part and parcel of every decision. Occasionally people (yes, still today—though they are not likely to tell you about it) encounter the satanic in dreams, auditions, apparitions, or visions. The image of Satan can be male or female, a supernatural power, a monster, or a pulsing blob of energy. We recognize the satanic, however, not by conventions of dress (the familiar red suit and horns), but by the numinous, dreadful, uncanny terror the image evokes. Even such experiences have an "as if" quality however; they are not literal representations of Satan but archetypal images appropriate to the aspect of Satan we are encountering on any given occasion.

When we fail to bring a committed ego to struggles for choice, and yield ourselves to compulsive gambling, or to overeating or drinking, or to sexual promiscuity, or to compliance with corporate directives we know are unethical—then to a degree we place ourselves in the power of autonomous complexes in the psyche or idolatrous institutions in the world. We do their bidding and are at their mercy, and as the popular expression says, "the Devil made us do it." But this is only because we have delivered ourselves straight into his hands. When we fail to make conscious, committed choices for God, we default on our "dominion" over the world, and Satan becomes like a holding company that has taken over billions of mortgages in arrears through foreclosure. The satanic is actualized as evil precisely by our *failure* to choose, and has no more power than we continue to give it. Hence it would be truer to say, "*We made the Devil do it*"!

We do not "create" Satan by our choices, however. Satan is an autonomous spirit that rises out of the depths of mystery in God. But by our choices we *do* determine which side Satan is on. Origen was condemned as a heretic for arguing that Satan might finally be redeemed. His humanitarian impulses certainly deserve respect, but that way of putting things leaves the real issue buried in eschatological myth. The truth of what he was saying is that *we must redeem Satan,* by bringing conscious, committed choice to the encounter. Only thus can Satan be freed from the sheer burden of unconsciousness, shadow and projection that an irresponsible humanity has laid on him. *We made Satan evil. Only we can restore him to his rightful role at God's left Hand.*

Evil is finally irrational. Our attempts to comprehend it are an odd mix of pastoral sensitivity and intellectual anxiety. Perhaps I have long since overspoken, and the only appropriate stance is silence before the mystery. But I must risk one more observation. Milton, in his *Paradise Lost*, portrayed Satan as such a complex, rebellious, Promethean spirit that despite all the punishments a just heaven might rain down on him, the readers' secret sympathies could scarcely help being attracted to him. Milton's God, by contrast, is a bit boring, too busy being Almighty to be very interesting. What got left out was the complexity and wiliness of *God*. Perhaps then we should distinguish four "moments" in the manifestation of the divine in reference to Satan:[28]

1. God as God
2. God as "Satan"
3. Satan as "God"
4. Satan as Satan

The unequivocal revelation of God or Satan in experience 1 and 4 is unambiguous, however much it may still require interpretation. The problem arises in distinguishing the second from the third. A great deal that is creative or innovative is initially resisted as evil, and God's new creation is rejected as the work of the devil (God as "Satan"). When Jesus turned aside the current messianic roles as satanic, and began to act on the basis of just those words that were proceeding from the mouth of God, the authorities declared him an enemy of God. When he cast out demons and declared this to be a sign of the inbreaking kingdom, he was accused of being in cahoots with Beelzebul. When he unmasked the evil of those blinded by the efficient normality of a satanic world, they said he was mad, or possessed by demons. When he declared sins forgiven he was called a blasphemer, and when he violated the Sabbath he was damned as a law-breaker. When he treated women as equals, or took children seriously, or ate with tax gatherers, or identified himself with harlots, how else could others regard him but as "satanic"?—as *long as they accepted the world as it was.* The God beyond god—that reality that lures us to ever greater creative transformations in order to liberate life to its fullness—instigates what those who obey "the god of this world" can only regard as evil.

In such a time, what is of Yahweh and what is of Satan becomes devilishly hard to unravel. Where are we experiencing evil disguised as the divine? Where are we experiencing the divine perceived by everyone as evil? How can we discern the difference? The struggle is most redemptive when one enters it fully committed to discovering and doing the will of God to the very limit; that is, to seeking the creative transformation latent in the situation in which one finds oneself at any given moment. It is the "satanic" aspect of God's will—justice, mercy, and truth misperceived as evil by the Powers That Be—that constitutes the threat and, simultaneously, the effectiveness of nonviolent civil disobedience. It is what produces horror among the "godly" when those whom they have judged outside the pale—blacks, Hispanics, gays—recognize their humanity and clamor for equal rights and recognition. It is this "satanic"-seeming aspect of the divine call that paralyzes our moral nerve when the question is raised about *our* joining a picket line outside a nuclear weapons plant, or going to jail for our beliefs. For how can we be certain that the voice we call "God" is not rationalized rebelliousness, or an unredeemed power complex, or an egoistic passion for publicity?

For Satan can also masquerade as God, and with so many masks (2 Cor.11:14)! William Blake made the classic statement of the problem of Satan as "God":

> Man must and will have Some Religion: if he has not the Religion of Jesus, he will have the religion of Satan, and will erect the synagogue of Satan, calling the Prince of this World, God, and destroying all who do not worship Satan under the Name of God. Will anyone say, "Where are those who worship Satan under the Name of God?" Where are they? Listen! Every Religion that Preaches Vengeance for Sin is the Religion of the Enemy and the Avenger and not the

Forgiver of Sin, and their God is Satan, Named by the Divine Name.[29]

Blake is not talking about Satanism (more on that shortly) but about Christian churches that behave satanically under the banner of Christ. To his criterion for discerning satanic "Christianity" we might add these: hostility toward those who are different; projecting evil out on others who are then demonized; claiming doctrinal certitude; breeding psychic dependency, unconsciousness, stagnation, fear, guilt, or hatred; depicting God as a monster (as in ascribing the death of loved ones to God). Satanic Christianity can be rigidly legalistic or morally slack—in either case substituting its view of morality for a living relationship with the God revealed by Jesus. But these are characteristics of much of what passes as Christianity!

The cost involved in the ethicalization of Yahweh was, as we saw earlier, the differentiation of "the Adversary" as an agent of divine justice and wrath. When, under the impact of apocalypticism, Satan became increasingly evil, the tendency to split Satan off altogether from the godhead became acute. Only if Satan's role as Evil One could be held in tension with his role as Servant could a genuine dualism be averted. In the history of Christianity, unfortunately, that tension snapped, and Satan became virtually an evil, rival God.

No such parallel development took place in Pharisaic Judaism in the same period, so we must ask what it was in the unique constitution of Christian faith that led to Satan's becoming so evil. Perhaps, as Jung has argued,[30] the identification of Jesus as the Christ who is all goodness and light led to a conception of God so bright-sided that the earlier complementarity of good and evil within God was obliterated, and Satan had to be pressed into service as the polar opposite of Christ, an antidivine force bent on destruction, sucking goodness and light into the abyss of everlasting night.

Justin Martyr (d. 165 c.e.) marks the turning point in that development. In Justin's theology, Satan was made responsible for every kind of evil in the world. Heretics are inspired by him; pagan rites that appear to be similar to Christian ones (baptism, eucharist), far from drawing from the same archetypal well, are conceived of as satanic parodies to confuse unbelievers. Satan is the cause of the persecution of Christians, the father of magic, the source of lust, the prince of demons.[31]

Something has gone wrong with the Christian archetype of God. Satan is now virtually autonomous from God. All paganism is diabolical; pagan gods are demons; demons operate in dreams. Evil, having been excluded from the now "perfect" godhead, is driven into the unconscious. Dreams, those oracles of *God* in the Old Testament, now become instruments of Satan, and the archetypal images cast up in sleep (the "gods") are devilish. No more clear statement of the collective psyche of Christendom would ever be articulated, though the split would continue to widen for two centuries.

Those Gnostics who sensed intuitively what was happening and reacted by stressing the dark side of God, or sexuality, or the feminine, were driven beyond the pale. *Gnosticism now became the Christian unconscious,* and would erupt in every century (the Catharii, the Albigensians, witchcraft, Satan worship). This repression of the dark side accounts for the remarkable voyeuristic quality in treatises on Satan, from the early theologians until today. Writer and reader alike are titillated by the "return of the repressed" under the safe guise of a pious exposition of Satan's perfidies. Indeed, Epiphanius (d. 403) was so awash with unconscious fascination with the forbidden evils of the Gnostic groups he wrote to refute that the editors of the *Nicene and Post-Nicene Fathers* refused to translate his exhaustive and deliciously obscene descriptions of the Gnostics' licentious practices. A great deal of his *Refutation of All Heresies* was, at an unconscious level, pornographic.

By the High Middle Ages, many people seem to have regarded the devil as a more insistent reality than God. Abbot Richalm of Schontal (early thirteenth century) had the gift of seeing demons. He saw them everywhere. They swarmed his monastery, interfered with devotions, caused the Abbot to nod and sleep in the choir, provoked the celebrant to wrath or indignation just before the hour of mass, or caused troublesome thoughts, snorting, coughing, or spitting. They plastered up the ears so that the brothers could not hear the reading of the monastic Rule.[32] All one's personal resistances, ambivalence, shadow, and unbelief are here conveniently repressed, projected, and reappear as hallucinated powers exterior to and other than the self, so that one need take no responsibility for or work on them directly. The spiritual life amounts to reinforcing repression and fighting the demons in the open field.

Witchcraft also reflects this peculiar split in the Christian psyche, aggravated by an even more basic split: the repression of women. One constant feature of the "confessions" of "witches" (almost invariably under torture) was the priests' insistence that they elaborate in great detail about their "intercourse" with Satan. It does not take advanced training in psychoanalysis to catch the scent of voyeurism here. By projecting on witches their own desires for illicit sex, these (celibate) inquisitors could live out in fantasy their own repressed desires while at the same time keeping them in check by the severity of the penalty visited upon their victims.

There is another side to witchcraft, however. Once God had been split off into "good" only, and Satan had been made totally evil, it was inevitable that certain people would gravitate toward the worship of the one side and not the other. To women who were denied access to power, especially to ordination to the priesthood, or who were not willing to suppress their sexuality, or who were rebellious against male authority, or who hated God for a particular evil suffered ostensibly at God's hands, or who were angry at the church, or frustrated at the inability to use their talents except at "women's" work, or greedy to the point of selling their souls to the devil in return for success, or who wanted revenge over a rival or a love potion for a lover, witchcraft and Satan worship represented an attractive gesture of defiance to a patriarchal God and to a male-dominated society. And it provided a means of seizing power against them. Besides all that, much of what of what was called witchcraft was simply the underground continuation of immemorial fertility cults, now shaped and colored in reaction to the dominant Christian religion.

It is in this context that we must view the surprising revival of Satan cults today. At least a part of their appeal derives from a reaction against the "God" of Christendom. Satanists do not doubt God; they *hate* God. But the "God" they hate is in certain respects deserving of hatred, insofar as the God-image has been used by moralistic Christians as a kind of introjected police power to censure and stifle aspects of peoples' own authentic creativity. In reaction to Christianity, Satanism is a kind of adolescent rebellion, a decomposition product of repressive Christianity. Its very one-sidedness, its sheer dependence on God to fuel its discontents, prevents it from ever achieving autonomy. For that reason Satan cults experience a high rate of turnover and a serious problem with backsliders, who simply outgrow the stage of rebellion and move on to something else.

Satanism also is a continuum. Its milder form is represented by Anton LaVey, who has capitalized on the "Playboy" mentality and franchised a middle-class Satanist denomination that practices enough ritual sexuality to make it exciting and yet affirms a negative form of the golden rule (do not do unto others what you do not want done to you) to garner a certain respectability and stave off chaos. The extreme forms of Satanism, however, involve the conscious, deliberate identification with evil as an act of religious devotion. Adolescent rebellion against God can be a necessary and freeing moment in a person's life-journey toward the God beyond the gods. But those who freely choose to embrace, worship, and surrender themselves to raw, senseless evil become the instruments of a primordial elemental force in themselves and the universe which has been darkened by millennia of wrong decisions, and which now, like a great blob of protoplasm constantly fed by the effluents of society, represents a power so horrendous that the very future of the planet hangs in the balance.

SATAN'S END

Origen's desire to see Satan redeemed at the final consummation was far more generous than the usual visions of Satan's eternal punishment. We have to hold the myth open to the possibility of Satan's conversion in order to honor the divine gift of freedom and the hope of the ultimate reconciliation of all things. But historical experience suggests a far more pessimistic climax. The degree of human commitment and consciousness necessary to redeem Satan is hard to envision as happening. Yet without such a response, how can we speak of the reign of God coming at all?

Perhaps the whole matter should be approached a different way. One of the climactic visions of the Book of Revelation (20:10) may provide the very clue we need:

> And the devil who had deceived them was thrown into the lake of fire and brimstone where the beast and the false prophet were, and they will be tormented day and night forever and ever.

This represents a second attempt at a final solution to the problem of evil. The first had been to chain Satan for a thousand years in the bottomless pit, "that he should deceive the *nations* no more." Satan's heart has always been in international politics. "After that he must be loosed for a little while" (Rev 20:3). The image of being chained in the bottomless pit could scarcely be more clearly one of psychological repression: out of sight, out of mind. And, as with all unconscious repression, it does not last: "He must be loosed."

That is what makes the second attempt so remarkable, both as a symbol of the achievement of individuation in John of Patmos, and of the sublimation of evil into the godhead. For this time Satan will not be consigned to the pit—which is precisely where repressive Christian theologies have tried to keep him—but to the lake of fire. The question that has not been asked is, *Where* is this lake? The assumed answer has been, In the underworld. But that is where Satan was consigned the first time around, and that did not work. A search through Revelation supplies the answer: those who worship the Beast "shall be tormented with fire and brimstone *in the presence of the holy angels and in the presence of the Lamb*" (Rev. 14:10). And where are they? Right before God's throne. The lake of fire bubbles and spews in the very presence of God! The lake of fire is nothing less than the sea of glass "mingled with fire" that stands before the throne of God (Rev. 4:6; 15:2). Satan and his unredeemed hosts crackle in the fires, not of the deep unconscious, where they inevitably must explode with volcanic fury (see what happens after Satan emerges from the bottomless pit in Rev. 20:7-10!), but in the fires of the heavenly throne room itself visualized as the heavenly counterpart of the Jerusalem temple.

> And I saw what appeared to be a sea of glass mingled with fire, and those who had conquered the beast and its image and the number of its name, standing beside the sea of glass with harps of God in their hands. And they sing.... (Rev. 15:2-3a)

What do these symbols mean? The satanic energy here burns in a perpetual transformation of satanic libido into heavenly passion (fire). If Satan is not so much a person, a being, a metaphysical entity, as a function in the divine economy, then the issue is not the inhuman torture of Satan as a person, but the transformation of Satan as an archetype. Does this not represent for the godhead what Freud declared to be the goal of all analysis: to move from the unconscious repression of negative elements to the integration of what can be redeemed and the *conscious repression* of what cannot? The craving of the addict may never be healed, but the addiction itself can be stopped. Inappropriate sexual desires may never cease, but their expression can be checked. The sense that one is unlovable, unworthy, or inadequate may never fully disappear, but we can refuse to let that drive us to perfectionism, despair, or overwork. Satan sublimated, burning forever in the lake of fire, the crystal sea: transformation comes not through the denial and repression of our evil, but by naming it, owning it and lifting it up to God.

In our own selves, this faithfully portrays the goal of all our striving: to face our own evil as courageously as we can; to love it into the light; to release the energy formerly devoted to restraining it; and to use that energy for the service of life. But there is also a residue of evil that can neither be cured nor integrated or humanized. *That* we can only bring before God to be burned forever (for it never burns up altogether; it is in fact a kind of fuel), trusting God to transform even our irredeemable evil into fiery light.

> And all shall be well and
> All manner of thing shall be well
> When the tongues of flame are in-folded
> Into the crowned knot of fire

And the fire and the rose are one.[33]

Notes

1. Morton Kelsey, "The Mythology of Evil," *Journal of Religion and Health* 13 (1974): 16.
2. See Paul Ricoeur, *The Symbolism of Evil* (New York: Harper & Row, 1967).
3. See the excellent study by Rivkah Scharf Kluger, *Satan in the Old Testament* (Evanston, Ill.: Northwestern Univ. Press, 1967).
4. Gerhard von Rad, "Diabolos," *TDNT* 2 (1964): 72–75.
5. Sheila Moon's fine phrase, *Joseph's Son* (Francestown, N.H.: Golden Quill Press, 1972), 20.
6. Kluger, *Satan in the Old Testament*, 76.
7. John B. Cobb, Jr., *Christ in a Pluralistic Age* (Philadelphia: Westminster Press, 1975), 84.
8. Trevor Ling, *The Significance of Satan* (London: SPCK, 1961), 38.
9. St. Ignatius Loyola, *The Spiritual Exercises,* trans. Anthony Mottola (Garden City, N.Y.: Image Books, 1964), 131–32.
10. Sidney Harris, *Word and Witness,* May 25, 1980.
11. Eccles. 10:20; Luke 20:20. See A. Lods, "Les origins de la figure de Satan, ses fonctions à la cour céleste" *Melanges syriens offerts a R. Dussaud*, II, *Bibliotheque archeologique et historique* 30/2 (1939): 649–60. See also C. Colpe, "Geister (Dämonen)," *Reallexikon für Antike und Christentum* 9 (1976): 569–70. See also A. L. Oppenheim, "The Eyes of the Lord," *Journal of the American Oriental Society* 88 (1968): 173–80.
12. Bernard J. Bamberger, *Fallen Angels* (Philadelphia: Jewish Publication Society of America, 1952), 42; Werner Foerster, "Diabolos," *TDNT* 2 (1964): 79.
13. Ibid., 83–84.
14. M. Scott Peck, *People of the Lie* (New York: Simon & Schuster, 1983), 78.
15. Peck's definition of Satan (*People of the Lie,* 207).
16. James Hillman, *Insearch* (New York: Charles Scribner's Sons, 1967), 90.
17. D. E. Wooldbridge, *The Mechanical Man* (New York: McGraw-Hill, 1968).
18. Bernal, cited by Brian Easlea, *Liberation and the Aims of Science* (Totowa, N.J.: Rowman & Littlefield, 1973), 326–27.
19. Cited by Easlea, *Liberation and the Aims of Science,* 261–62.
20. Ibid., 273.
21. Ibid., 267, italics mine.
22. Alfred North Whitehead, *Science in the Modern World* (New York: Mentor Books, 1948), 192.
23. Aleksandr I. Solzhenitsyn, *The Gulag Archipelago* III/Parts V-VII (New York: Harper & Row, 1976), chap. 5.
24. David Bakan, *Sigmund Freud and the Jewish Mystical Tradition,* 210–11; idem, *The Duality of Human Existence* (Skokie, Ill.: Rand McNally & Co., 1966), 67ff.; and idem, "Psychological Characteristics of Man Projected in the Image of Satan," in *On Method* (San Francisco: Jossey-Bass, 1967), 160–69.
25. Norman O. Brown, *Life Against Death: The Psychoanalytical Meaning of History* (Middletown, Conn.: Wesleyan Univ. Press, 1959), 204-9; cited by Peter Homans, *Theology After Freud* (New York: Hobbs-Merrill Co., 1970), 130–37.
26. Cited by Jean Lhermitte, *Diabolical Possession, True and False* (London: Bus & Oats, 1963), 9.
27. William Stringfellow, in *An Ethic for Christians and Other Aliens in a Strange Land* (Waco, Tex.: Word Books, 1973), 54–57, 132–33.

28. I learned this from Morton Kelsey.

29. William Blake, *Jerusalem,* plate 52, in *The Complete Writings of William Blake,* ed. Geoffrey Keynes (London: Oxford Univ. Press, 1966), 682.

30. See, for example, Jung's *Psychology and Religion: West and East,* 11 (1977), index entries under "devil" and "Satan."

31. Justin Martyr, *1 Apology* 1.54, 57; 2.5.

32. Edward Langton, *Satan, A Portrait* (London: Sheffington & Son, 1945), 72–73.

33. T. S. Eliot, *Four Quartets* (New York: Harcourt Brace Jovanovich, 1971), 59.

7

The Gods

Walter Wink argues that, contrary to popular belief, the ancient Hebrews were not monotheists, rather they were henotheists: they did not deny the existence of "the gods" but insisted that they had no primacy—that honor belonged only to Yahweh. The ancient Hebrews were "mono-Yahwists"—they worshiped only Yahweh, the High God who held sway over all the lesser gods. These lesser gods were subordinated to Yahweh, who assigned them to "the nations." They were not unambiguously evil; their function was to guide the nations they were assigned to in the ways of justice and to represent those nations in the heavenly council before God. If they failed in this function they were judged accordingly. The task of demonizing the gods was left to Christians. The eventual devolution of the gods to demons marked the conquest of paganism by the church. But, as Wink notes, the gods did not disappear, they "went underground" as "powerful archetypal images in the unconscious." These archetypes (gods) are real—they function as the "within" or "spirituality" of individual instinctive behavior on the one hand, and as the "collective spirituality" of a society and its institutions on the other. Wink turns to Carl Jung's notions of archetypes and the collective unconscious to examine the continuing role of the gods in the formation of persons and social institutions.

Source: Wink 1986: Excerpted from Chapter 5

The angels of the nations, as we saw in the previous chapter, are only a special category of heavenly powers elsewhere called gods, angels, or spirits. The language of the Powers in the New Testament period is so imprecise that it is often impossible to maintain distinctions between these spiritual entities. Generally speaking, what pagans called gods, Jews and Christians called angels or demons, and everyone spoke of them interchangeably as spirits. In this chapter we will examine how early Jews and Christians regarded the gods and incorporated them into their understanding of the Powers. Then we will ponder the meaning of the gods for our existence today.

Briefly, I will argue that the old gods of paganism are still very much alive, and that denial of this fact only guarantees their repression. Hidden from consciousness, they strike from concealment and craze or cripple us without our having the slightest comprehension as to what has happened. The gods never died, remarks Jung; they merely became diseases.[1] To the degree that Christianity has conspired in suppressing the gods and denying them the cautious respect and serious attention they deserve, it has unwittingly contributed to disease.

Roman Catholic and Orthodox Christians have been far more cognizant of the reality of the gods than have Protestants, who mistook the prophets' critique of idolatry—the false worship of gods—for a denial of their existence altogether. A fresh reading of the biblical sources and new insights from depth psychology now make a complete reassessment of the gods imperative.

The Gods Are Real

Christianity has not been uniformly hostile to the gods. It is well known, for example, that Catholic veneration of the saints and the elaboration of various orders of angels was a means of absorbing the religious impulses of polytheism into Christian devotion. Some of the "saints" are the old pagan gods taken over wholesale, without even a change of name (for example, Brigid, the Irish goddess of fire, smithcraft, and poetry, became St. Brigid) and at least one order of angels (the Virtues) had served an earlier hitch as equally impersonal and impassive Roman gods. In many other respects Christianity melded elements of paganism directly into its life. To cite but two further instances, pagan philosophy was taken over as the intellectual basis of Christian apologetics, and the orgiastic Roman Saturnalia was absorbed and neutralized by the celebration of a mass for Christ's birth.

On the whole, however, the pagan gods were ruthlessly suppressed. Christian theology was filtered through the monistic philosophies of Greece and Europe until it came in time to represent the belief that the gods never had any existence whatever. But "monotheism," if it is not purely a modern construct, could not have meant that to the ancient Hebrews, who regarded the gods of their neighbors as very real indeed.

The Israelites found three different solutions for dealing with the gods of the surrounding peoples: *syncretism, suppression,* and *subordination.*[2] *Syncretism* involved taking over alien beliefs, myths, and practices. Baal could be renamed

Yahweh; Canaanite mythological conceptions and expressions could be adopted, such as Baal's victory over Chaos or the concept of an assembly of gods presided over by a high god. Syncretism was unavoidable and advantageous; it made possible a degree of accommodation with the Canaanite inhabitants. But it involved dangers as well: the loss of the distinctive qualities of Israel's religious experience.

Consequently, others tended to champion the *suppression* of Baalism, stressing the uniqueness of Yahweh's covenant with Israel and of Israel's calling in history. Exclusion of Canaanite elements preserved the uniqueness of Israel's perception of Yahweh as the one God, but often within a narrowly nationalistic focus that was slow to acknowledge the universality of Yahweh's dominion and hence of Yahweh's objectivity in regard to Israel's fate among the nations. What reflection failed to grasp, repeated captivities taught. In time Israel came to perceive Yahweh as God of the nations and the universe who transcended the parochialism of both early Israel and its neighbors.

More characteristic of Israel's handling of the gods is *subordination.* Pure monotheistic thought is extremely rare in the Hebrew Scriptures. Second Isaiah alone denies the very existence of other gods. Even in Jeremiah, where Yahweh's sole reality is declared,[3] the prophet nevertheless pictures Yahweh as presiding over a heavenly council made up of the *bene elohim,* the "sons of God" who do Yahweh's bidding.[4] Yahweh is supreme over this host of subordinate powers, which include the gods of all the nations. The first commandment itself assumes this henotheistic belief. It does not deny the existence of other gods, but only their primacy: "You shall have no other gods before me" (Exod. 20:3). Other gods may be real, but they are of a different order of potency altogether: "Who is like thee, O Lord, among the gods?" (Exod. 15:11). By being made Yahweh's cabinet and chiefs of staff, the gods of the surrounding peoples were acknowledged to be real *in their own domain of influence,* but not ultimate. They possessed a certain degree of autonomy but were subject to Yahweh. "Ascribe to the Lord, O sons of gods (*elim*), ascribe to the Lord glory and strength" (Ps. 29:1, RSV margin). Those prophets and saints who saw Yahweh in vision were admitted to the divine throne room and took their places (temporarily) among the gods: "I give thee thanks, O Lord, with my whole heart; before the gods (*elohim*) I sing thy praise" (Ps. 138:1). "God has taken his place in the divine council; in the midst of the gods he holds judgment" (Ps. 82:1). "All gods bow down before him" (Ps. 97:7). In short, the gods of the peoples were, for the Hebrews, real, and Yahweh is their sovereign. "For the Lord is a great God, and a great King above all gods" (Ps. 95:3).

There is nothing unique in the Israelite conception of God presiding over a heavenly council made up of lesser gods. The same view is recorded in Canaan, Babylon, Egypt, and Greece. It is reflected, for example, in this prayer to the Babylonian moon-god Sin (c. 70 b.c.e.): "Bowed down in thy presence are the great gods; the decisions of the land are laid before thee; when the great god inquire of thee thou dost give counsel. They sit (in) their assembly (and) debate under thee...."[5]

This subordinationist conception did not, surprisingly, throw Israel open to the risk of encouraging the worship of other gods beside Yahweh. As Yehezkel Kaufmann points out, the gods were of a different order altogether. They were, even for the surrounding peoples, not the ultimate powers of the universe, but rather part of a realm that preceded them and which they did not create. They were as dependent on this prior realm as humans. They too must obey its decrees and laws. They may create the world and humanity, but they do so with preexisting stuff, and they do not comprise, singly or together, a divine will which governs and is the cause of all being. They themselves are generated out of the primordial substance, and therefore they are subject to sexual conditions, and engage in procreation. Since matter transcends them, they need food and drink. In subordinating such gods to Yahweh the Israelites were merely acknowledging the reality of a limited aspect of nature; they never even bothered to give them names.

Yahweh was of a different order entirely. Yahweh created the world, including the gods; Yahweh is subject to no law or necessity. Nothing is prior to Yahweh, all is created at Yahweh's word. Humanity was created for relationship with Yahweh in Yahweh's image; the gods have nothing to do with it.[6] Idolatry in Israel was thus not caused by including the gods in the heavenly council, but by foreign political alliances that established the cult of other gods in the king's house and even occasionally in the Jerusalem temple.

This "henotheistic" or "mono-Yahwist"[7] solution (which provided for belief in one high god served by lesser gods) offered the opportunity to subordinate and thus depotentiate the gods of the nations. Pagan deities were absorbed into the heavenly council and given the status of messengers or servants of Yahweh. Those gods who obeyed their Sovereign's will were members in good standing (Pss. 103:21; 148:1-6). Those gods who failed to do justice among their people were judged and sentenced to die like mortals (Ps. 82:1-7; Isa. 24:21).[8]

As we have seen already (chap. 4), the pagan gods were appointed by God over other nations and peoples to guide them into justice and serve as their ambassadors in the heavenly council. "When the Most High gave to the nations their inheritance, when he separated the sons of men, he fixed the bounds of the peoples according to the number of the sons of God" (Deut. 32:8). Israel alone would be God's special portion (v. 9), and Israel was therefore forbidden to worship the gods appointed over the nations. "Nor must you raise your eyes to the heavens and look up to the sun, the moon, and the stars, all the host of heaven, and be led on to bow down to them and worship them; *the Lord your God assigned these for the worship of the various peoples under heaven*" (Deut. 4:19 NEB, italics mine). These gods should have lifted the eyes of the pagans to contemplate in nature and history the workings of the Lord Most High, but the peoples instead fell to worshiping their own national gods as ultimate—an act that had immediate and devastating political consequences as well. Nevertheless, Israelites were not to speak evil of gods (Exod. 22:28 LXX), for Yahweh has ordained them for the nations.[9] As a hedge against the worship of the gods of the nations, it occurred to later Jewish writers to designate them simply as angels.

Philo represents the high-water mark of Jewish openness toward the existence of the gods. By identifying the Greek gods (*daimones*) as angels (not "demons"), he made possible a positive evaluation of Greek culture by means of allegory. "It is Moses' custom to give the name of angels (*aggelous*) to those whom other philosophers call *daimonas*, souls that is which fly and hover in the air. And let no one suppose that what is here said is a myth. . . . So if you realize that souls (*psychas*) and *daimonas* and angels are but different names for the same one underlying object, you will cast from you that most grievous burden, the fear of *daimones*."[10] These *daimones* must not be confused with the "demons" of the Gospels, which were petty, localized entities and uniformly evil. By contrast, in Greek thought the *daimones* were regarded as supernatural powers not specifically personified but which exercised an influence in human affairs. They were bearers of both good and ill; they maintained a profound ambivalence right into the New Testament period, despite attempts to rationalize them.

Philo provides a valuable glimpse into the intersection between the Greek and Jewish worlds when he writes:

> The common usage . . . is to give the name daimon to bad and good daimons alike. . . . And so, too, you also will not go wrong if you reckon as angels, not only those who are worthy of the name, who are ambassadors backwards and forwards between men and God and are rendered sacred and inviolate by reason of that glorious and

blameless ministry, but also those who are unholy and unworthy of the title. (*De gig. 16*)

This is advice, however, that most Jewish and Christian writers after him ignored. Those powers whom the Greeks called *daimones* or gods were neatly divided into two camps, good and evil. The first were called "angels," the second, "demons." The holy *daimones* of the Greeks now entered their unhappy and violent servitude as the "demons" of the Christian church, and responded to this denigration with all the virulence at their command.

The seeds for the demonization of the pagan gods, and hence their *de facto* expulsion from the heavenly council, lay already in Deut. 32:17—"they sacrificed to demons (*shedim*) which were no gods." But that line is followed by several others that affirm the reality of the gods: "To gods they had never known, to new gods that had come in of late, whom your fathers had never dreaded." The process of demonizing the gods gained impetus from Ps. 106:37 and from the LXX translation of Ps. 96:5. The Hebrew text of the latter had rendered a nice pun by saying that "all the gods (*elohim*) of the peoples are worthless (*elilim*)," not implying their nonexistence but rather their impotence.[11] The LXX chose to translate *elilim* by *daimonia*, which in the context can only have been intended pejoratively. *1 Enoch* and *Jubilees*, like the LXX also from the early second century b.c.e., witness to the increasing polemical utility Jews were finding in this demonic interpretation.[12] Paul takes this idea straight over into his epistles. "What pagans sacrifice they offer to demons and not to God" (1 Cor. 10:20).

Paul, however, did not endorse the monistic philosophies of most of his later interpreters, and did not therefore choose the easy solution of denying that gods exist altogether. His converts in Corinth apparently were tempted in that direction, however. Their logic seems to have run thus: If there is only one God, there are no other gods; if there are no gods, there can be no scruples about eating food sacrificed to idols.[13] But Paul regarded this "solution" to the problem of polytheism as too simplistic (though it later came to be the dominant view among Christians, and continues to be today). For the Corinthian solution had created friction in the church and jeopardized the faith of those whose previous experience of the gods had been more like possession, and who therefore knew them to be "real." So Paul made a concession for their sakes: there are indeed many gods and many lords, but Christians are under the one God and one Lord, Jesus Christ (1 Cor. 8:5-6). He is clearly avoiding metaphysics here; he is not interested in the ontological existence of gods, but in the existential fact that whatever is worshiped is indeed, for that person, a god. Some in that church had been so liberated from their former beliefs (or had been such disbelievers, even in gods) that gods no longer held any spells for them. These may eat food sacrificed to idols because they are freed from their power. But they should abstain from eating sacrificed meats in a temple banquet (8:10-13) or even at someone's private home (10:27-29) if doing so would tempt a fellow Christian who did not share this inner freedom to do the same.

After further reflection Paul hedges the last opinion. They should not eat in a temple at all, and for quite a different reason: by so doing they participate in partnership with the demons (1 Cor. 10:20). Despite their disbelief in the god, by their act they bring themselves into union with it. For the "weaker" brethren this might activate old patterns and deep stirrings over which they had no power. And yet Paul had asserted, however briefly, that the Christian is *in principle* free to eat in a pagan temple (1 Cor. 8:9). He could argue thus, not because he believed that the gods were non-existent, but because, as he says of the elements in Gal. 4:9, they were merely "weak and beggarly." This comes home with striking force in 1 Cor. 10:22. He is not afraid that the Christian will be overwhelmed by the numinous power of idols, but by the wrath of God. "Shall we provoke the Lord to jealousy? Are we stronger than"—not *they*, but—"he?" The gods conjure no fear in Paul, only God.

This equation, gods=demons, was the new formula by which paganism would be eradicated by the church. For the early apologists, "all the gods of the Greek and Roman mythology were supernatural and real, only malignant, beings," writes F. C. Conybeare.[14] Demonization of the gods, however, really represented a new departure. Israel, as we saw before, had dealt with the gods by means of syncretism, suppression, and subordination, often all three together. If, however, the gods are demons, there is really no further place for them in the heavenly council. They are merely "idols." The use of this term by the translators of the LXX was itself an act of derision, for Greeks did not use *eidolon* for gods. It meant "phantom, unsubstantial form, reflected image, fantasy." It had previously been used of ghosts, specters, or underworldly beings. Its use for the higher gods cast aspersions on their reality. The term was a weapon in the attack on the mythological foundations of the pagan worldview.[15]

The apocryphal Epistle of Jeremy (c. 316–306 b.c.e.) is typical of this Jewish polemic against idols. They are carved holding daggers or axes, says the author, yet are unable to deliver themselves from robbers. Their eyes are coated with dust stirred up by the feet of their worshipers, yet they cannot even wipe their own eyes. Bats, swallows, birds, even cats perch on their heads, and they are unable to prevent the predictable results. If they fall, someone has to right them, and if the temple burns, their priests escape but they themselves are consumed.

All this makes for very clever rhetoric, but it misses the mark. Among the masses of people, the gods may well have been regarded as identical with their representations. And such gods indeed "spoke," for they embodied the projections of their worshipers, projections which themselves arose out of the deep, collective unconscious of the people and the very structure of the psyche. In the Roman period, however, more sophisticated devotees were aware of the difference between the symbol and its referent. The pagan Maximus Tyrius (20 c.e.) knew perfectly well how to use images as genuine symbols:

> It is because we are not able to apprehend His [the god's] being that we lean upon words, and names, and animal forms, and representations of gold and ivory and silver, and plants and rivers, and mountain tops and groves. . . . It is like the case of lovers to whose sight the representations of their beloved give most pleasure, and pleasure, too, is given by a lyre of his, a javelin, a chair, a walk and, in short, everything which awakens the memory of the loved one.[16]

The weakness of the attack on idols is clear the moment we apply it to the Christian church, with its crosses, crucifixes, statues of Mary and the saints, depictions of God, Christ, the angels, and apostles in stained glass, and so forth. The Jews forbade all images, and were immune to the reversal of their argument against themselves, but Christians were not. As symbols, how do any of these differ from the images of paganism? Yet for a practicing Christian, such an argument has no force whatever. For the believer knows, or at least has faith, that there is a reality which the symbol expresses. And here is where the polemic against idols hit raw nerves. The pagan gods were too local, too identified with the devotion of certain *cities*. They were not prepared for a cosmopolis. And they were too fragmentary; there were too many, too vaguely specialized in their benefits, too various for a world converging on itself and needing a centralizing coherence.

In a living religion the image signifies the divine reality itself. It is a material expression of the being it evokes. It participates in the reality and conveys it. As the neo-Platonist Iamblichus (c. 330 c.e.) put it, "idols are divine and filled with the divine presence."[17] The image is like a hole dug in sand beside the sea, into which the whole sea presses. The sea is in the hole, but not the whole sea. The image is thus not empty, an "idol," except for a person for whom it evokes no reality. The images of any religion are "idols" to unbelievers or otherbelievers. For a devotee of Apollo or Artemis, the cross would have been an idol: empty, vain, nothing—or worse: repulsive, disgusting, hideous. In short, an idol is in the eye of the beholder and the charge of idolatry is always polemical, always born of a counterdevotion. It is an evaluation, not a description. It is a lethal instrument of ideological warfare.

Paganism's susceptibility to this attack lay in its own decline. For all too many people, the gods no longer spoke with any frequency; finally they scarcely spoke at all. Even the artisans who fashioned the images recognized this. They were honest workers. They began to portray the gods no longer as young, but aging.[18]

Where once the common workers in a city could appeal, through strikes and protests, to the gods and to their immediate representatives, aristocracy, now their appeals were brutally repressed without effecting change. They could no longer invoke the higher authority of the gods of the city to censure the tyranny of rulers; the rulers were now sent from Rome, and the gods would not help.[19]

It was not simply religious credibility that the gods had lost, but their capacity to cement society and to legitimate, correct, and chastise its rulers. Already weakened, the gods were delivered yet another blow by the withering criticism of philosophical rationalism. One last desperate pagan revival swept the second-century empire. When it ebbed, Christianity had already secured the future. Yet for all that it is not the case that the Greek gods represented a chaotic welter of contradictory or vying forces. On the contrary, the very term *theos* ("god") expressed what had been felt to be the *unity* of the religious world despite its multiplicity. "The Greek concept of God," writes Hermann Kleinknecht, "is essentially polytheistic, not in the sense of many individual gods, but in that of an ordered totality of gods, of a world of gods, which . . . forms an integrated nexus."[20]

Indeed, what polytheism provided, in its hierarchies of gods, their polar oppositions, and continual warfares and intrigues, was a mythological depiction of what we might today call fields of forces in both the psyche and the everyday world. "The Greek gods are simply basic forms of reality."[21]

Seen in that light, polytheism represents a piecemeal approach to divine unity. The Greeks apprehended the world as primordially many, but in the process of many cumulative experiences the gods acquired a consequent unity. Hence the movement of Greek religion toward *unity in multiplicity,* which it could only accomplish partially by its death and resurrection in Christianity. Israel, on the other hand, experienced God as primordially one, but in the process of unfolding the many potential forms God acquired a consequent multiplicity, which the primordial character absorbed into its own unity. Thus the movement of Israelite religion toward *multiplicity in unity,* evidenced by the proliferation of angels and the emergence of Satan and demons in apocalyptic Judaism. These momentous and ancient opposite movements of convergence finally collapsed upon each other in Christianity. The synthesis that was the result, though it might appear unintelligible to some, was in fact gemlike and dazzling in its simplicity and power: the holy Trinity.

But what had become of the gods? They had not simply been eclipsed by the rational elegance of the world they had helped to structure. The archetypal images no longer communicated the archetypes spontaneously. But the archetypes did not die. They went underground, partly as a consequence of their loss of numinosity as the traditional symbols were emptied of their power, and partly because they were hounded there by the uncompromising rhetoric of the Christian apologists and the suppressions of Christian emperors. Now they were "demons"—so they became demonic in the extreme. The gods were powerful archetypal images in the unconscious or invariant structures in nature or human society. Hence their demonization could lead only to a massive rebound in the form of obsession with the demonic.

By the year 1200, a monk like Caesarius could write his *Dialogus Miraculorum,* depicting a world infested with demons, where not even the crucifix was protection enough, where every forbidden human impulse was ascribed to ravenous exterior powers, where the common folk had no hope of overcoming their wiles, where only saints could expect to prevail against them, and then only through the greatest suffering.[22] The gods extracted a fierce revenge, almost eclipsing belief in the one God and terrifying a whole civilization from their impregnable stronghold in the core of the psyche, the bosom of nature, and the collective pathologies of society.

THE REHABILITATION OF THE GODS

The gods, like stars, have been put out of heaven, leaving no light for exploring the darkness. They have become part of the darkness themselves. The gods once named the shapes that came to meet us in the gloom; without them we are pummeled and maddened by forces we have never named and cannot tame. What else was mythology but a map of these dim regions where the elemental forces of the universe mingle without distinction? We need the gods back to guide us through this night of history and of our own souls.

The gods never died, they only became diseases, as Jung put it: "Zeus no longer rules Olympus but rather the solar plexus, and produces curious specimens for the doctor's consulting room, or disorders the brains of politicians and journalists who unwittingly let loose psychic epidemics on the world."[23]

The great archetypal powers of the soul have always behaved demonically whenever they were not channeled and propitiated as divinities. In a conjectural emendation to a missing section of Euripides' *The Bacchae,* the god Dionysus is depicted as crying out against the people of Thebes:

> Behold me, a god great and powerful, Dionysus, immortal son of Zeus and Semele! I come to the city of Seven Gates, to Thebes, whose men and women mocked me, denied my divinity, and refused to receive my holy rites. Now they clearly see the result of impious folly. The royal house is overthrown; the city's streets are full of guilty fear, as every Theban repents too late for blindness and blasphemy . . . for no god can see his worship scorned, and hear his name profaned, and not pursue vengeance to the utmost limit; that moral men may know that the gods are greater than they.[24]

This sense of being held fast by some overwhelmingly powerful, higher being is common to all religions. Jung chose the term "archetypes" as a more phenomenologically neutral way of speaking about what religions have called gods, spirits, angels, and demons. The archetypes are the numinous, structural elements of the psyche that preform our experience in certain typical ways. They are not inherited or eternal ideas but inherited *possibilities* of ideas, not a predetermined content but only a form. Like the axial system of a crystal, which does not determine the concrete shape of the individual crystal or its infinite variety of sizes or combinations with other crystals, but only its stereometric structure, so also the archetypes in themselves are empty and purely formal. They are predispositions to set reactions in universal situations. They are possibilities of representation which are provided by the very structure of the brain over the immense course of its evolution.[25] All human beings have mothers, fathers, grandparents, and experience hunger, sexual desire, fear, fury, and so forth. Endless repetition has engraved these experiences into our psychic constitution or collective memory, so that there are as many archetypes as there are typical situations in life.[26]

These archetypes possess a certain autonomy and specific energy which enable them to attract those contents best suited to themselves out of the conscious mind. Thus the archetypal image is at once both universal (insofar as it reflects a fundamental structure of human experience) and specific to the person and the culture to which it lends its symbols. The gods want to be known; they reveal themselves in the diaphanous imagery of dreams, to the end that their exile might be ended—or to put it in the more neutral language of the archetypes, that the libido (energy) committed to maintaining their autonomy might be integrated into a larger self by making the unconscious contents conscious.[27]

From this phenomenological point of view, the "god" archetype is the fullest expression of life-energy in the psyche and therefore has the greatest degree of energy attached to it. It is through this symbol that the individual may experience his or her relationship to the total life process. This function is so important that feeling accords it the highest value. Anything psychically powerful is invariably called "god," says Jung, and cannot but carry conviction and evoke faith. When the god-image is no longer vital, however, the intensity of libido-energy that is constellated is no longer channeled toward consciousness by the symbol, and the energy turns within, with the result that the individual is subject to the delusion that a superhuman power belongs to one's own or another's person.[28] The psychic danger of so much of the new religiousness today is its blithe conviction that we are divine, with no apparent awareness of the psychic inflation which that involves or the arduous task involved in encountering the divine image within us. Such spirituality is less a solution to our dis-ease than a symptom of it.

The collapse of the god-archetype for so many in our time has meant that the central thrust of life-energies in the self has been bereft of symbols of expression, and so has unconsciously been projected on more or less suitable human personalities—messianic figures in politics, movies, sports, entertainment, and therapy. The most catastrophic recoil of the gods in our time was Nazism, with its volcanic revival of the cult of the Norse god Wotan, and its hysterical adulation of Adolf Hitler. To the degree that the Christian God had died in the psyche of the German people, as Nietzsche had prophesied, to that degree vast sums of psychic energy were set loose to craze certain individuals with a lust for power and to inspire others to follow them blindly.[29]

But that is only an extreme case. All of us, from time to time, come under the spell of the gods, for they are images of personal and collective processes that are formative of life. On the one hand, they are personal insofar as they are to some degree the unconscious distillate of instinctual demands, the patterns of instinctual behavior.[30] They are, in terms of the general thesis of this work, the "within" or spirituality of the physical instincts. The gods, we might say, are, at the personal level, a psychic representation of our organisms craving for life.

No wonder the gods of the Greeks were lusty, furious, greedy, lascivious, erotic; they are the voices of the self's instinctual homeostatic processes. They provide feedback to the psychophysical system about compensatory needs that the ego is neglecting.

On the other hand, at the social level, aspects of the inner drama can be played out collectively, through myths, which function as the "dreams of a people." These myths are both guides and protectors through the bewildering maze of the unconscious, providing social support and sanction for an otherwise perilous and lonely journey. Myths can help us to sort out the bizarre eruptions from the depths, to identify their myriad voices and actors, to lend dignity to the humiliations of the ego by naming the assailant a god, and to promise a blessing to those who wrestle through the night.

When I speak of the gods as the "within" of instinctuality or as the collective spirituality of a society (including the gods or angels of nations and other corporate entities), I do not intend to reduce them to mere personifications of bodily or social processes. I could have said as easily that the instincts or social entities are the clothing of the gods. Gods, angels, and spirits on the one hand, and instincts and institutions on the other, are the inner and outer aspects of a single phenomenon that has both spiritual and material components, and is far more rich and complex than anything materialism has been able to say about the instincts or society. In the materialistic perspective gods are "only" the instincts, purely chemical and neurological reactions of the body. In that view the gods are rendered mere allegories of mechanical processes, and can fruitfully be dropped from the race's fund of resources. Or they are "only" naive projections of the regularities and requirements of the physical or social order. I am suggesting, on the contrary, that the gods are the "mentality" and "communicability" of the instincts or of institutions, their capacity to "speak" and thus provide information to an organism or a society. They are not rendered less real by being located, whether at Olympus or in the psyche. They are not a postulate or a hypothesis, but an experience. They are known through revelation, today just as in all times, in the dreams and visions of everyday people. They are not mere projections of subjective states. They are the very structures by which personality and society are formed. They are as real as anything in the world. Without them we would not exist.

After this book was completed I came upon Curtis Bennett's *God as Form: Essays in Greek Theology*, the best study of Greek religion that I have found. The gods, he argues, are necessary psychic forms for very real pressures and powers. They are the discrete categories, given shape by the imagination, for the powers which we encounter in the processes and events of the natural, social, and inner psychological environment. These forms are in the mind, but they are not simply human shapes assigned to immanent powers and energies. These forms, rather, are themselves precipitated by the pressures, energies and processes of the body and its world. As such they are indispensable images, because they alone historically carry the dramatic intuition of the relationship of a given individual to the unwilled and ungovernable processes of nature. We cannot relinquish the gods without relinquishing that intuition and hardening the delusion that individuals are self-determining.

On the contrary, urges Bennett, human existence is beyond the control of any of its individual expressions. The psyche is not self-determining; it is rather expressive of the powers that determine its history. The gods are not just projections. They are environmental powers as well as elsewhere determined elements in the individual psyche and its destiny. "Instead of being projections from the psyche of its hoped-for magic powers, the Greek gods denote the projection into the psyche in recognizable form and accent of all that determines its history; they are the mode of its realization of its own form, its own elements, and their place in the natural environment" (38–39). "As our dreams will forever show, we can not live without psychic projection, in the naturalistic sense, for realizing the elements of our own nature as independent of our authority" (35). For the same reason the anthropomorphic aspect of deity is essential: it is the way to see the power defined as it impinges on the individual mind. The image enables us to see what cannot be seen physically, *as if* it were seen physically.

Bennett also relates the gods to the instincts. "Instinct and capacity for the individual are realized in as-if human forms of enduring existence." They express the pressure of that instinct for self-expression in the individual of his or her non-individual endowment. There are, he remarks, no "instincts" or "needs" or "drives" any more than there "are" gods; all are processes rendered as psychic entities. The gods speak within, and one recognizes the experience precisely because it is not unique but generic, an external form. The human ego is only local, but the gods bespeak power, instincts, forms of action that automatically recall their manifold manifestations elsewhere, as immortal forms, gods. They therefore must "speak" as a "voice" communicating the extra-individual pressure or capacity of self-realization to the individual psyche.[31]

The gods live. Monotheism is constitutionally incapable of acknowledging this fact. Biblical henotheism has affirmed it all along. "Who among the sons of gods is like the Lord, a God feared in the council of the holy ones?" (Ps. 89:6-7). Even when we had suppressed the memory that Yahweh had a heavenly council, we continued in our worship and eucharists to chant, "Holy,

holy, holy is the Lord of *hosts*"—those hosts who were none other than the gods themselves. But now that the gods have returned—are we equal to their epiphany?

Relating to the Gods

One of the gods who has been playing special havoc with the psyches of moderns, though she is seldom given credit, is Aphrodite. She is the goddess of love, goddess of the holiness of the sexual act. Sexuality always has something *daimonic*, something uncanny, even sinister about it, some quality of numinosity, of the unintelligible, the superhuman. There are occasions when it uses us, compels us, drives us, even when our physical needs would appear to have been satisfied. There is more than biological urge involved here, something at the other end of the spectrum, more like a lure toward self-transcendence and individuation. For that reason intercourse often symbolizes in dreams the conjunction of opposites in a new increment of wholeness. The ecstasy of sexual union is "heavenly," insofar as it expresses the transcendent sanctity of the sexual act. More than this woman or this man is present. At that moment one communes with god.

It is important to note, as Curtis Bennett points out, that Aphrodite is neither sex personified nor an abstraction of sex. She is the form by which the psyche realizes that it is in the domain of sex. She is not the idealization of woman as a sex object, or a wish-fulfillment projected on a female form. For when she appears to Helen, enticing her to Paris, she nevertheless appears as a woman. She is rather the form presented to the psyche of the sexual need of one human being for another.[32]

Pagan worship sometimes externalized and literalized this psychic experience, enacting it with sacred "prostitutes" of both sexes. But the term of odium is ours; in their own context theirs was regarded as a "service to the gods." Our culture no longer builds shrines to the gods of sex, yet who has not known of couples enmeshed in furtive affairs that are invested by their participants with all the numinous qualities of powers divine? Now, as modern society has broken free of so much of its Puritan and Victorian restraint, pinups and pornography have become antimadonnas,[33] and sexual freedom is the new evangel. And Aphrodite is behind it all.

Christians are so accustomed to diatribes against her dangers—they are real, and we will get to them—that it seems only fair to point out that she can also bring blessings. She showers joy and a taste of eternity on people otherwise trapped in humdrum lives. And she can be a trickster used by God. Let me illustrate.

As a child, this man now in his midthirties had stuttered. His feet turned in. And his father had already had massive heart attacks. His older brothers would set into fights and then, when their father intervened, turn on him, terrifying this youngest child that they would cause his father's death. At night he would pray, O God, please make me better tomorrow, so that I won't be a burden to Dad.

Puberty hit this child who had to be good to save his father's life like a tornado. Powers reared up in him over which he had no control. Aphrodite—he himself used that word—ruled him like an autonomous force. He lived in terror that people would discover that he really was not good, that he was an evil boy swept away by sex. Nor had Aphrodite released him since.

Now he was thirty-five, telling his story. He felt no redemption in it. He could not embrace his demon. He could not even bring it into the presence of God. He was sure that having shared all this, no one could accept him. Yet he had been driven to say it all. One person responded, "Isn't it just the opposite of what you think? Wasn't this the only power in your world strong enough to shatter the tyranny of the 'good'? Wasn't Aphrodite the seducer who lured you out of the Castle of Phony Goodness? Wasn't she the thin margin between saintliness of a bogus sort, and your real humanity? And isn't this the reason why, when you shared all these things, one of us struck you incredulous by saying that she saw Christ in you right then? It is only because of Aphrodite that that sublime humanness shines through. She was God's grace to you. She had to be autonomous. Your world allowed no space for her otherwise. You need to love her for what she has done for you. That doesn't mean it's easy—you now have ahead the long hard task of integrating your sexuality at last. But you can do so now because you need no longer dread it as an external power beyond your control. You can honor it as a part of yourself that almost destroyed you trying to save you from becoming nothing more than an automaton of the good." He was thunderstruck. "I can't believe you are saying that to me," he murmured, then said it again. He seemed to become lighter as we watched. The burden of a lifetime was falling from him. His problem was far from solved—it had only finally been adequately identified—but for the first time he felt he had a fighting chance to overcome it.

What the poet Rilke declared of the god Orpheus is true here of Aphrodite as well: "And she obeys, even as she oversteps the bounds."[34] Aphrodite, however, has many faces. All the gods are ambivalent. She is content to incarnate herself in anyone and can be served by sexual alliances of every sort, wholly apart from any concern for morality, appropriateness, or the consequences. She is no monogamist. In American society, where people tend to vaunt themselves on their sexual freedom, what many experience is in fact sexual possession. They are *not free not to* engage in compulsive sexual fantasies, masturbation, or affairs, and are often unaware of the extent of their bondage until, by some means, they are liberated. The danger echoes still in Helen's plaint in the *Odyssey,* "It is Aphrodite who deceived me and brought me out of my village."[35] Jung points to Aphrodite's work: "When, for instance, a highly esteemed professor in his seventies abandons his family and runs off with a young red-headed actress, we know that the gods have claimed another victim."[36] And she has other aspects as well: her love of war (Ares was her husband), of orgies, of prostitution. She is far from archetypal femininity; hers is a masculinized image of sex as power, rebellion, lust, and conquest. We have to bridle her, bring her powers into the service of relationship, or else she may consume us.

Aphrodite is alive and well and inspiring a profitable sex industry grossing billions. Ares/Mars is alive and well and devouring more money, material, scientific creativity, and human flesh for past, present, and future wars than all the gods combined. Dionysus is alive and well and staging a major revival in voodoo, Macumba, the charismatic movement, the drug culture, the rock scene, and generally mocking to derision the rigid etiquette and emotional sterility of the traditional religions. Christians have been afraid to admit the existence of gods for fear people would succumb to worshiping them. That danger is great, but no greater than the opposite danger of denying their existence and being unconsciously tyrannized by them. The only sane course would appear to be to acknowledge their reality, learn their characteristics, raise to consciousness their ineluctable workings in our depths, and subject them to the sovereignty of the God of gods.

Besides the reality factor, there is the simple fact that Yahweh cannot symbolize all the ways in which we encounter the divine. There is no way of speaking of Yahweh as Cupid or Eros, for example, or as involved in the positive aspects of sexuality. Apart from the Song of Songs, one looks in vain for anything in Jewish or Christian sources that celebrates sexual intercourse. Little of the trickster quality of Hermes adheres to Yahweh; most of it was displaced on Satan, but humorlessly, with the result that the wonderful subterfuges by which we are beguiled into coming to terms with the darker aspects of ourselves are blamed on Satan and "righteously" resisted. And perhaps if we could perceive that much of the love for order and tradition that conventional Christianity ascribes to God is really more characteristic of Kronos/Saturn, then congregations might not absolutize familiar ways of doing things as much as they do.

I am aware that this openness toward the gods was not an option for the early church, picking its way through a world dense with idols. But our situation is fundamentally different. Ours is not a god-sotted world; it is god-bereft. The flames of secularism have destroyed much that is of value, but they have also incinerated great heaps of religious rubbish. Perhaps we are freer now to sort through the ashes to recover the finer metals refined in the fire. Furthermore, I believe that depth psychology now provides us for the first time with cognitive tools for relating to the gods without lapsing into their worship, and that these are already filtering down into a general cultural awareness. In short, I believe that Christianity can at last open itself to receive gifts from the other religions of the world.

And why should this not be the case? We believe that Jesus fulfilled the Law and the Prophets; why should he not also have fulfilled the myths of the pagans? I am not proposing syncretism, but merely the incorporation of the gods among the Powers where they belong, just as Ephraem Syrus said they should be. As such they are part of God's good creation, bearing all the marks of the Fall, yet still part of the divine economy and necessary for our development and redemption. Such a hermeneutical strategy simply carries on the ancient Israelite practice of conscripting the gods into the heavenly council. The gods are divested of ultimacy both by subordinating them to God and by ordering their myth within the foundational myth of the Judeo-Christian tradition. This "hierarchical principle of preference among values," as Paul Ricoeur puts it, makes it possible for us to remain deeply rooted in our primary myth and still appropriate values drawn from any other complementary mythic source.[37]

I am not the least bit interested in reviving polytheism. People today are lost enough without being thrown into a wilderness of vying spiritual powers, none of which possesses ultimacy though all alike claim it. The great revelation given Israel to give the nations, that there is one God beyond the gods, is the single greatest treasure the world possesses. Monotheism is an abasement of that gift. It snaps the tension between multiplicity and unity, declares for unity alone, and teaches unbridled intolerance toward all other opinions. And it also has induced a simplistic notion of the self as indivisible and one, denying us the very guides whose aid we must enlist to find our way through the bewildering labyrinth of personal development and collective life. The henotheistic or mono-Yahwist view of the Bible, on the other hand, acknowledges the rich multiplicity of Powers in the soul and in the world, yet encompasses them all within an integrative principle of coherence.

Perhaps the time has come to recast the henotheistic metaphor of God as a king presiding over his court into a new, less patriarchal, hierarchical, and antiquarian image. Not all forms of coordination require central control, after all. An ecosystem, for example, has a most intricate coordination of synergistic actions, yet there is no central power. A market economy can likewise rely on Adam Smith's "invisible hand" to weave together the pursuits of individual economic agents into a coherent fabric of exchange. In each case the control is in the total system, not some key point in it, much as the self cannot be located in any central point in the body, but pervades the whole. The picture of God as King requires a controller outside the system or atop its hierarchical apex, directing the whole. It is only in direct contests of power that a directing authority is required at the center. It may be that the very power-system of civilized society has entrapped us into conceiving God as a despot anxious to maintain ascendancy, demanding unquestioning obedience, and served by a heavenly army (the original meaning of "Lord of *hosts*"). For the very epitome of centralized control is the military organization, with its pyramid of power and centralized chain of command. What the ancients designated by "King," we are free to reconceive as the System of the systems, the Soul of the cosmos, the Mother of all, the Life of life, the I AM still and forever, the Eternal.

However we choose to speak of God, we should be clear that God is not merely the sum of all the gods, or the complex of opposites, but the dynamism that thrusts toward their synthesis. Along each loop of the spiral of life we encounter the gods arrayed in polar opposition. On each revolution we confront them again, over and over—the same archetypal patterns, the same neurotic complexes, the same cultural or political compulsions. Each god is ambivalent, possessing its own component of good and evil. Our capacity to be faithful in these encounters and to transform that bit of evil and encompass that bit of good adds incrementally to the total available energy and being of the self and the world. As the spiral widens in its gyre, life is enhanced.

The problem of false worship of the gods stems from the fact that as the "within" of instinctuality or the collective compulsions of society, they encounter us with such almighty power that we not only fail to resist but are awed into submission. We worship what enslaves us, forging our own chains. This lies at the heart of Paul's critique of the gods. He could not take the easy route of denying the gods' existence, as the Corinthians were doing. He knew their power to *enslave*. "Indeed, there are many gods and many lords—yet for us there is one God. . . ." How then, he cries in another place, "can you turn back again to the weak and beggarly elements, whose slaves you want to be once more?"[38] Such idolatry mislocates the reverence due to the Creator and lodges it in a power that is only a subaspect of creation. Whenever this happens, the god does become demonic, just as the apologists said—but without their realizing that the demonic quality does not inhere in the gods but in the way we *relate* to the gods. When we worship them we abdicate our lives to them, thus destroying the creative tension that the ego must maintain with and against them in order to wrest from them their blessings for the self.

How then can we relate to the gods without inundation? Much depends on *ego* and *altar*. The archetypes should be honored, but honored at a distance, as a fire that can consume, as a force that both blesses with its presence and inflicts itself as curse. The ego (the conscious aspect of the self) must therefore not only participate in living forward the pattern provided by the archetype, says Murray Stein; it must at the same time monitor the process as a cautious and interested observer. Without this dual consciousness, the participatory "I" is simply a puppet of the archetype, and the pattern simply repeats itself rather than providing the key for release. Yielding to the archetype can be pathological. If the mythology lives us, instead of our living it, we can fall into a state of inflation, possession, bondage, one-sidedness, and stereotypy.[39] All the more soul-wise cultures have shown an acute sense of the "perils of the soul" and of the dangerousness and general unreliability of the gods, Jung remarks. Hence one ought to avoid at all costs identification or union with the god, for as psychosis and certain contemporary events demonstrate, the consequences are terrifying.[40]

Thus forewarned, the ego's next task is to find the god's blessing—to read, in the disgusting compulsiveness of our neurotic behavior or the crippling effects of our diseases, some divine rune that unravels its meaning. Our mistaken quest for perfection ill-prepares us to find the healing value in the very inferior and unacceptable aspects of ourselves that we have so long tried to flee, deny, crush, amputate, or disown. But it is just there that the God of gods waits to be discovered, in the integration of autonomous parts of ourselves into the total selfhood to which we are called.

Such integration will require sacrifice. We must therefore have an *altar*. But what is the proper gift? The ego is desperately trying to hold its own, overmatched by a god—and we are told that the ego must itself be sacrificed. That it must abandon control, so that the entire Gestalt of the self can absorb, digest and integrate this new thing. But that can only be done on faith that something or someone is in charge, greater and better than the ego. It demands trust that there is a higher will in this encounter, working to augment life. Here both the ego and the gods must bow, and be ordered under an organic principle that transcends them both. The "altar" frees us to honor the gods without worshiping them, to keep our distance and yet relate to them. This is the religious task of the ego: to worship only the God of gods, weaver of life's purposes.

Honor the gods; worship God. Something of the same formula animated the anti-iconoclasts in the great controversy over icons. The Seventh Ecumenical Council at Nicaea in 787 adopted the distinction between reverence (*proskynesi*) and the true worship of faith (*latreia*). The first could be offered as a form of veneration before icons of Christ, Mary, and saints. This was no different in kind from the *proskynesis* performed in the East before bishops or the emperor and empress. But *latreia*, true worship, was appropriate only to God.[41] Psalm 29 goes one step further. We are to order the gods to worship Yahweh!

> Ascribe to the Lord, O sons of gods,
> ascribe to the Lord glory and strength.
> Ascribe to the Lord the glory of his name;
> worship the Lord in holy array.
> (Ps. 29:1-2, RSV marginal reading)

This is finally the only way to keep the gods in their place—to remind them of their fealty to their sovereign. (And here, too, despite every attempt to recast the image, the metaphor of kingship *means* something so central to the life of faith that one wonders if we will ever be able to dispense with it.) The gods too are creatures. When we do not command the gods to worship thus, we forget ourselves and worship them. When that happens, they are potentiated as autonomous powers. They become disobedient to the divine will, possessing us with all the irresistible force of a neurotic complex or a political obsession. It is *our* task to keep them in their seats in the heavenly council, ours to signal their praise to Yahweh. What a glorious picture of the role of choice, of our own role in helping to determine the good or evil of the gods!

The gods live. They are real but not ultimate, transcendent but not absolute, suprahuman but not superior to humans, more powerful than we yet subject to our responses, worthy of honor yet never to be worshiped, manifestations of the divine yet never to be identified with godhead. If we do not acknowledge them they compel us from concealment. If we demonize them we lose their blessing. If we worship them we risk possession by what is fragmentary and lose our relatedness to the whole.

Perhaps it will be the case that in the twisting and surprising turns of our development it may be our fate to have as our dancing partner for a few spins one of the great gods. But it is still the Fiddler that calls the tunes. The trick is staying in the dance—do not, oh do not let the god escort you off the floor and out into the dark. Stay in close earshot to the music, keep moving with the beat, and the Fiddler will see you through.

Notes

1. Carl Jung, *Alchemical Studies,* CW 13 (1968), 37.
2. I am following G. B. Caird's helpful discussion in *Principalities and Powers* (Oxford: Clarendon Press, 1956), 2–8.
3. Jer. 5:7; 10:2-16.
4. Jer. 23:18, 22; see also Isa. 63:9.
5. Gerald Cooke, "The Sons of (the) God(s)," *Zeitschrift für die alttestamentliche Wissenschaft* 76 (1964): 22–47.
6. Yehezkel Kaufmann, *The Religion of Israel* (Chicago: Univ. of Chicago Press,1960), 21–59.
7. Norman Gottwald's designation (*The Tribes of Yahweh: A Sociology of the Religion of Liberated Israel 1250-1050* b.c.e. [Maryknoll, N.Y.: Orbis Books, 1979], 679).
8. B. W. Anderson, "Hosts, Host of Heaven," *IBD* 2:655–56.
9. R. P. C. Hanson, "The Christian Attitude to Pagan Religions up to the Time of Constantine the Great," *ANRW* II.23.2 (1980): 951.
10. Philo, *De gig.* 6.16. See *De fuga* 212: "Angels are God's household-servants, and are deemed gods by those whose existence is still one of toil and bondage." Also, *De spec. leg.* 1.13–20.
11. Henry Ansgar Kelly, *The Devil, Demonology and Witchcraft* (Garden City, N.Y.: Doubleday & Co., 1968), 12–13.
12. 1 *Enoch* 19:1.
13. Hans Conzelmann, *1 Corinthians,* Hermeneia (Philadelphia: Fortress Press, 1975), 142.
14. F. C. Conybeare, "The Demonology of the New Testament," *Jewish Quarterly Review* 8/9 (1896/97): 608.
15. W. Kern, S. J., "Die antizipierte Entideologisierung oder die 'Weltelemente' des Galater-und Kolosserbriefes Heute," *Zeitschrift far Katholische Theologie* 96 (1974): 200ff.
16. Maximus Tyrius 8.10; cited by W. R. Halliday, *The Pagan Background of Christianity* (Liverpool: Liverpool University Press, 1955), 7–8.
17. Cited by Photius, *Bibl.*215. For a general discussion, E. R. Dodds, *The Greeks and the Irrational*(Berkeley and Los Angeles: Univ. of California Press, 1951), 292–95 and 306 n. 87.
18. Campbell Bonner, "Religious Feeling in Later Paganism," *Harvard Theological Review* 30 (1937): 139.
19. James M. Fennelly, "The Primitive Christian Values of Salvation and Patterns of Conversion," in *Man and His Salvation,* ed. Eric J. Sharpe and John R. Hinnells (Manchester: Manchester Univ. Press, 1973), 117–118.
20. Hermann Kleinknecht, "Theos," *TDNT* 3 (1965): 67.
21. Ibid., 68.
22. Cited by Norman Cohn, *Europe's Inner Demons* (New York: New American Library, 1975), 68–71.
23. Jung, *Alchemical Studies,* 37.

24. Euripides, *Bacchae*. This is a translator's reconstruction of the lacuna at line 1329; I have been unable to discover whose. It is, however, consistent with and a summary of the entire play.

25. Carl Jung, "Concerning the Archetypes and the Anima Concept," *The Archetypes and the Collective Unconscious*, CW 9/1 [1971], 66, 58.

26. Ibid., 48.

27. Jung, "General Aspects of Psychoanalysis," in *Freud and Psychoanalysis*, CW 4 (1961), 232.

28. Jung, *Symbols of Transformation*, CW 5 (1970), 64; Ira Progoff, *Jung's Psychology and Its Social Meaning* (Garden City, N.Y.: Doubleday & Co., Anchor Books, 1973), 182.

29. Progoff, *Jung's Psychology*, 186ff.

30. Jung, "The Concept of the Collective Unconscious," 44; idem, *Aion*, CW 9/2 (1979), 179.

31. Curtis Bennett, *God as Form* (Albany: State Univ. of New York Press, 1976).

32. Bennett, *God as Form*, 31.

33. Kern, "Die antizipierte Entideologisierung," 204.

34. See Rainer Maria Rilke, "The Sonnets to Orpheus," first series, no. 5, in *Duino Elegies and the Sonnets to Orpheus*, trans. A. Paulin, Jr. (Boston: Houghton Mifflin, 1977), 93.

35. Homer, *Odyssey* 4.260–61.

36. Jung, "The Archetypes of the Collective Unconscious," in *The Archetypes and the Collective Unconscious*, 30.

37. Paul Ricoeur's remarks on this subject are still an unmined treasure of insights for the question of religious pluralism (*The Symbolism of Evil* [New York: Harper & Row, 1967], 248, 308–30).

38. 1 Cor. 8:5-6; Gal. 4:9 (au. trans.).

39. Murray Stein, "Hephaistos: A Pattern of introversion," in *Facing the Gods*, James Hillman et al. (Irving, Tex.: Spring Publications, 1980), 84–85.

40. Jung, "Psychological Aspects of the Mother Archetype," 103–4.

41. Hans-Ruedi Weber, *Experiments with Bible Study* (Geneva: World Council of Churches: 1981), 22–23.

PART IV

Engaging the Powers

8

Introduction

In the final volume of the Powers trilogy, Walter Wink takes as his task "engaging" the Powers in such a way that their negative (evil) and positive (good) functions are held together. His belief is that they can be redeemed in order that they might be reclaimed for the "humanizing purposes of God." Wink here briefly describes five competing worldviews—the ancient, the spiritualistic, the materialistic, the theological, and the integral. To varying degrees, each of these worldviews finds adherents today, but Wink argues that only the integral worldview is adequate to the task of engaging the Powers redemptively. Like the ancient worldview, the integral worldview affirms the inner and outer aspect of all things but does not see the inner or spiritual aspect as the earthly counterpart of heavenly realities. Rather, the integral worldview sees the inner spirituality of things as "inextricably related to an outer concretion or physical manifestation." This conceptual move allows Wink to introduce the concept of "domination systems," and assert that the real spiritual force we experience within domination systems emanates from actual institutions, structures and systems. Theologically, the utility of the Powers for examining structural/systemic evil is clear.

Source: Wink 1992: Introduction

FUGITIVE.	The beast is in the king.
JOURNEYER.	The beast is in the king?
FUGITIVE.	But the king doesn't see it. In the palace only the slaves see the beast.
JOURNEYER.	But the king sent me to kill the beast. To bring back its claws!

FUGITIVE.	The king was a liar. He told you to "get claws" So you would believe there were claws. He told you to "kill it" So you would believe it could be killed. But the beast has no claws. It can't be killed. In the palace we killed the king.
JOURNEYER.	You killed the king!
FUGITIVE.	But there was still the beast. We put a doll on the throne. *But* there was still the beast. We destroyed the doll *But* there was still the beast.
JOURNEYER.	In my village we need help. In my village they are forgetting.
FUGITIVE.	But if the beast has no claws, If the beast can't be killed—
JOURNEYER.	Still, I have to find the beast Whatever it is, Or isn't.

—Jean Claude von Itallie, *A Fable*[1]

One of the most pressing questions facing the world today is, How can we oppose evil without creating new evils and being made evil ourselves?

It is my conviction that any attempt to face the problem of evil in society from a New Testament perspective must be bound up with an understanding of what the Bible calls the "Principalities and Powers." I am also convinced that no social ethic can be constructed on New Testament grounds without recognition of the role of these Powers in sustaining and subverting human life.

The Powers, unfortunately, have long since been identified as an order of angelic beings in heaven, or as demons flapping about in the sky. Most people have simply consigned them to the dustbin of superstition. Others, sensing the tremendous potential in the concept of the Powers for interpreting social reality, have identified them without remainder as institutions, structures, and systems. The Powers certainly are the latter, but they are more, and it is that "more" that holds the clue to their profundity. In the biblical view they are both visible *and* invisible, earthly *and* heavenly, spiritual *and* institutional. The Powers possess an outer, physical manifestation (buildings, portfolios, personnel, trucks, fax machines) and an inner spirituality, or corporate culture, or collective personality. The Powers are the simultaneity of an outer, visible structure and an inner, spiritual reality. The Powers, properly speaking, are not just the spirituality of institutions, but their outer manifestations as well. The New Testament uses the language of power to refer now to the outer aspect, now to the inner aspect, now to both together, as I have shown in *Naming the Powers*. It is the spiritual aspect, however, that is so hard for people inured to materialism to grasp.

Perhaps this understanding of the Powers can be clarified by a comparison of worldviews, since our perception of the Powers is colored to a great extent by the way we view the world.

1. THE ANCIENT WORLDVIEW

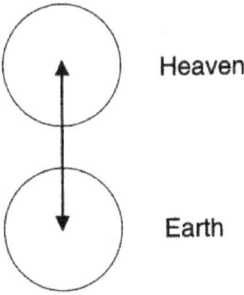

1. The Ancient Worldview.

This is the worldview reflected in the Bible (see fig. 1). In this conception, everything earthly has its heavenly counterpart, and everything heavenly has its earthly counterpart. Every event is thus a simultaneity of both dimensions of reality. If war begins on earth, then there must be, at the same time, war in heaven between the angels of the nations involved on earth. Likewise, events initiated in heaven would be mirrored on earth. There is nothing uniquely biblical about this imagery. It was shaped not only by the writers of the Bible, but also by Greeks, Romans, Egyptians, Babylonians, Assyrians,

Sumerians—indeed, by everyone in the ancient world—and it is still held by large numbers of people in Africa, Asia, and Latin America. It is a profoundly true picture of reality.

2. THE SPIRITUALISTIC WORLDVIEW

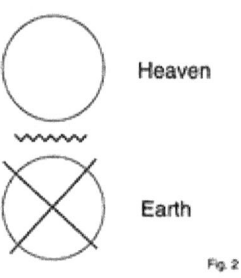

2. *The Spiritualistic Worldview.*

Fig. 2

What distinguishes this worldview (see fig. 2) from all other types is that it divides human beings into "soul" and "body"; one understands oneself as the same as one's "soul" and other than one's "body." In this account, the created order is evil, false, corrupted. Creation was itself the fall. Matter is either indifferent or downright evil. Earthly life is presided over by imperfect and evil Powers. When the soul leaves its heavenly bliss, and is entrapped in the body, as a result of sexual intercourse, it forgets its divine origins and falls into lust, ignorance, and heaviness. The body is a place of exile and punishment, but also of temptation and contamination. Salvation comes through the knowledge of one's heavenly origins and the secret of the way back. This worldview is usually associated with Gnosticism, Manichaeism, some forms of Neoplatonism, and in regard to sexuality, Puritanism. (Something of the same picture would fit some forms of Eastern religions, except that they would see the world not as evil but as illusion.)

3. THE MATERIALISTIC WORLDVIEW

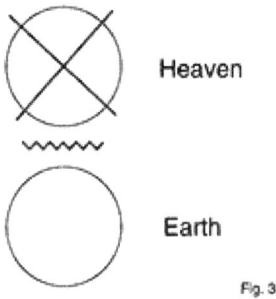

3. The Materialistic Worldview.

Fig. 3

This view (see fig. 3) became prominent in the Enlightenment, but is as old as Democritus (ca. 460–ca. 370 b.c.e.), and is in many ways the antithesis of the world-rejection of spiritualism. In this view, there is no heaven, no spiritual world, no God, no soul—nothing but material existence and what can be known through the five senses and reason. The spiritual world is an illusion. There is no higher self; we are mere complexities of matter, and when we die we cease to exist except as the chemicals and atoms that once constituted us. This materialistic worldview has penetrated deeply even into many Christians, causing them to ignore the spiritual dimensions of systems or the spiritual resources of faith.

4. THE "THEOLOGICAL "WORLDVIEW"

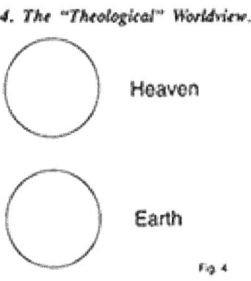

4. The "Theological" Worldview.

Fig. 4

In reaction to materialism, Christian theologians invented the supernatural realm (see fig. 4). Acknowledging that this supersensible realm could not be known by the senses, they conceded earthly reality to modern science and preserved a privileged "spiritual" realm immune to confirmation or refutation at the cost of an integral view of reality and the simultaneity of heavenly and earthly aspects of existence. This view of the religious realm as hermetically sealed and immune to challenge from the sciences has been held not only by the Christian center and right, but by most of theological liberalism and neoorthodoxy.

5. AN INTEGRAL WORLDVIEW.

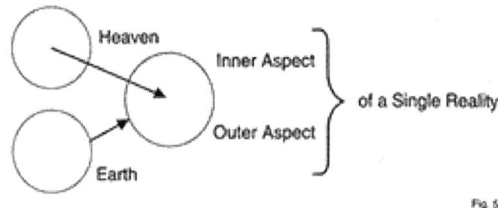

Fig. 5

This new worldview (see fig. 5) is emerging from a confluence of sources: the reflections of Carl Jung, Teilhard de Chardin, Morton Kelsey, Thomas Berry, Matthew Fox, process philosophy, and the new physics. It sees everything as having an outer and an inner aspect. It attempts to take seriously the spiritual insights of the ancient or biblical worldview by affirming a withinness or interiority in all things, but sees this inner spiritual reality as inextricably related to an outer concretion or physical manifestation. It is no more intrinsically "Christian" than the ancient worldview, but I believe it makes the biblical data more intelligible for people today than any other available worldview, including the ancient.

The integral worldview that is emerging in our time takes seriously all the aspects of the ancient worldview, but combines them in a different way. Both images are spatial. The idea of heaven as "up" is a natural, almost unavoidable way of indicating transcendence. But in the West, which has been irremediably touched by modern science, few of us can any longer actually think that God, the angels, and departed spirits are somewhere in the sky, as most ancients literally did. (And some people today who disbelieve still do—including atheists. Remember the glee of the Soviet cosmonauts in announcing to the world that they had encountered no supernatural beings in space?)

The image of the spiritual as "withinness" is not, however, a flat, limited, dimensionless point. It is a within coterminous with the universe—an inner realm every bit as rich and extensive as the outer realm. The psychologist Carl Jung spoke of this rich inner dimension as the collective unconscious, meaning by that a realm of largely unexplored spiritual reality linking everyone to everything. The amazement of mystics at the discovery of this realm within is matched only by the amazement of physicists upon discovering that the "final" building block of matter, the atom, has an interiority also, and that the electrons and protons they had once thought so substantial are not best described as matter but as energy-events: what we might call, from the perspective of this book, spiritmatter. It appears that everything, from photons to subatomic particles to corporations to empires, has both an outer and an inner aspect.

My thesis is that what people in the world of the Bible experienced and called "Principalities and Powers" was in fact real. They were discerning the actual spirituality at the center of the political, economic, and cultural institutions of their day. The spiritual aspect of the Powers is not simply a "personification" of institutional qualities that would exist whether they were personified or not. On the contrary, the spirituality of an institution exists as a real aspect of the institution even when it is not perceived as such. Institutions have an actual spiritual ethos, and we neglect this aspect of institutional life to our peril.

When people speak to me about their experiences of evil in the world, they often use the language of the ancient worldview, treating demons and angels as separate beings residing in the sky somewhere, rather than as the spirituality of institutions and systems. When I suggest restating the same thought using the new integral worldview, they often respond, "Oh, yes, that's what I meant." But it is not at all what they have said. In fact, they have just said something utterly different. I can only explain this anomalous behavior, not as woolly thinking (these are generally exceptionally perceptive people, or they would not have discerned these spiritual realities), but as an indication that this new integral worldview has only just come of age, and that the old conceptuality is repeated merely for lack of a better one. When a more adequate language is suggested, it is instantly recognized, not as a *new* idea to which they capitulate, but as *what they wanted to say all along*, and simply lacked the vocabulary for saying. People are groping for a more adequate language to talk about spiritual realities than the tradition provides. I conclude that a very rapid and fundamental sea change has been taking place in our worldview that has passed largely unrecognized but is everywhere felt. A new conceptual worldview is *already* in place, latently, and can be triggered by its mere articulation.

The less-known aspect of the Powers is the *spiritual* or *invisible* dimension. It is generally only indirectly perceptible, by means of projection. In New Testament times, people did not read the spirituality of an institution straight off from its outer manifestations. Instead, they projected its *felt* or intuited spiritual qualities onto the screen of the universe, and perceived them as cosmic forces reigning from the sky.

There were, in the first century, both Jews and Christians who perceived in the Roman Empire a demonic spirituality that they called Sammael or Satan.[2] But they encountered this spirit in the actual institutional forms of Roman life: legions, governors, crucifixions, payment of tribute, Roman sacred emblems and standards, and so forth. The spirit that they perceived existed right at the heart of the empire, but their worldview equipped them to discern that spirit only by intuiting it and then projecting it out, in visionary form, as a spiritual being residing in heaven and representing Rome in the heavenly council.

In the ancient worldview, where earthly and heavenly realities were inextricably united, this view of the Powers worked effectively. But modern Westerners are, on the whole, incapable of maintaining that worldview. What we usually encounter instead is either fundamentalist treatments of the Powers as demons in the air, wholly divorced from their concretions in the physical or political world (the theological worldview), or denials that this spiritual dimension even exists (the materialistic worldview).

What is necessary is to complete the projection process by *withdrawing* the projections and recognizing that the real spiritual force that we are experiencing is emanating from an actual institution. In the ancient worldview, a seer or prophet was able to sense the diseased spirituality of an institution or state, and then bring that spirituality to awareness by projecting it in visionary form onto the heavenly realm and depicting it (even *seeing* it) as a demon on high. Our task today, working with a unitary worldview, is to withdraw that projection from on high and locate it in the institution in which it actually resides.

Projection is not a falsification of reality. It is sometimes the only way we have of knowing certain internal things. The demons projected on the screen of the cosmos really are demonic, and play havoc with humanity; only they are not up there, but over there, in the socio-spiritual entities that make up the one-and-only real world. Thus the New Testament insists that demons can have no effect unless they are able to embody themselves in people (Mark 1:21-28 par.; Matt. 12:43-45 // Luke 11:24-26), or pigs (Mark 5:1-20 par.), or political systems (Revelation 12–13).

Visitors to Nazi Germany in the late 1930s spoke of the palpable evil in the "air," of a pervading "atmosphere" that hung over the entire land, full of foreboding and menace. Those who leave South Africa remark on the sense of an enormous weight of anxiety and tension that drops off their shoulders as the plane leaves South African airspace. People who remember the assassination of President John F. Kennedy will still recall a feeling of darkness over the face of the nation that lasted for days. These "spirits" are real, but they are not independent operatives from on high; they are the actual spirituality of the nations involved, and the sheer intensity of evil renders them, for a brief time, almost visible.

It is merely a habit of thought that makes people think of the Powers as personal beings. In fact, many of the spiritual powers and gods of the ancient world were not conceived of as personal at all (the Lares, the Penates, Virtue, Victory, Providence, and so forth). Even the angels in Judaism were impersonal agents of God. For a long time the Jews resisted naming the angels for fear they would detract from the sole sovereignty of God. The entire interest of early Judaism was in the angels' function, not in their personal characteristics, which we see emerging only in late apocalyptic literature.

I prefer to think of the Powers as impersonal entities, though I know of no way to settle the question except dogmatically. It is a natural human tendency to personalize anything that seems to act intentionally. But we are now discovering from computer viruses that certain systemic processes are self-replicating and "contagious," behaving almost willfully even though they are quite impersonal. Generally, I have bracketed the question of the metaphysical status of the Powers, and have instead treated them phenomenologically—that is, I have attempted to describe the *experiences* that got called "Satan," "demons," "powers," "angels," and the like. Thus I speak of "demons" as the actual spirituality of systems and structures that have betrayed their divine vocations. I use the expression "the Domination System" to indicate what happens when an entire network of Powers becomes integrated around idolatrous values. And I refer to "Satan" as the world-encompassing spirit of the Domination System. Do these entities possess actual metaphysical *being*, or are they the "corporate personality" or ethos or gestalt of a group, having no independent existence apart from the group? I leave that for the reader to decide. My main objection to personalizing demons is that they then are regarded as having a "body" or form separate from the physical and historical institutions of which, on my theory, they are the actual interiority. Therefore I prefer to regard them as the impersonal spiritual realities at the center of institutional life.

Think, for example, of a riot at a soccer game, in which, for a few frenzied minutes, people who in their ordinary lives behave quite decently on the whole suddenly find themselves bludgeoning and even killing opponents whose only sin was rooting for the other team. Afterwards people often act bewildered, and wonder what could have possessed them. Was it a Riot Demon that leaped upon them from the sky, or was it something intrinsic to the social situation: a "spirituality" that crystallized suddenly, precipitated by the outer permissiveness, heavy drinking, a violent ethos, a triggering incident, the inner violence of the fans? And when the riot subsides, does the Riot Demon rocket back to heaven, or does the spirituality of the rioters simply dissipate as they are scattered, subdued, or arrested?

Frank Peretti's best-selling novel, *This Present Darkness*,[3] grandly illustrates the hopelessness of trying to repristinate the ancient worldview today. While I appreciate his treatment of the interconnection of heavenly and earth reality, the role of human freedom, the centrality of prayer, the angels of cities and nations and the subtle coincidence of demonic promptings and people's words or thoughts, what we are served up is a consistently paranoid view of reality. With such a worldview one cannot help seeing demons everywhere, even among the saints. Rather than learning from our enemies, this view causes one to dismiss them as possessed by Satan. The author is welcome to his politics; but it is one thing to regard the United Nations as a dangerous idea, and another to portray it as a conspiracy of the Devil. We have here a case of the total projection of evil out on others. The view of evil is scary but finally trivial; his demons are simply imaginary bad people with wings, and the really mammoth and crushing evils of our day—racism, sexism, political oppression, degradation, militarism, patriarchy, homelessness, economic greed—are not even mentioned. It is simply Pentecostal political naïveté writ large on the universe.

But equally naive is the blind refusal to recognize the reality of the demonic in this most demonic of centuries. The relevance of the Powers for an understanding of structural evil should by now begin to be clear. Any attempt to transform a social system without addressing both its spirituality and its outer forms is doomed to failure. Only by confronting the spirituality of an institution *and* its concretions can the total entity be transformed, and that requires a kind of spiritual discernment and praxis that the materialistic ethos in which we live knows nothing about.

To put the thesis of these three volumes in its simplest form:

> The Powers are good.
> The Powers are fallen.
> The Powers must be redeemed.

These three statements must be held together, for each, by itself, is not only untrue but downright mischievous. We cannot affirm governments or universities or businesses to be good unless at the same time we recognize that they are fallen. We cannot face their malignant intractability and oppressiveness unless we remember that they are simultaneously a part of God's good creation. And reflection on their creation and fall will appear only to legitimate these Powers and blast hope for change unless we assert at the same time that these Powers can and must be redeemed.

Hobbes got it wrong when he argued that governments are necessary because people are evil and need to be defended from each other. For governments are also necessary because people are good and need to be organized to assist each other to meet each other's needs. Rousseau got it wrong when he argued that people are born good and that institutions make them evil. For institutions also socialize them to prevent them from doing harm to one another and to think of the common good. Marx got it wrong when he argued that people are basically good and are alienated by capitalist means of production. For communist means of production have alienated them every bit as much and failed to make good on the promise to produce new, nonalienated human beings.

Perhaps these comments shed light on the title of this volume. I could not name it "Confronting the Powers," or "Combating the Powers," or "Overcoming the Powers," because they are not simply evil. They can be not only benign but quite positive. (One of the friendliest, most helpful people in my community is a bureaucrat—the postmaster.) Thus the title, *Engaging the Powers*. It is precisely because the Powers have been created in, through, and for the humanizing purposes of God in Christ that they must be honored, criticized, resisted, and redeemed. Let us then engage these Powers, not just to understand them, but to see them changed.

Notes

1. Jean Claude von Hallie et al., *A Fable* (New York: Dramatists Play Service, 1976), 28–29.
2. I. P. Culianu, "The Angels of the Nations and the Origins of Gnostic Dualism," in *Studies in Gnosticism and Hellenistic Religions* (Festschrift for Gilles Quispel), ed. R. van den Broek and M. J. Vermaseren (Leiden: E. J. Brill, 1981), 78–91.
3. *Frank Peretti, This Present Darkness (Westchester, Ill.: Crossway Books, 1986). He has also published Piercing the Darkness with the same press, 1989.*

9

The Myth of the Domination System

In this first chapter of Engaging the Powers, *Walter Wink makes the surprising but demonstrable assertion that the religion of ancient Babylon, with its "myth of redemptive violence," is alive and well in every nook and cranny of American life. This myth provides the ground for the domination system(s) that have bedeviled the lives of the many while securing privilege, power and possessions for the few. Not surprisingly, most of us are unaware of it for the simple fact that, as Wink declares in his opening sentence, "Violence is the ethos of our times" (one might argue of all times) and thus just the way things unquestionably are. Wink points to the way culture inculcates children with the myth of redemptive violence through comics and cartoons, television and movies, video games and media broadcasts of real-time violence. With children so thoroughly socialized to accept violence, it is, Wink argues, not at all surprising that they come to accept violence as a reasonable way to maintain order, confront "evil" and resolve conflict. The consequences are that children come to see evil as without rather than within themselves, and into adulthood tend to "scapegoat others . . . for all that is wrong in the world." As disturbing as this is, more disturbing is the trend in contemporary "entertainment" to present violence as an end in itself, which leaves us with the myth of violence without redemption. Finally, Wink addresses the relationship between redemptive violence and both the "national security state" and the escalation of nationalistic goals, goals that largely serve the interests of the dominant class. With an entire culture socialized to accept violence as a legitimate if not moral response to perceived threats from "without," it is not at all difficult for the domination system to co-opt the "traditions, rites, customs, and symbols of Christianity" and subordinate them to the interests of dominant structures and systems—most often to the disadvantage of the non-privileged.*

Source: Wink 1992: Excerpted from Chapter 1

Violence is the ethos of our times. It is the spirituality of the modern world. It has been accorded the status of a religion, demanding from its devotees an absolute obedience to death. Its followers are not aware, however, that the devotion they pay to violence is a form of religious piety. Violence is so successful as a myth precisely because it does not seem to be mythic in the least. Violence simply appears to be the nature of things. It is what works. It is inevitable, the last and, often, the first resort in conflicts. It is embraced with equal alacrity by people on the left and on the right, by religious liberals as well as religious conservatives. The threat of violence, it is believed, is alone able to deter aggressors. It secured us forty-five years of a balance of terror. We learned to trust the Bomb to grant us peace.

The roots of this devotion to violence are deep, and we will be well rewarded if we trace them to their source. When we do, we will discover that the religion of Babylon—one of the world's oldest, continuously surviving religions—is thriving as never before in every sector of contemporary American life, even in our synagogues and churches. It, and not Christianity, is the real religion of America. I will suggest that this myth of redemptive violence undergirds American popular culture, civil religion, nationalism, and foreign policy, and that it lies coiled like an ancient serpent at the root of the system of domination that has characterized human existence since well before Babylon ruled supreme. In order to get our bearings, however, we have to go back to the mythic source.

The Myth of Redemptive Violence

Jesus taught the love of enemies, but Babylonian religion taught their extermination. Violence was for the religion of ancient Mesopotamia what love was for Jesus: the central dynamic of existence. For this early civilization, life was as cruel as the floods and droughts and storms that swept the Fertile Crescent. Recurrent warfare between the various city-states in the region exhausted resources. Chaos threatened every achievement of humanity. The myth that enshrined that culture's sense of life was the *Enuma Elish,* dated to around 1250 b.c.e. in the versions that have survived, but based on traditions considerably older.

In the beginning, according to this myth, Apsu and Tiamat (the sweet- and saltwater oceans) bear Mummu (the mist). From them also issue the younger gods, whose frolicking makes so much noise that the elder gods cannot sleep and so resolve to kill them. This plot of the elder gods is discovered, Ea kills Apsu, and his wife Tiamat pledges revenge. Ea and the younger gods in terror turn for salvation to their youngest, Marduk. He exacts a steep price: if he succeeds, he must be given chief and undisputed power in the assembly of the gods. Having extorted this promise, he catches Tiamat in a net, drives an evil wind down her throat, shoots an arrow that bursts her distended belly and pierces her heart; he then splits her skull with a club, and scatters her blood in out-ofthe-way places. He stretches out her corpse full length, and from it creates the cosmos.[1]

We are indebted to Paul Ricoeur for his profound commentary on this myth.[2] He points out that in the Babylonian myth, creation is an act of violence: Tiamat, "mother of them all," is murdered and dismembered; from her cadaver the world is formed. Order is established by means of disorder. Creation is a violent victory over an enemy older than creation. The origin of evil precedes the origin of things. Chaos (symbolized by Tiamat) is prior to order (represented by Marduk, god of Babylon). Evil is prior to good. Violence inheres in the godhead. Evil is an ineradicable constituent of ultimate reality, and possesses ontological priority over good.

The biblical myth is diametrically opposed to all this. There, a good God creates a good creation. Chaos does not resist order. Good is ontologically prior to evil. Neither evil nor violence is a part of the creation, but both enter as a result of the first couple's sin and the machinations of the serpent. A basically good reality is thus corrupted by free decisions reached by creatures. In this far more complex and subtle explanation of the origins of things, evil for the first time emerges as a problem requiring solution.

In the Babylonian myth, however, there is no "problem of evil." Evil is simply a primordial fact. The simplicity of its picture of reality commended it widely, and its basic mythic structure spread as far as Syria, Phoenicia, Egypt, Greece, Rome, Germany, Ireland, and India. Typically, a male war god residing in the sky—Wotan, Zeus, or Indra, for example—fights a decisive battle with a female divine being, usually depicted as a monster or dragon, residing in the sea or abyss.[3] Having vanquished the original Enemy by war and murder, the victor fashions a cosmos from the monster's corpse. Cosmic order equals the violent suppression of the feminine, and is mirrored in the social order by the subjection of women to men. Male supremacy and contempt for the womanly is explicit in the *Enuma Elish:* "What male is this who has pressed his fight against thee? It is but Tiamat, a woman that flies at thee with weapons!"[4]

At the same time, Marduk's accession to supremacy over the gods means the ascendancy of Babylon over earlier city-states like Nippur and Eridu. Heavenly events are mirrored by earthly events, and what happens above happens below.

After the world has been created, the story continues, the gods imprisoned by Marduk for siding with Tiamat complain of the poor meal service in their jail. Marduk and Ea therefore execute one of the captive gods, and from his blood, Ea creates human beings to be servants to the gods.

The implications are clear: humanity is created from the blood of a murdered god. Our very origin is violence. Killing is in our blood. Humanity is not the originator of evil, but merely finds evil already present and perpetuates it. Our origins are divine, to be sure, since we are made from a god, but from the blood of an assassinated god.[5] We are the consequence of deicide. Human beings are thus naturally incapable of peaceful coexistence; order must continually be imposed upon us from on high. Nor are we created to subdue the earth and have dominion over it as God's regents; we exist but to serve as slaves of the gods and of their earthly regents. The tasks of humanity are to till the soil, to produce foods for sacrifice to the gods (represented by the king and the priestly caste), to build the sacred city Babylon, and to fight and, if necessary, to die in the king's wars. Such a myth reflects a highly centralized state in which the king rules as Marduk's representative on earth. Resistance to the king is treason against the gods. Unquestioning obedience is the highest virtue, and order the highest religious value. "The king's word is right; his utterance, like that of a god, cannot be changed!"[6]

In their ritual the Babylonians reenacted the original battle by which world order was won and chaos subdued. This victory was celebrated liturgically in the New Year's Festival, when the king ceremonially played the part of Marduk, reasserting that victory and staving off for another year the dreaded reversion of all things into formlessness and disorder.

This ritual is not only cultic, therefore, but military. As Marduk's representative on earth, the king's task is to subdue all those enemies who threaten the tranquility that he has established on behalf of the god. The whole cosmos is a state, and the god rules through the king. Politics arises within the divine sphere itself. Salvation *is* politics: identifying with the god of order against the god of chaos, and offering oneself up for the holy war required to impose order and rule on the peoples round about. And because chaos threatens repeatedly, in the form of barbarian attacks, an ever-expanding imperial policy is the automatic correlate of Marduk's ascendancy over all the gods.

Do you begin to sense where all this is leading? An added dimension of depth was given the myth when Marduk (represented by the king) was pictured as undergoing ritual humiliation at the New Year's Festival. The priest strikes the king's face and pulls his ears. This action may have been associated with death and lamentation as the god descends into the underworld. The people, thrown into confusion, weep for him as for a suffering and dying god. Creation reverts to chaos (winter). With the aid of the ritual the god is revived, liberated, and released (spring). His enthronement is reenacted and the people celebrate the victory over chaos in a magnificent feast. Finally, a sacred marriage revives all the life-giving forces in nature and humanity.[7] This motif of the "suffering of the hero" is central to our own contemporary depictions of the myth, as we shall see.

The ultimate outcome of this type of myth, remarks Ricoeur, is a theology of war founded on the identification of the enemy with the powers that the god has vanquished and continues to vanquish in the drama of creation. Every coherent theology of holy war ultimately reverts to this basic mythological type.[8]

The relation of King versus Enemy becomes the political relation par excellence. According to this theology, the Enemy is evil and war is her punishment. Unlike the biblical myth, which sees evil as an intrusion into a good creation and war as a consequence of the Fall, this myth regards war as present from the beginning.

This ancient mythic structure has been variously called the Babylonian creation story, the combat myth, the ideology of zealous nationalism, and the myth of redemptive violence. The distinctive feature of the myth is the victory of order over chaos by means of violence. This myth is the original religion of the status quo, the first articulation of "might makes right." It is the basic ideology of the Domination System. The gods favor those who conquer. Conversely, whoever conquers must have the favor of the gods. The mass of people exists to perpetuate that power and privilege which the gods have conferred upon the king, the aristocracy, and the priesthood. Religion exists to legitimate power and privilege. Life is combat. Any form of order is preferable to chaos, according to this myth. Ours is neither a perfect nor a perfectible world; it is a theater of perpetual conflict in which the prize goes to the strong. Peace through war, security through strength: these are the core convictions that arise from this ancient historical religion.

This myth also inadvertently reveals the price men have paid for the power they acquired over women: complete servitude to their earthly rulers and heavenly gods. Women for their part were identified with inertia, chaos, and anarchy. Now "Woman is to man as nature is to culture"—the ideology that rationalizes the subordination of women in patriarchal societies by presenting their subordination as if it were a natural fate.[9]

This primordial myth is far from defunct. It is as universally present and earnestly believed today as at any time in its long and bloody history. I will now suggest that it is the dominant myth in contemporary America (more influential by far than Judaism or Christianity), that it enshrines a cult of violence at the very heart of public life, and that even those who seek to oppose its oppressive violence often do so using the very same means.

The Myth of Redemptive Violence in Popular Culture Today

The myth of redemptive violence inundates us on every side. We are awash in it yet seldom perceive it. We will look presently at its impact on foreign policy, nationalism, the Cold War, militarism, the media, and televangelism, but first we must identify its simplest, most pervasive, and most influential form, where it captures the imaginations of each new generation: children's comics and cartoon shows.

Here is how the myth of redemptive violence structures the standard comic strip or television cartoon sequence. An indestructible good guy is unalterably opposed to an irreformable and equally indestructible bad guy. Nothing can kill the good guy, though for the first three-quarters of the strip or show he (rarely she) suffers grievously, appearing hopelessly trapped, until somehow the hero breaks free, vanquishes the villain, and restores order until the next installment. Nothing finally destroys the bad guy or prevents his reappearance, whether he is soundly trounced, jailed, drowned, or shot into outer space.

I am not referring to programs that do not feature violence, but to what I would call the "classic" type of cartoon, where the mythic pattern of redemptive violence is straightforward. Examples would include Teenage Mutant Ninja Turtles, Superman, Superwoman, Mighty Mouse, Captain Marvel, Captain America, Green Hornet, Lone Ranger, Superfriends, Courageous Cat, Submariner, Batman and Robin, Roadrunner and Wile E. Coyote, Darkwing Duck, and Tom and Jerry. A variation on the classic theme is provided by humorous antiheroes, whose bumbling incompetence guarantees their victory despite themselves (Underdog, Super Chicken, the Banana Splits, Super Six, GoGo Gophers, Wackey Racers). Then there is a more recent twist, where an evil or failed individual undergoes a transformation into a monstrous creature who—amazingly—does good (Spider Man, The Hulk, Iron Man, the Herculoids). It is almost as if people believe that heroes of sterling character can no longer arise in our society, and that goodness can be produced only by a freak of technology (such as electrocution or chemicals). All these cartoons, however, adhere rigidly to the mythic structure, no matter how cleverly or originally it is represented.

Few cartoon shows have run longer or been more influential than Popeye and Bluto. In a typical segment, Bluto abducts a screaming and kicking Olive

Oyl, Popeye's girlfriend. When Popeye attempts to rescue her, the massive Bluto beats his diminutive opponent to a pulp, while Olive Oyl helplessly wrings her hands. At the last moment, as our hero oozes to the floor, and Bluto is trying, in effect, to rape Olive Oyl, a can of spinach pops from Popeye's pocket and spills into his mouth. Transformed by this gracious infusion of power, he easily demolishes the villain and rescues his beloved. The format never varies. Neither party ever gains any insight or learns from these encounters. Violence does not teach Bluto to honor Olive Oyl's humanity, and repeated pummelings do not teach Popeye to swallow his spinach *before* the fight.

Only the names have changed. Marduk subdues Tiamat through violence, and though he defeats Tiamat, chaos incessantly reasserts itself, and is kept at bay only by repeated battles and by the repetition of the New Year's Festival, where the heavenly combat myth is ritually reenacted. The structure of the combat myth is thus faithfully repeated on television week after week: a superior force representing chaos attacks aggressively; the champion fights back, defensively, only to be humiliated in apparent defeat; the evil power satisfies its lusts while the hero is incapacitated; the hero escapes, defeats the evil power decisively, and reaffirms order over chaos. Willis Elliott's observation underscores the seriousness of this entertainment: "Cosmogony [the birth of the cosmos] is egogony [the birth of the individual person]: you are being birthed through how you see 'all things' as being birthed." Therefore, "*Whoever controls the cosmogony controls the children.*"[10]

The psychodynamics of the television cartoon or comic book are marvelously simple: children identify with the good guy so that they can think of themselves as good. This enables them to project onto the bad guy their own repressed anger, violence, rebelliousness, or lust, and then vicariously to enjoy their own evil by watching the bad guy initially prevail. (This segment of the show actually consumes all but the closing minutes, and thus allows ample time for indulging the dark side of the self.) When the good guy finally wins, viewers are then able to reassert control over their own inner tendencies, repress them, and reestablish a sense of goodness. Salvation is guaranteed through identification with the hero.

This structure cannot be altered. Bluto does not simply lose more often—he must *always* lose. Otherwise this entire view of reality would collapse. The good guys must always win. In order to suppress the fear of erupting chaos the same mythic pattern must be endlessly repeated in a myriad of variations that *never in any way alter the basic structure.*

Cartoon strips like Superman and Dick Tracy have been enormously successful in resolving the guilt feelings of the reader or viewer by providing totally evil, often deformed and inhuman scapegoats on whom one can externalize the evil side of one's own personality and disown it without coming to any insight or awareness of its presence within oneself. The villain's punishment provides catharsis; one forswears the villain's ways and heaps condemnation on him in a guilt-free orgy of aggression.[11] No premium is put on reasoning, persuasion, negotiation, or diplomacy. There can be no compromise with an absolute evil. Evil must be totally annihilated or totally converted. As Dick Tracy said on the day following Robert Kennedy's assassination (quite by coincidence; the strip had already been drawn earlier), "Violence is golden when it's used to put evil down."

Cartoon and comic heroes cast no shadows. They are immortals; they cannot be killed. They are not beset by the ordinary temptations, never take advantage of damsels in distress, accept no bribes, usually receive no remuneration, and generally live above the realm of sin. Repentance and confession are as alien to them as the love of enemies and nonviolence. As Ariel Dorfman puts it, "The Lone Ranger himself contains not a single internal contradiction."[12]

Superman, for his part, intervenes in the lives of the people he encounters without ever challenging them to evaluate their beliefs and values or expose themselves to the anguish of transformation. He merely manipulates the environment. Villains are relegated to outer darkness but not redeemed from their bondage to evil or restored to true humanity.[13]

Batman, who lacks the godlike qualities of Superman, compensates with commitment. To avenge the murder of his parents he swears to spend "the rest of my life warring on all criminals." He will, in short, be a vigilante. He communicates well with the police commissioner, to be sure, but "the Caped Crusader" is answerable to no one in his role as a self-appointed crime-stopper.

His is a sacred vow, binding him to holy war on all the vermin of evil. His motives are not generous at all. He wants revenge.[14] In this respect Batman parallels the classic gunfighters of the "western," who settle old scores by shoot-outs, never by due process of law. The law, in fact, is suspect, too weak to prevail in the conditions of near-anarchy that fiction has misrepresented as the Wild West. The gunfighter must take matters into his own hands, just as, in the anarchic situation of the big city, a beleaguered citizen finally rises up against the crooks and muggers and creates justice out of the barrel of a gun (the movie *Dirty Harry* and, in real life, Bernard Goetz).

As Robert Jewett points out, this vigilantism betrays a profound distrust of democratic institutions, and of the reliance on human intelligence and civic responsibility that are basic to the democratic hope. It regards the general public as passive and unwise, incapable of discerning evil and making a rational response (as in the film *High Noon*). Public resources are inadequate, so the message goes; we need a messiah, an armed redeemer, someone who has the strength of character and conviction to transcend the legal restraints of democratic institutions and save us from an evil easily identifiable in villainous persons.

These vigilantes who deliver us by taking the law into their own hands will somehow do so without encouraging lawlessness. They will kill and leave town, thus ridding us of guilt. They will show selfless and surpassing concern for the health of our communities, but they will never have to practice citizenship, or deal with the ambiguity of political decisions. They neither run for office nor vote. They will reignite in us a consuming love for impartial justice, but they will do so by means of a mission of personal vengeance that eliminates due process of law.

The possibility that an innocent person is being executed by our violent redeemers is removed by having the outlaw draw first, or shoot from ambush. The villain dresses in dark clothing, is swarthy, unshaven, and filthy, and his personality is stereotyped so as to eliminate any possibility of audience sympathy. The death of such evil beings is necessary in order to cleanse society of a stain. The viewer, far from feeling remorse at another human being's death, is actually made euphoric.[15] Such villains cannot be handled by democratic means; they are far too powerful, for they are archetypally endowed with the transcendent qualities of Tiamat. So great a threat requires a Marduk, an avenger, a man on a white horse.

Rather than shoring up democracy, the strongman methods of the superheroes of popular culture reflect nostalgia for simpler solutions. They bypass constitutional guarantees of legal procedure in arrest, or the tenet that a person is to be regarded as innocent until proven guilty. What we see instead is a mounting impatience with the laborious processes of civilized life and a restless eagerness to embrace violent solutions. Better to mete out instant, summary justice than risk the red tape and delays and bumbling of the courts.[16] The yearning for a messianic redeemer who will set things right is thus, in its essence, a totalitarian fantasy.

The myth literally replays itself, without any awareness on the part of those who repeat it, under the guise of completely secular stories. Take the movie *Jaws*, for example. Recall that in the Babylonian myth, Marduk spread a net over

Tiamat, and when she opened her jaws to devour him, "he drove in the evil wind so she could not close her lips. . . . He let fly an arrow, it pierced her belly." With her destruction, order is restored. The community is saved by an act of redemptive violence.

In the movie *Jaws*, Police Chief Brody encounters a shark larger by one-third than any known shark, of which a preview says, "It is as if nature had concentrated all its forces of evil in a single being." Brody kicks an oxygen tank into the attacking shark's throat, then fires a bullet that explodes the tank, thus forcing into the shark's body a wind that bursts it open. Brody is transformed into a superhero, chaos is subdued, and the island is restored to a tourist's paradise.[17]

Or take the spy thriller. In the service of one's country, the spy is permitted to murder, seduce, lie, steal, commit illegal entry, tap phones without a court order, and otherwise do anything necessary to protect the values of Christian civilization (the James Bond movies, "Mission: Impossible," etc.). This genre was literally enacted under the Reagan administration by Lt. Col. Oliver North and his colleagues in the Iran-Contra scandals. These men lied to Congress and the American people, possibly withheld vital information and decisions from their own president, appropriated funds for their own private use, and condoned drug running to finance their adventures—all in the name of a rabid patriotism that scorned democratic restraints or public accountability.

The basic attitude is summed up in an episode of that ultimate spoof on the spy thriller, "Get Smart." As I recall the scene decades after viewing it, the show ends with the villain being tricked by a loaded cigarette and blown off a cliff to his death on the rocks below. Agent 99 watches in horror, then comments, "You know, Max, sometimes I think we're no better than they are, the way we murder and kill and destroy people." To which Smart retorts, "Why, 99, you know we have to murder and kill and destroy in order to preserve everything that's good in the world."

And who are 99 and Smart fighting, week after week? An international conspiracy of evil intent called KAOS. And for whom do they work? CONTROL. The archetype is able to reproduce itself, not only in the public media, but in actual history. In the mid-1970s, Congressman Les Aspin uncovered a secret CIA operation intended to disrupt domestic dissident groups in the 1960s. Though its work was expressly forbidden by law, this surveillance operation infiltrated fully legal antiwar groups and organizations that were attempting to rectify injustices, and sought to undermine them, often by trying to provoke violence. The name of the program: OPERATION CHAOS.[18] History itself becomes mythic.

How is it possible that this ancient archetypal structure still possesses such power in a modern, secular, scientific culture? Thanks to the American penchant for letting viewer interest determine programming, the story lines of cartoons, television shows, comics, and movies tend to gravitate to the lowest common denominator of mythic simplicity. The head of programming at a major network was asked to describe the thinking process that led to the network's selection of programs. He answered: There was no thinking process whatsoever. Television and film producers provide whatever fare the ratings and box offices tell them will generate the most immediate profit.[19] With important exceptions (Mr. Rogers, Captain Kangaroo, Sesame Street, and a few of the more benign cartoons . . .), the entertainment industry does not create materials that will be good for children to watch—material that will inculcate high values, ethical standards, honesty, truthfulness, mutual care and consideration, responsibility, and nobility of character. Instead, what children themselves prefer determines what is produced. The myth of redemptive violence is the simplest, laziest, most exciting, uncomplicated, irrational, and primitive depiction of evil the world has ever known. Furthermore, its orientation toward evil is one into which virtually all modern children (boys especially) are socialized in the process of maturation. The myth that lay like a threshold across the path of burgeoning empires also lies across the path of each individual bred in such societies. Children select this mythic structure because they have already been led, by culturally reinforced cues and role models, to resonate with its simplistic view of reality. Its ubiquity is not the result of a conspiracy of Babylonian priests secretly buying up the mass media with Iraqi oil money, but a function of inculcated values endlessly reinforced by the Domination System.

Once children have been indoctrinated into the expectations of a dominator society, they may never outgrow the need to locate all evil outside themselves. Even as adults they tend to scapegoat others (the Commies, the Americans, the gays, the straights, the blacks, the whites) for all that is wrong in the world.

They continue to depend on group identification and the upholding of social norms for a sense of well-being. There is a cultic dimension to our television violence, involving the public in a reaffirmation of group values through the ritualization of collective ideas.[20] It is tragic that the mass media, which could be so effectively used (and occasionally are) to help people mature beyond the infantilisms of scapegoating behavior, have been made the chief exponent of the myth of redemptive violence.

In a period when Christian Sunday schools are dwindling, the myth of redemptive violence has won children's voluntary acquiescence to a regimen of religious indoctrination more exhaustive and effective than any in the history of religions. Estimates vary widely, but the average child is reported to log roughly thirty-six thousand hours of television by age eighteen, including some fifteen thousand murders.[21] In prime-time evening shows, our children are served up about sixteen entertaining acts of violence (two of them lethal) every night; on the weekend the number of violent acts almost doubles (thirty). By age sixteen, the average child spends as much time watching television as in school.[22]

What church or synagogue can even remotely match the myth of redemptive violence in hours spent with children or quality of presentation? (Think of the typical "children's sermon"—how bland by comparison!)

No other religious system has ever remotely rivaled the myth of redemptive violence in its ability to catechize its young so totally. From the earliest age children are awash in depictions of violence as the ultimate solution in human conflicts. Nor does saturation in the myth end with the close of adolescence. There is no rite of passage from adolescent to adult status in the national cult of violence, but rather a years-long acclimatization to adult television and movie fare. Not all shows for children or adults are based on violence, of course. Reality is far more complex than the simplicities of this myth, and maturer minds will demand more subtle, nuanced, complex presentations. But the basic structure of the combat myth underlies the pap to which a great many adults turn in order to escape the harsher realities of their everyday lives: spy thrillers, westerns, cop shows, and combat programs. It is as if we must watch so much "redemptive" violence to reassure ourselves, against the deluge of facts to the contrary in our day-to-day lives, that reality really is that simple.

With the right kinds of support, children might outgrow the simplicities of the myth of redemptive violence. Our modern tragedy is that just when boys ought to be transcending it, they are hit by an even more sophisticated barrage of unmitigated violence—violence so explicit and sexually sadistic that it cannot even be shown on television. I refer to a new wave of ever more brutal comic books, video games, and home videos. Recently I spent an hour browsing through a mall comic shop, examining such fare as The Uncanny X-Men, Swamp Thing, War of the Worlds, The Warlock Five, The Avengers, The Spectre, Shattered Earth, Scout: War Shaman, The Punisher, Gun Fury, The Huntress, Dr. Fate, The Blood Sword, and so on: an entire store devoted to the promulgation of a paranoid view of reality, where the initiation of violence is the only protection against those plotting our doom. And boys are almost the exclusive readership. "Over the last decade, comics have forsaken campy repartee and outlandishly byzantine plots for a steady diet of remorseless violence."[23]

Likewise, the "video nasties," such as *The Texas Chain Saw Massacre, The Evil Dead,* or *Zombie Flesh-Eaters,* have reached new levels of inventiveness in brutality. "Adult only" home videos such as these have been viewed by one quarter of British children aged seven to eight; by age ten, half have seen them, if not at home, then at a friend's. Many have their first introduction to explicit sex in these films, in the form of rape, followed by decapitation, dismemberment, and cannibalism. With alarming frequency, crimes are being committed that are modeled after video violence.[24]

If such shows only provided a needed catharsis of violence, they might be defensible. But virtually all of the seven hundred studies done by 1984, along with those since, conclude that video violence increases substantially the degree to which adolescent boys engage in serious violence themselves.[25] In the past, villains tended to be depicted as undesirable models; the less human the model, the weaker the tendency to copy the model's behavior. Marduk is humanoid; Tiamat is a monster with seven heads. Marduk therefore attracts the greater identification. But realistic human figures portrayed as wholly evil on videos invite the very identification that earlier myths and fairy tales tried to deflect.

To the degree that programs present violence in the context of close personal relationships, show violence being done by "good" guys in the maintenance of law and order, or feature gratuitous violence, they appear to incite actual violent behavior. Violence is largely learned behavior. Unlike imaginative tales, these brutalities are not enacted in the manner of playful pretense in some remote fantasyland. They are carried out in familiar environments: in homes, bedrooms, railway trains, and back streets.[26] There is a quantum leap from a child's singing, "They all ran after the farmer's wife, she cut off their tails with a carving knife," seated securely on mother's lap, to a child's watching an adult woman be decapitated in utter realism, from the killer's angle of vision, in the solitude of one's home while one's parents are away at work.

Perhaps most disturbing, many of these video films do not portray the age-old confrontation of good versus evil, with the "bad guys" eventually being overcome by the good. What we find is far more crude: simply the assault of pure evil. It is the Babylonian religion without Marduk, myth without redemption. Redemptive violence gives way to violence as an end in itself—not a religion that uses violence in the pursuit of order and salvation, but a religion in which violence has become the ultimate concern, an elixir, sheer titillation, an addictive high, a substitute for relationships. Violence is no longer the means to a higher good, namely order; violence itself becomes the goal.

Teachers report increased violence in children: rejection of fair play, greater cruelty, far more frequent and previously unthinkable verbal and physical attacks on teachers, fistfights between two boys replaced by a whole circle of children kicking one child on the ground, games that imitate video violence with the stronger playing the heroes and the weaker forced to play the villains.[27] "*We are beginning to create a generation of children with a different set of values from previous ones,*" the authors of *Video Violence and Children* conclude.[28]

Perhaps we are just witnessing one of many oscillations in the intensity of violence throughout history. Violence in earlier times was chronic and highly public. Whole cities came out to be entertained by executions. Perhaps for some people violence has always been an end in itself. It would be naive to expect a gradual reduction in violence even if more egalitarian values were to take hold. Such values will instead incite a ruthless reaction. The Gospels anticipate an escalation of violence, not its decline, as the Epoch of Domination enters its final countdown to supersession.

But there is an even more significant aspect of the myth of redemptive violence that we have not developed: its contribution to the maintenance of international conflict.

Redemptive Violence and the National Security State

In every age, the myth of redemptive violence reappears in one form or another as a religion dedicated to the support of the powerful and privileged through violence. In the original Babylonian story, the price Marduk exacts for killing Tiamat is rulership over the pantheon of the gods. In that myth the council of the gods, and their mode of governing the universe, exactly reproduces the structure of Hammurabi's kingdom.

An older way of evaluating this correspondence between heavenly and earthly powers was to regard the gods as merely cosmic personifications that disguise the power arrangements of the state. The myth was thus seen as a mystification of actual power relations that provided divine legitimacy for oppressive earthly institutions.

In the first volume of this series I suggested that this reductionistic reading misses the mark.[29] The gods are not a fictive masking of the power of the human *state—they are its actual spirituality.* The *Enuma Elish* depicts the ascendancy of Marduk, the youngest god, to supreme authority over the other gods in the heavenly council, simultaneous with the ascendancy of the king of

Babylon over the surrounding region. That myth, far from mystifying power relations, shows by the precise correspondence between heavenly and earthly events that it has faithfully and accurately brought to expression the actual power relations at work. As above, so below: Babylon is explicitly said to be "a likeness on earth of what he [Marduk] has wrought in heaven" (*Enuma Elish* VI.113; so also VI.104: "Let his command be supreme above and below"). This masks nothing. The myth plainly shows, for everyone to see, that Babylon has acquired hegemony over the other city-states in Mesopotamia. It states clearly that the king acts on behalf of Marduk to suppress chaos and impose order. The state is a mirror of cosmic order; therefore, resistance or rebellion is a crime against heaven.

We saw earlier that in the myth of redemptive violence, the survival and welfare of the nation are elevated as the highest earthly and heavenly good. There can be no other gods before the nation. This myth not only establishes a patriotic religion at the heart of the state, but also gives that nation's imperialistic imperative divine sanction. As Georges Khodr notes, all war is metaphysical; one can only go to war religiously.[30] The myth of redemptive violence is thus the spirituality of militarism. By divine right the state has the power to order its citizens to sacrifice their lives to maintain the privileges enjoyed by the few. By divine decree it utilizes violence to cleanse the world of evil opponents who resist the nation's sway. Wealth and prosperity are the right of those who rule in such a state. And the name of God—any god, the Christian God included—can be invoked as having specially blessed and favored the supremacy of the chosen nation and its ruling caste.[31]

The unique contemporary form of Western redemptive violence (the Soviet Union had already shaped its own version under Lenin and Stalin) was sired by the Cold War. In 1947, the United States created new political institutions that would drastically alter the character and even the future prospects of democracy: the National Security Council and the Central Intelligence Agency. To propagate national security doctrine, the National War College was established in Washington in 1948. Through its doors have passed thousands of military and police officers from Latin America and other "Third World" nations. These institutions were but the outer form of a new Power being spawned: the national security system. Every Power, as we have seen in *Naming the Powers*, has an inner spirituality as well as outer institutional forms. The spirituality of the national security system is the ideology of the national security state.

José Comblin has trenchantly analyzed this relatively new development within the history of nationalism in *The Church and the National Security State*.[32]

According to this doctrine, "the survival of the nation is the absolute goal. National strategy intends to incorporate the whole nation into the national survival plan, to make it the total and unconditional object of each citizen's life." On this view, all times are times of war. Peace is nothing more than the conventional name given to the continuation of war by other means. All politics is a politics of war. In Chile or South Africa or El Salvador, what this means in actual practice is that the army and its weapons are not used against outer geopolitical threats so much as against *their own people*.

The national security ideology is thus nationalism raised to ultimacy. Origen long ago warned Christians that the greatest temptation was participation in the national cults, which were nothing less than idolatrous worship paid to the angels of the nations as if they were God.[33] Though our contemporary idolaters never tire of speaking about the democracy and Christianity that they are defending with dictatorship and war (and the war never ends), the real faith of these National Securocrats is redemptive violence. As Brazilian General Golbery do Couto e Silva, one of the most influential geopolitical thinkers, put it,

> To be nationalist is to be always ready to give up any doctrine, any theory, any ideology, feelings, passions, ideals, and values, as soon as they appear as incompatible with the supreme loyalty, which is due to the Nation above everything else. Nationalism is, must be, and cannot possibly be other than an Absolute One in itself, and its purpose is as well an Absolute End—at least as long as the Nation continues as such. There is no place, nor should there be, nor could there be place for nationalism as a simple instrument to another purpose that transcends it.[34]

Since such a nationalism cannot accept the existence of a higher power, it must destroy any forms of Christian faith that go beyond mere cultural inheritance. Nevertheless, national security ideologues saturate their language with religious platitudes. Their documents are drenched with phrases cribbed from the Bible and from papal encyclicals, and they may even be active attenders of church. But it is clear that what they mean by Christianity is merely the perpetuation of the privileges of a tiny capitalistic minority by whatever means necessary. It is new-old redemptive violence, the Domination System pure and simple.

Here is a cool and reflective rendition of the creed of regenerative violence from a contemporary spokesman from the American religious right:

> That it is a privilege to engage in God's wars is clearly seen in the Psalms, perhaps nowhere better than in Ps. 149:5-7, where the saints sing for joy on their beds while they contemplate warring against God's enemies, or Ps. 58:10, "The righteous will rejoice when he sees the vengeance; he will wash his feet in the blood of the wicked." Those who cannot say "Amen" to such sentiments have not yet learned to think God's thoughts after him.... We have no problem rejoicing in His judgments, or in seeing it a privilege to be called to execute them.... The righteous ... are called by God's law to exercise a holy "violence" against certain of the wicked, thereby manifesting God's wrath.[35]

Zealous nationalism of this stripe cannot simply be dismissed as aberrant, however; it is, indeed, "biblical." The Bible is full of bloodthirsty deeds of Yahweh, and those who wish to "think God's thoughts after him" can easily multiply references: the "ban" requiring the total destruction of every living being at Ai and Jericho; the atrocities committed by Jehu in the name of the prophet Elisha; Phinehas's zeal in murdering a couple whose sin was racial intermarriage; the picture of sinners being tortured in fire and brimstone for all eternity that Matthew has added to his sources; the lust for vengeance in the Book of Revelation—all these and many, many more examples attest to the success of the myth of redemptive violence in penetrating the Bible itself.

The Rev. Gerald Derstine, defending U.S. government aid to the Contras fighting in Nicaragua, commented, "God uses war to cleanse the earth from wickedness. When it's time for a war, God allows certain evils to be exterminated."[36] The same orientation recently led the Rev. R. L. Hymers to pray with his congregation for the death of Supreme Court justices who support legalized abortion, and for God to remove ailing justice Harry Blackmun "in any way that God sees fit."[37] Televangelists like Pat Robertson and Jerry Falwell are only a little less crude in their support for apartheid, their opposition to disarmament, and their advocacy of militarism. The national security church thus becomes the kept court chaplain of the national security state.

The myth of redemptive violence thus uses the traditions, rites, customs, and symbols of Christianity in order to enhance the power of a wealthy elite and the goals of the nation narrowly defined. It has no interest in compassion for the poor, or for more equitable economic arrangements, or for the love of enemies. It merely uses the shell of religion—a shell that can be filled with the blasphemous doctrine of the national security state. Emptied of their prophetic vitality, these outer forms are then manipulated to legitimate a power system intent on the preservation of privilege at all costs.[38]

Why then do large masses of the nonprivileged submit to such a myth? Why, for example, do blue-collar workers, who are among those most victimized by the ruling elite, continue not only to support their oppressors but also to be among their most vociferous fans? The answer is quite simple: the promise of salvation. The myth of redemptive violence offers salvation through identification with Marduk and his earthly regents.

The modern individual, stripped of the values, rites, and customs that give a sense of belonging to traditional cultures, is the easy victim of the fads of style, opinion, and prejudice fostered by the communications media. At once isolated and yet absorbed into the masses, people live under the illusion that the views and feelings they have acquired by attending to the media are their own.[39] Overwhelmed by the giantism of corporations, bureaucracies, universities, the military, and celebrities, individuals sense that the only escape from utter insignificance lies in identifying with these giants and idolizing them as the true bearers of their own human identity.

Salvation through identification: whether it be in cartoon shows or westerns or confrontation with a foreign power, one's personal well-being is tied inextricably with the fortunes of the hero-leader. Right and wrong scarcely enter the picture. Everything depends on victory, success, the thrill of belonging to a nation capable of imposing its will in the heavenly council and among the nations. For the alternative—ownership of one's own evil and acknowledgment of God in the enemy—is for many simply too high a price to pay.

This longing to identify with a winner was glaringly evident during the Persian Gulf War. The orgy of patriotism unleashed in the United States revealed how strongly people wanted to be able to think well of their nation again. Here at last was what seemed to many a truly "just" war, and its incomparably successful military prosecution led to a flood of self-congratulatory euphoria. But for many people patriotism was merely a mask for a shame that they wanted to bury: our defeat in Vietnam; our failure domestically to provide adequate jobs, housing, education, and safety; and, perhaps most important, our failure to live by our own professed ideals. All that ambivalence could be submerged under a tide of national pride. Salvation comes, not by insight, repentance, and truth, but by identification with American military might: the Marduk solution. And the tragedy is that violence proved so incredibly "successful" for the Allies. Why consider nonviolent sanctions when our smart bombs are wiser than our diplomats?

The structure of the ancient combat myth is not then just the basis of comics and cartoons; it is the framework of much that passes as foreign policy. Subdue Tiamat, the argument runs, and a new world order will prevail. It is so simple, so unarguable, so irresistible. Before such a prospect, who would think of negotiating a peace that requires all parties involved to concede their own culpability for the crisis and to surrender advantages they have gained unjustly?

When the Viet Cong overran Ben Tre, a city of 35,000, American bombers were ordered to level the entire city on the grounds that "it became necessary to destroy the town to save it." As absurdly contradictory as such statements may appear to us today, they fit precisely the structure of the mystique of violence.[40] As Richard Slotkin put it, the myth of regenerative violence is the structuring metaphor of the American experience.[41]

Is there no escape from this myth of redemptive violence? Yes, there is, but it is difficult. To face the fear of enemies would finally require us to acknowledge our own inner evil, and that would cost us all our hard-earned self-esteem. *We* would have to change, laboriously, struggling daily to transform or redeem our shadow side. We would have to see ourselves as no different in kind from our enemy (however different we may be in degree). It would mean seeing God in the enemy as we learn to see God in ourselves—a God who loves and forgives and can transform even the most evil person or society in the world. Such insight would require conversion from the myth of redemptive violence to the God proclaimed by the prophets and by Jesus. We would have to abandon our preferential option for violence and replace it with a preferential option for the oppressed. We could no longer rely on absolute weapons for the utter annihilation of an absolute enemy. We could no longer justify unchristian means to preserve at all costs the hollow shell of a "Christian civilization" that has, in effect, been filled with the creed of redemptive violence.

The myth of redemptive violence is nationalism become absolute. This myth speaks *for* God; it does not listen for God to speak. It invokes the sovereignty of God as its own; it does not entertain the prophetic possibility of radical denunciation and negation by God. It misappropriates the language, symbols and scriptures of Christianity. It does not seek God in order to change; it claims God in order to prevent change. Its God is not the impartial ruler of all nations but a biased and partial tribal god worshiped as an idol. Its metaphor is not the journey but a fortress. Its symbol is not the cross but a rod of iron. Its offer is not forgiveness but victory. Its good news is not the unconditional love of enemies but their final liquidation. Its salvation is not a new heart but a successful foreign policy. It usurps the revelation of God's purposes for humanity in Jesus. It is blasphemous. It is idolatrous.

And it is immensely popular.

I love my country passionately; that is why I want to see it do right. There is a valid place for a sensible patriotism. But from a Christian point of view, true patriotism acknowledges God's sovereignty over all the nations, and holds a healthy respect for God's judgments on the pretensions of any power that seeks to impose its will on others. There is a place for a sense of destiny as a nation. But it can be authentically embraced and pursued only if we separate ourselves from the legacy of the combat myth and "enter a long twilight struggle against what is dark within ourselves."[42] There is a divine vocation for the United States (and every other nation) to perform in human affairs. But it can perform that task, paradoxically, only by abandoning its messianic zeal and accepting a more limited role within the family of nations.

Notes

1. Text in James B. Pritchard, *Ancient Near Eastern Texts Relating to the Old Testament*, 3d ed. (Princeton: Princeton Univ. Press, 1969), 60–72.
2. Paul Ricoeur, *The Symbolism of Evil* (New York: Harper & Row, 1967), 175–210.
3. James A. Aho, *Religious Mythology and the Art of War* (Westport, Conn.: Greenwood Press, 1981), 60.
4. *Enuma Elish* II.110–11 (Pritchard, *Ancient Near Eastern Texts*, 64).
5. Ricoeur, *Symbolism of Evil*, 178, 180.
6. Text in *Revue d'assyriologie et d'archéologie orientale* 17 (1920): 132; the translation is by Jacobsen, *Before Philosophy*, 218.
7. See Ricoeur, *Symbolism of Evil*, 193.
8. Ricouer, *Symbolism of Evil*, 198.
9. Ruby Rohrlich, "State Formation in Sumer and the Subjection of Women," *Feminist Studies* 6/1 (Spring 1980): 76–102.
10. Willis Elliott, "Thinksheet," no. 2196, November 8, 1987.
11. Arthur Asa Berger, *The Comic-Stripped American* (Baltimore: Penguin Books, 1973), 128.
12. Ariel Dorfman, *The Empire's Old Clothes* (New York: Pantheon Books, 1983), 97.
13. John T. Gallaway, Jr., *The Gospel According to Superman* (Philadelphia: A. J. Holman, 1973), 93; Dick Davis, "Interventions," unpublished paper, p. 4.
14. Berger, *Comic-Stripped American*, 161.
15. Ibid.
16. Marshall McLuhan, *The Mechanical Bride*, cited by Berger, *Comic-Stripped American*, 158.
17. Robert Jewett and Sheldon Lawrence, *American Monomyth* (University Press of America, 1988), 157.
18. *New York Times*, August 7, 1975, 16.
19. Michael N. Nagler, *America Without Violence* (Covelo, Calif.: Island Press, 1982), 27.
20. Andrew J. McKenna, "The Law's Delay: Cinema and Sacrifice," *Legal Studies Forum* 15/3 (1991): 199–213.
21. *U.S. News and World Report*, October 27, 1986, 64.
22. William F. Fore, "Media Violence: Hazardous to Our Health," *Christian Century* 102 (Sept. 25, 1985): 836.

23. Joe Queenan, "Drawing on the Dark Side," *New York Times Magazine,* April 30, 1989, 32–34, 79, 86.

24. Geoffrey Barlow and Alison Hill, eds., *Video Violence and Children* (New York: St. Martins Press, 1985), 67.

25. Ibid.

26. Geoffrey Barlow and Alison Hill, *Video Violence and Children* (New York: Macmillan 1986), 89.

27. Ibid., 152–58.

28. Ibid., 152.

29. *Naming the Powers,* 131–37.

30. Georges Khodr, "Violence and the Gospel," *Cross Currents* 37 (Winter 1987–88): 405.

31. Jose Miguez Bonino, *Toward a Christian Political Ethic* (Philadelphia: Fortress Press, 1983), 86.

32. Jose Camblin, *The Church and the National Security State* (Maryknoll, N.Y.: Orbis Books, 1984), 64–98.

33. Jean Danielou, *Origen* (New York: Sheed & Ward, 1955), 234.

34. Cited by Camblin, *The Church and the National Security State,* 18.

35. James B. Jordan, "Pacifism and the Old Testament," in *The Theology of Christian Resistance,* ed. Gary North (Tyler, Tex.: Geneva Divinity School Press, 1983), 90, 92.

36. *Berkshire Eagle,* April 20, 1987, A4.

37. Ibid., July 27, 1987, A10.

38. José Comblin, *The Church and the National Security State* (Maryknoll, N.Y.: Orbis Books, 1984), 107.

39. See Jacques Ellul, *Propaganda: The Formation of Men's Attitudes* (New York: Vintage Books, 1973).

40. Robert Jewett, *Captain America Complex: The Dilemma of Zealous Nationalism* (Rochester, Vermont: 1984), 210–11.

41. Richard Slotkin, *Regeneration through Violence* (Middletown, Conn.: Wesleyan Univ. Press, 1973), 5.

42. Jewett, *Captain America Complex,* 253.

10

The Nature of the Domination System

At the beginning of this penultimate chapter of Part One of Engaging the Powers, *Walter Wink makes three significant assertions regarding the Powers: they are good; they are fallen; they can and will be redeemed. These assertions are corollary to the assertion that God created the Powers and thus they cannot be inherently evil and beyond redemption. The Powers function as the necessary structures and systems that make social life possible; when, however, they are raised through idolatry to the level of ultimacy, evil results. The notion that all created beings, including the Powers, are created good, but have fallen, allows Wink to affirm that neither humankind nor the Powers—the social structures and systems that order life for good or for ill—are intrinsically evil. Therefore both persons and social structures and systems can be redeemed. This conviction, which Wink carefully grounds biblically, is at the heart of his insistence on aggressive nonviolent resistance to evil and "tough love" of enemies. It is counter to the gospel to seek the extermination of created beings capable of being redeemed. Evangelism, then, for Wink, is two-pronged in that it seeks both the conversion/transformation of individuals and the conversion/transformation of society. Jesus' proclamation of the kingdom or reign of God was a denunciation of the Domination System of his time and all times, while simultaneously pointing to their transformation from self-idolatry to the humanizing processes of God for which they were created.*

Source: Wink 1992: Excerpted from Chapter 4

> *The greatness of Christianity lies in its being hated by the Domination System (kosmos), not in its being convincing to it.*
> —Ignatius of Antioch, To the Romans 3:3

The good news is that God not only liberates us from the Powers, but liberates the Powers as well. The gospel is not a dualistic myth of good and evil forces vying for ascendancy, as in the myth of redemptive violence. It is a sublimely subtle drama about the intertwining of good and evil in all of historical reality. The Powers are not simply evil. They are a bulwark against anarchy, and a patron, repository, and inspirer of art. They inculcate values that encourage interdependency, mutual care, and social cohesiveness. They encourage submission of personal desires to the general good of everyone. Their evil is not intrinsic, but rather the result of idolatry. Therefore they can be redeemed. The New Testament presents this insight as a drama in three simultaneous acts:

> The powers are good
> The powers are fallen
> The powers will be redeemed

The Powers Are Good

In the hymn of the cosmic Christ in Col. 1:16-17, the Powers are described as having been created in, through, and for Christ. "For in him all things in heaven and on earth were created, things visible and invisible, whether thrones or dominions or rulers or powers—all things have been created through him and for him. He himself is before all things, and in him all things hold together."

The Colossians hymn is the brash assertion, against the grain of human suffering, that the Principalities and Powers that visit the world with so much evil are not autonomous, not independent, not eternal, not utterly depraved. The social structures of reality are creations of God. Because they are creatures, they are mortal, limited, responsible to God, and made to serve the humanizing purposes of God in the world.

In the verses that precede the hymn of Colossians these Powers are referred to collectively as "the dominion of darkness" from which believers have been delivered (Col. 1:13). Ernst Käsemann has argued that this hymn was sung at the liturgy of baptism, and that it marks a change of spheres of influence, from the sphere of darkness (Col. 1:12-14 being added to give the hymn a "liturgical introduction") to the sphere of light. Believers are delivered from the Domination System and freed from the enslaving power of the old aeon. "In baptism the Christian changes from one jurisdiction to another. Henceforth he belongs not to the cosmos, but to the Cosmocrator."[1]

Following the hymn, likewise, Paul reminds his readers that they were "once estranged and hostile in mind, doing evil deeds" (1:21). The context therefore makes clear, whereas the hymn itself does so only by allusion (v. 20), that these Powers are or have become hostile to the purposes of God in their creation.

Nevertheless, the hymn itself celebrates their creation in, through, and for Christ. They are not demonized as utterly evil; they are the good creations of a good God, and God, in the Genesis story of creation, creates no demons. But their rationale for existence is to serve the human needs and values revealed as ultimate by the identification of Jesus with Wisdom and Christ.

These Powers are the necessary social structures of human life, and it is not a matter of indifference to God that they exist. God *made* them. And all this is asserted—chanted, intoned, sung—into the teeth of the everyday experience of institutional and structural evil. Without institutionalization, ideas never materialize into action. Institutions are indispensable for human existence, and they have a right to be concerned about their own survival. But they must keep this concern penultimate, not ultimate. For this reason, von Rad reminds us, the account of creation in Genesis does not end in chapter 2, with the creation of the world, but in chapter 10, with the creation of the nations. The meaning is clear: humanity is not possible apart from its social institutions.[2] Subsystems, like people, continually need to weigh their needs against the needs of the system as a whole. "Order is not sufficient," wrote Whitehead. "What is required is something much more complex. It is order entering upon novelty; so that the massiveness of order does not degenerate into mere repetition; and so that the novelty is always reflected upon a background of system."[3]

Even in their apostasy and dereliction from their created vocation, the Powers are incapable of separating themselves from the principle of coherence. When subsystems idolatrously violate the harmony of the whole by elevating their own purposes to ultimacy, they are still no more able to achieve autonomy than a cancer can live apart from its host. Like a cancer, again, they are able to do evil only by means of processes imbedded in them as a result of their good creation.

We must be careful here. To assert that God created the Powers does not imply that God endorses any particular Power at any given time. God did not create capitalism or socialism, but there must be some kind of economic system. The simultaneity of creation, fall, and redemption means that God at one and the same time *upholds* a given political or economic system, since some such system is required to support human life; *condemns* that system insofar as it is destructive of full human actualization; and *presses for its transformation* into a more humane order. Conservatives stress the first, revolutionaries the second, reformers the third. The Christian is expected to hold together all three.

This is the point, and perhaps only this, of Rom. 13:1-7 ("Be subject to the governing authorities"). It does not legitimate blind obedience to an oppressive system. It says, rather, that governments are indispensable for the preservation of social order and protection against criminals and invaders. They are supposed to be a terror not to good conduct, but to bad (vv. 3-4). Oppressive regimes, however, are just the reverse: they reward bad conduct and are a terror to those who do good.

To say that the Powers are created in, through, and for the cosmic Christ, then, does not imply endorsement of any particular economic or political system. What the hymn sings is recognition that it is God's plan for us to live in interrelationship with each other, and to this end God has determined that there will be subsystems whose sole purpose is to serve the human needs of the One who exemplifies and encompasses humanity.

An institution may place its own good above the general welfare. A corporation may cut corners on costs by producing defective products that endanger lives. Union leadership may become more preoccupied with extending its personal advantages than fighting for better working conditions for the rank and file. The point of the Colossians hymn is not that anything goes, but that no matter how greedy or idolatrous an institution becomes, it cannot escape the encompassing care and judgment of the One in and through and for whom it was created. In that One "all things hold together" (Col.1:17)—lit., "receive their systemic place"—*synistēmi*, the source of our word "system"). The Powers are inextricably locked into God's system, whose human face is revealed in Christ. They are answerable to God. And that means that every subsystem in the world is, in principle, redeemable.

We may pollute our water supply and the air we breathe with no regard for the future; but we are systemically inseparable from the ecosystem, and the judgment of the system rebounds on us in escalating carcinogenic illnesses. A nation can behave as if it did not belong to the world-system of nations, as did Nazi Germany, and can attempt to subordinate the system to itself; but its very attempt to do so mobilizes the wrath of the nations against it and brings about its own collapse. No subsystem that aspires to the status of God's system itself can long remain viable. The myth of Satan's rebellion and expulsion from heaven symbolically depicts the fate of any creature that lusts after ultimate power and authority.

The bound-togetherness celebrated by this hymn thus serves as the foundation of the ethic of nonviolence and the love of enemies. Nothing is outside the redemptive care and transforming love of God. The Powers are not intrinsically evil; they are only fallen. What sinks can be made to rise again. We are freed, then, from the temptation to satanize the perpetrators of evil. We can love our nation or church or school, not blindly, but critically, recalling it to its own highest self-professed ideals and identities. We can challenge these institutions to live up to the vocation that is theirs by virtue of their sheer createdness. We can oppose their actions while honoring their necessity. For example, a factory is polluting the air and water of our city, and we want it cleaned up. We can engage in that struggle knowing that its employees need jobs, and that their families also are at risk from the pollution, just as ours are. We can talk without hatred to the hard-nosed representatives of the plant, because we know that they, and we, and this factory, are encompassed by the love of God, and exist to serve the One in and through and for whom we were all created. We do not have to struggle to bring this plant into the orbit of God's system. It is already there. We have only to remind its managers that it exists to serve values beyond itself (though this "reminding" may require a protracted boycott or strike).

Adam Smith himself acknowledged this when he wrote that the ultimate goal of a business is not to make a profit. Profit is just the means. The goal is the general welfare. It is part of the church's task to remind corporations and businesses that profit is *not* the "bottom line," that as "creatures" of God they have as their divine vocation the achievement of human benefaction (Eph. 3:10). They do not exist for themselves. They were bought with a price (Col. 1:20). They belong to the God who ordains sufficiency for all.

The Powers Are Fallen

Talk of the Fall is not popular in a period when certain New Age and Eastern gurus are proclaiming our divinity; when secularism, by virtue of denying the spiritual realm, is incapable of conceiving of radical evil; when in legitimate reaction to the morbid Christian overemphasis on sin and guilt, many are emphasizing the goodness of creation and the open-endedness of our potentials (an emphasis I endorse).

Nevertheless, the doctrine of the Fall is essential for understanding both ourselves and the Powers. And, curiously enough, it is part of the good news, a source of immense relief, and a sentinel against seduction. I submit (1) that the doctrine of the Fall provides an account of evil that acknowledges its brute reality while preserving the sovereignty and goodness of God and the creation; (2) that it is not just a temporal myth and thus did not simply happen "once upon a time," but is also a structural aspect of all personal and social existence; (3) that the doctrine of the Fall frees us from delusions about the perfectibility of ourselves and our institutions; and (4) that it reminds us that we cannot be saved from the Powers by anything within the Power System, but only by something that transcends it.

In the first place, the doctrine of the Fall affirms the radicality of evil. Frankly, most of us, myself included, simply do not *want* to believe in radical evil. The implications are too terrible. It violates the reasonable, middle-class paradigm to learn that children are kidnapped for prostitution rings, Satan cults, and pornographic "snuff" movies (where actual murders are filmed).[4] And like most people when their paradigm is challenged, we question the data rather than our presuppositions. (I am thinking of those who deny that the Holocaust ever happened.) Thus when a friend of ours went to his colleagues in the peace community for support in dealing with a victim of satanic abuse, they responded by regarding him as deranged. Evil of such magnitude could not exist—this from people opposing the most insane evil of all, nuclear weapons!

Evil is within us (in Jungian terms, the personal "shadow") and among us (as collective "shadow"), but much of that can be raised to consciousness and transformed. We are speaking now of a deeper evil—a layer of sludge beneath the murky waters that can be characterized only as a hellish hatred of the light, of truth, of kindness and compassion, a brute lust for annihilation. It is the sedimentation of thousands of years of human choices for evil (not *wrong* choices merely, but actual choices *for* evil) that has precipitated Satan as the spirituality of evil. Call it what you will, it is real. The doctrine of the Fall is merely a mute pointer to that sludge, lest we deny its reality and foolishly attempt to erect a society on this base.

Second, talk about a Fall is mythical language. It is true that the myth is presented sequentially, as if it can be segmented into three chronological phases: once the Powers were good, then they fell, and in the future (tomorrow, next year, at the end of time) they will be redeemed. But the biblical myth is both temporal and does manifest all three aspects simultaneously: it performs a necessary function and is created in, through, and for Christ; it is fallen; and it may experience moments when it becomes transparent to the purposes for which it was created. It is possible, right in the midst of the old reality, for both people and Powers to live in relative emancipation from the power of death.[5]

Past, present, and future are temporal realities, yet they are also gathered into the eternal now of today. The Creation, Fall, and Final Judgment are now, as the flat perspective of history opens out into the depth of eternity. The final subjugation of the Powers under Christ's feet will happen (1 Cor. 15:24-25), but it is already, in anticipation, experienced now (Eph. 1:19-23), in the new reality of resurrection existence. "Now is the judgment of the Domination System (*kosmos*), now shall the ruler of that System (*kosmos*) be cast out" (John 12:31*). The "heavenly" becomes efficacious now; we have already been raised up with Christ and made to sit "with him in the heavenly places" (Eph. 2:6). The final restoration of all things in harmonious unity is tasted now, fragmentarily, deliciously—and gone. The reign of God is not "built," but sampled. We have a foretaste, an appetizer, an aperitif, a down payment (Rom. 8:23; 2 Cor. 1:22; 5:5; Eph. 1:14). We "have tasted the goodness of the word of God and the powers of the age to come" (Heb. 6:5). There may be no measurable progress (yes, some things do get better over time, but others get worse). There are just these blinding (or feeble) flashes of the beyond in our midst; just these moments of lucidity, when a subsystem offers itself to the whole; just these acts of sacrificial love, costly reminders of the cross at the heart of reality.

It is precisely this simultaneity of Creation, Fall, and Redemption, freed from literalistic temporalizing, that delivers us from naïveté regarding our personal or social powers for transformation. It liberates us from the illusion that at least some institutions are "good" and viable and within human direction, or can be rendered so by discipline or reform or revolution or displacement.[6] The Powers are at one and the same time ordained by God and in the power of Satan. They can, to some degree, be humanized, but they are still fallen. They can be open to transcendence, but they will still do evil. They may be benign, but within a Domination System of general malignancy. As Reinhold Niebuhr once remarked, no society ever achieved peace without incorporating a degree of injustice in its harmony,[7] and that will prove to be as true in the immediate future as in all previous periods.

The powers are good, fallen, and redeemable all at once; and they were good, they fell, and they will be redeemed in God's domination-free order that is coming. This tension between the timeless and the temporal enables us to eye each successive sincerity, each new utopian solution or structural arrangement, with dispassionate realism. It can prevent our being swept away by new visions of transformation that as yet have no history of failures (as they surely will). It leads us to expect each new intervention for good to bring in its wake unintended consequences, some of them evil. We can join in struggles for social justice without being suckered by slogans promising what cannot be delivered and without crumbling under the inevitable setbacks and reverses. We can work for a society which will not make people good, but in which it will be easier for them to be good.

Third, the doctrine of the Fall frees us from delusions about the perfectibility of ourselves and our institutions, and from the diabolical belief that we are responsible for everything that happens. The very success of a reform effort helps to produce its decline, since the improved situation reduces the public outrage necessary to sustain opinion and activity on behalf of change. Social progress is thus self-limiting; every movement forward is usually followed by at least some movement back. Furthermore, we are usually able to understand only the system that is crumbling, not the one emerging. This means that our perception of reality generally arrives too late to save a society, but just in time to explain its demise.

Dreams of perfection are fatal to social change movements. As Michael Lerner points out, despite their vision of a better society, such movements are made up of idealists who are far from perfect. They are attempting to change a society that has already profoundly conditioned them to believe themselves unworthy of love, and the system to be incapable of change. Consequently, they tend to act in ways that engender despair, causing them to choose tactics that alienate the very people they need to affect. Driven by their ideals, they denigrate their own accomplishments as inadequate, as if they should have been able to do more. Or they change the goal just as they are close to realizing it so that they never get to celebrate victories along the way. They burn themselves trying to live in utopian fashion with all their old socialization intact. They believe they should be able to overcome their racist and sexist attitudes of will. Then, when they experience the persistence of these attitudes, they turn on each other with demands for movement purity. Rather than recognizing that we are all racist or sexist or undemocratic as a result of our social upbringing, and developing ways to assist people gently in the needed transformation, the movement declares that anyone with these attitudes is a traitor or a deviant. When they can no longer stand their own hypocrisy or that of others, many drop out to enter psychotherapy, meditate, or earn money. The Powers once again, acting from concealment, entice courageous and dedicated people to blame their own personal inadequacies for what are in fact systemically induced delusions. Here the traditional religions can come to our aid, Lerner insists, since they, almost alone in our society, are able to mount a consistent counter-cultural critique of domination.[8]

The non-perfectibility of the world does not make us passive. We still act by the best lights we have. It only makes us modest, so that we can be expectant toward God. And modesty is an enormous relief. It is the infallible sign that one has been awakened from dreams of perfection. The Powers can be redeemed, but not made flawless. And when we no longer have to believe that we must make everything happen ourselves, we are well-positioned to live in anticipation of miracles.

Finally, the doctrine of the Fall reminds us that we cannot be saved from the Powers by anything within the Power System, but only by something that transcends it. The notion of the Fall is good news. No doubt the doctrine of the Fall has been perverted to justify the worst kinds of oppression, on the grounds that our inherent sinfulness must be kept under check by government, and that any order is better than the risk of chaos that every attempt at change harbors. If the gospel is understood to teach that people are basically rotten, one is unlikely to look to it for resources to reconcile them or to create more equitable social structures. Worst of all, the doctrine of the Fall has occasionally been debased to the bizarre idea of total depravity: the notion that there is nothing good in us, that we are incapable of any good whatever.

All that is perversity. The gladsome doctrine of the Fall does not say that people and the social order are utterly sinful or basically wicked or incapable of good. It teaches quite the opposite: people and the Powers are *not* evil by nature; evil is, on the contrary, unnatural, a disorder, a perversion. We, and the Powers, are the good creations of a good God. By contrast, there is in Scripture no account of the creation of the demons. Unlike the Powers, the demonic is not a constituent part of the universe. Its emergence is always an event in time, the consequence of wrong choices. An institution becomes demonic when it abandons its divine vocation for the pursuit of its own idolatrous goals. But what has become perverted in time can be redeemed in time.

Evil is not our essence. God intended us for better things. "Fallenness" does not touch our essence, but it characterizes our existence. No one can escape it. "Good" and "bad" people alike are fallen. The tax collectors and harlots are fallen, but so are the scribes and Pharisees and Jesus' disciples. Saints are fallen, together with sinners. The church is fallen along with the empire. "Fallen" simply means that we all live under the conditions of the Domination System.

The Fall does not revoke the gift of life, or the vocation to live humanly in the midst of a fallen creation. The Fall does not mean that everything we do is evil, vain, or hopeless, but merely that it is all ambiguous, tainted with egocentricity, subject to deflection from its divine goal, or capable of being co-opted toward other ends. All that distinguishes Christians is the confidence that we have been reconciled with God in the very midst of a fallen world.

Paradoxically, those in the grip of the cultural trance woven over us by the Domination System are usually unaware of the full depth of their soul-sickness. It is only after we experience liberation from primary socialization to the world-system that we realize how terribly we have violated our authentic personhood—and how violated we have been. For we are not just sinners, but the sinned against. We not only have defected from higher values, but we have been trained, schooled, cajoled, and bullied into defecting from them by the combined onslaught of much that goes to make up our world. In part, our sin is that we acquiesced in this socialization.

Like addicts who cannot tell how distorted their perceptions have become until they get off drugs, we too cannot recognize the depth of our alienation from life until we are well on the way toward healing. Like addicts, we are not completely "redeemed," with all our former cravings gone and the damage we have done to ourselves and others all undone. We continue to live redemptively as fallen people in a fallen world, as God's good creations. Like addicts, again, we cannot redeem ourselves from a system whose malignancy we scarcely recognize and whose blandishments we have come to crave. We need revelation, to see our state, and liberation, to be freed from it. We, too, like other addicts, must turn over our lives to a higher power, not just another of the Powers but the God who transcends the Powers.[9] For no Power, in the act of freeing us from another Power, can deliver us from itself.

The simultaneity persists: we and the Powers are good, fallen, and redeemed, all at the same time. We do not escape into utopia. The doctrine of the Fall keeps our feet anchored firmly in the harsh reality of the one and only world, known in both its inner and outer aspects, even as God continues to work in us transformations we were not even aware, in our estranged state, that were needed or were possible.

The Powers Will Be Redeemed

A devout Roman Catholic charismatic in Chile attempted to persuade me that Christians have no business trying to change structures, that we are simply called to change individuals and that as a consequence of changed individuals, the structures will automatically change. Jesus himself, she asserted, did not try to reform the structures of first-century society. He was not a revolutionary, nor did he propose alternative institutions. Political science is a field of great complexity requiring specialist knowledge. Christians have no business telling politicians what to do or how to do it. The church's task is to nurture persons who feel called to politics and are steeped in Christian values.

THE IRREDUCIBILITY OF THE PERSONAL TO THE SOCIAL

Comments like these contain an element of truth. There is sometimes a leavening process in institutions as individuals change. People can make a difference in the way an office or factory or nation is run. Gorbachev has had an immense impact on the history of our time. One person's integrity can have a marked effect in checking a dozen employees' dishonesty. We must never deny the incredible power of a few dedicated people. Almost every major reform can be traced back to a single person or a small group of people who were outraged by wrong. It is true that Christians often have no grasp of the complexity of issues, even when they have made their best efforts to be informed, and that many "Christian" solutions have given rise to new and sometimes even greater evils. One thinks of the Latin American "Christian Democratic" parties, which so often have been neither. The church *can* have a salutary effect on society by nurturing people with special callings in the secular world, and must forswear the grandiosity of thinking that it has a solution for every problem.

Nor may the individual ever be treated as of lesser value than the social system. Changed people, reconciled with God and in process of transformation, are at the very core of the gospel message. The harmony of the whole is not worth the involuntary sacrifice of a single life. The problem of society lies far too deep to be settled through mere systemic changes, as Václav Havel insisted when his was one of the few voices of dissent in Czechoslovakia before the collapse of communism there. He deplored the willingness of those who, for the sake of fundamental social change, were always ready to sacrifice things less fundamental—like human beings. "A better system will not automatically ensure a better life. In fact the opposite is true: only by creating a better life can a better system be developed."[10] The main rationale for changing structures is precisely in order to liberate people from whatever deprives them of the opportunity to realize as fully as possible their own God-given potential. Our freedom under God means that, in the final analysis, each person is responsible for choosing life, regardless of the structure.

Grant this much to my Chilean friend: we must not reduce the personal to the social. No structural change will, *of necessity,* produce good or transformed people. I have considerable sympathy with conservative groups in the mainline American denominations who fault church leadership for ignoring evangelism altogether or redefining it as struggles for social justice. Ultimately, as liberation theologian Domingos Barbé comments, the sickness of our world is a spiritual illness that comes from a lack of a living relationship with God.[11] Without reestablishing that relationship, there can be no deep and lasting social change. Many people do need to undergo a change of heart. God must supplant the upstart ego. People do need to be "reborn" from their primary socialization in an alienated and alienating system—though conservatives are generally too acculturated themselves to go that far—and take on the radical values of God's nonviolent commonwealth.

Our times have produced tragic illusions about the power of new systems to create new people. The abolition of slavery in the American South did not produce transformed people, however much it may have improved the former slaves' lot and theoretically enhanced their capacity to achieve their true potentials. Soviet communism did not lead to the much-vaunted "New Man" (sic), but to an actual decline in human happiness and fulfillment. No doubt private property prompts greed, but greed is also observable where private property has been abolished. In intentional communes, fathers still molest their daughters sexually, treasurers abscond with community funds, and envy over the fairness of the distribution of power and goods persists. Social arrangements can perhaps help reduce the profitability and attraction of sin, but they cannot make it disappear.

Human misery is caused by institutions, but these institutions are maintained by human beings. We are made evil by our institutions, yes; but our institutions are also made evil by us. Not all sin can be projected outside the self; it is within us as well, far deeper than mere socialization. *It is, in part, what makes socialization necessary.*

Marx had rightly stressed that the self is "the ensemble of social relations." But that is not all it is. The self is that ensemble of social relations which also knows itself to be primordially grounded in being-itself, to have a name uttered over it, or within it, from all eternity. No state, or family, or employer can reach all the way to the core of our beings; and it is this residual irreducibility of the self to the social that makes it possible to resist society, to oppose the Powers, to transcend our own socialization. Much as we might like to lay the blame for all evil on the rise of the Domination System, we cannot do so without at the same time sacrificing responsibility and freedom. We are not merely socialized in sin, or sinned against; we also *choose* to sin, and it is this ontological capacity to sin that, paradoxically, insures our human freedom.[12]

Marx, Rousseau, Ernest Becker, Eisler, Schmookler, and a host of others want to bring humanity the good news that evil is not our fault, that it is all a confidence trick played on us by the structures we innocently and unwittingly created to dike ourselves against the rising flood of civilized anarchy. But anyone who has looked deeply within knows that not all evil has been introjected into us by the means of production or the government or patriarchy or the structures of society. Some evil would remain in our souls regardless of the social system. Otherwise, how can we account for the creation of these alienating structures in the first place? No arrangement of social cooperation, in which power controls power and anarchy is tamed, will produce human beings free from the lust for power.

Humanity longs for a world where the travail of personal transformation will not be necessary, where the arduous effort to develop a virtuous character can be avoided, where our neighbors will be judged by the standards we idealize but have exempted ourselves from achieving. Behind all such dreams of a perfected social structure lies the nightmare of totalitarianism. At what cost in personal freedoms must the dream of an anarchy-free society be bought? Unless people as well as their systems are changed, the crystal utopias of our fantasies will continue to dawn blood-drenched and inhospitable.

For once our dreams of paradise start to turn into reality, comments Milan Kundera, reflecting on his experience under Polish communism, people start to crop up here and there who stand in its way.

> So the rulers of paradise have to build a little gulag on the side of Eden. In the course of time this gulag grows ever bigger and more perfect, while the adjoining paradise gets ever smaller and poorer. . . . Hell is already contained in the dream of paradise and if we wish to understand the essence of hell we must examine the essence of the paradise from which it originated. It is extremely easy to condemn gulags, but to reject the totalitarian poesy which leads to the gulag by way of paradise is as difficult as ever. [13]

We must not, then, confuse any coming epoch (the Age of Aquarius, a harmonic convergence, a world federation of states, or whatever) with the reign of God. While history lasts, God's New Creation remains the transcendent criterion by which every system is judged. And any new social order instituted by human beings, whatever its form, will inevitably be a new, possibly better, but still pervasively fallen society. Such attempts may be able to ameliorate evil; that is the proper function of politics. But they will also recast evil into other forms.

The Fall is not a temporal event, the reach of whose effects we might someday, by sheer perseverance, outrun. It is mythic, which means it is always present. Whatever redemption, social change, improvement of working conditions, or restructuring of government that takes place within history will take place under the conditions of the Fall.

Evil finally can be dealt with only through myth. And here the biblical myth repeatedly reveals its capacity to unveil the *not said* and the *not-yet-thought*. The objection above, that evil cannot be wholly ascribed to our social or political or economic or religious systems, or all of them in concert, is not just an inference from the experience of the evil within ourselves. It is also a deduction from the narratives of the Fall in Genesis. The first fall is that of the man and the woman: human sin is ontologically prior to all social systems and structures. Therefore, it cannot be reduced to social determinism, but is an act of willful rebellion against God (Genesis 3).

The second fall is that of the angels: there is a rupture in the very spirituality of the universe (Gen. 6:1-4). Human sin cannot therefore account for all evil. There is a "withinness" or spirituality in things that is capable of covetousness and insatiable greed.

The third fall is that of the nations: the systems and structures that exist to protect human life become idolatrous and unjust, and subordinate the people they exist to serve to ends not ordained by God (Genesis 11).

Together, these three mythical tableaux from Genesis provide a vast panorama for contemplation. They prevent us from reducing people to society or society to people, the spiritual to the structural or the structural to the spiritual. They negate every attempt to blame evil solely on humanity (as most theology still insists on doing), solely on spiritual powers (as pentecostalism sometimes does), or solely on institutions and systems (as materialism does). Together these stories tell how evil came into a good world created by a good God, and they offer inexhaustible resources for discernment in the complex flux of everyday life.

The Irreducibility of the Social to the Personal

The problem with my Chilean friend's approach is not so much with what it affirms as what it leaves out. It ignores altogether the implications of Eph. 6:12 and all the companion references to the Powers: "For our struggle is not against human foes, but against cosmic powers, against the authorities and potentates of this dark age, against the superhuman forces of evil in the heavenly realms" (REB). As long as these Powers were thought of personalistically—that is, as long as they were themselves reduced to the categories of individualism and imagined as demonic beings assaulting us from the sky—their institutional and systemic dimension was mystified, and belief in the demonic had no political consequences. But once we recognize that these spiritual forces are *the interiority of earthly institutions or structures or systems,* then the social dimension of the gospel becomes immediately evident. These Powers with which we contend—and the biblical writer assumes we are all engaged in that struggle—are the inner *and* outer manifestations of political, economic, religious, and cultural institutions. Despite any excellences these institutions may individually possess, they are collectively caught up in a world-system blind to its Creator and drunk on self-aggrandizement. They are at one and the same time divinely ordained, and acolytes of the kingdom of death.

The principle of the irreducibility of persons to systems must therefore be matched by its opposite: the irreducibility of systems to persons. Structures have their own laws, their own trends and tendencies, quite independent of the human agents involved in them. The laws relevant to collectivities cannot be reduced to those of individuals, just as the laws of engineering that regulate the functioning of a tractor cannot be reduced to the laws of physics and chemistry that determine the behavior of the individual molecules and atoms that make up its parts. There are hierarchies of laws. People are the atoms and molecules of social systems. Every person is subject to the "laws" of personal development. But their interactions in a transnational corporation may have very little to do with the way their personal development is progressing. (I am told that over half of the managers of the Fortune 500 companies have had sensitivity training. Has the world noticed a difference?) The host of junior and senior managers surely vary in skill, maturity, and ethical integrity, but they are to a very high degree interchangeable and replaceable.

And what *motivates them* is almost irrelevant. They need not be greedy for profit at all; *the system is greedy on their behalf.* Berdyaev once remarked that social changes cannot wait until people are made morally perfect. "The putting of an end to torture of the weak by the strong cannot await the moral perfection of the strong. . . . The weak must be supported by actions which change the structure of society."[14]

Even the moral concern of a few is usually insufficient to change an oppressive system. The owner of a business, for example, may undergo an experience of spiritual rebirth, and genuinely desire to humanize the conditions under which her employees work. But she encounters immediately a fixed constraint: cost. If she deviates too much from the general norm for wages and benefits, the cost of the product will price her out of business. So she must be extremely cautious in introducing fundamental change, because her business is dependent on a world economic system that is utterly indifferent to her ethical concerns. This is not to dismiss the value of that one business person's attempt to be more humane. That attempt, within the narrow range of her freedom, may be the thin margin between making work pleasant for her workers or miserable.

Her free choices can have a limited effect on her employees' satisfaction in life. And that is by no means negligible. New management styles have helped to humanize existence in some workplaces. But she cannot raise salaries sharply and still remain competitive when a factory owner in Taiwan or South Korea is making the same product with teenage girl laborers paid one-tenth of the salary and working twelve or fourteen hours a day six days a week. The system is greedy on her behalf, and if she rejects the system's values she may be ejected by the system. It is not just that people are making choices about how they will behave in the economic system: the system is also making choices about who will remain viable in the system. We do not contend against flesh and blood, but against the world rulers of this present darkness.

That example is rather simple. Consider now the more complex case of an agricultural researcher at a state agricultural experiment station. He typically hails from a farm or at least a small-town agricultural service community. The researcher has a genuine desire to serve the farmer by making farming easier and more profitable. Let us even imagine that the researcher feels this as a genuine vocation from God, as my Chilean friend would put it.

But now watch how the Powers strip from his hands the very capacity to fulfill his vocation. The researcher responds directly to the needs of the farmers. But these needs are *imposed on* the farmer by the system of production and marketing for farm products. That means he virtually has to use a tractor instead of a horse to plow and cultivate. He must till more acres to insure profitability and justify the cost of the tractor. He must buy commercial fertilizer because he no longer can produce enough manure locally, and he must buy a harvesting machine because he is farming more acreage, and an adequate labor force is costly and undependable.

So the farmer calls on the researcher to develop seeds with higher yields, and herbicides to kill the weeds. The researcher responds with a will, determined to serve the farmer. But all these demands are dictated, not by the farmer, but by the technological innovations that must be used in order to maintain profitability in a market in which competitors are taking advantage of these technological innovations also.

And our researcher? With the best will in the world, he perseveres in producing a hybrid corn seed that will increase yields for the farmer. But this backs the farmer into even greater dependency on the four seed companies that supply most of the U.S. corn belt. Since hybrids do not breed true, the farmer must now buy new seed each year instead of harvesting his own seed from the choice stock of his own crop. All this takes money; in the past seventy-eight years the average farmer's indebtedness increased eightyfold.[15]

The agricultural researcher does not intend to drive his clients into debt, yet this is the unintended result of his endeavors on the farmer's behalf. And since all such highly mechanized farmers can now produce tremendous yields, the price of corn drops, they cannot pay off their debts, and the bank forecloses.

The tragedy is that many farmers blame themselves entirely for what is in large part a systemic catastrophe. They feel shame for a failure that has all the inevitability of an avalanche. Our individualistic blinders cause us to seek private causes for public malfunctions. It is easier, for them and us, to blame bankrupted farmers for their own personal incompetence than to unmask the system that is doing them in. (And we have not even considered the role of agribusiness and the U.S. Congress in the farm debacle!)

We in the West have a tendency to think of people as primary and social institutions as secondary, as if the latter were an arbitrary and inessential framework invented by human beings. Studies of birds, dolphins, whales, and primates have shown, however, that social organization is by no means a human invention. We emerged as humans already graced with a broad repertoire of social institutions. Ervin Laszlo goes so far as to call these institutions "natural systems," because they are apparently as intrinsically and indispensably human as the need for food, drink, and sexual expression.[16]

As long as human societies were small, minimal organization was required. Even with the emergence of the great empires of the Near East, Egypt, and China in the Bronze and Early Iron ages, where the king was identified with the high god, we find little awareness of the intermediate Powers that so profoundly determine human existence. Polytheism, to be sure, reflected a keen awareness of the multiplicity of Powers that shape the human psyche, but these primary intuitions were not given sociopolitical expression until the time of Alexander the Great, at least in the region in which the biblical religions took their rise.

With the sudden collapse of the city-states and the emergence of the Hellenistic cosmopolis, people were simultaneously stripped of the religious cosmologies that had sustained them and plunged into a world of vast and imponderable forces vying for supremacy. For the first time, the language of Principalities and Powers emerged as a way of identifying the *experiences* people were having of new spiritual forces embodied in the social and political institutions of Alexander's successors. If these spiritual Powers had been there all along, how can we account for their being identified so late? If they had eternal metaphysical status, why were they stored up so long and released only in the Hellenistic age? But if they were *new* spirits, the interiority of new social forces identified as the result of new perceptions, then their emergence precisely at that moment in history makes perfect sense.

These forces were not altogether new. The Hebrew Bible was already familiar with angels of the nations, for example (Deut. 32:8-9, a very ancient text; see also 2 Sam. 5:24; Ps. 82:1-8). But the range and ubiquity of these forces for the first time came to awareness in the post-Alexandrine era. And what those capable of discernment testified is that these Powers were beyond simple human control.

This sense that affairs have passed out of human hands into those of suprahuman Powers increased in the Roman period. A change of emperor might affect the ordinary Roman incidentally for good or evil, comments Harold Mattingly, but it was really the system that mattered, and the system changed very little whatever particular occupant might be enthroned in the seat of the Caesars.[17] The office of the emperor seemed to possess a power independent of its incumbent: "It was inevitable that the system should come to tyrannize over each Emperor of the moment, that caprice, never to be completely excluded, mattered less and less, that the Emperor should end by being as much a prisoner of his office as the meanest serf among his subjects."[18] A highly placed officer at the Pentagon expressed to me the same sentiments: "Sometimes it feels like it's just a massive system that got going and no one knows how it happened or how to stop it."

For we are not contending against mere human beings, but against suprahuman systems and forces, against "the *spirituality (pneumatika)* of the evil Powers in the invisible order." The modern sociologist Peter Blau concurs that institutions seem to be beyond human control: "Once firmly organized, an organization tends to assume an identity of its own which makes it independent of the people who have founded it or of those who constitute its membership."[19]

People establish institutions, but they are in turn themselves molded by the institutions they have established. We come into a world already institutionally organized, often for injustice. "I suppose that at first, it was people who invented borders," writes the Russian poet Yevgeny Yevtushenko, "and then borders started to invent people."[20]

"Fate" means literally "what is spoken"—not what we speak, but what is spoken over us to predetermine our future by blocking our free access to the reality we would choose. [21] It refers to the fact that not only individuals, but whole groups, classes, and races can find themselves in a state of physical or psychic detention. We are each defined in part by the sum total of possibilities that are denied to us, that is, by a future more or less blocked off.[22] The final triumph of the Powers, then, is to cause us to will to be where we have been detained.

To be created by God means that no system can totally determine us. But there is such a thing as "natal alienation," as someone has called it: the experience of being born into a world in which one is condemned in advance, by virtue of one's skin color, or gender, or disability, or malnutrition, or a mother's addiction, or AIDS, to a future more or less blocked off. We are talking here about not just an occasional aberration but about hundreds of millions of people. If South African "Bantu education" has been intentionally geared to teach just enough to train blacks for work in the mines but not enough for them to achieve competitive parity with whites, how free are they to "be all that they can be" under God?

Jesus denounced the Domination System of his day and proclaimed the advent of the reign of God, which *would transform every aspect of reality, even the social framework of existence.* To this end he founded an anti-structure[23] that provided a haven for those whose encounter with Jesus left them nowhere else to go (prostitutes, toll collectors, "sinners," the landless). It bodied forth a new existence under God, freed from legalism and the purity code. It also liberated people from the alienating spirituality of the Hellenistic ethos. And it set in motion a permanent revolution against the Power System whose consequences we are still only beginning to grasp to this day.

Our charismatic friend in Chile regarded Jesus as only the savior of souls, not the savior of the world. Her Jesus was not the bringer of the New Order into this time and space, but a redeemer who saves people from this time and space into an afterlife. The proclaimer of God's reign on earth had become, for her, the divine broker who negotiates our forgiveness for personal infractions of the moral code. Christianity was, in her eyes, a fairly private affair, a matter of "spiritual life" only, which left uncriticized and unopposed a System exemplified in Chile, at the very moment we were speaking, by the iron-fisted dictator, Gen. Augusto Pinochet. The General had nothing to fear from her.

The Jesus who died at the hands of the Powers died every bit as much for the Powers as he died for people. The statement in Col. 1:20 that God was pleased to reconcile to himself all things, whether on earth or in heaven, by making peace through the blood of the cross, cannot apply just to people, since we are not in "heaven." It must mean the Powers referred to in v. 16, in both their visible and invisible aspects, as the reiteration of the phrase "on earth or in heaven" (1:16, 20) makes clear. It is these Powers that Christ reconciles to God through his death on the cross. That death is not, then, merely an unmasking and exposure of the Powers for what they are (Col. 2:15), but an effort to transform the Powers into what they are meant to be.

Philippians 3:21 further specifies: Christ will transform the world "by the power that also enables him to make all things subject to himself." The paradox of the cross, however, prevents this from being just another dream by the powerless of a reversal of power. The one who subjects all things to himself is precisely the same one who abandoned all mimetic rivalry with God—"who, though he was in the form of God, did not regard equality with God as something to be exploited"—and emptied himself of all desire to dominate, taking the form of the oppressed, identifying himself with the enslaved, and suffering a criminal's death (Phil. 2:6-8*). Subjection to such a ruler means the end of all subjugation. The rulership thus constituted is not a domination hierarchy but an enabling or actualizing hierarchy.[24] It is not pyramidal but organic, not imposed but restorative. It is presided over by naked, defenseless truth—the Crucified—not by a divine dictator. Christ makes all things subject to himself, not by coercion, but by healing diseased reality and restoring its balance and integrity.

Reinhold Niebuhr taught that organizations reflect the lowest common denominator of morality of their members, and are therefore less moral than most of the people that make them up.[25] This is depressingly true of a great many groups; if it is the whole story, however, hopes for transforming institutions are incredibly slim. But in fact we all know of groups that lift people to a *higher* level than the individuals who compose them: Alcoholics Anonymous and groups for addicts of other kinds; or certain intentional Christian communities like the Latin American base communities, or Ground Zero, Church of the Savior, Sojourners, Koinonia Farm and the Iona Community. Many clergy feel they have been able to help improve the churches they have served, as do many business executives their companies. Even this side of the reign of God, institutions can be impacted for the better.

The gospel is not a message of personal salvation *from* the world, but a message of *a world transfigured, right down to its basic structures.* Redemption means actually being liberated from the oppression of the Powers, being forgiven for one's own sin and for complicity with the Powers, and being engaged in liberating the Powers themselves from their bondage to idolatry. The good news is nothing less than a cosmic salvation, a restitution of all things (Acts 3:21), when God will "gather up all things in him [Christ], things in heaven and things on earth" (Eph. 1:10). This universal rectification will entail both a healing and a subordination of rebellious structures, systems, and institutions to their rightful places, in service to the One in and through and for whom they exist.

Redemption of the Powers requires neutralizing their proclivity to evil and bringing them into subjection to Christ ("under his feet," 1 Cor. 15:24-27; Eph. 1 22; Heb. 10:12-13). The Powers will enter the heavenly city, redeemed, transformed (Rev. 22:2), bearing as their "glory" all the artistic, cultural, political, scientific, and spiritual contributions whereby they have enriched the world (Rev. 21:24). On this side of the New Jerusalem they will remain relatively good and evil, none perfect, none totally depraved. But some will become so destructively demonic in their self-idolization that they must be resisted with all our might.

The understanding that the Powers are created, fallen, and redeemable helps negotiate a truce between two camps long at odds. The one argues that all governmental, economic, educational, and cultural systems are intrinsically evil, though capable of some limited good. This position is held by some Amish, Mennonites, and others from the Anabaptist tradition. The other insists that governments and other public institutions are not just post-Fall phenomena but intrinsic elements of God's creation, and therefore capable not only of reform but even of being "christianized." This position is associated with the Calvinist tradition, but is also characteristic of Catholicism and most mainline Protestants.[26]

Without such a truce, the invidious "either/or" of the debate leaves us either abandoning the Powers to secularity or installing an establishment Christianity: either withdrawal or theocracy. Instead of these two extremes, the New Testament view of the Powers gives us a broad continuum of possible emphases, adaptable to every situation. There are no prepackaged answers that tell us how Christians should engage the Powers. One person may be called to try to reorganize the office where she works in a more humane fashion; another may have to walk out to protest sexual harassment. One may run for political office; another may despair of the electoral system and work to overthrow it. But all live in the paradox of "as if not," as being in but not of the Domination System. "Come out of her, my people" (Rev. 18:4) may be our marching orders, but so may be the call to assume secular office (as with Joseph and Daniel). Spiritual discernment takes the place of fixed rules. As Jacques Ellul argues, there really is no such thing as a "Christian ethic," only the ethical inventiveness of Christians.[27]

Social entities *can* be changed, but they can only be fundamentally changed by strategies that address the socio-spiritual nature of institutions. Since we are not out to destroy people but to change the systems that hold even their beneficiaries in thrall, we must take as our spiritual weapons the "whole armor of God," the nonviolent armament of which Ephesians so eloquently speaks:

truth, justice, peace, faith, salvation, the word of God, and above all, prayer (Eph. 6:10-20). That is, the church's peculiar calling is to discern and engage both the structure and the spirituality of oppressive institutions.

Have I ended by agreeing with my Chilean charismatic friend? We are certainly of one mind that the church's unique task is spiritual. We differ only in the recognition that part of the church's evangelistic task is proclaiming to the Principalities and Powers in the heavenly places the manifold wisdom of God (Eph. 3:10). And that means addressing the spirituality of actual institutions that have rebelled against their divine vocations and have made themselves gods.

We are slowly beginning to read the events of our time in ways that honor both the social and the personal. The irreducibility of the personal to the social, and the irreducibility of the social to the personal: these two principles form an indissoluble and necessary duality that must be maintained against all simplistic attempts at individualistic *or* sociological reductionism. God's will is the transformation of people *and* society. Individuals will enter the New Jerusalem, but so also their nations, redeemed and healed by the leaves of the tree of life (Rev. 21: 24-26; 22:2). Evangelism and social struggle are the twin pincers of a single movement for world transformation.

The Powers are good, the Powers are fallen, but the Powers will be redeemed. That is a hope worthy of the One in and through and for whom all things exist, and whose praises we hymn in anticipation of the final restitution of all things in the embrace of divine love.

Notes

1. Ernst Käsemann, "A Primitive Christian Baptismal Liturgy," in *Essays on New Testament Themes* (London: SCM Press, 1964), 162.

2. Gerhard von Rad, *Old Testament Theology*, 2 vols. (New York: Harper & Row, 1962–65), 1:161–65.

3. A. N. Whitehead, *Process and Reality*, corrected edition, ed. David Ray Griffin and Donald W. Sherburne (New York: The Free Press, 1978), 339.

4. See Kathleen L. Roney-Wilson, "Deeper and Darker: Satanic Child Abuse," *Journal of Christian Healing* 1211 (Spring 1990): 9–12.

5. William Stringfellow, *An Ethic for Christians and Other Aliens in a Strange Land* (Waco, Tex.: Word, Inc., 1973), 43.

6. Ibid., 83.

7. Reinhold Niebuhr, *Moral Man and Immoral Society* (New York: Charles Scribner's Sons, 1932), 129.

8. Michael Lerner, *Surplus Powerlessness* (Atlantic Highlands, N.J.: Humanities Press International, 1991), 266–86.

9. See Anne Wilson Schaef, *When Society Becomes an Addict* (San Francisco: Harper & Row, 1987).

10. *Václav Havel or Living in Truth,* ed. Jan Vladislav (Boston: Faber & Faber, 1987), 70, 92.

11. Domingos Barbé, "The Spiritual Basis of Nonviolence," in *Relentless Persistence,* ed. Philip McManus and Gerald Schlabach (Philadelphia: New Society Publications, 1991), 272.

12. Joel Kovel, *History and Spirit* (Boston: Beacon Press, 1991), 167.

13. Philip Roth, interview with Milan Kundera, *New York Times Book Review,* November 30, 1980, 78, 80.

14. Nicolas Berdyaev, *Slavery and Freedom* (New York: Charles Scribner's Sons, 1944), 208.

15. From 0 in 1910 to ,000 in 1988, not adjusted for inflation. Source: *National Financial Summary, Economic Indicators of the Farm Sector* (Washington, D.C.: U.S. Dept. of Agriculture, December 31, 1988), 67.

16. Ervin Laszlo, *The Systems View of the World* (New York: George Braziller, 1972), 23.

17. Harold Mattingly, *The Man in the Roman Street* (New York: Numismatic Review, 1947), 96.

18. Harold Mattingly, *Christianity in the Roman Empire* (New Zealand: University of Otago Press, 1955), 10.

19. Peter Blau, cited by Rubem Alvez, "From Paradise to the Desert: Autobiographical Musings," in *Frontiers of Theology in Latin America,* ed. Rosino Giliellini (Maryknoll, N.Y.: Orbis Books, 1979), 296. Peter Berger and Thomas Luckmann, *The Social Construction of Reality* (Garden City, N.Y.: Doubleday, 1966), 78—a highly influential but extraordinarily reductionistic work.

20. From "Fuku," in *Almost at the End*(London: Marion Boyars, 1987), 41.

21. James M. Robinson, "Kerygma and History in the New Testament," in *The Bible in Modern Scholarship,* ed. J. Philip Hyatt (Nashville: Abingdon Press, 1965), 117.

22. Hazel E. Barnes, "Introduction," in Jean Paul Sartre, *Search for a Method* (New York: Alfred A. Knopf, 1967), xxiii.

23. Victor Turner's designation, in *Dramas, Fields and Metaphors* (Ithaca: Cornell Univ. Press, 1974), 298.

24. Riane Eisler, *The Chalice and the Blade* (San Francisco: Harper & Row, 1987), 205 n. 5.

25. Reinhold Niebuhr, *Moral Man and Immoral Society.*

26. See the helpful discussion by Richard J. Mouw, *Politics and the Biblical Drama* (Grand Rapids: Wm. B. Eerdmans, 1976), 85–116.

27. Darrell J. Fasching, "The Dialectic of Apocalyptic and Utopia in the Theological Ethics of Jacques Ellul," paper delivered at the annual meeting of the American Academy of Religion in Boston, November 1987, p. 5.

11

Jesus' Third Way: Nonviolent Engagement

In this chapter, Walter Wink addresses what, for him, is a central tactic in strategies for engaging the Powers—nonviolence. He is quick to point out that nonviolence is not pacifism; it is not submissive acquiescence to the Powers That Be and their oppressive and exploitative structures and systems. As an alternative to stereotypical responses to evil—fight (meeting violence with violence) and flight (passivity and submission)—Wink offers what he calls "Jesus' third way," the way of creative, aggressive, coercive nonviolent resistance. It seeks, on the one hand, to shame and convert the oppressor while, on the other hand, restoring self-esteem, dignity and initiative to the oppressed. Using Jesus' teaching in Matt. 5:38-42 (turn the other cheek, give your cloak, go the second mile), Wink argues that Jesus is not suggesting that the victims of oppression cooperate in their subjugation. Rather, he is calling for creative responses to oppression that assert the worth of the oppressed while unmasking the Domination System and its beneficiaries, showing them up publicly for what they really are. Wink pays particular attention to Matt. 5:39b—"But I say to you, Do not resist an evildoer"—and demonstrates convincingly that "do not resist" is better translated as "do not violently resist." This leaves room for aggressive nonviolent engagement with evil, with the caveat that one not become the evil one resists. In Peter's terms, "Do not repay evil for evil" (1 Pet. 3:9)—do not repay violence with violence.

Source: Wink 1992: Excerpted from Chapter 9

> We have assumed the name of peacemakers, but we have been, by and large, unwilling to pay any significant price. And because we want the peace with half a heart and half a life and will, the war, of course, continues, because the waging of

> war, by its very nature, is total—but the waging of peace, by our own cowardice, is partial. So a whole will and a whole heart and a whole national life bent toward war prevail over the velleities of peace.... "Of course, let us have the peace," we cry, "but at the same time let us have normalcy, let us lose nothing, let our lives stand intact, let us know neither prison nor ill repute nor disruption of ties...." There is no peace because there are no peacemakers. There are no makers of peace because the making of peace is at least as costly as the making of war—at least as exigent, at least as disruptive, at least as liable to bring disgrace and prison and death in its wake.
>
> –Daniel Berrigan, *No Bars to Manhood*[1]

Human evolution has provided the species with two deeply instinctual responses to violence: flight or fight. Jesus offers a third way: nonviolent direct action.[2] The classic text is Matt. 5:38-42:

> [38] You have heard that it was said, "An eye for an eye and a tooth for a tooth." [39] But I say to you, do not resist and evildoer. But if anyone strikes you on the right cheek, turn the other also; [40] and if anyone wants to sue you and take your coat, give your cloak as well; [41] and if anyone forces you to go one mile, go also the second mile. [42] Give to everyone who begs from you, and do not refuse anyone who wants to borrow from you. (See also Luke 6:29-30.)

Christians have, on the whole, simply ignored this teaching. It has seemed impractical, masochistic, suicidal—an invitation to bullies and spouse-batterers to wipe up the floor with their supine Christian victims. Some who have tried to follow Jesus' words have understood it to mean nonresistance: let the oppressor perpetrate evil unopposed. Even scholars have swallowed the eat-humble-pie reading of this text: "It is better to surrender everything and go through life naked than to insist on one's legal rights," to cite only one of scores of these commentators from Augustine right up to the present.[3] Interpreted thus, the passage has become the basis for systematic training in cowardice, as Christians are taught to acquiesce to evil.

Cowardice is scarcely a term one associates with Jesus. Either he failed to make himself clear, or we have misunderstood him. There is plenty of cause to believe the latter. Let us set aside for the moment the thesis statement (vv. 38-39a), and focus on the three practical examples he gives.

Jesus on Nonviolent Engagement

1. *Turn the Other Cheek.* "If anyone strikes you on the right cheek, turn the other also." Why the *right* cheek? A blow by the right fist in that right-handed world would land on the *left* cheek of the opponent. An open-handed slap would also strike the left cheek. To hit the right cheek with a fist would require using the left hand, but in that society the left hand was used only for unclean tasks. Even to gesture with the left hand at Qumran carried the penalty of ten days' penance. The only way one could naturally strike the right cheek with the right hand would be with the back of the hand. We are dealing here with insult, not a fistfight. The intention is clearly not to injure but to humiliate, to put someone in his or her place. One normally did not strike a peer thus, and if one did the fine was exorbitant. The mishnaic tractate *Baba Kamma* specifies the various fines for striking an equal: for slugging with a fist, 4 *zuz* (a *zuz* was a day's wage); for slapping, 200 *zuz;* but "if [he struck him] with the back of his hand he must pay him 400 *zuz.*" But damages for indignity were not paid to slaves who were struck (8:1-7).[4]

A backhand slap was the usual way of admonishing inferiors. Masters backhanded slaves; husbands, wives; parents, children; men, women; Romans, Jews. *We have here a set of unequal relations, in each of which retaliation would invite retribution.* The only normal response would be cowering submission. Part of the confusion surrounding these sayings arises from the failure to ask who Jesus' audience was. In all three of the examples in Matt. 5:39b-41, Jesus' listeners are not those who strike, initiate lawsuits, or impose forced labor, but their victims ("If anyone strikes *you* . . . wants to sue *you* . . . forces *you* to go one mile . . ."). There are among his hearers people who were subjected to these very indignities, forced to stifle outrage at their dehumanizing treatment by the hierarchical system of class, race, gender, age, and status, and as a result of imperial occupation.

Why then does he counsel these already humiliated people to turn the other cheek? Because this action robs the oppressor of the power to humiliate. The person who turns the other cheek is saying, in effect, "Try again. Your first blow failed to achieve its intended effect. I deny you the power to humiliate me. I am a human being just like you. Your status does not alter that fact. You cannot demean me."

Such a response would create enormous difficulties for the striker. Purely logistically, how would he hit the other cheek now turned to him? He cannot backhand it with his right hand (one only need try this to see the problem). If he hits with a fist, he makes the other his equal, acknowledging him as a peer. But the point of the back of the hand is to reinforce institutionalized inequality. Even if the superior orders the person flogged for such "cheeky" behavior (this is certainly no way to *avoid* conflict!), the point has been irrevocably made. He has been given notice that this underling is in fact a human being. In that world of honor and shaming, he has been rendered impotent to instill shame in a subordinate. He has been stripped of his power to dehumanize the other. As Gandhi taught, "The first principle of nonviolent action is that of noncooperation with everything humiliating."[5]

This very type of action had already been performed by Jesus' own contemporaries. Shortly after Pilate was appointed procurator in Judea (26 c.e.), he introduced into Jerusalem by night "the busts of the emperor that were attached to the military standards,"[6] which Jews regarded as idols and thus a desecration of the holy city. Crowds of Jews rushed to Pilate's headquarters in Caesarea to implore him to remove the standards. When he refused, they fell prostrate and remained there for five days and nights. On the sixth day, Pilate summoned the multitude to the stadium on the pretext of giving them an answer. Instead, they found themselves surrounded by soldiers, three deep.

> Pilate, after threatening to cut them down, if they refused to admit Caesar's images, signaled to the soldiers to draw their swords. Thereupon the Jews, as by concerted action, flung themselves in a body on the ground, extended their necks, and exclaimed that they were ready rather to die then to transgress the law. Overcome with astonishment at such intense religious zeal, Pilate gave orders for the immediate removal of the standards from Jerusalem.[7]

Jesus was not, then, articulating a notion alien to his people, but elevating it from occasional and spontaneous use to a central element in the coming of God's Reign.

2. *Give the Undergarment.* The second example Jesus gives is set in a court of law. Someone is being sued for his outer garment. Who would do that, and under what circumstances? The Hebrew Scriptures provide the clues.

> If you lend money to my people, to the poor among you, you shall not deal with them as a creditor; you shall not exact interest from them. If ever you take your neighbor's cloak (LXX, *himation*) in pawn, you shall restore it before the sun goes down; for it may be your neighbor's only clothing (*himation*) to use as cover; in what else shall that person sleep? And if your neighbor cries out to me, I will listen, for I am compassionate.
>
> (Exod. 22:25-27; LXX 22:24-26)
>
> When you make your neighbor a loan of any kind, you shall not go into the house to take the pledge. You shall wait outside, while the person to whom you are making the loan brings the pledge out to you. *If the person is poor,* you shall not sleep in the garment given you as the pledge. You shall give the pledge back by sunset, so that your neighbor may sleep in the cloak and bless you. . . . You shall not . . . take a widow's garment (*himation*) in pledge.
>
> (Deut. 24:10-13, 17)
>
> They who trample the head of the poor into the dust of the earth . . . lay themselves down beside every altar upon garments (*himatia*) taken in pledge.
>
> (Amos 2:7-8; see also Ezek. 18:5-9)

Only the poorest of the poor would have nothing but a garment to give as collateral for a loan. Jewish law strictly required its return every evening at sunset. Matthew and Luke disagree whether it is the outer garment (Luke) or the undergarment (Matthew) that is being seized. But the Jewish practice of giving the outer garment as a pledge (it alone would be useful as a blanket for sleeping) makes it clear that Luke's order is correct, even though he does not preserve the legal setting. In all Greek usage, according to Liddell-Scott, *himation* is "always an outer garment . . . worn above the *chitōn,*" whereas the *chitōn* is a "garment worn next to the skin."[8] S. Safrai and M. Stern describe normal Jewish dress: an outer garment or cloak of wool and an undergarment or tunic of linen.[9] To avoid confusion I will simply refer to the "outer garment" and the "undergarment."

The situation Jesus speaks to is all too familiar to his hearers: the debtor has sunk ever deeper into poverty, the debt cannot be repaid, and his creditor has summoned him to court (*krithēnai*) to exact repayment by legal means.

Indebtedness was endemic in first-century Palestine. Jesus' parables are full of debtors struggling to salvage their lives. Heavy debt was not, however, a natural calamity that had overtaken the incompetent. It was the direct consequence of Roman imperial policy. Emperors had taxed the wealthy so stringently to fund their wars that the rich began seeking nonliquid investments to secure their wealth. Land was best, but it was ancestrally owned and passed down over generations, and no peasant would voluntarily relinquish it. Exorbitant interest, however, could be used to drive landowners ever deeper into debt. And debt, coupled with the high taxation required by Herod Antipas to pay Rome tribute, created the economic leverage to pry Galilean peasants loose from their land. By the time of Jesus we see this process already far advanced: large estates owned by absentee landlords, managed by stewards, and worked by tenant farmers, day laborers, and slaves. It is no accident that the first act of the Jewish revolutionaries in 66 c.e. was to burn the Temple treasury, where the record of debts was kept.[10]

It is to this situation that Jesus speaks. His hearers are the poor ("if anyone would sue *you*"). They share a rankling hatred for a system that subjects them to humiliation by stripping them of their lands, their goods, finally even their outer garments.

Why then does Jesus counsel them to give over their undergarments as well? This would mean stripping off all their clothing and marching out of court stark naked! Imagine the guffaws this saying must have evoked. There stands the creditor, covered with shame, the poor debtor's outer garment in the one hand, and his undergarment in the other. The tables have suddenly been turned on the creditor. The debtor had no hope of winning the case; the law was entirely in the creditor's favor. But the poor man has transcended this attempt to humiliate him. He has risen above shame. At the same time he has registered a stunning protest against the system that created his debt. He has said in effect, "You want my robe? Here, take everything! Now you've got all I have except my body. Is that what you'll take next?"

Nakedness was taboo in Judaism, and shame fell less on the naked party than on the person viewing or causing the nakedness (Gen. 9:20-27). By stripping, the debtor has brought the creditor under the same prohibition that led to the curse of Canaan. And much as Isaiah had "walked naked and barefoot for three years" as a prophetic sign (Isa. 20:1-6), so the debtor parades his nakedness in prophetic protest against a system that has deliberately rendered him destitute. Imagine him leaving the court, naked. His friends and neighbors, aghast, inquire what happened. He explains. They join his growing procession, which now resembles a victory parade. The entire system by which debtors are oppressed has been publicly unmasked. The creditor is revealed to be not a legitimate moneylender but a party to the reduction of an entire social class to landlessness, destitution, and abasement. This unmasking is not simply punitive, therefore; it offers the creditor a chance to see, perhaps for the first time in his life, what his practices cause, and to repent.

The Powers That Be literally stand on their dignity. Nothing depotentiates them faster than deft lampooning. By refusing to be awed by their power, the powerless are emboldened to seize the initiative, even where structural change is not immediately possible. This message, far from being a counsel to perfection unattainable in this life, is a practical, strategic measure for empowering the oppressed, and it is being lived out all over the world today by powerless people ready to take their history into their own hands.

Jesus provides here a hint of how to take on the entire system by unmasking its essential cruelty and burlesquing its pretensions to justice. Here is a poor man who will no longer be treated as a sponge to be squeezed dry by the rich. He accepts the laws as they stand, pushes them to absurdity, and reveals them for what they have become. He strips naked, walks out before his fellows, and leaves this creditor, and the whole economic edifice that he represents, stark naked.

3. *Go the Second Mile.* "If one of the occupation troops forces (*angareusei*) you to carry his pack one mile, carry it two miles" (Matt. 5:41, TEV). Jesus' third example is drawn from the relatively enlightened practice of limiting the amount of forced or impressed labor (*angareia*) that Roman soldiers could levy on subject peoples to a single mile. The term *angareia* is probably Persian, and became a loanword in Aramaic, Greek, and Latin. Josephus mentions it in reference to the Seleucid ruler Demetrius, who, in order to enlist Jewish support for his bid to be king, promised, among other things, that "the Jews' beasts of burden shall not be requisitioned (*angareuesthai*) for our army" (*Ant.* 13.52). More familiar is the passion narrative, where the soldiers "compel"

(*angareuousin*) Simon of Cyrene to carry Jesus' cross (Mark 15:21 // Matt. 27:32). Such forced service was a constant feature in Palestine from Persian to late Roman times, and whoever was found on the street could be compelled into service.[11] Most cases of impressment involved the need of the postal service for animals and the need of soldiers for civilians to help carry their packs. The situation in Matthew is clearly the latter. It is not a matter of requisitioning animals but people.

This forced labor was a cause of bitter resentment for all Roman subjects. "*Angareia* is like death," complains one source.[12] The sheer frequency, even into the late empire, of legislation proscribing the misuse of the *angareia* shows how regularly the practice was used and its regulations violated. An inscription of 49 c.e. from Egypt orders that Roman "soldiers of any degree when passing through the several districts are not to make any requisitions or to employ forced transport (*angarei*) unless they have the prefect's written authority"[13]—a rescript clearly made necessary by soldiers abusing their privileges. Another decree from Egypt in 133–137 c.e. documents this abuse: "Many soldiers without written requisition are travelling about in the country, demanding ships, beasts of burden, and men, beyond anything authorized, sometimes seizing things by force . . . to the point of *showing abuse and threats to private citizens,* the result is that the military is associated with arrogance and injustice."[14] In order to minimize resentment in the conquered lands, Rome made at least some effort to punish violators of the laws regarding impressment.

The Theodosian Code devotes an entire section to *angareia*.[15] Among its ordinances are these:

> If any person while making a journey should consider that he may abstract an ox that is not assigned to the public post but dedicated to the plow, he shall be *arrested with due force* by the rural police . . . and he shall be haled before the judge [normally the governor]. (8.5.1, 315 c.e.)

> By this interdict We forbid that any person should deem that they may request pack animals and supplementary posthorses. But if any person should rashly act so presumptuously, *he shall be punished very severely.* (8.5.6, 354 c.e.)

> When any *legion* is proceeding to its destination, it shall not hereafter attempt to appropriate more than two posthorses (*angariae*), and only

for the sake of any who are sick. (8.5.11, 360 c.e., my emphasis throughout)

Late as these regulations are, they reflect a situation that had changed little since the time of the Persians. Armies had to move through countries with dispatch. Some legionnaires bought their own slaves to help carry their packs of sixty to eighty-five pounds (not including weapons). The majority of the rank and file, however, had to depend on impressed civilians. There are vivid accounts of whole villages fleeing to avoid being forced to carry soldiers' baggage, and of richer towns prepared to pay large sums to escape having Roman soldiers billeted on them for winter.[16]

With few exceptions, the commanding general of a legion personally administered justice in serious cases, and all other cases were left to the disciplinary control of his subordinates. Centurions (commanders of 100 men) had almost limitless authority in dealing with routine cases of discipline. This accounts for the curious fact that there is very little codified military law, and that which exists is late. Roman military historians are agreed, however, that military law changed very little in its essential character throughout the imperial period.

No account survives to us today of the penalties to be meted out to a soldier for forcing a civilian to carry his pack more than the permitted mile, but there are at least hints. "If in winter quarters, in camp, or *on the march, either* an officer or a soldier does injury to a civilian, and does not fully repair the same, he shall pay the damage twofold."[17] This is about as mild a penalty, however, as one can find. Josephus's comment is surely exaggerated, even if it states the popular impression: Roman military forces "have laws which punish with death not merely desertion of the ranks, but even a slight neglect of duty" (*War* 3.102–8). Between these extremes there was deprivation of pay, a ration of barley instead of wheat, reduction in rank, dishonorable discharge, being forced to camp outside the fortifications, or to stand all day before the general's tent holding a clod in one's hands, or to stand barefoot in public places. But the most frequent punishment by far was flogging.[18]

The frequency with which decrees were issued to curb misuse of the *angareia* indicates how lax discipline on this point was. Perhaps the soldier might receive only a rebuke. But the point is that the soldier *does not know what will happen.*

It is in this context of Roman military occupation that Jesus speaks. He does not counsel revolt. One does not "befriend" the soldier, draw him aside, and drive a knife into his ribs. Jesus was surely aware of the futility of armed insurrection against Roman imperial might; he certainly did nothing to encourage those whose hatred of Rome was near to flaming into violence.

But why carry his pack a second mile? Is this not to rebound to the opposite extreme of aiding and abetting the enemy? Not at all. The question here, as in the two previous instances, is how the oppressed can recover the initiative and assert their human dignity in a situation that cannot for the time being be changed. The rules are Caesar's, but how one responds to the rules is God's, and Caesar has no power over that.

Imagine then the soldier's surprise when, at the next mile marker, he reluctantly reaches to assume his pack, and the civilian says, "Oh no, let me carry it another mile." Why would he want to do that? What is he up to? Normally, soldiers have to coerce people to carry their packs, but this Jew does so cheerfully, and will not stop! Is this a provocation? Is he insulting the legionnaire's strength? Being kind? Trying to get him disciplined for seeming to violate the rules of impressment? Will this civilian file a complaint? Create trouble?

From a situation of servile impressment, the oppressed have suddenly seized the initiative. They have taken back the power of choice. The soldier is thrown off balance by being deprived of the predictability of his victim's response. He has never dealt with such a problem before. Now he has been forced into making a decision for which nothing in his previous experience has prepared him. If he has enjoyed feeling superior to the vanquished, he will not enjoy it today. Imagine the situation of a Roman infantryman pleading with a Jew to give back his pack! The humor of this scene may have escaped us, but it could scarcely have been lost on Jesus' hearers, who must have been regaled at the prospect of thus discomfiting their oppressors.

Jesus does not encourage Jews to walk a second mile in order to build up merit in heaven, or to exercise a supererogatory piety, or to kill the soldier with kindness. He is helping an oppressed people find a way to protest and neutralize an onerous practice despised throughout the empire. He is not giving a nonpolitical message of spiritual world-transcendence. He is formulating a worldly spirituality in which the people at the bottom of society or under the thumb of imperial power learn to recover their humanity.

One could easily misuse Jesus' advice vindictively; that is why it must not be separated from the command to love enemies, which is integrally connected with it in both Matthew and Luke. But love is not averse to taking the law and using its oppressive momentum to throw the soldier into a region of uncertainty and anxiety where he has never been before.

Such tactics can seldom be repeated. One can imagine that within days after the incidents that Jesus sought to provoke, the Powers That Be would pass new laws: penalties for nakedness in court, flogging for carrying a pack more than a mile! One must be creative, improvising new tactics to keep the opponent off balance.

To those whose lifelong pattern has been to cringe before their masters, Jesus offers a way to liberate themselves from servile actions and a servile mentality. And he asserts that they can do this *before* there is a revolution. There is no need to wait until Rome has been defeated, or peasants are landed and slaves freed. They can begin to behave with dignity and recovered humanity now, even under the unchanged conditions of the old order. Jesus' sense of divine immediacy has social implications. The reign of God is already breaking into the world, and it comes, not as an imposition from on high, but as the leaven slowly causing the dough to rise (Matt. 13:33 // Luke 13:20-21). Jesus' teaching on nonviolence is thus of a piece with his proclamation of the dawning of the reign of God.

In the conditions of first-century Palestine, a political revolution against the Romans could only be catastrophic, as the events of 66-70 c.e. would prove. Jesus does not propose armed revolution. But he does lay the foundations for a social revolution, as Richard A. Horsley has pointed out. And a social revolution becomes political when it reaches a critical threshold of acceptance; this in fact did happen to the Roman Empire as the Christian church overcame it from below.[19]

Nor were peasants and slaves in a position to transform the economic system by frontal assault. But they could begin to act from an already recovered dignity and freedom and the ultimate consequences of such acts could only be revolutionary. To that end, Jesus spoke repeatedly of a voluntary remission of debts.[20]

It is entirely appropriate, then, that the saying on debts in Matt. 5:42 // Luke 6:30 // *Gos. Thom.* 95 has been added to this block of sayings. Jesus counsels his hearers not just to practice alms and to lend money, even to bad risks, but to lend without expecting interest or even the return of the principal. Such radical egalitarian sharing would be necessary to rescue impoverished Palestinian peasants from their plight; one need not posit an imminent end of history as the cause for such astonishing generosity. And yet none of this is new; Jesus is merely issuing a prophetic summons to Israel pertaining to the sabbatical year enshrined in Torah, adapted to a new situation.

Such radical sharing would be necessary in order to restore true community. For the risky defiance of the Powers that Jesus advocates would inevitably issue punitive economic sanctions and physical punishment against individuals. They would need economic support; Matthew's "Give to everyone who *asks* [*aitounti*—not necessarily *begs*] of you" may simply refer to this need for mutual sustenance. Staggering interest and taxes isolated peasants, who went under one by one. This was a standard tactic of imperial "divide and rule" strategy.[21]

Jesus' solution was neither utopian nor apocalyptic. It was simple realism. Nothing less could halt or reverse the economic decline of Jewish peasants than a complete suspension of usury and debt and a restoration of economic equality through outright grants, a pattern actually implemented in the earliest Christian community, according to the Book of Acts.

Just on the grounds of sheer originality, the examples of unarmed direct action in Matt. 5:39b-41would appear to have originated with Jesus. No one, not only in the first century, but in all of human history, ever advocated defiance of oppressors by turning the cheek, stripping oneself naked in court, or jeopardizing a soldier by carrying his pack a second mile. For three centuries, the early church observed Jesus' command to nonviolence. But nowhere in the early church, to say nothing of the early fathers, do we find statements similar to these in their humor and originality. These sayings are, in fact, so radical, so unprecedented, and so threatening, that it has taken all these centuries just to begin to grasp their implications.

The Thesis Statement: Do Not Mirror Evil

A more difficult problem is the meaning of *antistēnai* in Matt. 5:39a. It is translated "resist" in almost all versions (NRSV: "Do not resist an evildoer"). That meaning of the word is certainly well-attested, but its use in this passage is insupportable. Purely on logical grounds, "resist not" does not fit the aggressive nonviolent actions described in the three following examples. Since in these three instances Jesus provides strategies for resisting oppression, it is altogether inconsistent for him to counsel people in almost the same breath not to resist it. Has Matthew added the term, or has it been mistranslated?

Matthew 5:39a also seems to suggest false alternatives: one either resists evil, or resists not. Fight or flight. No other possibilities appear to exist; if Jesus commands us not to resist, then the only other choice would appear to be passivity, complicity in our own oppression, surrender. Submission to evil appears to be the will of God. *And this is precisely the way most Christians have interpreted this passage.* "Turn the other cheek" is understood as enjoining supine acquiescence when someone behaves violently toward us. "Give your undergarment as well" has encouraged people to go limp in the face of injustice and hand over the last thing they own. "Going the second mile" has been turned into a platitude meaning nothing more than "extend yourself." Rather than encouraging the oppressed to resist their oppressors, these revolutionary statements have been heard as injunctions to collude in one's own despoiling.

What the translators have not noted, however, is how frequently *anthistēmi* is used as a military term. Resistance implies "counteractive aggression," a response to hostilities initiated by someone else. Liddell-Scott defines *anthistēmi* as to "*set against* esp. in battle, *withstand*." Ephesians 6:13 is exemplary of its military usage: "Therefore take up the whole armor of God, so that you may be able to withstand [*antistēnai*, lit., to draw up battle ranks against the enemy] on that evil day, and having done everything, to stand firm [*stēnai*, lit., to close ranks and continue to fight]." The term is used in the LXX primarily for armed resistance in military encounters (44 out of 71 times). Josephus uses *anthistēmi* for violent struggle 15 out of 17 times, Philo 4 out of 10. As James W. Douglass notes, Jesus' answer is set against the backdrop of the burning question of forcible resistance to Rome. In that context, "resistance" could have only one meaning: lethal violence. 22

In short, *antistēnai* means more in Matt. 5:39a than simply to "stand against" or "resist." It means to resist *violently,* to revolt or rebel, to engage in an insurrection. The logic of the text requires such a meaning: on the one hand, do not continue to be supine and complicit in your oppression; but on the other hand, do not react violently to it either. Rather, find a third way, a way that is neither submission nor assault, neither flight nor fight, a way that can secure your human dignity and begin to change the power equation, even now, before the revolution. Turn your cheek, thus indicating to the one who backhands you that his attempts to shame you into servility have failed. Strip naked and parade out of court, thus taking the momentum of the law and the whole debt economy and flipping them, jujitsu-like, in a burlesque of legality. Walk a second mile, surprising the occupation troops with a sudden challenge to their control. These are, of course, not rules to be followed legalistically, but examples to spark an infinite variety of creative responses in new and changed circumstances. They break the cycle of humiliation with humor and even ridicule, exposing the injustice of the System. They recover for the poor a modicum of initiative that can force the oppressor to see them in a new light.

There is good reason to suspect that the original form of this saying about resistance is best preserved in the New Testament epistles. In Romans 12 we find more allusions to Jesus' teaching than anywhere else in all Paul's letters. Among them are:

12:14—"Bless those who persecute you; bless and do not curse them"; cf. Matt. 5:44 // Luke 6:28.
12:15—"Rejoice with those who rejoice, weep with those who weep"; cf. Matt. 5:4, 12 // Luke 6:21, 23.
12:17—"Do not repay anyone evil for evil" and 12:21—"Do not be overcome by evil, but overcome evil with good"; cf. Matt. 5:39a.

Both 1 Thess. 5:15 ("See that none of you repays evil for evil") and 1 Pet. 3:9 ("Do not repay evil for evil or abuse for abuse; but, on the contrary, repay with a blessing") preserve the same saying as Rom. 12:17. We appear to have here an extremely early fixed catechetical tradition, predating even the earliest preserved epistle.[23] The teaching on nonviolence thus clearly antedates the Jewish War and was not a reaction to it.

The expression "Repay no one evil for evil" conveys precisely the sense we were driven to for Matt. 5:39a: Do not mirror evil. The examples that follow in 5:39b-41 in fact presuppose some such sense. Could this ancient catechetical tradition have originally stood, then, in Matthew's tradition? If "Do not repay evil for evil" and "Do not forcibly resist evil" have equivalent meanings, could they simply be different versions of the same tradition? We can now, for the first time, answer a cautious yes to that question. George Howard has recently discovered what he regards as an early Hebrew text of the Gospel of Matthew, which reads at 5:39a, "But I say to you, *do not repay evil for evil*." [24] If this remarkable find is indeed as ancient as Howard argues, it reinforces our suspicion that Matt. 5:39a and the catechetical saying in Rom. 12:17; 1 Thess. 5:15; and 1 Pet. 3:9 are indeed derived from the same tradition. And even if this text is not as early as Howard thinks, its very existence, from *any* period, proves that at least one Hebrew version regarded "Do not repay evil for evil" as the proper way to read Matt. 5:39a.

If this line of argument is correct, then the original version of v. 39a was something closer to "Do not repay evil for evil." This is the sense that vv. 39b-42 require. The logic of Jesus' examples in Matt. 5:39b-42 goes beyond both inaction and overreaction, capitulation and murderous counterviolence, to a new response, fired in the crucible of love, that promises to liberate the oppressed from evil even as it frees the oppressor from sin. "Do not react violently to evil, do not counter evil in kind, do not let evil dictate the terms of your opposition, do not let violence draw you into mimetic rivalry"—this is the revolutionary principle, recognized from earliest times, that Jesus articulates as the basis for nonviolently engaging the Powers.

Perhaps the alternatives we are discussing can be more graphically presented by a chart:

Jesus' Third Way

- Seize the moral initiative
- Find a creative alternative to violence
- Assert your own humanity and dignity as a person
- Meet force with ridicule or humor
- Break the cycle of humiliation
- Refuse to submit or accept the inferior position
- Expose the injustice of the system
- Take control of the power dynamic
- Shame the oppressor into repentance
- Stand your ground
- Make the Powers make decisions for which they are not prepared
- Recognize your own power
- Be willing to suffer instead of retaliate
- Force the oppressor to see you in a new light
- Deprive the oppressor of a situation where a show of force is effective
- Be willing to undergo the penalty of breaking unjust laws
- Die to fear of the old order and its rules
- Seek the oppressor's transformation

Flight	Fight
Submission	Armed revolt
Passivity	Violent rebellion
Withdrawal	Direct retaliation
Surrender	Revenge

Gandhi insisted that no one join him who was not willing to take up arms to fight for independence. They could not freely renounce what they had not entertained. One cannot pass directly from "Flight" to "Jesus' Third Way." One needs to pass through the "fight" stage, if only to discover one's own inner strength and capacity for violence (see fig. 1). One need not actually become violent, but one does need to know one's fury at injustice and care enough to be willing to fight and, if necessary, die for its eradication. Only then can such a person freely renounce violence and embrace active nonviolence.

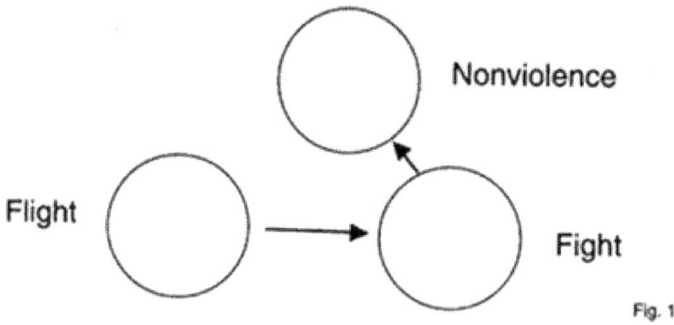

Fig. 1

It is dangerous to be engaged in nonviolent struggle beside people who have not yet learned about their inner violence.

Jesus' third way did not arise out of a vacuum. It was a logical development of Israel's idealized concept of the holy war. One line of Israel's development can be seen as the movement from (1) submission, to (2) holy war, to (3) prophetic peacemaking. As Paul Valliere observes, the Genesis creation narratives are extraordinary, compared with other creation accounts from that time and area, precisely because of their refusal to count war as part of the nature of things. War is not the means used to subdue the cosmos, as in Hesiod's *Theogony* or the Babylonian *Enuma Elish*. Peace is the norm of the cosmos from the beginning. "Holy war" enters the narrative as God's sovereign act of liberating the Hebrew slaves from Egypt without their striking a blow. God, and God alone, fought on their behalf. God would drive out the inhabitants of Canaan by means of hornets, terror, panic, or pestilence, not the sword (Exod. 23:28; Deut. 7:20; Josh. 24:12). Jericho's walls collapsed after ritual, not military, action (though the mopping-up operation was carried out by Hebrew warriors—Joshua 6), and God overcame the Midianites by means of three hundred men armed only with torches and trumpets (Judges 7). Even the "ban," the practice of "devoting" booty to God by destroying it, can be seen as the imposition of extremely ascetical limits on the enjoyment of the fruits of war. (It also reveals the depth to which the myth of redemptive violence had penetrated Israel's theology and politics.) At least one strand of Israelite reflection regarded holy war, not as a war fought for or in the name of God, but as *a war that God alone fights.*

With its defection to monarchy, however, Israel began waging political wars that the false prophets tried to legitimate as holy. Israel came to trust in military might rather than God (Hos. 10:13); yet God continued to offer to save the people, but not "by bow, or by sword, or by war, or by horses, or by horsemen" (Hos. 1:7; see also Zech. 4:6). The unique contribution of the true prophets was their refusal to turn holy war into political war. This led them at times to declare that God was waging holy war *against* faithless Israel. They recognized the impossibility of maintaining a standing army and concluding treaties with foreign powers while still preserving Israel's utter reliance on God alone to fight for them. The prophets turned to a kind of "prophetic pacifism." Holy war came to be seen as a contest fought not with the sword but with the divine word: truth against power. In a new twist on the warrior asceticism of old, the Hebrew prophets waged solitary moral combat against virtually an entire people who were convinced that wars of national defense, liberation, or conquest were their only hope of salvation. Israel had succumbed to the myth of redemptive violence, but the prophets had discovered that the word of God was a mighty sword that cut both ways, for and against God's people (cf. Heb. 4:12).[25]

Out of the heart of that prophetic tradition, Jesus engaged the Domination System in both its outer and spiritual manifestations. His teaching on nonviolence forms the charter for a way of being in the world that breaks the spiral of violence. Jesus here reveals a way to fight evil with all our power without being transformed into the very evil we fight. It is a way—the only way possible—of not becoming what we hate. "Do not counter evil in kind"—this insight is the distilled essence, stated with sublime simplicity, of the experience of those Jews who had, in Jesus' very lifetime, so courageously and effectively practiced nonviolent direct action against Rome. Jesus, in short, abhors both passivity and violence. He articulates, out of the history of his own people's struggles, a way by which evil can be opposed without being mirrored, the oppressor resisted without being emulated, and the enemy neutralized without being destroyed. Those who have lived by Jesus' words—Leo Tolstoy, Mohandas K. Gandhi, Martin Luther King, Jr., Dorothy Day, César Chavez, Adolpho Pérez Esquivel—point us to a new way of confronting evil whose potential for personal and social transformation we are only beginning to grasp today.

Making Jesus' Teaching Operational

Nothing is deadlier to the spirit of Jesus' teaching on nonviolence than regarding it legalistically. Women beaten by their husbands are told to "turn the other cheek" and let the man continue to brutalize them, with no reference to Jesus' actual intention. If we reenter the freedom Jesus sought to establish in these sayings, we would rather counsel the battered to seize the initiative, force her husband to recognize her rights, expose his behavior publicly, and break the vicious cycle of humiliation, guilt, and bruising.

In the American legal context, according to the social workers I have consulted, the most loving thing a battered wife could do might be to have her husband arrested. This would bring the issue out into the open, put him under a court injunction that would mean jail if the violence continues, position him so that his self-interest is served by joining a therapy group for batterers, and thus potentially begin a process that would not only deliver the woman from being battered, but free the man from battering as well. I cite this suggestion because it is at the antipodes to our sentimental notions of what love entails. Perhaps there are better ways; but they will certainly involve tough love, not the limp collusion that so often masquerades as Christian.

To require a boy who is being bullied at school literally to "turn the other cheek" can simply encourage cowardice. Of course, a nonviolent solution would be preferable, and one can usually be found. But it is a fundamental rule of the life of the spirit that people cannot sacrifice something they do not have. Jesus did not invite slaves to abandon their sense of dignity as a way of mortifying the ego; their egos had been mortified a thousand times, so much so that the vast majority had internalized a sense of their inferiority. They could not give up their self-esteem for the sake of God; they had been robbed of it long since by the very structure of servitude. It was precisely to restore that dignity and self-esteem that Jesus counseled nonviolent assertiveness.

If, then, a boy is willing and able to fight, even at the cost of great pain, then one might have a right to encourage him to renounce violence and seek a third way. But to duck violence under cover of the gospel, without having found the inner strength to fight for one's own rights, is both dishonest and craven. Gandhi was adamant that nothing could be done with a coward, but that from a violent person one could make a nonviolent one. "I do believe that, where there is only a choice between cowardice and violence, I would advise violence. . . . But I believe that nonviolence is infinitely superior to violence."[26] "At every meeting I repeated the warning that unless they felt that in nonviolence they had come into possession of a force infinitely superior to the one they had and in the use of which they were adept, they should have nothing to do with nonviolence and resume the arms they possessed before."[27]

Early on, before he had become fully committed to satyagraha, Gandhi so despaired of teaching his people the art of courageous nonviolence that he even proposed that they enlist in the army, reasoning that men who had risked their lives on the battlefield would be better prepared to risk their lives in a nonviolent struggle.[28] Something of the same militancy can be seen in Jesus' call to a potential disciple in Luke 9:60, where discipleship is comparable to the conscripting of recruits for a holy war. In normal circumstances, no grounds exist that justify flouting the filial obligation to bury one's father; but if the issue is war or something even more urgent (the reign of God), there is no time for normal obligations.

What looks to the entire world like passivity may in fact be the third way. When Jackie Robinson became the first black player in major league baseball, Branch Rickey of the Brooklyn Dodgers pressed this intensely competitive athlete to agree that for three years he would take whatever abuse was heaped on him without a word. Robinson finally said, "Mr. Rickey, are you looking for a negro who is afraid to fight back?" Rickey replied, "I'm looking for a ballplayer with guts enough not to fight back."[29]

Humor and wit can help preserve the humanity of all parties in a conflict. Once, a squatter community in South Africa found its shelter infested with lice. When the authorities refused to fumigate it, the leadership committee took bags full of lice-infested blankets to the administrator's office and dumped them on his floor. They got immediate action.[30]

A black woman was walking on a South African street with her children, when a white man, passing, spat in her face. She stopped and said, "Thank you, and now for the children." He was so nonplused he was unable to respond.

Sometimes the wit can have a barb, as when Bishop Desmond Tutu was walking by a construction site on a temporary sidewalk the width of one person. A white man appeared at the other end, recognized Tutu, and said, "I don't give way to gorillas." At which Tutu stepped aside, made a deep sweeping gesture, and said, "Ah yes, but I do."

Ridicule even has a role in shocking people awake to the meaning of their acts. One of the world's most peaceful peoples, the Mbuti, hunter-gatherers of northeast Zaïre, defuse anger through laughter. If a group of children making noise wake a man from his nap, who then shouts at or slaps a child, all the children come rushing together and play the adult role, shouting and slapping each other. The adult, seeing himself ridiculed this way, must either retreat or join the laughter in his own self-ridicule.[31]

Similarly, Chinese students, forbidden to demonstrate against government policy, donned masks of the communist leadership and carried signs: "Support Martial Law," "Support Dictatorship," "Support Inflation."

During the struggle of Solidarity in Poland, one group dressed in Santa Claus outfits distributed scarce sanitary napkins to women as a way of dramatizing the difficulty of obtaining essentials. When these Santas were arrested, other Santas showed up at jail insisting that the others were frauds, that they were the *real* Santas.

Gandhi spoke of entering jail as a bridegroom enters his bride's chamber, as a way of stressing the importance of being fearless of the government's punishment. So when he was arrested during the civil disobedience campaign of 1930, a mass meeting was organized to *congratulate* the government for arresting him. It is difficult for a government to arrest well-wishers![32]

Jesus does not proclaim a nonviolence for the perfect, but for the violent. His is a practical, achievable nonviolence that can be performed by ordinary people. The beatitude about the meek can be translated as "Blessed are the *nonviolent,* for they shall inherit the earth" (Matt. 5:5).[33] Jesus' way is not individualistic, but collective; it usually involves the actions of organizations, communities, social classes, or racial groups. Not just young men of war-making age, but all sectors of the population can participate, from babies to the elderly. "Tradition here is for the men to keep the women in their houses," said Murabak Awad during the Palestinian *Intifada.* "But now husbands are allowing their wives out, to engage in political activity. The women are pouring all their energy into it. Nonviolent action can draw all of the population together and create a powerful unity."[34]

Nor is Jesus' third way averse to using coercion. His way aims at converting the opponent; failing that, it hopes for accommodation, where the opponent is willing to make some changes simply to get the protesters off his back. But if that too fails, nonviolence entails coercion: the opponent is forced to make change rather than suffer the loss of power, even though he remains hostile.[35] But Jesus' way does not employ violent coercion.

As Barbara Deming puts it, in nonviolence one "exerts force upon the other, not tearing him away from himself but tearing from him only that which is not properly his own, the strength which has been loaned to him by all those who have been giving him obedience."[36] The civil rights marchers who crossed the bridge in Selma, Alabama, without a parade permit forced the authorities to decide between two courses, either of which would damage their position: either they allowed the blacks to march, thus recognizing the legitimacy of their protest; or they forcibly stopped it, thus exposing their own endemic violence for all the world to see. The choice of violence proved to be catastrophic for white supremacy and a major victory for the marchers, despite the injuries incurred.

Finally, nonviolence must not be misconstrued as a way of avoiding conflict. The "peace" that the gospel brings is never the absence of conflict, but an ineffable divine reassurance within the heart of conflict: a peace that passes understanding. Christians have all too often called for "nonviolence" when they really meant tranquility. Nonviolence, in fact, seeks out conflict, elicits conflict, exacerbates conflict, in order to bring it out into the open and lance its poisonous sores. It is not idealistic or sentimental about evil; it does not coddle or cajole aggressors, but moves against perceived injustice proactively, with the same alacrity as the most hawkish militarist.

As Eisler reminds us, a partnership society is not a society devoid of conflict. It values conflict as the inevitable price of freedom. But it handles conflict nonviolently. The Domination System, by contrast, deals with conflict by suppressing it.[37] Democracy is a state of perpetual low-level conflict—severe enough to agitate citizens into action, and mild enough to prevent that action from boiling over into violence.

The programmatic task of what we might call the "Jesus project" in the decades ahead will require moving from largely reactive, episodic, and occasional nonviolent actions to an aggressive, sustained movement. Our goal must be the training of millions of nonviolent activists who are ready, at a moment's notice, to swing into action on behalf of the humanizing purposes of God.

That struggle is not the sole preserve of Christians, of course; some of the greatest exponents of nonviolence have been non-Christian: the Hindu Gandhi, the Muslim Abdul Ghaffar Khan, the Buddhist Thich Nhat Hanh. These exponents of nonviolence have helped awaken us to its centrality in our own tradition.

And the world, and the church, are waking up! What an exciting prospect! What an auspicious opportunity! What a time to be alive!

Notes

1. Daniel Berrigan, *No Bars to Manhood* (Garden City, N.Y.: Doubleday, 1970), 57–58.

2. For a more detailed exegetical study of this passage see my article, "Neither Passivity nor Violence: Jesus' Third Way," *Forum* 7 (1991): 5–28.

3. Eduard Schweizer, *The Good News according to Matthew* (London: SPCK, 1976), 130.

4. *The Ancient Near East: An Anthology of Texts and Pictures,* ed. James B. Pritchard (Princeton: Princeton Univ. Press, 1969), 161.

5. Gandhi, in *Harijan,*March 10, 1946; cited by Mark Juergensmeyer, *Fighting with Gandhi* (San Francisco: Harper & Row, 1984), 43.

6. Josephus, *Ant.* 18.55.

7. Josephus, *War* 2.169–74.

8. H. G. Liddell and R. Scott, A *Greek-English Lexicon,* 9th ed. (Oxford: Clarendon Press, 1958), 829

9. See S. Safrai and M. Stern, eds., *The Jewish People in the First Century* (Philadelphia: Fortress Press, 1987), I.2.797–98.

10. Josephus, *War* 2.427.

11. M. Rostovtzeff, "Angariae," *Klio. Beitriige zur alten Geschichte* 6 (1906): 249–58.

12. T. J. B. *Metz.* 6.3, 11a, cited by Paul Fiebig, *"angareuō,"* *Zeitschrift fur die neutestamentliche Wissenschaft* 18 (1918): 64–72.

13. *Corpus Inscriptionum Graecarum.* no. 4956, A21, cited by Edwin Hatch, *Essays in Biblical Greek* (Amsterdam: Philo, [1889] 1970), 37.

14. *Papyri greci e latini* 446 (133–137 c.e.), cited by Ramsay MacMullen, *Soldier and Civilian in the Late Roman Empire* (Cambridge: Harvard Univ. Press, 1963), 89 n. 42, my emphasis.

15. *The Theodosian Code,* ed. Clyde Pharr (Princeton: Princeton Univ. Press, 1952), sections 8.5.1, 2, 6, 7, 8.1, 11, 66.

16. Michael Grant, The *Army of the Caesars* (London: Weidenfeld & Nicolson, 1974), xxi–xxx.

17. Maurice, *Strategikon* 7.3, my emphasis; cited by C. E. Brand, *Roman Military Laws* (Austin: Univ. of Texas, 1968), 21. See also 4.10 (Brand, 195).

18. Brand, *Roman Military Laws* 104–6.

19. Horsley, *Jesus and the Spiral of Violence* (San Francisco: Harper & Row, 1987), 318–26.

20. See Sharon H. Ringe, *Jesus, Liberation, and the Biblical Jubilee,* Overtures to Biblical Theology (Philadelphia: Fortress, 1985).

21. Horsley, *Jesus and the Spiral of Violence,* 32.

22. James W. Douglass, *The Non-Violent Cross* (New York: Macmillan, 1968), 193.

23. Victor Paul Furnish, *The Love Commandment in the New Testament* (Nashville: Abingdon Press, 1972), 106; C. E. B. Cranfield, *The Epistle to the Romans,* International Critical Commentary, 2 vols. (Edinburgh: T & T Clark, 1975–79), 1:645.

24. George Howard, *The Gospel of Matthew according to a Primitive Hebrew Text* (Macon: Mercer Univ. Press, 1987), 20–21.

25. Paul Valliere, *Holy War and Pentecostal Peace* (New York: Seabury Press, 1983), 46–86.

26. Devi Prasad, "Gandhi's Attitude Towards Violent Struggles for Freedom, *"International Fellowship of Reconciliation Report,* April 1980, 20; citing *Young India,* 11 August 1920.

27. Gandhi, in Joan V. Bondurant, *Conquest of Violence* (Princeton: Princeton Univ. Press, 1958), 139.

28. Eknath Easwaran, *A Man to Match His Mountains: Badshah Khan, Nonviolent Soldier of Islam* (Petaluma, Calif.: Nilgiri Press, 1984), 194.

29. *The New York Times,* April 12, 1987, 8.

30. Africa Watch Committee, *No Neutral Ground: South Africa's Confrontation with the Activist Churches* (New York: Human Rights Watch, 1989), 65.

31. Colin M. Turnbull, "The Politics of Non-Aggression (Zaire)," in *Teaching Non-Aggression,* ed. Ashley Montague (New York: Oxford Univ. Press, 1978), 187–91.

32. George Lakey, *Powerful Peacemaking* (Philadelphia: New Society Publishers, 1987), 112.

33. Bernard Haring, *The Healing Power of Peace* (New York: Paulist Press, 1986), 25.

34. Marjorie Hope and James Young, "Christians and Nonviolent Resistance in the Occupied Territories," *Christian Century* 105 (April 27, 1988): 432.

35. Rob Fairmichael, "Nonviolent Methods;' *Dawn Train* 9 (Belfast, N. Ireland, 1990), 29–30.

36. Barbara Deming, "On Revolution and Equilibrium," cited by Robert L. Holmes, *Nonviolence in Theory and Practice* (Belmont, Calif.: Wadsworth Publishing Co., 1990), 101.

37. Riane Eisler and David Love, *The Partnership Way* (San Francisco: Harper San Francisco, 1990), 116.

12

The Acid Test: Loving Enemies

Walter Wink suggests with great seriousness that the primary spiritual question of our age is, "How can we find God in our enemies?" The answers to this provocative question just might save us from self-destruction and prevent those who resist domination from establishing new dominations that perpetuate the cycle of violence and oppression. Love for enemies humanizes aggressive nonviolence, which, apart from such love, can cynically degenerate into a strategy for revenge rather than for transformation of the personal and the social. By identifying love of enemies as the rationale for nonviolent resistance to evil, Wink grounds both the struggles for social, political and economic justice and for the worth and dignity of all people—even that of the oppressor—in the "very nature of God" as Jesus understood and experienced it. Our very createdness places us in solidarity with our enemies, but our solidarity with our enemies goes beyond the fact that, like us, our enemies are creations of a good and loving God. We also find solidarity with our enemies in fallenness, in brokenness, in sinfulness, in evil. As Wink notes, "If God were not compassionate toward us, we would be lost. And if God is compassionate toward us, with all our unredeemed evil, then God must treat our enemies the same way"—and so should we. Wink asserts that enemies bring invaluable gifts to us. They provide a dynamic whereby we, by recognizing and peeling back our projections upon them, might encounter and acknowledge our own shadow, thereby opening us to their humanity and our own.

Source: Wink 1992: Excerpted from Chapter 14

> *Why this sudden unrest and confusion?*
> *(How solemn their faces have become.)*
> *Why are the streets and squares clearing quickly,*
> *And all return in their homes, so deep in thought?*

> *Because night is here but the barbarians*
> *have not come.*
> *Some people arrived from the frontiers,*
> *And they said that there are no longer any*
> *barbarians.*
> *And now what shall become of us without*
> *any barbarians?*
> *Those people were kind of a solution.*
> —C. P. Cavafy, "Expecting the Barbarians"[1]

In the spiritual renaissance that I believe is coming to birth, it will not be the message of Paul that this time galvanizes hearts, as in the Reformation and the Wesleyan revival, but the human figure of Jesus. And in the teaching of Jesus, the sayings on nonviolence and love of enemies will hold a central place. Not because they are more true than any others, but because they are the only means known for overcoming domination without creating new dominations.

I submit that the ultimate religious question today should no longer be the Reformation's question, "How can I find a gracious God?" but rather, "How can we find God in our enemies?" What guilt was for Luther, the enemy has become for us: the goad that can drive us to God. What has often been a purely private affair—justification by faith through grace—has now, in our age, grown to embrace the world. As John Stoner comments, we can no more save ourselves from our enemies than we can save ourselves from sin, but God's amazing grace offers to save us from both.[2]

There is, in fact, no other way to God for our time but through the enemy, for loving the enemy has become the key both to human survival in the nuclear age and to personal transformation. The end of the Cold War has eased, not solved, the nuclear crisis, which now shows signs of proliferation to smaller states not constrained by the danger of total war. Now border disputes and acts of aggression can be settled by nuclear brinkmanship, terrorism, or holocaust. Today, more than ever, we must turn to the God who causes the sun to rise on the evil and on the good, or we may have no more sunrises.

Jesus' teachings about nonviolent direct action and love of enemies are also the acid tests of true Christianity. Just as in the lore of exorcism the Devil cannot bear to utter the name of God, so our false prophets today cannot tolerate mention of the love of enemies. The Rev. Greg Dixon, a former state chairman and National Secretary for the Moral Majority, recently urged his followers to pray for the death of their opponents, claiming, "We're tired of turning the other cheek . . . good heavens, that's all that we have done."[3] The Rev. Jerry Falwell and his allies are champions of the warrior mentality and of peace through strength; Jesus' way of creative nonviolence is for them indistinguishable from supine cowardice. As James A. Sanders reminds us, no false prophet can ever conceive of God as being God also of the enemy.[4]

Jesus' way of nonviolence and love of enemies has frequently been dismissed as impractical, idealistic, and out of touch with the need of nations and oppressed peoples to defend themselves. No such irrelevancy is charged against the myth of redemptive violence, however, despite the fact that it fails at least half the time. Its exaltation of the salvific powers of killing, and the privileged position it is accorded by intellectuals and politicians alike (to say nothing of theologians), make redemptive violence the preferred myth of Marxists and capitalists, fascists and leftists, atheists and churchgoers alike. Redemptive violence is the prevailing ideology of the Institute of Religion and Democracy and segments of the World Council of Churches, of *Christianity Today* and *Christianity and Crisis,* of much of liberation theology and much of conservative theology.

Then came 1989–1990, years of unprecedented political change, years of miracles, surpassing any such concentration of political transformations in human history, even the Exodus. In 1989 alone, thirteen nations comprising 1,695,100,000 people, over 32 percent of humanity, experienced nonviolent revolutions that succeeded beyond anyone's wildest expectations in every case but China, and were completely nonviolent (on the part of the participants) in every case but Romania and parts of the southern U.S.S.R. The nations involved were Poland, East Germany, Hungary, Czechoslovakia, Bulgaria, Romania, Albania, Yugoslavia, Mongolia, the Soviet Union, Brazil, Chile, and China. Since then Nepal, Palau, and Madagascar have undergone nonviolent struggles, Latvia, Lithuania, and Estonia have achieved independence nonviolently, the Soviet Union has dissolved into a commonwealth of republics, and more than a dozen countries have moved toward multiparty democracy, including Mongolia, Gabon, Bangladesh, Benin, and Algeria. If we add all the countries touched by major nonviolent actions just since 1986 (the Philippines, South Korea, South Africa, Israel, Burma, New Caledonia, and New Zealand), and the other nonviolent struggles of our century—the independence movements of India and Ghana, the overthrow of the Shah in Iran, the struggle against authoritarian governments and landowners in Argentina and Mexico, and the civil rights, United Farm Worker, anti-Vietnam and antinuclear movements in the United States—the figure reaches 3,337,400,000: a staggering 64 percent of humanity!

All this in the teeth of the assertion, endlessly repeated, that nonviolence does not work in the "real" world.

It appears as if the nonviolent way articulated by Jesus as the heart of the gospel message has finally found an unwitting following. The dream of abolishing war, like child sacrifice and exposure, gladiatorial combat, slavery, cannibalism, colonialism, and dueling, seems to be finally approaching the first stages of realization. The significance of what is happening needs to be set in the widest possible frame. Humanity has arisen, it would appear, as the means by which the evolutionary process has become conscious of itself. And what emerged with Jesus, according to Gerd Theissen, is the decisive protest against the brutality of natural selection, a protest that had already been proclaimed with increasing clarity in the religion of Israel, beginning with the mass exodus of the Hebrew slaves from Egypt. Jesus rejects selection of the "fittest," both in nature and in culture, and declares in favor of those whom the natural process seeks to winnow out: the meek, the poor, the crippled, the sick, the retarded, outcasts, pariahs, and the possessed.[5]

Jesus was not the first to practice nonviolence; indeed, he clearly learned it from his own people. But his manner of incarnating nonviolence marked an evolutionary breakthrough that rejected the pattern of domination of the weak by the strong. He offers the weak a way of affirming their essential humanity, not sometime in the far-off future, but here, now, in precisely the situation of oppression itself.

Solidarity in Poland proved that Jesus' nonviolent way could be lived even under the circumstances of a communist regime and martial law. People said to one another, in effect, "Start doing the things you think should be done, and start being what you think society should become. Do you believe in freedom of speech? Then speak freely. Do you love the truth? Then tell it. Do you believe in an open society? Then act in the open. Do you believe in a decent and humane society? Then behave decently and humanely." This behavior actually caught on, leading to an "epidemic of freedom in the closed society." By acting "as if" Poland were already a free country, Solidarity *created* a free country. The "as if" ceased to be pretense and became actuality. Within ten years, Solidarity had taken over the government. This is not only a graphic example of a social revolution becoming a political revolution, but it constitutes, in Jonathan Schell's words, a new chapter in the history of revolution: a revolution in revolution.[6]

Nonviolent direct action can be used for causes some of us would not support, though the requirement that one voluntarily suffer the consequences tends to weed out trivial or selfish expressions of it. Likewise, it can be used for revenge or to manipulate or humiliate others without concern for their genuine wellbeing. Without love for enemies, nonviolence would be just another arrow in the quiver of coercive force. The rationale for Jesus' nonviolent way is neither the short-term effectiveness of nonviolent strategies, nor the long-term self-interest of the species, but rather the very nature of God.

God Is All-Inclusive

We are to love our enemies, says Jesus, because God does. God makes the "sun rise on the evil and on the good, and sends rain on the righteous and on the unrighteous" (Matt. 5:45). We are to love our enemies and pray for those who persecute us, so that we may be children of this strange Father-Mother, who "is kind to the ungrateful and the wicked" (Luke 6:35).

Much of what passes as religion denies the existence of such a God. Is not "God" precisely that moral force in the universe that rewards the good and punishes the evil? This had been the message of John the Baptist, and it would later be the message of the church. In John's preaching, God is depicted as verging on a massive and final counteroffensive against evil in which all evil will be exterminated. One whole side of reality will be wiped out. Ostensibly John has chaffy people in mind. God will obliterate them by fire (Matt. 3:7-12 // Luke 3:7-18).

Jesus, by contrast, understood judgment not as an end, but as a beginning. The penitential river of fire was not to consume but to purify, not to annihilate but to redeem. Divine judgment is intended, not to destroy, but to awaken people to the devastating truth about their lives. Jesus seizes the apocalyptic vision of impending doom and hurls it into time, into the present encounter with God's unexpected and unaccountable forgiveness. Judgment now no longer is the last crushing word on a failed life, but the first word of a new creation. Jesus lived this new creation out in his table fellowship with those whom the religious establishment had branded outcasts, sinners, and renegades: the enemies of God. He did not wait for them to repent, become respectable, and do works of restitution in hopes of gaining divine forgiveness and human restoration. Instead he audaciously bursts upon these sinners with the declaration that their sins have been forgiven, prior to their repentance, prior to any acts of restitution or reconciliation. Everything is reversed: You are forgiven; now you can repent! God loves you; now you can lift your eyes to

God! The enmity is over. You were enemies and yet God accepts you! There is nothing you must do to earn this. You need only accept it.

The radicalism of Jesus' image of God is hidden by the self-evident picture he draws from nature. God clearly does not favor some with sunshine and rain, and others with darkness and drought, depending on their righteousness. Yet, in fact, society has in every possible way created the impression that only some are in God's favor and the others out. By dress, color, nationality, wealth, gender, sexual preference, education, language, looks, and health, others are meant to recognize instantly whether we are blessed or cursed, beloved or rejected.

There are enormous benefits for going along with this selective grading of human beings, and severe penalties inflicted for its rejection. For these accidents of genetics and class determine one's social location and power, and anyone who tampers with them undermines the foundations of unequal privilege. To say that God does not sit atop the pyramid of power legitimating the entire edifice, does not favor some and reject others, is to expose the entire structure as a human contrivance established in defiance of God's very nature.

Jesus' laconic mention of God's all-inclusive parental care is thus charged with an unexpected consequence for human behavior: we can love our enemies, because God does. If we wish to correspond to the central reality of the universe, we will behave as God behaves—and God embraces all, evenhandedly. This radical vision of God, already perceived by the Hebrew prophets but never popular among the resident Powers, is the basis for true human community.

Our solidarity with our enemies lies not just in our common parentage under God, but also in our common evil. God "is kind to the ungrateful and the wicked." We too, like them, live in enmity against what God desires for the world. We would like to identify ourselves as "just" and "good," but we are a mix of just and unjust, good and evil. If God were not compassionate toward us, we would be lost. And if God is compassionate toward us, with all our unredeemed evil, then God must treat our enemies the same way. As we begin to acknowledge our own inner shadow, we become more tolerant of the shadow in others. As we begin to love the enemy within, we develop the compassion we need to love the enemy without.

If however, we believe that the God who loves us hates those whom we hate, we insert an insidious doubt into our own selves. Unconsciously we know that a deity hostile toward others is potentially hostile to us as well.[7] And we know, better than anyone, that there is plenty of cause for such hostility. If God did not send sun and rain on everyone equally, God would not only not love everyone, but love no one.

Against Perfectionism

The climactic assertion in Matthew's statement about loving enemies runs, "Be perfect, therefore, as your heavenly Father is perfect" (5:48). The gospel appears to be saying two opposite things in a single breath: God loves everyone, good and bad alike, unconditionally; and God's love is conditional after all: we must be perfect. This closing line seems to fly in the face of everything Jesus has just taught. If I am not perfect then what? Rejection, isolation, the fires of hell! Our heavenly Parent no longer seems to be kind to the ungrateful and the wicked, but has now become exceedingly choosy: a God that no sensible person would want as a parent, a God who measures out love on an exact scale of deserving, a God whose love must be earned, whose wrath must be placated, whose tendencies to reject must be mollified, whose incapacity for unconditional love, mercy, and grace must be borne as a permanent wound in the Christian's psyche.

It may come as immediate relief to learn that *Jesus could not have said, "Be perfect."* There was no such word, or even concept, in Aramaic or Hebrew. And for good reason. The Second Commandment had forbidden the making of graven images (Exod. 20:4). Israel consequently never developed the visual arts. The word used by Matthew, *teleios*, was, however, a Greek aesthetic term. It described the perfect geometric form, or the perfect sculpture. It was seldom used in ethical discourse, since moral perfection is not within the grasp of human beings, and would even have been regarded, in Greek piety, as a form of hybris.

Matthew appears to have taken *teleios* over from the Greek translation of Deut. 18:13, where the term was used to render the Hebrew word *tamim* ("whole, complete, finished, entire, to have integrity"). The NRSV translates it, "You must remain completely loyal to the Lord your God." In Israel, the closest thing to the notion of perfection was being without blemish. This was a purely negative and functional idea. A man ugly beyond tolerance could still officiate at a Jewish sacrifice as long as he was not maimed, diseased, or deformed. There were no positive norms of beauty, only negative criteria of exclusion.

Among the Greeks, perfection did not accrue to people, but to works of art. In the Middle Ages, Greek and Hebrew thought coalesced, with sin taking the place of blemish. Perfection was negatively defined as not behaving, or even not thinking, in certain ways. But the sense of sin was so profound that moral perfectionism was no factor at all except among the "spiritual athletes," the ascetics, who made it their whole life's task to achieve moral perfection. It was not until the Enlightenment, with its reintroduction of Greek aesthetic norms in neoclassical art and its search for universals, that widespread moralistic perfectionism became really imaginable. The merger of Protestant religious egalitarianism and Enlightenment rational equalitarianism now for the first time made the ideal of sinlessness—a heresy on its face—not only a cultural goal but a profound obsession. The fact that many Protestant churches officially espoused justification by grace alone scarcely checked the advance of perfectionistic moralism. The Enlightenment ideal of humanity perfecting itself had so deeply penetrated Western culture that deviance was defined as failure to live up to social norms that one now had no excuse (such as human sinfulness) for violating, and that offered no restitution (such as forgiveness). Thus perfectionism is not simply a characteristic of Protestantism, but an artifact of Western culture generally.[8]

Placed in its context within the rest of the paragraph, Jesus' saying about behaving like God becomes abundantly clear. We are not to be perfect, but, like God, all-encompassing, loving even those who have least claim or right to our love. Even toward enemies we are to be indiscriminate, all-inclusive, forgiving, understanding. We are to regard the enemy as beloved of God every bit as much as we. We are to be compassionate, as God is compassionate.

This saying underscores Jesus' rejection of the holiness code as it was interpreted by his contemporaries. Mercy (God's all-inclusive love) is deliberately contrasted with exclusivity and segregation. His hearers could scarcely miss the echo of Lev. 19:2 here, except that its "Be holy, for I the Lord your God am holy" has been altered to headline Jesus' new emphasis: "Be merciful, just as your Father is merciful," as Luke so much more effectively renders it (6:36).[9]

A gesture of embrace makes the point physiologically a thousand times more eloquently than any words. Jesus wants us to behave toward enemies as he has discovered God does.

Jesus does not call for "wholeness," though that would have been a better translation than "perfect." For "wholeness" places all the focus on us, and Jesus points us away from ourselves to love our *enemies*. All-inclusive love is his goal, even if broken, contaminated by elements of our own unredeemed shadow, intermittent. Again the gesture: embracing *everyone*. To do so is not to be perfect. It is, according to Jesus, an entirely possible human act, because with the command God supplies the power to do it. He is not urging us to a perfection of being-in-ourselves, but to abandon all dreams of perfection and to embrace those we feel are least perfect, least deserving, and most threatening to our lives. "You therefore must be all-inclusive, as your heavenly Abba is all-inclusive."

Jesus is not demanding of us a perfection that we cannot attain and so driving us, by the cudgel of law, into the arms of grace. Yet there is a role for grace here: the inbreaking reign of God, which makes what was impossible under the Domination System suddenly achievable. We cannot will ourselves into such new behaviors, for the will is merely the total organized personality of the moment, and the strength of will depends not on exhortation or trying harder, but on the strength of the factors that enter into its organization.[10] What frees us for the radical new behaviors of the new social order that Jesus proclaimed is not a willing, but a giving of ourselves wholly to the God who reveals and brings this new reality. That full self-offering to God creates a new organization of the personality, so that now "the one who believes in me will also do the works that I do and, in fact, will do greater works than these, because I am going to the Father" (John 14:12).

Of course we will fail to realize the fullness of Jesus' vision. We will compromise it, and whittle him down to our size to avoid the possibilities that a larger life might prompt in us. We may cling to our class, racial, and gender interests and rationalize them with the purest of orthodoxy. God forgives all that, in advance. And because we are forgiven, we can repent. But that forgiveness is no inducement to stay trapped in our conditioning, for we are now free from having to measure up to other people's standards of what is required for our salvation. We are animated by love, excitement, and the "hunger and thirst after justice" that draws us continually to transcend our social location for the sake of that better world for which we long.

The perfectionist misreading of Jesus' text about loving enemies leads to a crowning irony: the attempt to will to love enemies in order to become perfect makes the love of enemies a psychological impossibility. If we have to be perfect in order to earn God's grudging love, then what do we do with those aspects of ourselves that are not perfect and that we know will never be? What do we do with our tempers, our lust, our cowardice, our greed, our indifference to the suffering of others? If we wish to continue the game of perfectionism at all (and it is a game, played on us to our detriment by the Great Deluder), we must repress all that evil. Out of sight, out of mind—but not out of the psyche! Then, when we encounter people who remind us of the things we hate about ourselves and have repressed, we will involuntarily project onto them what has been evoked in our own unconscious. We are therefore systematically prevented from loving our enemies because we need them as targets for our projections. By thus discharging our hatred on external enemies, we can achieve a partial release from the pent-up energy festering in the unconscious. The perfectionist reading of this text thus stands Jesus' intention on its head, and makes all-inclusive love of enemies literally impossible.

Perfectionism has a secret and unacknowledged *need* for enemies. Perfectionists are perfect only by comparison. They must have someone to look down on. But this is the structure that first gave birth to the ancient Babylonian myth of redemptive violence. Reality is split into two parts, good and evil, and salvation resides in identifying oneself wholly with the good side and projecting all one's evil on the bad. This approach can last only so long as insight about one's shadow side can be prevented.

Paul Tillich once commented, that "the weakness of the fanatic is that those whom he fights have a secret hold upon him."[11] When we project our evil onto others, we establish a symbiotic relationship with them as our enemies. We *require* enemies, and are secretly fascinated by their evil, which at some level we wish we could do. Secretly, worshipers of order are always votaries of chaos. They may publicly praise Marduk, but in the private citadels of the unconscious they adore Tiamat. Without an enemy, without conflict, without some external threat to unify the people, there is no incentive to pay taxes for a standing army. Marduk must have a Tiamat to subdue, or else he will have to invent one. Nothing threatens order so much as peace. Peace, as William Graham Sumner once remarked, is the problem that war is required to solve.[12] It will be interesting, with the ending of the Cold War, to see what new parade of scapegoats, enemies, and barbarians are invented to carry the national shadow. Saddam Hussein has already performed that role splendidly. Who will be next?

The Enemy's Gift

Once the spell of the perfectionist reading has been broken, we begin to see just how far from perfect Jesus assumed we are. "Why do you see the speck in your neighbor's eye, but do not notice the log in your own eye? Or how can you say to your neighbor, 'Let me take the speck out of your eye,' while the log is in your own eye? You hypocrite, first take the log out of your own eye, and then you will see clearly to take the speck out of your neighbor's eye" (Matt. 7:3-5 // Luke 6:41-42).

This is the earliest known teaching of projection. We have scarcely begun to trace the implications of Jesus' discovery of projection; his entire understanding of evil is the fruit of it. The "splinter" in the other's eye is a chip off the same log that is in one's own eye. We see in the other what we would not see in ourselves. But why is it a *log* in the eye of the beholder? Normally we say, "I may be (somewhat bad—a splinter), but *that* person is (really bad—a log)." Why has Jesus inverted that conventional way of putting it?

Because the log in my eye totally blinds me. I can see nothing objectively. Remove the log, and I can see to help my neighbor remove his or her splinter. In workshops on this theme June and I invite people to name an enemy and list all the things they dislike about that person (or group or movement or nation). Then we ask them to go through that list and ask how many of those characteristics are true also of them (or our group or movement or nation). The common elements identify our projections. These can be taken into our meditation, prayer, and spiritual guidance, to see what they have to teach us about ourselves. (Not all elements will be common. Some people may be objectively hostile. Our scores may range from zero to one hundred percent.)

One pastor wrote of his "enemy," "He wants to be in on every decision whether he is involved or not." This was one of the characteristics he had ticked off his list that was also true of him. The "enemy" was a lay leader who insisted that every decision made by any duly authorized group in the church had to be confirmed by him. The pastor, who saw the same tendency in himself, acknowledged that both he and the lay leader had a deep need to control everything.

> "Why do you need to control everything?" he was asked.
> "Because if things go wrong I'll get blamed."
> "What fear lies behind that need to control everything?"
> "The fear that everything will just crumble. That I'll be a failure who's not loved."
> "Can you think back to times in your life when you've felt this way?" He could. "Now, put yourself in your enemy's shoes. What fear drives him to need so much control?"
> "He's a retired farmer who milked five hundred cows a day. That's a big operation. He's sixty-six, and he's just turned the farm over to his son. I think he feels his life is slipping away from him. And here I come trying to force him to release control on the whole church, too!"

The pastor needed to discover this dynamic because it was important to stop this man's autocratic behavior. But it was also necessary to be aware of his own tendencies to autocracy. Otherwise they would simply get locked in the unconscious power struggle. But he must not give in to the other man either. He needs to assert his authority as a spiritual leader of the church. But to sense the pain and panic, the desperation of this man, will make it easier to love and understand him.

Another, a woman deeply involved in struggles for political justice, related that her enemy was President Reagan. The common quality they shared was self-righteousness.

> "How do you manifest self-righteousness?" she was asked.
> "I always feel I am right," she said.
> "Why do you need to feel you're right all the time, since it's unlikely that you are?"
> "I want God to love me."
> "What is the fear behind your social passion?"
> "That I won't do enough to be loved."
> "What do you think drives Reagan to be self-righteous, then?"
> "I suppose the same fear."
> "How would it change your attitude if you realized that you and Reagan are no different in kind from each other— different in content, yes, but no different in kind?"

She did not like this idea, but she herself had established the commonality from the outset. Gradually her face softened. The realization was humbling, deflating—the recognition that she and Reagan were one humanity together.

These "revelations" (and they are precisely that) need to be treasured, because that is the gift our enemy may be able to bring us: *to see aspects of ourselves that we cannot discover any other way than through our enemies.* Our friends seldom tell us these things; they are our friends precisely because they are able to overlook or ignore this part of us. The enemy is thus not merely a hurdle to be leaped on the way to God. The enemy *can be* the way to God. We cannot come to terms with our shadow except through our enemies, for we have almost no other access to those unacceptable parts of ourselves that need redeeming except through the mirror that our enemies hold up to us. This then is another, more intimate reason for loving our enemies: we are dependent on our enemies for our very individuation. We may not be able to be whole people without them.

How painfully humiliating: we not only may have a role in transforming our enemies, but our enemies can play a role in transforming us. As we become aware of our projections on our enemies, we are freed from the fear that we will overreact murderously toward them. We are able to develop an objective rage at the injustices they are perpetrating while still seeing them as children of God. The energy squandered nursing hatred becomes available to God for confronting the wrong or transforming the relationship.

An understanding of the Powers makes forgiveness of our enemies easier. If our oppressors "know not what they do," if they too are also victims of the delusional system, then the real target of our hate and anger can be the System itself rather than those who carry out its bidding. "For our struggle is not against enemies of blood and flesh, but against the rulers, against the authorities, against the cosmic powers of this present darkness, against the spiritual forces of evil in the heavenly places" (Eph. 6:12).

A Catalan, Llius Mario Xirinacs, exhibits this understanding in a letter he wrote to his torturer in 1976:

> You have beaten me, arrested me, and insulted me very often. Do you know what I think, for example, when I am crouching on the ground with my hands on my head, protecting myself from your dreadful truncheon-blows? I feel extremely sad to see you obliged to hit me. It grieves me to be the occasion through which you lose your human dignity by hitting an innocent, defenseless companion. I am ashamed at the accumulation of advantages which have enabled me to choose not to go to the police under this regime, whereas you, because there was no other way out, because you come from a region which is exploited by people from my class, find yourself obliged to play this wretched part. On the one hand, myself full of possibilities, on the other, you, having fallen into the fateful trap, and reduced to being the hired strongman of the truly privileged. Injustice has made me into a man of studies, and made you into men of violence.[13]

With these words the author heaped "burning coals on their heads" (Rom. 12:20). This much-misunderstood saying does not advocate a sugarcoated vengeance. On the contrary, as Jean Goss-Mayr notes from the vantage point of a lifetime of nonviolent experience, Paul rightly stresses the aggressive nature of nonviolent love of enemies. "If we refuse to heap burning coals onto our enemies, that is, to set fire to their consciences with our own capacity for loving, they will never recognize what they are doing."[14] Douglas J. Elwood thus proposes translating Rom. 12:20, "for by doing this you will make him *burn with shame*."[15]

In some ways we may *need* enemies. On purely sociological grounds, churches would be much healthier if they had a stronger sense of their enemies.

Enemies define what the church is against. They help provide its solidarity and identity.[16]

Mainline and liberal churches should quit caterwauling about the growth of conservative churches and *be themselves* over against them. For the mainline and liberal churches have never been good at evangelism. They have always depended to a large measure for new members on people disillusioned with the authoritarianism and intellectual poverty of fundamentalism. Instead of watering down their liberal beliefs in order to seem conservative, churches with a relevant liberal or centrist message should flaunt it. They need those conservative churches in order to survive.

Love Transforms

Identifying enemies runs the risk, however, of freezing them in their role, and of blocking their conversion. Treating people as enemies will help create enemy-like reactions in them. Too great an emphasis on liberating the oppressed, too big a focus on success in nonviolent campaigns, too pragmatic an orientation to nonviolent struggle, can have the effect of dehumanizing the opponent in our minds and acts. One peace activist observed,

> We were committed to the idea of dialogue because it is an important part of our pacifist creed. But when people like Selective Service employees or career military officers actually responded to us, we withdrew from dialogue. We were afraid to acknowledge the hold that the ideals we once embraced, and which they were still living by, still had on us. We were afraid to acknowledge the similarity between the war's impact on their lives and its impact on ours. Although we kept talking about our desire for dialogue, what we really wanted was to make civil disobedience demonstrations and verbal confrontations with non-pacifists into rituals affirming our own purity.[17]

Henry Mottu's experience was similar:

> When I was twenty years old and went to jail [in Switzerland for refusing the draft] . . . I more or less consciously had the tendency simply to reverse the biblical word as if Jesus would have said: Hate your neighbor (the Swiss bankers) and love your enemy (the foreign

workers, the communists). But you see, you cannot simply reverse Jesus' maxim and suddenly fall in love with those who are not your people, who are far away, and hate the very people who used to be your neighbors. In other words, I chose to fight the battles of others, not my own battles, and I brought love of the enemies into play only to be able to hate my neighbors with a good conscience.[18]

Loving our enemies has become, in our time, the criterion of true Christian faith. It may seem impossible, yet it can be done. At no point is the inrush of divine grace so immediately and concretely perceptible as in those moments when we let go our hatred and relax into God's love. No miracle is so awesome, so necessary, and so frequent.

Ten years after the end of World War II, Hildegard and Jean Goss-Mayr met with a group of Polish Christians in Warsaw. At one point they asked, "Would you be willing to meet with Christians from West Germany? They want to ask forgiveness for what Germany did to Poland during the war and to begin to build a new relationship."

First there was silence. Then someone vehemently spoke up: "Jean and Hildegard, we love you, you are our friends, but what you are asking is impossible. Each stone of Warsaw is soaked in Polish blood! We cannot forgive!" Even after ten years, the wounds of war were just too deep.

Before the group parted for the evening, the Goss-Mayrs suggested they say the Lord's Prayer together. All joined in willingly. But at the point of praying "forgive us our sins as we forgive . . . ," the group suddenly halted their prayer. Out of the silence, the one who had spoken most vehemently said softly, "I must say yes to you. I could no more pray the Our Father, I could no longer call myself a Christian, if I refuse to forgive. Humanly speaking, I cannot do it, but God will give us his strength!" A year and a half later, the Polish and West German Christians met in Vienna. Friendships made at that meeting continue today.[19]

The command to love our enemies reminds us that our first task toward oppressors is pastoral: to help them recover their humanity. Quite possibly the struggle, and the oppression that gave it rise, have dehumanized the oppressed as well, causing them to demonize their enemies. It is not enough to become politically free; we must also become human. Nonviolence presents a chance for all parties to rise above their present condition and become more of what God created them to be. There is a spirit of generosity that is willing to submit to outrages and injustice, not in a cowardly fear of retaliation, but in order, if possible, to awaken God in the other's soul.

Joe Seremane, who was tortured almost to death by the South African police, said that, for him, Jesus' saying about doing kindness to one of "the least of these" (Matt. 25:10) refers to those in the security forces who have diminished the image of God in themselves. "So God will ask me how I treated the least of these"—his torturers!

As we stop dividing the world into "us" and "them" we can begin to see that the enemy is not monolithic; that some in the opposition feel conflict and guilt over their stance, and can be won by persuasion; that there is "that of God" in everyone that can be appealed to *if* opponents recognize we are not out to destroy them. There were many reasons for the fall of the Allende regime in Chile, some of them quite sinister; but one reason CIA pressure and rightwing opposition was effective is that the middle class began to believe leftist rhetoric that the bourgeois were enemies of the Marxist state and ought to be liquidated. To alienate so large a sector of the public, with no attempt at dialogue and persuasion, simply invited disaster.

Loving enemies is also a way of living in expectation of miracles. No one anticipated the radical new directions inaugurated by Gorbachev in the Soviet Union or de Klerk in South Africa. No one in their wildest dreams would have predicted that the secret society that has ruled South Africa since apartheid was officially launched, the Broederbond, would turn out to be quietly directing apartheid's dismantling and trying to control the reactions of the white public.[20]

People can and do change, and their change can make a fundamental difference. We must pray for our enemies, because somewhere within them is a profound longing to become synchronized with the divine Source of us both. And deep within them, that Source is trying to stir up the desire to be just.

It takes a bit of growing to recognize that our attempts at social change will never succeed until we learn to utilize the truth and strengths in our adversaries, rather than reacting to them with the brutalizing dynamics of violence. Nonviolence, at its best, seeks to activate the truth in people rather than to coerce them into *our* program. Nonviolent direct action can be misused merely to surface the worst in our opponents. We can instead help them grow toward the Light by being open to them, affirming their humanity, and praying for their transformation.

Notes

1. C. P. Cavafy, *The Complete Poems of Cavafy,* trans. Rae Dalven (New York: Harcourt, Brace & World, 1961), 19.

2. From remarks made at a meeting of peace activists at Kirkridge Retreat Center, Bangor, Pa., in 1986.

3. Cited in an undated mailing from People for the American Way.

4. James A. Sanders, "Hermeneutics in True and False Prophecy," in *From Sacred Story to Sacred Text* (Philadelphia: Fortress Press, 1987), 103.

5. Gerd Theissen, *Biblical Faith: An Evolutionary Approach* (Philadelphia: Fortress Press, 1985), 112–19.

6. Jonathan Schell, "Reflections: A Better Today," *The New Yorker,* February 3, 1986, 47, 57, 60.

7. Edwin A. Hallsten, "The Commandment That Kills—Paul and Prohibition," a paper presented to the Colloquium on Religion and Violence, New Orleans, November 16, 1990.

8. I am unable to find the source of this historical reflection, but vaguely recall hearing it from Cornel West.

9. Marcus Borg, *Conflict, Holiness and Politics in the Teachings of Jesus* (NewYork: Edwin Mellen Press, 1984), 128.

10. Reinhold Niebuhr, *An Interpretation of Christian Ethics* (New York: Living Age Books, 1956), 193.

11. Paul Tillich, *The Courage to Be* (New Haven: Yale Univ. Press, 1964), 50.

12. Cited by Robert E. Park, "The Social Function of War," in *War: Studies in Psychology, Sociology, Anthropology,* ed. Leon Bramson and George W. Goethals, rev. ed. (New York: Basic Books, 1968), 243.

13. Cited in Jean and Hildegard Goss-Mayr, *A Non-Violent Lifestyle,* ed. Gerard Houver (London: Marshall Morgan Scott, 1989), 91–92.

14. Ibid., 28.

15. Douglas J. Elwood, *Toward a Theology of People Power* (Queson City, Philippines: New Day Publishers, 1988,) 12.

16. Carl S. Dudley and Earle Hilgert, *New Testament Tensions and the Contemporary Church* (Philadelphia: Fortress Press, 1987), 114–17.

17. Chuck Noell, "Rediscovering Dialogue," *Fellowship* 42 (August–September 1976): 15.

18. Henry Mottu, sermon at the Union Theological Seminary, New York City, February 9, 1972.

19. Jim Forest, *Making Enemies Friends* (New York: Crossroad, 1988), 76–78.

20. Christopher S. Wren, "A Secret Society of Mrikaners Helps to Dismantle Apartheid," *New York Times,* October 30, 1990, A9.

PART V

The Human Being

13

Introduction

In this introduction to The Human Being: Jesus and the Enigma of the Son of the Man, *Walter Wink indicates that his purpose is to construct a "Christology from below." It is not a purely academic enterprise; he has a much more practical purpose. He is driven by his conviction that an encounter with the human Jesus just might enable us to learn something about becoming human ourselves. He gives us a series of questions, the answers to which he hopes to uncover, but he does not presume to be able to deliver "the historical Jesus" at the end of his study. The historical Jesus is beyond our grasp, but Wink will be satisfied if his work contributes "to a new myth: the myth of the human Jesus"—a narrative that facilitates the humanizing work of God.*

Source: Wink 2002: Introduction

> The historical Jesus will be to our time
> a stranger and an enigma.
> —*Albert Schweitzer*

I am puzzled that a species that has subjected virtually the entire universe to its analytical gaze and that has penetrated to the tiniest constituents of matter still knows next to nothing about how to become human. I am greatly agitated that our society seems to be losing the battle for humanization. Violence, domination, killing, disrespect, terror, environmental degradation, and want have reached intolerable levels. Likewise, I am bewildered, having lived the greater part of my life, that I know so little about becoming human myself. I am shocked that I am still largely an amalgam of conventions and opinions and so little in touch with my real thoughts and feelings. Who am I? What might I become? Why have so many of us sold out to miniaturized versions of ourselves?

These are some of the questions that prompt this study of the biblical expression "the son of the man." The farther I penetrate into the mystery of this term, the more profound and provocative it seems. I have struggled with this puzzle long enough to suspect that the real reward lies not in deciphering the riddle but in wrestling with it. It may be that "the son of the man" is a genuine enigma, an irreducible riddle. But nothing so piques the curiosity of humans as the inexplicable. Perhaps our curiosity is a symptom of a desire to become more human. Like those who have gone before and who will follow, I rise to the bait.

In this book, I explore the hypothesis that this opaque figure, the son of the man, is a catalyst for human transformation: unchanging and unchanged, yet changing those who dare to come in contact with it. It seems that within us, deeply buried or just below the surface, is something that knows better than we the contours of our true face, or that "new name that no one knows except the one who receives it," as Rev. 2:17 hints.

A word, then, about the spirit in which I conduct this inquiry. This book shares in a growing effort to cast the original truths of Christianity in molds that have more appeal for people in our day. For my part, I have been searching the records of Judaism and Christianity to see if there are other ways to interpret, and to live out, the original impulse of Jesus. I want to reflect both exegetically and theologically on how that impulse, which Jesus inaugurated, can open us to the present possibilities of the past. I do so as one deeply committed to what Jesus revealed. I believe that the churches have to a tragic extent abandoned elements of that revelation. I do not, however, wish to throw the whole enterprise overboard. The Gospels continue to feed me, as does all of Scripture, even the worst parts, and some churches are impressively faithful. But if Scripture is to speak to those who find its words dust, we will have to radically reconstitute our reading.

My supposition is that something terrible has gone wrong in Christian history. The churches have too often failed to continue Jesus' mission. I grant that the church fathers sometimes understood the implications of the gospel better than the earliest Christians who lacked the perspective of hindsight. But there is a disappointing side as well: anti-Semitism, collaboration with oppressive political regimes, the establishment of hierarchical power arrangements in the churches, the squeezing of women from leadership positions, the abandonment of radical egalitarianism, and the rule of patriarchy in church affairs. Those of us who are to varying degrees disillusioned by the churches feel that it is not only our right but our sacred obligation to delve deeply into the church's records to find answers to these legitimate and urgent questions:

- Before he was worshiped as God incarnate, how did Jesus struggle to incarnate God?
- Before he became identified as the source of all healing, how did he relate to, and how did he teach his disciples to relate to, the healing Source?
- Before forgiveness became a function solely of his cross, how did he understand people to have been forgiven?
- Before the kingdom of God became a compensatory afterlife or a future utopia adorned with all the political trappings that Jesus resolutely rejected, what did he mean by "the kingdom"?
- Before he became identified as Messiah, how did he relate to the profound meaning in the messianic image?
- Before he himself was made the sole mediator between God and humanity, how did Jesus experience and communicate the presence of God?

It is, of course, conceivable that the surviving data do not permit us to distinguish the Jesus of the Gospels from the gospel of Jesus. It is my judgment, however, that there is sufficient evidence to develop an alternative mode of access to Jesus. Specifically, traces in the Gospels provide flashes of authenticity that seem incontrovertibly to go back to Jesus or to a memory of him equally true. When we finish our quest, however, we will not have the historical Jesus "as he really was," for such a feat is impossible. If we are successful, we will have contributed, through historical reflection and interpretation, to a new myth: *the myth of the human Jesus.*

Toward that end, I have attempted to construct a Christology from below, using the son-of-the-man sayings as my guide. Our itinerary starts with the use of the expression in the Hebrew Scriptures and in later, non-canonical data. Then I focus on the pre-Easter and post-Easter son-of-the-man sayings ascribed to Jesus. I conclude with the striking parallels in Jewish mysticism and Gnosticism that show that the son of the man was an archetypal phenomenon touching even non-Christians in the ancient world. But first I turn to the presuppositions and methods that undergird this book.

14

The Human Being in the Quest for the Historical Jesus

In the opening chapter of The Human Being, *Walter Wink returns to several issues he raised almost thirty years earlier in* The Bible in Human Transformation—*the continuing "bankruptcy" of historical-critical biblical study, the false consciousness of objectivism, and the intention of the biblical material to both evoke and strengthen faith in the service of both personal and social transformation or humanization. As Wink sees it, it is precisely the "heritage of positivism and objectivism" that prevents potentially transformative encounters with the text and the reality that stands behind the text. Wink juxtaposes two "myths": the "Christ myth," with its accretions of dogma over 2000 years that mask the humanity of Jesus, and the "myth of the human Jesus," which is still being constructed. (As Wink uses the term, myth "refers to those founding narratives that provide whole societies [groups and individuals] with orientation to the world.") For Wink, the "quest for the historical Jesus" that has occupied biblical scholars for the past 200 years is not a quest for the incarnated God-man; rather it is the quest for the human Jesus. The "Christ myth," the narrative of the incarnated God-man, has been co-opted by numerous domination systems over the last two millennia to sanction oppressive and exploitative structures that privilege the few to the disadvantage of the many. In Wink's compelling exegesis, the human Jesus condemned the many forms in which social, political and economic domination are manifest. Over the centuries, the church has both cooperated with and sanctioned domination, and Wink is driven to "humanize" the church by recovering the human Jesus' "original impulse" and positioning it over against the "almost inhuman Christ of dogma" and orthodoxy.*

Source: Wink 2002: Chapter 1

A. The End of Objectivism

What stands in the way of new/ancient readings of Scripture is the heritage of positivism and objectivism—the belief that we can handle these radioactive texts without ourselves being irradiated. Biblical scholars have been exceedingly slow to grasp the implications of the Heisenberg principle: that the observer is always a part of the field being observed, and disturbs that field by the very act of observation. In terms of the interpretive task, this means that there can be no question of an objective view of Jesus "as he really was." "Objective view" is itself an oxymoron; every view is subjective, from a particular angle of vision. We always encounter the biblical text with interests. We always have a stake in our reading of it. We always have angles of vision, which can be helpful or harmful in interpreting texts. "Historical writing does not treat reality; it treats the interpreter's relation to it," according to Brian Stock.[1] "All history," said the poet Wallace Stevens, "is modern history." All meaning, says Lynn Poland, is present meaning.[2] "All truly creative scholarship in the humanities is autobiographical," says Wendy Doniger O'Flaherty.[3] "Historical criticism is a form of criticism of the present," according to Walter Kasper.[4] All that is true, but only partially. For historical criticism still can help us understand that past that holds out present meaning.

According to Hal Childs of the Guild for Psychological Studies, the past is not an object we can observe. It is an idea we have in the present about the past. History is constantly being rewritten from within history. Thus there is no absolute perspective available outside of history that could provide a final truth of history.[5] Childs contends that Jesus of Nazareth, as a real person who once lived but who now no longer exists, is unapproachable by historical-critical methods. Obviously it is possible to continue to reinterpret the documents that reveal his onetime presence in history. But this is a reinterpretation of meaning in the present and not a reconstruction of the past. Following Jung, Childs believes that whether we can ever know what happened in the past is, in the final analysis, undecidable. All we can know is the past's effect on us today.

While I agree with much of Childs's critique, I believe he goes too far when he declares that the past is unapproachable by historical methods. Historical criticism still can help us recover an understanding of a past that holds present meaning. The text is a brute fact, not a Rorschach inkblot onto which any conceivable interpretation can be read. The great if limited value of the historical-critical approach is that it debunks arbitrary notions of what the text might mean. From every hypothesis and reconstruction it demands warrants, or reasonable evidence, within the text. Arguments can sometimes be falsified by historical and literary data. Not just anything goes, but only positions that other scholars can examine and debate. In order to discern the past in its present meaning, it is essential that we have as accurate a picture of the past as possible. We do not need "a final truth of history," but only approximate truth, backed up by evidence.

We can find meaning in the present, not *instead of* a reconstruction of the past, but *by means of* a reconstruction of the past. There is not just one horizon—the present—but two—the past and present. It is their interplay and dialogue, often tacit and unconscious, that provides meaning. This built-in, self-critical aspect of historical method prevents pure subjectivity. So I want two things at once: to overcome the objectivist illusion that disinterested exegesis is possible; and to affirm the present meaning of the past by means of the most rigorous exegesis possible.

The *present* meaning of the historical Jesus has been the unconscious agenda of the Jesus-quest these past two centuries. Driving that enormous undertaking was an inchoate desire among Christian scholars to recover something numinous and lost *within themselves,* and within contemporary religion. The means used in this quest, however, were not capable of rejuvenating the springs of faith. In fact, the historical approach became a kind of Midas touch. The very act of projecting that longing for the numinous back into the first century concealed its present motivation. This meant that the Jesus found in the past, however much a projection of modern religious ideals, could not then be brought forward into the present. To do so would have violated those scientific principles that had been used to recover Jesus in his original setting. Having found him again, in all his compelling modernity, scholars had to abandon him to the past. For no one was aware, until Albert Schweitzer exposed it, that the driving force behind this scholarly exertion was a modern longing to be encountered by the divine. Scholarship pretended to be able to dispense with that longing through its objectivist methodology and detached attitude. Paradoxically, the Jesus they found by scholarly means was located on the far side of an unbridgeable gulf—the past—a gulf created by the very method scholars had chosen to recover Jesus as their contemporary.

No legitimate quest for the historical Jesus is possible as long as the real motives behind the quest are denied. Once the false objectivity of historians has been renounced, however, we can acknowledge that most scholars study the past *in order to change its effect on the present.*

B. The Myth of God Incarnate versus the Myth of the Human Jesus

It is not, however, a choice between the human, nonmythological Jesus versus the divine, mythological Christ. For *both* are archetypal images. The human Jesus of the quest has already entered into the archetype of humanness, and seems to have affected people even during Jesus' active ministry. Indeed, the son of man was already archetypally charged as early as Ezekiel 1 and Daniel 7.[6]

The quest of the historical Jesus, then, functions in service of the myth of the human Jesus. It attempts to recover the humanity of Jesus in order to liberate it from the accretions of dogma that have made Jesus a God-Man. For two centuries, scholars have believed that they were simply going behind the gospel traditions to these traditions' earliest forms. But the scandalous lack of historical consensus reveals the true situation: they were not recovering Jesus as he really was; rather, they were forging the myth of the human Jesus. This statement is as true of "unbelievers" as "believers," as true of liberals as conservatives. Ultimately, we find ourselves reading the myth of the human Jesus in the light of our own personal myths.

No wonder there was no scholarly consensus. Every picture of Jesus that scholars produced was inevitably invested with that scholar's projections onto Jesus, positive or negative. Since these projections were by definition unconscious, and disguised the scholar's personal needs and interests, we scholars often became dogmatic about our exegetical conclusions when only tentative answers were appropriate. We had to be dogmatic, it seemed; the myth of the human Jesus that we were unwittingly helping to fashion offered us a kind of salvation. Since the driving spirit behind the quest was the hope of discovering our own humanness in God, the very meaning of our lives hung in the balance. And because scholars brought their own set of needs to the quest, there could never be unanimity as to the historical-critical results. Our contributions to the quest, then, are not "the truth" about Jesus, but rather personal probes of various value into the humanity of Jesus. Each contribution, however subjective, adds to the wild proliferation of flowers and weeds that make up the riotous garden of Jesus studies.

I in no way deplore these efforts to construct a new, liberating Jesus-myth. I believe it is the most important theological enterprise since the Protestant Reformation, urgently to be pursued. The problem is that many scholars believed they were producing objective historiography rather than creating a necessary new myth. That myth, to be sure, draws on historical methodologies. But it marshals those methodologies in the service of what I hope will become a powerful mythic alternative to the Christ-myth that we have known these past two thousand years. *Historical criticism is essential for Jesus research because the myth of the human Jesus is itself historically constructed.* As Bruce Malina puts it, "While history must be imaginative, it should not be imaginary."[7]

In short, the quest for the *historical* Jesus all along has been the quest for the *human* Jesus. There is no need for consensus or unanimity on what constitutes authentic Jesus tradition. The myth of the human Jesus is a wide field with room for many divergent views. Yet it is a field with boundaries. It is still possible to reject, on historical-critical grounds, constructions that are not supported by the text—though there will be disagreement even over the boundaries. It is not the case, then, that we scholars initiated the quest for the human Jesus. Rather, the archetype of the Human Being initiated the quest as long ago as Ezekiel, and, if some scholars are right, even earlier, in myths of the Primal Man. And the archetype continues to provide the dynamic impetus that has driven that quest. We are not the drivers, but the driven.

The Jesus-quest, however, faces two major limitations: the paucity of the biblical data, and the poverty of ourselves. The myth of the human Jesus cannot simply be spun out of the air, because that myth insists on the historicity of the human Jesus. The myth itself demands that we provide warrants for all our assertions and a plausible synthesis of the data. I believe that fallible persons such as ourselves can nevertheless exercise those critical judgments and, in so doing, provide information about the human Jesus. It is precisely that wager that leads exegetes to engross themselves in the "extremely verbatim reading" of which the mystics spoke. We cannot abandon the historical method, because it provides one of the most powerful tools we have for constructing the myth of the human Jesus.

Scholars seek to rectify the limitation on our data by turning over every leaf in search of new information about the ancient world. Newly discovered texts, new ways of reading texts, new disciplines applied to the texts, all provide invaluable aid in understanding Jesus' world and his relation to it. Such research participates in perpetual feedback, in which our interpretation of solitary sayings and deeds of Jesus continually modify our overall picture of him, while our overall picture in turn exercises a powerful influence on the way we read the solitary pieces.

It is by now a truism that information with which to write a biography of Jesus, or even to profile his personality, is inadequate. It is also true that scholarly reconstructions of the *teaching* of Jesus (for which we have considerably more data) do not carry the religious impact of the mythologized Gospels. *That is why we must attempt to recover the archetypal meaning of the "son of the man." Only then can we hope to offer an alternative to the perfect, almost inhuman Christ of dogma that has dominated these two millennia of Christian orthodoxy.* As Richard Rohr, OFM, comments, "without sacred mythology, all we have left is private pathology: my little story disconnected from any group story and surely disconnected from any Great Story."[8]

What I and others similarly inclined are trying to do is to move Christianity in a more humane direction. For that task we seek a Jesus who is not the omnipotent God in a man-suit, but someone like us, who looked for God at the center of his life and called the world to join him. What we do not know how to do, or even whether it can be done, is to position ourselves to experience the Human Being as numinously activating, religiously compelling, and spiritually transformative. If such a thing is possible, then new liturgies, music, meditative practices, disciplines, and commitments will spring up spontaneously.

Even if we are able to recover something of the human Jesus, we might still be subject to the second limitation mentioned above: the poverty of our selves. No matter how vast our knowledge of Jesus' historical period, unless we are also addressing our spiritual inadequacies we will be unable to proceed closer to the mystery of Human Being. We will continue to circle its perimeter, accumulating more information without being changed by the encounter.

No scholar can construct a picture of Jesus beyond the level of spiritual awareness that they have attained. No reconstruction outstrips its reconstructor. We cannot explain truths we have not yet understood. We cannot present insights that we have not yet grasped. Our picture of Jesus reflects not only Jesus, but the person portraying Jesus. If we are spiritual infants or adolescents, whole realms of human reality will simply escape us. As Gerald O'Collins remarked, writing about Jesus betrays what we have experienced and done as human beings.[9] Or as a very wise black woman in Texas once said to me, "You can't no more give someone something you ain't got than you can come back from somewhere you ain't been."

The Jesus-quest as it manifests itself today entails a high but necessary cost, and that is self-exposure, self-mortification, and personal transformation. Once we step out from behind the screen of historical objectivism into Heisenberg's universe, we become as much the subject of study as Jesus.

After all, "Jesus," "quest," and "Scripture" are not merely artifacts for study or names for an inquiry. They are great religious impulses and archetypal powers, and they are not just "out there" in the texts to be studied, but already "in here," in the self that is fascinated, repelled, driven, wounded, and possibly healed by these realities.

C. The Myth of History

The historical-critical method cannot deliver Jesus as he really was. But we should never have demanded that it do so. Its real contribution has been to sift through the Jesus traditions in order to establish the elements of a reconstruction. We can create the myth of the human Jesus because, as W. Taylor Stevenson has noted, the historical approach is basically a *mythic* way of perceiving the world. The idea of history *is* our modern myth.

To be sure, the myth of history is falsified when we pass from claiming that reality is historical in nature, to insisting that reality can only be discerned by use of historical method.[10] Historical investigation cannot, for example, establish whether one person truly loves another, or is acting from the motives she gives for her behavior. Historical study, while indispensable, is incapable of providing the kind of insights that can make the Bible come alive with the power to facilitate transformation—which is the manifest intention behind its writing and preservation in the first place. Every historical image of Jesus that is created serves the myth of the human Jesus, because today we *are* constituted by the myth of history. As Hal Childs commented to me,

> A significant dimension of our ontology today, our core being, is the myth of history. This is why "history" is so important to us, why it is so important to perceive and portray Jesus historically. We conceive of ourselves as historical beings; history is our being. History does not mean "true facts." It is a grand narrative with ontological status, which because of its ontological status feels absolutely real at a pre-reflective level within us, as our being. I am trying to make this myth more conscious, but because it is still mostly unconscious, or we are mostly unconscious to it, there is ongoing confusion as we try to think about it.

However much scholars differ on details, and however much they quibble over interpretations, most agree that Jesus really was a human being, and that our historical findings can help recover aspects of his humanity. Because traditional Christianity suppressed his humanness in favor of his divinity, the recovery of Jesus' full humanity is felt as a remedial and even, for some, as a sacred task.

That Jesus really lived is, to be sure, required, not by some putative historical science, but by the Christian myth itself. Faith is not dependent on historiography. But it can certainly be helped by it. Historical criticism can fashion alternative images of Jesus that can free us from oppressive pictures spawned by churches that themselves are too often oppressive. Critical scholarship can help us recover Jesus' critique of domination. Scholarship also lets us appreciate Jesus without an overlay of dogma that claims absolute truth and that negates the value of other approaches to understanding Jesus.

Bruce Chilton's recent *Rabbi Jesus* is an excellent example of the careful use of historiography to paint a plausible picture of Jesus. It is full of speculation, informed guesses, and novelistic narrative. Because Chilton has performed such exhaustive research, and because he has tethered his imagination to reliable facts from the period and its places, he is able to make a significant contribution to the quest for the human Jesus. In a society in which, for many, the great living myths have lost their cogency, what we once held as beliefs can now be held self-consciously as "true fiction," as "creative nonfiction," or as "myths" in quotation marks. We no longer have to defend our meaning-stories, notes mythologist Betty Sue Flowers. We simply watch them evolve as we tell them and live in the present created by the future we tell. [11]

D. Jesus' Original Impulse

My goal in studying the Gospels is to recover what Jesus unleashed—the original impulse that prompted the spread of his message into new contexts that required new formulations, in his spirit. In this book I have attempted to develop a perspective on Jesus using the historical-critical method and a critique of domination. I have developed that critique more fully in chapter 6 of *Engaging the Powers*.[12] To summarize that critique briefly, Jesus condemned all forms of domination:

- patriarchy and the oppression of women and children;
- the economic exploitation and the impoverishment of entire classes of people;
- the family as chief instrument for the socialization of children into oppressive roles and values;
- hierarchical power arrangements that disadvantage the weak while benefiting the strong;
- the subversion of the law by the defenders of privilege;
- rules of purity that keep people separated;
- racial superiority and ethnocentrism;
- the entire sacrificial system with its belief in sacral violence.

Jesus proclaimed the Reign of God (or God's "Domination-Free Order"), not only as coming in the future, but as having already dawned in his healings and exorcisms and his preaching of good news to the poor. He created a new family, based not on bloodlines, but on doing the will of God. He espoused nonviolence as a means for breaking the spiral of violence without creating new forms of violence. He called people to repent of their collusion in the Domination System and sought to heal them from the various ways the system had dehumanized them.

In my analysis of texts in this book I privilege Jesus' critique of domination over all other viewpoints because, after a lifetime of study, I have found it to be the most radical and comprehensive framework for understanding what he was about. Using a critique of the Domination System as my critical lens enables me to recover emphases lost as the gospel was domesticated in the early church. Although occasionally Jesus' teachings were further radicalized (as in Stephen's speech in Acts 7 or in the opening of the church to include Gentiles), the more pronounced tendency of the tradition was to accommodate the gospel to structures of domination (for example, the treatment of women in later New Testament writings). This critique of domination does not replace the historical criteria worked out by New Testament scholars. It does provide the primary criterion for discerning what was revelatory in Jesus' life and message.

I should add that I am using "revelatory" not in a theological but in an epistemological sense. I regard a "revelation" as any new idea that bursts upon the world with sufficient force to bring about positive change in people and history. A revelation begins as a private, subjective *experience* that happens to individuals. But if it has cogency, it becomes a public, historic occasion. What we call a revelation is a positive mutation in the history of thought or being. Buddha was a revealer, as was Lao-Tzu, Zoroaster, Muhammad, St. Francis, Karl Marx, Sigmund Freud, Mohandas Gandhi, Teilhard de Chardin, Carl Jung, and others, some of far less fame and accomplishment. But it was Jesus who exposed the Domination System with such devastating effect and envisioned God as nonviolent and all-inclusive. There were antecedent revelations, of course, but the revelation Jesus brought was so at odds with the world's power arrangements that we have yet to take its measure.

I am concerned not so much with whether Jesus actually said something, but with whether it is true, regardless of who said it. If truth is our goal rather than historicity, then revelation is a far more appropriate category than facticity for weighing the impact of Jesus. If a statement is revelatory, if it provides insights about becoming more fully human, if it exposes the Domination System for what it is, then we may call it "true." But we should not assume that something is true because Jesus said it. Rather, he would have said it because he thought it was true. Some sayings later developed by various churches are no doubt true; it is even conceivable that some things Jesus said are not true, though most of these would have been filtered out in transmitting the tradition. (The church did courageously retain passages that were clearly disconfirmed, such as the second coming, Mark 9:1 par.) The myth of the human Jesus *requires* that Jesus must have made mistakes, have had flaws in his personality, sinned, and otherwise exhibited imperfect (that is, human) behavior. But the issue of historicity, while occasionally crucial, is far less significant than consistency *with the original impulse of Jesus,* whether articulated by him or by his followers later. That impulse was the spirit that drove Jesus to challenge his own religious tradition and those who were its protectors. Working from the vantage point provided by a critique of domination, the criteria of historicity can, when needed, isolate texts that illuminate the human Jesus. To be sure, this involves us in a hermeneutical spiral (*not* a circle), in which the fragments are interpreted by that critique, and that critique is modified by the fragments, and on and on. All historical work proceeds in this manner. Indeed, failure to continue the spiral is to abort the entire enterprise. Consequently, if a critique of domination fails to account for significant elements of the tradition, it would have to be modified or abandoned altogether.

The presence of a particular critical perspective does not spell the end of objectivity; we are still required to provide warrants for our claims. Once one abandons the chimera of disinterestedness, however, objectivity is free to become what it should have been all along: just another name for simple honesty and the willingness, as Schweitzer demonstrated, to be changed by what we discover.

I listen intently to the Book. But I do not acquiesce in it. I rail at it. I make accusations. I censure it for endorsing patriarchalism, violence, anti-Judaism, homophobia, and slavery. It rails back at me, accusing me of greed, presumption, narcissism, and cowardice. We wrestle. We roll on the ground, neither of us capitulating, until it wounds my thigh with "new-ancient" words. And the Holy Spirit is there the whole time, strengthening us both.

Such wrestling ensures that our pictures of Jesus are not mere repetitions of the prevailing fashion. They can be a groping for plenitude, an attempt to carry on the mission of Jesus, and an effort to transcend the influence of the Domination System. In the end, we may not just be conforming Jesus to ourselves, but in some faint way conforming ourselves to the truth revealed by Jesus.

My deepest interest in encountering Jesus is not to confirm my own prejudices (though I certainly do that), but to be delivered from a stunted soul, a limited mind, and an unjust social order. No doubt a part of me wants to whittle Jesus down to my size so that I can avoid painful, even costly, change. But another part of me is exhilarated by the possibility of becoming more human. So I listen in order to be transformed. Somehow the gospel itself has the power to activate in people that "hunger and thirst for righteousness" of which Matt. 5:6 speaks (whether it is Jesus or someone of the same mind speaking). There are people who want to be involved in inaugurating God's domination-free order, even if it costs their lives. *Respondeo etsi mutabor*: I respond though I must change.[13] And in my better moments, I respond *in order to change*. Truth is, had Jesus never lived, we could not have invented him.

Notes

1. Brian Stock, *Listening for the* Text: *On the Uses of the Past* (Baltimore: Johns Hopkins University Press, 1990), 80–81.

2. Lynn M. Poland, "The New Criticism, Neoorthodoxy, and the New Testament," *Journal of Religion* 65 (1985): 473.

3. Wendy Doniger O'Flaherty, "The uses and Misuses of Other Peoples' Myths," *JMR* 54 (1986): 219–39.

4. Walter Kasper, cited in Hal Childs, *The Myth of the Historical Jesus and the Evolution of Consciousness,* SBL Dissertation Series 179 (Atlanta: Scholars Press, 2000), 85.

5. Childs, *The Myth of the Historical Jesus,* 227–28.

6. I use "son of man" when referring to the expression in the Hebrew Bible or intertestamental writings, since there the expression lacks definite articles. I use "the son of the man" when dealing with the New Testament and later writings, since that is what the Greek says.

7. Bruce J. Malina, *The Social Gospel of Jesus: The Kingdom of God in Mediterranean Perspective* (Minneapolis: Fortress Press, 2001), 7.

8. Richard Rohr, "Let Us Be Up and Building," *Radical Grace* 6 (1993): 1.

9. Gerald O'Collins, *Interpreting Jesus* (London: G. Chapman, 1983), x

10. W. Taylor Stevenson, *History as Myth* (New York: Seabury Press, 1969), 6.

11. Bruce Chilton, *Rabbi Jesus* (New York: Doubleday, 2000); Betty Sue Flowers, "Practicing Politics in the Economic Myth," *The Salt Journal* 2 (2000): 53.

12. Walter Wink, *Engaging the Powers: Discernment and Resistance in a World of Domination* (Minneapolis: Fortress Press, 1992).

13. Eugen Rosenstock-Huessy, "Elrewell to Descartes," *Out of Revolution* (New York: William Morrow, 1969), 751.

15

Jesus and the Human Being

In keeping with his focus on the intention/role of the text in personal and social transformation, Walter Wink begins this chapter on Jesus and the Human Being with the insight (credited to Elizabeth Howes) that the biblical notion of the son of the man is an "archetypal image" that functions as a "catalytic agent in the service of the Self." As an archetypal image, the "Human Being" drives one toward an emerging and transformative consciousness of "the Human One," authentic humanity, God within us as God was within Jesus. To explore the ways in which the image of the Human Being catalyzes transformation, Wink examines son-of-the-man sayings in the biblical stories about Jesus. His exegesis leads him to posit that the son of the man was not originally a Christological title (although post-Easter theology made it so). Rather, he argues for a collective son of the man including, for example, the disciples. These early followers of Jesus, in the freedom they experienced in relation to him, exercised the same authority Jesus exercised to heal, to forgive, and to challenge the Domination System in the service of both human need and worth. To quote from a chapter not included in this volume, "Jesus incarnated the Human Being and taught his disciples to do the same." This "numinous reality" is encountered in those texts where Jesus speaks of the "son of the man." In a concluding section of the chapter, Wink examines the various atonement theories that have been employed to explain how redemption occurs. He rejects Anselm's "blood atonement" theory, but finds degrees of truth in the several New Testament theories of the atonement to the degree that they have to do with forgiveness and transformed life. Wink concludes that what finally matters is the relationship between one's Christology and one's anthropology. Clearly he is most comfortable with a low Christology (a fully human Jesus) and a low anthropology (humankind with the potential of becoming more fully human in the manner of Jesus).

Source: Wink 2002: Excerpted from Chapter 5

A number of scholars early in the twentieth century were convinced that the biblical "son of man" was an offshoot of Iranian mythology about an "Urmensch," or Primal Man.[1] Subsequent research has exposed the synthetic nature of this "myth," which never existed in the form proposed. Despite the absence of such a hypothetical myth in pre-Christian sources, however, there is something irreducibly mythic about this enigmatic "son of man." It glows with a halo of overdetermined meaning. It possesses singular numinosity, but has no story. There is no drama of creation, redemption, or the founding of a people; there is no narrative, no pattern. We seem to have a mythic figure without a myth. It was the seminal contribution of Elizabeth Boyden Howes to develop the insight that the "son of the man" was not a title, nickname, circumlocution, or myth, but an *archetypal image*. As such, she saw, the image functions as a symbol of wholeness, less august and almighty than the Messiah or Christ, more mundane and daily than the heroes of myth. She saw the image more as a catalytic agent of transformation in the service of the Self than as a symbol of the Self as such.[2] We turn first, then, to an examination of the son-of-the-man saying in the story of the plucking of grain on the sabbath.

A. Plucking Grain on the Sabbath: Mark 2:23-28 // Matt. 12:1-8 // Luke 6:1-5

> [23] One sabbath he was going through the grainfields; and as they made their way his disciples began to pluck heads of grain. [24] The Pharisees said to him, "Look, why are they doing what is not lawful on the sabbath?" [25] And he said to them, "Have you never read what David did when he and his companions where hungry and in need of food? [26] He entered the house of God, when Abiathar was high priest, and ate the bread of the Presence, which it is not lawful for any but the priests to eat, and he gave some to his companions." [27] Then he said to them, "The sabbath was made for humankind, and not humankind for the sabbath; [28] so the son of the man is lord even of the sabbath." (Mark 2:23-28)

This passage has been regarded as inauthentic by a number of scholars. Their reasons include the fact that not Jesus' behavior, but that of his disciples, is being criticized, suggesting a setting in the early church in its controversy with Judaism over the law; the example of David depends on David's violating the law, whereas Jesus has done nothing; David did not act on a sabbath; David took the initiative on his followers' behalf, whereas Jesus' disciples act on their own; no reason is given for the Pharisees' presence in a field on a sabbath; in v. 28 one's relationship to Jesus determines one's right to break the sabbath, rather than one's special needs; "and he said to them" in v. 27 is usually the mark of a suture between independent traditions.[3]

Each of these objections has counterobjections. A teacher going to bat for his disciples is scarcely unusual in any age, but especially in a movement as controversial as Jesus'. David had to have acted on a sabbath, since the sabbath was the only day that Ahimelech (Mark erroneously reads "Abiathar") would have had only the shewbread available for feeding David and his companions. The appeal to David's example, while not exact, was nevertheless a real parallel, in that regulations meant to safeguard something holy (the shewbread) were set aside for David and his men, just as regulations meant to safeguard something holy (the sabbath) are now set aside for Jesus and those with him.[4] Pharisees would not have had to walk out to the fields since the fields ran right up to the houses in Galilean villages; fields commonly had public pathways running through them, and one could avoid violating the sabbath rule against traveling more than two thousand cubits between villages by taking shortcuts through the fields.[5] Hellenistic Jewish and Gentile Christians seem to have left the issue of sabbath observance behind quite early (it is not an issue in the Pauline correspondence or in the rules set down for Gentiles in Acts 15:29). Besides, the text assumes the validity of the sabbath; had the church created the narrative, they would more likely have made it a contest between the Jewish sabbath and the Christian "Lord's day," or Sunday. The earliest Christians kept the sabbath; any controversy would be over the proper interpretation of the law. Later Christians did not keep the sabbath at all.[6] And as for the phrase "then he said to them," this might simply be a rhetorical device to heighten the solemnity of the saying that follows; Luke retains it even though he drops Mark's v. 27. The objection that v. 27 refers to humanity in general, while v. 28 deals just with the authority of Jesus, presupposes the identification of Jesus with the son of the man, and that is precisely what I am contesting here.

If v. 27 refers to human beings in general ("the sabbath was made for humankind, and not humankind for the sabbath"), then, says Oscar Cullmann, we would expect v. 28 also to say that humanity in general (here, "son of Adam" might fit) is lord of the sabbath, since the sabbath was made for the sake of human beings.⁷ That construction would then feature synonymous parallelism between the terms "human" and "child of the human" as we find it in the Hebrew Scriptures, especially the Psalms. Reverse synonymous parallelism is what we have, once we abandon the notion that "the son of the man" here is a Christological title.

The disciples, whom Mark often portrays as dunces, are depicted here as having grasped the authority that Jesus had engendered in them, or, rather, that he had helped them discover in themselves. They had made no provision for meals on the sabbath, though they obviously knew it was coming. But being part of Jesus' peripatetic retinue made such preparations difficult, if not impossible. Jesus is shown backing up their actions by a statement giving them even more magisterial authority. Even if we conclude that the followers of Jesus fabricated this story, the result is the same: unauthorized disciples of Jesus discover the power latent within them to become "lords of the sabbath."

Elsewhere, the disciples are shown assuming the same authority as Jesus. As the Human Being, Jesus places himself above the practice of fasting (Matt. 11:18), and his disciples claim the same authority for themselves (Mark 2:18-20). The Human Being is not alone in having left home to preach the kingdom (Luke 9:58); his disciples have done so too (Mark 10:28). The Human Being is persecuted (Mark 9:31); so are the disciples (Matt. 10:19).⁸ That some of this information reflects later church practice is undeniable. But I can only regard the sheer sovereignty exercised by these untutored peasants as a consequence of the creative impulse of Jesus, whether all of these sayings go back to Jesus or not.

Furthermore, Jesus is not making claims about himself in this narrative. In appealing to the behavior of David, Jesus does *not* make an argument from the lesser to the greater: if David could take the law into his own hands, how much more *the Son of David?* Instead, the focus shifts to the son of the man (compare Mark 8:29, 31). Not David's status, but only David's need and the need of his companions is appealed to. The assertion that the sabbath was made for humankind, not humankind for the sabbath, seems to place human need over divine law. A statement like this could lead to endless mischief; no wonder both Matthew and Luke, and some manuscripts of Mark, omit it! Not only that, but a son of the man can even violate the tradition's understanding of the role of the son of the man: "Happy is the man (*'enosh*) who does this [maintains justice], the son of man (*ben 'adam*) who holds it fast, who *keeps the sabbath, not profaning it*" (Isa. 56:2). Yet this Galilean "son of the man" and his followers have no scruples about interpreting the sabbath according to need, since they are "lords of the sabbath." Jesus might seem to be saying that humanity is the measure of all things. If so, it would take little to refute him. Humanity is alienated from the cosmos, a wolf at the throat of its neighbors, a rebel against God and the requirements of the ecosystem, and a threat to every living species. Humanity can least of all be the measure of all things! It is not humanity as such, but the Human Being that is the lord even of the sabbath.

What constituted a sabbath violation was the focus of ongoing debate in Judaism. Many liberal rabbis would have agreed with Jesus that human need takes precedence over sabbath observance. The only question, then, would have been whether the disciples' need was serious or trivial. Jesus is not condemning the law here, or abrogating it, or declaring himself and his followers above the law and beyond good and evil. The passage assumes that keeping the Sabbath is normative. The question is not whether to keep the sabbath, but when and how. Jesus presses behind the issue of obedience and examines the origin of the sabbath itself. Why did the first Hebrews celebrate the sabbath? Was it in order to fulfill a commandment or to give former slaves, who had never known rest, a day of rest each week (Exod. 5:12-15)? In the later creation story of Genesis 1, even God enjoys a day of rest; sabbath is part of the rhythm of the cosmos. Therefore it is not an onerous obligation but a blessed gift, one that Judaism has now given to the world. Jesus honors its purpose, but reminds his hearers that the sabbath was itself created to serve the needs of human beings, not human beings to serve the sabbath.

Jesus drives to an apprehension of what it means to keep the Sabbath, within and out. To operate out of consciousness of the Human Being, which by definition indicates that *more* than personal need is involved, is to function out of the heart of the sabbath. If only need is involved, one breaks the law without understanding the depth of the sabbath.[9] If this is the most sacred of all Jewish institutions (since the sabbath alone was created on the seventh day), then one can say, "Institutions have been created to serve human beings, not human beings to serve institutions."

A Jewish saying from a later period states, "The Sabbath is delivered to you, and you are not delivered to the Sabbath." But I suspect that few rabbis would have considered the plucking episode to be an occasion serious enough to warrant Sabbath suspension. If everyone began to behave this way, it would not be long before the Sabbath was ignored in all but name—as has happened in our own time. Why then does Jesus defend the disciples' behavior?

On this occasion, they have placed the urgency of proclaiming Jesus' gospel to all Israel above the preparations for the sabbath, and so they do what the very poor are allowed to do: to pluck and eat standing grain by hand, but not to gather it in their pockets (Deut. 23:25). Technically, they were reaping, an activity prohibited on the Sabbath. But the disciples judged, with the freedom in which they had been established before God by Jesus, that the infraction was too trivial to count.

But was it? Numbers 15:32-36 recounts an episode during the Exodus when a man who was gathering sticks on the sabbath was stoned to death, showing how seriously Israelites regarded such infractions.

How then does one prevent this freedom from turning into antinomian license? The world has witnessed to the breaking point the narcissistic insistence that the individual's needs transcend all other considerations in the universe. Once need has been elevated above law, law is subject to infinite qualification, until anarchy prevails. What does it mean, then, that the Human Being is lord even of the sabbath?

The sabbath was indeed made for everyone, but not everyone knows how to keep the Sabbath. The Human Being knows, because the Human Being in us can know what God wants. Laws structure freedom. If we are serving that which the law serves, then we have freedom of choice, even if it means breaking the law (or, as here, interpreting for oneself what constitutes violation of the law). But if we are not serving that which the law serves, then we are obligated to obey the law. Law deals with the unredeemed aspect of persons, and insofar as we are all unredeemed, to that degree we are and must remain under law. So this freedom is the opposite of lawlessness (Howes).

One very valuable Greek manuscript of the New Testament, Codex Bezae (D), has a surprising reading after Luke 6:4, just before the statement about the Human Being being lord of the sabbath: "On the same day he saw someone working on the Sabbath and said to him: *'anthrōpe* (Human Being), if you know what you are doing, you are blessed; but if you do not know, you are cursed and a transgressor of the law.'"

This comment is remarkable for its positive evaluation of work. The Greeks despised manual labor and handed it over to slaves; those who entered the study of philosophy were required to give up work. In the Bezae saying work is not only not inconsistent with the sabbath, but can even be considered to merit divine blessing.[10] Ernst Hammel notes the uncharacteristic assumption that an unlettered peasant might be able to know the will of God in a concrete situation, or that she might be capable of interpreting the law for herself. Equally striking is that Jesus is not shown formulating his own opinion. He neither denounces the law nor imposes a new rule. No direct information is given about the position Jesus himself takes, nor is advice given to his hearers. "It is exactly the point where the historic Jesus stood which is brought out in the saying. The Law is not declared null and void, but freedom and independence are required and demanded for those who have an inkling of God—the very independence that led to Jesus' downfall and condemnation."[11] This apocryphal saying in Codex Bezae implicitly critiques all human institutions, calling them back to their created purposes, and it continues the creative impulse of Jesus by freeing people to become human. I regard the Codex Bezae story as true whether Jesus said it or not.

Jesus does not call on his disciples to let conscience be their guide, because their consciences had long since taken on the conventional values of society. In most cases, conscience is nothing else than the cultural superego. (One thinks of Huckleberry Fin grappling with his conscience over whether to turn in the runaway slave Jim. All the data in his conscience represented the internalized values of Southern slaveholding, so that his decision to save Jim is made in violation of everything that his conscience has been taught is right.[12] But that must mean that there is a transcendent dimension to conscience that is not socialized, but that represents the ineradicable image of God in us. Huck responded out of that higher impulse.) The Human Being is not the offspring of the Domination System, or of this old and fading order. It is something of God within us, "that aspect of the Self which has about it the moral quality of being able to function through the ego in concrete everyday decisions" (Howes).[13] The Human Being seems to be encoded with the specificity of the *imago Dei* in each person, in a non-standardized form capable of infinite variation within fixed patterning. "To be oneself means to realize God's idea of one's self."[14] The religious task of the ego is to encourage the growth and nurturance of this inner element of discernment. Jesus responded to what God was doing in the outer reality, but he was able to do so only because he was responding out of something deep inside himself as well.

We need sabbaths in order to foster the Human Being within. If we are not in touch with the Human Being, then nothing is lord of the sabbath, and we lose relatedness to the sabbath as a healing interval in our lives and communities. Perhaps the Human Being is most especially lord of the *sabbath*— of the centering, renewing spaces in which our lives get restored and related again to the Source. The man who is plowing, if *he knows what he is doing*, is not an anarchist violating the law; he may in fact be *keeping* the sabbath.

To place so much premium on consciousness is terrifying. Are we to weigh every decision in the light of the Human Being? Might Jesus have also said (or might we): "On the same day he saw someone *keeping* the sabbath, and said to him: Man, if you know what you are doing, you are blessed, but if you do not know, you are cursed and a transgressor of the law"?

What then can we say about the Human Being in the plucking story? The son of the man cannot simply be a name for Jesus, for it is not Jesus but his disciples who show themselves to be "lords of the sabbath." Thus, the son of the man here cannot represent "I" or "this fellow" either. It could mean "I and anyone else like me," but that leaves us without any idea of the expression's *content*. The Human Being here exhibits a breathtaking authority, an authority fearlessly assumed by a common artisan and by his motley band of disciples. The scandal, says José Cárdenas Pallares, is that Jesus places the whole of the law in the service of a few poor people, subordinating the law to the welfare of any human being who is hungry and in need. "For Jesus nothing, not even the most sacred law, may be allowed to obstruct the liberation of the human being." After all, the law of Moses was originally intended for the benefit of an oppressed slave people.[15]

The sabbath was the most revered practice in Israel. It had more weight than all the other commandments of the law combined.[22] If the Human Being is lord even of the sabbath, then it is in principle lord of every law touching the lives of humanity. It knows not only what we need, but the fullness toward which God is drawing us. Elizabeth Howes comments:

> [T]he term "Son of man" is related to but is not the same as the archetype of the Self. . . . It was used by Jesus to describe the main image which dominated his life and which can be found by others, as it describes in a rather rare way the Self as it operated through him. The "Son of man" phrase describes the Self *at work in concrete life,* a Self lived existentially, not as a hope or a vision; but it is not the same as the Self. We have thus a picture of God coming into humanity lived as the Son of man by Jesus.[16]

Thus Jesus could speak of himself as the Human Being, but also of anyone else (the peasant plowman, for example, or Jesus' grain-plucking disciples) who could respond out of the higher self, even if it violated current morality. Such sovereign freedom, placed in the hands of the underclasses, inevitably strikes terror in the hearts of those entrusted with the tranquility of society. The dramatic location of the initiation of the death plot against Jesus, only a few verses after the story of the plucking of the grain in Mark (3:6), may or may not be chronologically exact, but it is logically appropriate.

It was not simply the religious and political authorities, however, who trembled at the human cost of such freedom. Some in the early churches also blanched at so much moral discretion being placed at the disposal of common people. I have already noted that Matthew and Luke omit Mark 2:27 ("the sabbath was made for humankind . . ."), and so do a few manuscripts of Mark itself. By deleting that verse, Matthew and Luke have converted the saying into its opposite: the assertion that Jesus *alone* as son of man is lord of the sabbath. Once "the son of the man" had been flattened into a mere equivalent of Son of God and Christ/Messiah, no other reading seemed possible.

Matthew additionally enhances the Christological centrality of Jesus by inserting, "Or have you not read in the law that on the sabbath the priests in the temple break the sabbath and yet are guiltless? I tell you, something greater than the temple is here" (12:5-6). Whereas special *need* had originally justified the breach or suspension of the law, now one's relationship with a special *person* does so—a person endowed with a transcendent authority shared by no one else.

Once all authority becomes vested only in Jesus, however, what happens to the sovereign freedom that he evoked in his disciples? What becomes of the freedom to "judge for yourselves what is right" (Luke 12:57)? It is indeed awesome how Christology has been used to avoid the clear intent of Jesus! So the astonishing freedom of the Human Being was sabotaged in the interests of institutional harmony and rule by law.

And Feuerbach chuckled.

B. The Healing of the Paralytic: Mark 2:1-12 // Matt. 9:1-8 // Luke 5:17-26

> ¹ When he returned to Capernaum after some days, it was reported that he was at home. ² So many gathered around that there was no longer room for them, not even in front of the door; and he was speaking the word to them. ³ Then some people came, bringing to him a paralyzed man, carried by four of them. ⁴ And when they could not bring him to Jesus because of the crowd, they removed the roof above him; and after having dug through it, they let down the mat on which the paralytic lay. ⁵ When Jesus saw their faith, he said to the paralytic, "Son, your sins are forgiven." ⁶ Now some of the scribes were sitting there, questioning in their hearts, ⁷ "Why does this fellow speak in this way? It is blasphemy! Who can forgive sins but God alone?" ⁸ At once Jesus perceived in his spirit that they were discussing these questions among themselves; and he said to them, "Why do you raise such questions in your hearts? ⁹ Which is easier,

to say to the paralytic, 'Your sins are forgiven,' or to say, 'Stand up and take your mat and walk'? ¹⁰ But so that you may know that the Son of the Man has authority on earth to forgive sins"—he said to the paralytic— ¹¹"I say to you, stand up, take your mat and go to your home." ¹²And he stood up, and immediately took the mat and went out before all of them; so that they were all amazed and glorified God, saying, "We have never seen anything like this!"

This seemingly simple account is the focus of a complex debate about its historicity. Many scholars believe that Mark 2:5b-10 has been added, thus turning what was a simple healing narrative (1-5a, 11-12) into a compound healing-and-conflict story. The alleged insertion is full of Markan vocabulary; the repetition of the phrase "he said to the paralytic" in 5a and 10b has the appearance of an editorial link; the transition between 10 and 11 seems awkward; the universal acclaim at the end of the story ignores the scribes, who were most certainly not mollified, and takes account only of the act of healing, not the forgiveness; and the implication that the man's sin had caused his sickness seems at odds with Jesus' attitude elsewhere (e.g., Luke 13:10-17). The most influential argument against the passage's integrity, however, pertains to its form: two discrete forms are juxtaposed, a healing story (regarded as primitive) and a conflict story (assumed to reflect later church struggles with the Jews).

These arguments, however, are not conclusive. Markan vocabulary appears in vv. 1-5a as well;[17] the repetition of "he said to the paralytic" is good storytelling technique (see Exod. 4:4); the putative "awkwardness" of the transition from vv. 10 to 11 escaped the notice of both Matthew and Luke, who faithfully reproduced it while freely making other changes to improve or condense Mark; the acclaim at the end that ignores the scribes also is repeated by Matthew and Luke, who apparently enjoyed the total eclipse of Jesus' opponents, even though the opponents' unabated hostility would very shortly lead to a death plot (Mark 3:6 par.); and Mark probably intended the crowd's amazement to include the act of forgiving sins. The structure of this passage also argues for its integrity as a unit.

Ched Myers notes a neat echoing that no one else, to my knowledge, has seen:

A C 2:2 Jesus was *teaching* them the Word . . .
B D 2:6 Scribes were *reasoning* in their hearts . . .

B C 2:7 Scribes: "Why does this man *teach* this?"
A D 2:8 Jesus: "Why do you *reason* thus in your hearts?"[18]

Note the ABBA structure of the speakers (technically known as "chiasmus") coexisting with the CDCD sequence of the verbs. For this structure to work, however, v. 2 (the healing) must have coexisted with vv. 6, 7, and 8 (the controversy) from the beginning, for the structure of the saying is not a redactional superimposition but is intrinsic to the narrative. And v. 9, which is in the heart of the conflict story, refers to the contemplated healing.[19] Are we to ascribe this tight construction to the chance juxtaposition of two independent narratives, or to the redactional work of a scribe (Mark) who is already roundly accused of making awkward transitions in vv. 5 and 10? This passage has suffered from the worst kind of form criticism, which simplistically separated the healing narrative from the controversy story.[20] There is no doubt that such forms are standard. But if the healing precipitated conflict, then the two forms naturally belong together. And we know from other stories (including the Fourth Gospel's independent version of the same story, John 5:1-18) that Jesus' healings created enormous controversy. The Gospel "forms" are not Procrustean beds into which every lively and unpredictable story must be crushed, but "typical" frameworks that are not always appropriate. They are not causes but effects.

It is worth pausing over the form-critical issue, because this text has been something of a showpiece for the form-critical approach. Let me tell a brief healing story. "A boy was beaten up, received multiple injuries, and was rushed to the hospital, where the doctors had to take forty-six stitches to sew him up. After some days in the hospital they released him, still a bit groggy, but mending." There you have all the elements of a healing narrative: description of the problem, encounter with the healer, the healing act, and evidence of healing. What I did not tell was that he was a twelve-year-old black boy in Harlem, and the injuries were delivered by three white policemen, and that their brutal beating of him set off furious protests, including the trashing of some stores, a march on precinct headquarters, and charges from black leaders.

So there you have it: a healing story *intrinsically* yoked with a conflict story. This happens all the time. Jesus' healings seem to have created controversy on more than one occasion. To recall an early criticism of the extension of form criticism beyond its capacities, "Judgments of form cannot lead to judgments of historicity." To which we might add, the story should suggest the form; the form should not be imposed on the story. When form criticism does move from judgments of form to judgments of historicity, it invariably becomes impaled on circular reasoning: this passage reflects a hypothetical community, which in turn is seen as creating this passage to meet the needs of that community. The enigmatic is explained by the imaginary. The capacity to fantasize plausible contexts in the early church's life does not make them historical.

Most significant, however, are the data from the independently transmitted story of a healed paralytic in the signs source of John's Gospel.[21] Here we find the almost identical words ("Jesus said to him, 'Stand up, take your mat and walk.' At once the man was made well, and he took up his mat and began to walk," John 5:8-9a). In addition, the man's illness is associated with his having sinned ("Do not sin any more," John 5:14), and the healing story is subordinated to a conflict narrative (5:1, 9b-47). In the center of that conflict, Jesus says that the Father "has given him authority to execute judgment because he is a son of man" (5:27). Only this once is the phrase anarthrous (lacking a definite article). Apparently, John believes that authority has been given to *everyone* who will claim it. This is very similar to Mark 2:10 ("the son of the man has authority on earth to forgive sins"). Most scholars believe that John's Gospel was written independently of the Synoptic Gospels, though drawing on common traditions. If so, then it must have used a source in which the healing narrative and the conflict story were already joined.

This is the only "son of the man" saying connected with forgiveness (or with healing, for that matter). If Jesus had not made that connection, how would it have occurred to people in the early church to do so? Some argue that the church wished to authorize its right to declare sins forgiven by dragging in the son-of-the-man title; but that assumes that they were already declaring sins forgiven (and that the son of the man was a title). How did they get started, if it was not Jesus' own initiative? The scandal is exacerbated by the fact that, not just Jesus, but also his followers, were authorized to declare the sins of people forgiven. And the three Synoptic Gospels concur that these scribes regarded Jesus' declaration of forgiveness at least as unambiguous blasphemy.[22]

The collective implications of this story are made most clear by Matthew who ends his version with the statement, "and they glorified God who had given such authority to *human beings*" (9:8). We would have expected Matthew, of all the evangelists, to conclude that sentence with "Jesus" or "the Christ." Matthew clearly understands the term as collective. (The Greek term *anthrōpois* here is equivalent to the Hebrew *bene 'adam*, "sons of man.") Any person who knows that God forgives sins has the authority to declare another person's sins forgiven. They would know this ostensibly because they had experienced it. Matthew no doubt was thinking about the church as the community that had received this revelation, but it would in principle include *anyone* who knows this revelation to be true. Matthew believed that Jesus intended to share this authority to forgive with his followers. That much is clear from Matt. 16:19 and 18:18, as well as 9:8. The authority to heal and exorcise was also given to the disciples (Mark 6:7-13 par.; Luke 10:9, 17-20).

According to Matthew, then, "the son of the man" in this narrative is not limited to Jesus, but indicates any person who "knows" God's will regarding forgiveness, indeed, who knows God's very nature, that God is, at the core, forgiving. This forgiveness is not attained or earned. One does not, as in both Jewish and Christian liturgies, need to repent first before receiving words of absolution. Jesus does not offer forgiveness to those who repent and promise to do works of restitution. He declares people forgiven before they repent, as in this story. There were, in that society, people who were by trade or ill fortune categorically incapable of doing works of restitution (toll collectors, prostitutes, shepherds, attendants at bathhouses, weavers, tanners, robbers), who were regarded as sinners because of their occupations. To these he declares: Your sins are forgiven (Luke 18:9-14)! Now you can repent! As Mark summarizes Jesus' message, "The time is fulfilled, and the kingdom of God has come near; repent, and believe in the good news" (Mark 1:15). Repentance is possible because God has drawn near in the proclamation of Jesus.

We must cling to Matt. 9:8 with all our might, because it is one of the few passages in which we can know unequivocally that at least one of the evangelists understands the Human Being in a collective sense.[23] It is not then merely a title for Jesus, or a form of humble self-designation, or a circumlocution for "I," though it would be possible to understand it as "I and anyone else like me." But even that is too limiting. The early Christians had the clear sense that the Human Being is not restricted to Jesus, but that it is an authority they are permitted to assume themselves: the authority to heal and to forgive sins. Perhaps that is why Jesus does not say, "But that you may know that I am the son of the man. . . ."

This is the point T. W. Manson made in 1931, though few endorsed it. Arguing from the explicitly collective nature of *ben 'adam* in Psalm 80 and *bar enash* in Dan. 7:13, Manson suggested a "communal interpretation" of the Human Being. The "son of the man" is "an ideal figure and stands for the manifestation of the Kingdom of God on earth in a people wholly devoted to their heavenly king."[24] Jesus' mission was to create the kingdom of the saints of the Most High—a fully human community that honored the integrity and uniqueness of all people. Jesus and his disciples *together* "should be the Son of Man, the Remnant that saves by service and self-sacrifice, the organ of God's redemptive purpose in the world."[25] "He and they together, so long as they adhere to him, constitute the 'Son of Man' . . . . 'Son of Man' should be read throughout and understood to connote 'the people of the saints of the Most High' and to denote Jesus and his disciples."[26] When Jesus speaks of the sufferings of the Human Being, then, he means something in which he and his followers would share (Mark 8:34-35). "By dying Jesus has brought the Son of Man into existence, given to that dream-figure a body, a local habitation, and a name. It is the Church, his own body, of which he is the head."[27]

Manson's ideas won little acceptance largely because he was unable to provide sufficient textual evidence for his corporate Human Being concept. In a peculiar form of self-immolation, he dismissed the two texts that support his thesis most powerfully: Mark 2:1-12 and 2:23-28.[28] I have already demonstrated that Matthew understood the Human Being corporately in 9:8; this is a rare fact about which there can be no doubt. And the authority exercised by the *disciples* is what Jesus refers to in Mark 2:23-28. Armed with these two texts, we are able to make Manson's case for the collective son of the man more strongly than Manson himself.

The story of the paralytic furthers the sense of sovereign authority that we found in the account of plucking the grain on the sabbath. Surprisingly, in contrast to Ezekiel, Jesus never appeals to God's authority to authenticate his mission. He never says, "Thus says the Lord." In Mark 11:27-33 par., a conflict narrative of highest authenticity, Jesus is depicted as *refusing* to claim divine authority for his mission. This attitude is counter to the trend of the developing church. He clearly implies that his authority is "from heaven," but will not say so, indicating only that it has the same source as John's. This exalted evaluation of John is also opposite the church's tendency (Matt. 11:11b // Luke 7:28b; John 3:27-30). There was no reason for such reticence by Jesus; the long history of prophets in Israel had more than adequately prepared Jews to take seriously a person who claimed to speak on behalf of God, saying, "thus says the Lord." That Jesus *never* appealed to God's authority for anything he said or did is as remarkable as the divine authority that clearly shines through his words and deeds.

We must not overlook the implications of his reticence. He refused to stake the truth of his ministry on external authority, even God's. He spoke, as Mark reports people as saying, with authority, and not as the scribes (1:22). The scribes worked from texts, exegetically—like Christians! They appealed to Scripture to buttress their arguments—like Christians! (Feuerbach would have loved it!) But Jesus simply spoke with authority. And he taught his disciples to do the same.

Why then does Jesus say that the Human Being forgives, instead of God forgiving (as his entire tradition would lead us to expect)? Apparently the Human Being is authorized to act on God's behalf. Jesus does not contemplate a God outside the universe intervening to heal the paralytic, but as a power that can be evoked in suffering human beings themselves. That power is put into action by faith-acts: take up your bed and walk! What Jesus says arouses the Human Being in the other. Jesus knows that the Human Being has its locus in himself, but it also has its locus in the paralytic. The Human Being seems to function as the mediator of God's intent for our becoming whole.

When the church ceased to read the reference to the Human Being here as universal empowerment to forgive sins, and took it instead as a Christological title more or less equivalent to Christ and Son of God, the authority to declare people reconciled to God ceased to be common property of the New Humanity established by Jesus. Instead it became the sole prerogative of Jesus and, through ordination, of those who continued to represent him as the official leaders of the church. With ordination, the rank-and-file members were stripped of the authority to declare others forgiven on behalf of God. The "laity" became passive recipients of grace and thus emptied themselves once again into transcendence.

C. Foxes Have Dens: Luke 9:58 // Matt. 8:20 // Gos. Thom. 86

^{58} And Jesus said to him, "Foxes have dens, and the birds of the sky have nests; but this mother's son has nowhere to rest his head." (Scholars Version, modified)

This is the only son-of-the-man saying that has multiple independent attestations (Q and *Gos. Thom.* 86). It appears to be authentic. The problem is making sense of it. Is it a disguised political swipe: foxes ("that fox [Herod]," Luke 13:32) have their lairs, and those marching under the Roman eagle (Luke 17:37) have their encampments, but the human and humane ruler is deemed "a worm and no man," and denied his proper homage and habitation?[29] It is not difficult to imagine Jesus giving expression to the hardships imposed by his itinerant mission. But why would he or his disciples have repeated what looks like a self-pitying complaint, and why would it have been preserved in collections of sayings intended to challenge others to a permanent commitment towards God's rule whatever comes?[30] "For Jesus to use the mere lack of a bed to call his own," says Mahlon Smith, "even if it was a fact of his chosen lifestyle, to declare that vermin and scavengers had more than he, makes him seem not only bitter but petty."[31] "If you can't stand the heat, stay out of the kitchen!" Besides, we do know that he had a home in Nazareth (Mark 1:9) and, later, Capernaum (Mark 2:1).[32] Nor is it plausible that Jesus was a Cynic sage complaining of hardship.

Superficially at least, Jesus and his disciples may have resembled the Cynic philosophers who wandered the world barefooted, sleeping on the ground, with only a threadbare cloak, a begging bag, and a staff. Yet the Gospel writers seem to be deliberately depicting the disciples as "anti-Cynics," in Richard Horsley's apt characterization: no purse, no bag, no staff, and no sandals; and "greet no one on the road."[33] The Cynic Diogenes (d. 323 b.c.e.) liked to proclaim himself

> Without a city, without a home, bereft of fatherland, a beggar and a vagabond, living from day to day.[34]

There are other similarities: voluntary poverty, indifference to what one eats or drinks; unconcern for etiquette; rebellion against law and custom; simplicity; rejection of fame, family, social distinction, and respectable clothing; a significant role for women; iconoclasm; missionary zeal to convert and proselytize; wandering disciples; subversion of existing authorities; occasionally a large response among the poorer classes; and persecution and martyrdom at the hands of the emperors Nero and Domitian. Some similarities are due to the same type of lifestyles. For example, the Cynic Crates writes: "I don't have one country as my refuge, nor a single roof, but every land has a city and house ready to entertain me" (compare Mark 10:28-30).[35]

The differences, however, are glaring. Most of the Cynics had no god, and the rest, at best, expressed indifference or atheism. Among the Cynics there was no worship; no mysteries; no rituals; no healings; no exorcisms; in most cases, no prayers; no dogmas; no punishments after death; no eschatology; no anthropomorphisms; little concern for community; the use of put-downs, sarcasm, shaming, and derogatory laughter; deliberate provocation to shake hearers out of complacency, such as public masturbating, urinating, farting, spitting on people, defecating, and copulating; defense of cannibalism, incest, free love; self-mastery and self-sufficiency as opposed to dependence on God; living according to nature rather than custom; the wearing of filthy garments and the refusal to take baths; unconcern for where one sleeps, or how one satisfies one's sexual desires; and behind all these practices, the quest for freedom and happiness.[36] No doubt some Cynics lacked the brass to offend deliberately;

some were more pious, some even referred to God as Father of all.³⁷ But the Cynic reputation was not built on etiquette.

On top of these observations is the difficulty of determining what documents can be regarded as Cynic, and which contain authentic Cynic statements. Derek Krueger faults scholars who wish to portray Jesus as a Jewish Cynic preacher for sanitizing the bawdy aspects of Cynic behavior. "It is not surprising that studies attempting to draw parallels between texts about Diogenes and texts about Jesus are unlikely to focus on stories of Cynics' spitting, farting, or defecating."³⁸ Besides these points, by making Jesus a Cynic sage, these scholars take him out of his natural Jewish milieu of prophets and wisdom teachers, exegetes and rabbis, and place him in a Greco-Roman context. The result is a Jesus who is more philosopher than preacher, more loner than leader, more humanist than Hasid. The result is a very un-Jewish Jesus. Christians and even Jesus might have borrowed aspects of generalized Cynic behavior and teaching. But I doubt it constituted a very high degree of borrowing.

More must be at stake in this saying about homelessness than simply grumpiness. Arthur Dewey suggests that we are missing the joke, and that Jesus is having some fun at our expense: "Ah yes, that son of man who exists at the pinnacle of creation as Psalm 8 avers—and not a cot to sleep on!" Jesus neither identifies with nor dissociates himself from the Human Being here. He can speak as if the Human Being were he, as if it were other than he, as if it included his disciples, or as if it included this prospective disciple. The title demands as much of them as it does of him. Here again we see indications that the Human Being could denote Jesus and, at the same time, have a collective meaning that took in those following Jesus' way. He does not say, "*I* have no place to lay my head," nor "*I the son of the man* have no place to lay my head," but "the son of the man has no place to lay *its* head." Insofar as Jesus, and others, live the existential uncertainty of the Human Being, they have incarnated it. Such incarnation can be the realization that we can live out of an interior center, secure yet flexible, capable of enduring tension, with a tolerance for ambiguity, anxiety, and conflict, traveling like turtles with our homes on our backs.³⁹ Dogmatic religion exists to protect people from this anxious, insecure openness to the possibilities of the moment.

Whatever else it signifies, the Human Being represents the urge to actualize the self, inner and outer. The Powers are what prevent our becoming. The Human Being is the lure toward our becoming. The Reign of God—God's domination-free order—is the goal of our becoming. Becoming means fidelity to the uniqueness of our own selves. As Jung put it, "Personality is the supreme realization of the innate idiosyncrasy of a living being."

> To develop one's own personality is indeed an unpopular undertaking, a deviation that is highly uncongenial to the herd. . . . To the [person] in the street it has always seemed miraculous that anyone should turn aside from the beaten track with its known destinations, and strike out on the steep and narrow path leading into the unknown. Hence it was always believed that such a [person], if not actually crazy, was possessed by a daemon or a god.[40]

Were such persons crazy? Or were they merely stubborn seekers following the impulse of the Human Being, who has no place to lay its head?

D. Blasphemy against the Human Being: Luke 12:10 // Matt. 12:31-32 // Gos. Thom. 44

> [10] And everyone who speaks a word against the son of the man will be forgiven; but whoever blasphemes against the Holy Spirit will not be forgiven.

On the basis of dissimilarity alone, this passage should be judged authentic, since Jesus does not demonize his opponents, as the church was later to do, even in the Gospels (Matthew 23). Furthermore, Jesus does not treat "speaking against" or blaspheming the son of man as unforgivable, in contrast to the later tendency of the church. Mark has changed "the son of man" to a plural, so as to avoid the suggestion that it is permissible to curse the Human Being. As far as Mark is concerned, it is not permissible. It is inconceivable that a church that regarded Jesus as "*the* son of the man," exalted to the right hand of God, the judge of the world, the Messiah, Son of God, and God, would *invent* a saying as mischievous as this. As James D. G. Dunn suggests, a prophet might dare to blaspheme Jesus on the authority of the risen Christ, but no church would have recognized it as an authentic prophetic saying. We know exactly how they would have responded, because we have their response: "No one speaking by the Spirit of God ever says 'Let Jesus be cursed!'" (1 Cor. 12:3).[41] So while we can imagine the uses to which such a saying could be put after it was accepted into the tradition, I find it difficult to imagine any other source for the saying itself but Jesus.

In the Markan framework, which Matthew follows, Jesus has been accused by a deputation of scribes from Jerusalem of "having Beelzebul." This charge is not one of possession, but of possessing: he is alleged to have brought a demonic spirit under his power to do his bidding. We can see from the Greek Magical Papyri what this entailed. A magician acquires an "assistant" (variously referred to as a demon, angel or god) who is adjured to obey its master in every regard. "He [the spirit] sends dreams, he brings women, men . . . he kills, he destroys, he stirs up winds from the earth, he carries gold, silver, bronze, and he gives them to you whenever the need arises." This demon also "stops very many evil [demons]"—just what the scribes charge Jesus with doing. The scribes are, in short, accusing him of evil magic, and of using evil powers to gain control of people—a power the papyrus expressly promises: "And you will be [worshiped] as a god since you have a god as a friend."[42]

To this charge, Jesus gives a series of devastating rebuttals that probably had no effect. Of interest for our purposes is what he does *not* say. He makes no appeal to any divine or messianic status or authority. He unambiguously regards himself as the one who brings the Reign of God, but he just as clearly indicates that he does so, not by his own power, but by the "finger of God," the power of the Holy Spirit.[43] He does not reverse the argument against his opponents and insist that they are the ones in collusion with the devil. Nor is there the slightest suggestion, notes Douglas Hare, that the vilified son of the man is destined to become a heavenly figure, the eschatological judge, who will give these detractors their comeuppance.[44] On the contrary, Jesus tries to explain the illogic of their position and amazingly concedes them the right to criticize and even blaspheme the Human Being ("everyone who speaks a word against the son of the man will be forgiven"). He simply adds the warning that they should look to their own souls to see if they are not perhaps themselves the blasphemers, despite their sincere defense of God. He thus avoids satanizing his opponents, remaining open to the possibility of their transformation, convinced that the God who heals the sick and casts out demons can even convert those who defend God. He makes his case by a series of statements that assume his hearers' capacity to recognize the truth when they are shown the truth: "How can Satan . . . If a kingdom . . . if a house . . . if Satan has risen . . . if I cast out demons . . . if it is by the Spirit . . . how can one enter?"

His hearers' case against him, however, is pretty persuasive: the devil, in order to deceive people, has raised a false prophet and given him power over demons. Why shouldn't Satan sacrifice a few demons if thereby he can gain a kingdom? The position of the investigatory commission is understandable: they recognize Jesus' power, sense its numinosity and fascination to the crowds, judge his ministry to be destructive to the ancestral religion, and therefore infer that his inspiration is Satan. But rather than confronting Jesus, they were "going around saying" (*elegon*, imperfect, Mark 3:22) their charge to the people, behind his back.

Jesus' refusal to deny their charge outright is astonishing. Does it mean that he is willing to acknowledge that he might have a malevolent element at work in him ("No one is good but God alone," Mark 10:18)? If so, one might conclude that he saw the same sinister element at work in everyone; this at least is the memory of the Johannine community (John 2:24-25). This vivid sense of the universality of sin could be the presupposition of his teaching on loving enemies. He is clear that, in the name of the Human Being, he can make wrong decisions. Decisions are fallible. Therefore one may speak against the Human Being, precisely because it is not identical with the Holy Spirit.

It is curious that he does not say, "Everyone who speaks a word against *me* will be forgiven." He could easily have referred to himself directly. There was no reason of modesty or humility to disguise himself by a third-person reference, since the passage makes no claims about him. Quite the opposite—the Human Being, whatever it is, can be blasphemed. Jesus surely saw his mission as part of a process of transforming life. He attempted to live by the power of the Holy Spirit within him (Matt. 12:28 // Luke 11:20). His choice of "the son of the man" instead of "me" here means that we have three entities to account for: Jesus, the Human Being, and the Holy Spirit. Jesus resists identifying either with an emergent archetypal image of what it means to be human (the Human Being) or with the immanent power of the life-transformative process (the Holy Spirit).

But why then is it permissible to blaspheme the one and not the other? In terms of modern depth psychology we might say it is because the Human Being is not the Self. The latter is the totality, the complete human integrated with all that is. Psychologically speaking, the Self is indistinguishable from God (though not theologically speaking!). The Human Being seems to be more mundane, more a process of emerging consciousness than consciousness itself. It is, as it were, a mediator between the Self and the ego, seeking to bring the depths of the Self to consciousness, on the one hand, and to keep the ego faithfully attending to the Self's longing to incarnate on the other. The Human Being pursues the will of God through trial and error and consequently is bound to make mistakes. Therefore the Human Being may be "spoken against," even corrected or condemned.

The Holy Spirit, on the other hand, is the divine immanence urging us toward our full humanity. In this text, specifically, blasphemy against the Holy

Spirit is consciously calling good evil. Sin is the opposite: calling evil good. Everyone does the latter, says Elizabeth Howes, and this passage assures us that all such sins are forgiven. But to consciously recognize the good and to damn it as evil so devastates the moral sense that one may never recover.[45] The architects of Nazism possessed a moral sense so atrophied that most of them later were unable to repent. Blasphemy against the Holy Spirit must be extremely rare. In blasphemy, one cuts off the possibility of forgiveness, because forgiveness flows from an interaction with the Source; blasphemy is calling the Source itself evil.

This passage about blaspheming the son of the man has, unfortunately, been used to terrify people who are only too certain that whatever sin they have committed is precisely the unnamed "unforgiveable sin." But Jesus is not talking about sin here; that one is anxious shows that the moral sense has not been destroyed. Anyone who can feel guilt can still repent. Even more insidious has been the use of this saying to damn the Jews, who rejected Jesus and had to be disposed of so the church could assume their role as God's chosen people. Tragically, churches have all too often ended up in the same role as the scribes in this story, defending "God" and "religion" against "blasphemers" and "heretics." How sad, when so often these "sinners" only sin was to call the churches to look at their apostasy, a call coming from the one who taught that it was forgivable to badmouth the Human Being.

E. A Glutton and a Drunkard: Luke 7:31-35 // Matt. 11:16-19

> [31] To what then will I compare the people of this generation, and what are they like? [32] They are like children sitting in the marketplace and calling to one another, "We played the flute for you, and you did not dance; we wailed, and you did not weep." [33] For John the Baptist has come eating no bread and drinking no wine, and you say, "He has a demon"; [34] the Son of Man has come eating and drinking, and you say, "Look, a glutton and a drunkard, a friend of tax collectors and sinners!" [35] Nevertheless, wisdom is vindicated by all her children.

This passage certainly belongs to the myth of the human Jesus. In the first place, it is intrinsically improbable that the early church would have created a tradition in which Jesus is labeled a "glutton and drunkard" and not also have included a vehement *denial* of that charge. But Jesus seems to *accept* the charge, and even, in a perverse sort of way, revels in it.

Second, this saying subtly balances Jesus' solidarity with John and his marked differences from John in a way that is nonpolemical. John and Jesus are portrayed fighting on a common front on *equal* terms, but in opposite ways. This runs counter to the tendency, already in Q but present in all four Gospels and Acts, to circumscribe John's role and to establish his inferiority to Jesus.

Third, there is no reason to doubt that Jesus ate with tax (toll) collectors and sinners. There are too many references to them in the Gospels (twenty-five!).[46] Jesus' friendship with tax collectors and sinners was scandalous and an embarrassment to the church. There is no conceivable reason why the church would have manufactured Jesus' contact with socially stigmatized people and every reason to see in that behavior something characteristic of his companionship with the marginalized. The church was simply unable to maintain this radical aspect of Jesus' ministry for any time. Paul is already struggling over who can be included, who excluded, from the community and its meals (1 Cor. 5:9-13; 6:9-11).

Fourth, "a glutton and a drunkard" is the precise charge leveled against a rebellious son in Deut. 21:20, and it is the prelude to his being stoned to death. By applying the expression to Jesus, his opponents imply that he deserves to be stoned. But that is not the way Jesus was executed. So why would the church have invented an allusion to Jesus' execution if it was not the manner by which he was actually killed? Therefore, this passage has a claim to antedate the death of Jesus.

Fifth, one of the earliest evaluations of Jesus by some branches of the early church may have been based on the figure of Wisdom in the Book of Proverbs. Luke reflects that early belief, in which Jesus is not identified with Wisdom, but is merely one of her children, twinned with John, who is therefore portrayed as Jesus' equal (7:35). Both are prophets sent by Wisdom and rejected by the rulers. Matthew changes the phrase to "Wisdom is justified by her *deeds*," suggesting that Jesus is himself Wisdom incarnate. Luke has no interest in a Wisdom Christology, so the presence of this saying in his Gospel must mark an early tradition.

Sixth, the passage can be retranslated into Aramaic poetry featuring the *kina* or lament meter: a three-beat cry answered by a shorter two-beat echo. There is also a rhyming wordplay between *raqqēdtūn* ("dance") and *arqēdtūn*("lament").[47] And there is antithetical parallelism in Luke 7:33-34. This would suggest a Palestinian, or at least Aramaic, origin for the saying.

Seventh, there are a staggering number of references in the Gospels to meals. Jesus seems to have had a predilection for table fellowship and good times. He comes across here as humorously self-ironical and paints a "Falstaffian" (if you will pardon the anachronism) image of himself—an image assiduously avoided by later church iconographers.

There are, however, several negative arguments as well. The first is the lack of integration between vv. 31-32 and 33-35. The structure is

THIS GENERATION = CHILDREN CALLING

A	Counter A
we piped	*you did not dance*
B	Counter B
we wailed	*you did not weep*
A'	Counter A'
For John was ascetic	*he has a demon*
B'	Counter B'
Jesus ate and drank	*a glutton and a drunk*

The problem with this otherwise beautiful structure is that "this generation/children" are doing the piping in v. 32, whereas John and Jesus are doing it in vv. 33-34. The problem may have been created by inadequate integration of the following adage in v. 32. In any case, the saying is confusing. Since it is already found in Q, the Q community or its predecessors may have joined the two pieces infelicitously. Verses 33-35 would then at least antedate Q.

The Q source shows no awareness of the contradiction, so perhaps it focuses on a different logic, as captured by Patrick J. Hartin:

Premise 1: The children of this generation opposed John and Jesus.
Premise 2: John and Jesus are the children of Sophia.
Conclusion: The children of this generation oppose Sophia's children.[48]

A second problem is the statement that the son of man "has come." Does this indicate Christian reflection on Jesus' coming from God? Rudolf Bultmann, who has reservations about these verses, nevertheless grants that "there are no possible grounds for objecting to the idea that Jesus could have spoken in the first person about himself and his coming; that need be no more than what befits his prophetic self-consciousness."[49] Jeremias believes that the underlying Aramaic *'atayit* has nothing of the intentionality of later reflection, but simply means, "it is my task."[50] "Came" is also used of John (Matt. 11:18; 21:32); for both figures, the word simply implies vocation. The Scholars Version of the New Testament paraphrases "come" in Mark 1:38 as "that's what I came for," and in the present passage as "John the Baptist appeared on the scene. . . . The son of Adam appeared on the scene."[51]

What then shall we make of Jesus' use here of "the son of the man" (or of Wisdom's child, Luke 7:3)? It could be a circumlocution for "I"; it could be a third-person self-reference with a gesture ("this fellow," pointing to himself). It could *not* be the equivalent of "a human being" or "mortal" or "I and anyone else in my situation," since Jesus' speech points specifically to the actions of Jesus alone. But we learned from earlier passages that this identity need not be without remainder. Jesus could refer to himself as the Human Being, but he could also be referring to the gathered community. Logically, A (Jesus) is B (the Human Being), but B is more than A.

The "Human Being" here is virtually identical with Divine Wisdom in Wisd. Sol. 7:27:

> Although she is but one, she can do all things,
> and while remaining in herself, she renews all things;
> in every generation she passes into holy souls
> and makes them friends of God, and prophets.

Wisdom is a catalytic agent, who changes things without herself being changed, and who inspires the prophets. So Ezekiel, John, and Jesus are all her children, all of them prophets, all of them catalysts of change. Jesus portrays himself here, mockingly, as a bon vivant who enjoys good food and drink. But he is not necessarily admitting to debauchery. This may be what Frederick Danker calls an "opposition logion," in which Jesus takes the complaint of an opponent and turns it into a self-affirmation.[52]

The issue is not really culinary excess but eating with people deemed social inferiors, pariahs, outcasts, and deviants. Jesus seems to wish to make the point that his behavior is not simply whimsical, or rebellious, or countercultural posturing, but that it is a direct consequence of his divine calling. "The Human Being" has come eating and drinking"—and "come" here refers to his divine destiny—because his meals with the marginalized and rejected are a manifestation of God's domination-free order as a present reality. Wisdom's Child is God's emissary sent to those never invited to the banquet (Luke 14). The Human Being "comes" among them as an archetypal mutation, as an eruption of joie de vivre from the center of a celebratory universe, and all are invited. Jesus comes out of that side of Judaism that could later declare (here, rather heavy-handedly), "We will have to give account on the judgment day of every good thing which we refused to enjoy when we might have done so."

Most amazing about Jesus here is that he not only is unafraid of pleasure, but that he is willing to risk his life for this kind of happiness with these kinds of people. For his effort, he is branded a "disobedient son," a "glutton and a drunk," an expression that, as we saw, implies the penalty of stoning. Jesus proudly accepts the reproach and ascribes the genesis of his behavior to Wisdom herself, whose child he unapologetically is. But he does not claim that he alone has truth. John the Baptist came following an ascetic path, and that is one of Wisdom's ways as well. The problem with "this generation" is that it is prepared to follow neither path, but petulantly pouts, seated firmly on the ground, demanding that its prophets do their bidding. They will answer neither John's call to repent nor Jesus' invitation to the messianic feast that has already begun, even under the conditions of the domination system.

God's all-inclusiveness explicitly includes God's feminine or female aspect here: the figure of Wisdom. Luke preserves the earlier tradition, in which Jesus and John are both Wisdom's children. Matthew identifies Jesus with Wisdom, thus replacing her with the male Jesus. Elsewhere Wisdom is crowded out by the male Logos (Col. 1:15-20; John 1:1-18). This masculinizing of the Godhead meant the suppression of the female aspect of Wisdom in the Godhead. This process took place alongside the general devaluation of the feminine and of females in Christianity. In the long run, Christian churches would abandon the Wisdom tradition's acceptance of ambiguity and inclusiveness in favor of an all-male Trinity and a rigid orthodoxy.[53] Consequently, churches are often the last place where most "tax collectors and sinners" feel welcome or wanted.

F. The Human Being Refuses Signs:

Mark 8:11-12 // Matt. 16:1-4; Luke 11:29-30 // Matt. 12:38-40

> [11] The Pharisees came and began to argue with him, asking him for a sign from heaven, to test him. [12] And he sighed deeply in his spirit

and said, "Why does this generation ask for a sign? Truly I tell you, no sign will be given to this generation." (Mark 8:11-12)

Here Jesus refuses any kind of sign that would externally authenticate his divine mission. If he has already, right before the people's eyes, healed the sick, cast out demons, and brought an authoritative message from God, what sort of "sign" could surpass these? So he refuses. Q, however, has a different form of the tradition:

> [29] When the crowds were increasing, he began to say, "This generation is an evil generation; it asks for a sign, but no sign will be given to it except the sign of Jonah. [30] For just as Jonah became a sign to the people of Nineveh, so the Son of Man will be to this generation. (Luke 11:29-30)

Specifically, Jesus identifies his preaching of repentance with Jonah's. "The Son of Man *will be* to this generation what Jonah was to the Ninevites, namely, a sign, and he will be the *only* sign to be given to it," writes A. J. B. Higgins. Consequently, Higgins sees no essential difference in meaning between the prediction of the sign of Jonah in Q and the refusal of any sign at all in Mark 8:12.[54] The point seems to be that one's standing in the last judgment will be determined by one's response to Jesus' preaching of repentance now, in "this generation." Wisdom's Child will not come in the future to judge; rather, he is the present standard by which one will be judged in the future. Repentance—literally "getting a new mind," a mind that goes beyond one's old ways of thinking—is the doorway to the dawning Reign of God. It is not possible to stand outside the door and to view God's Reign, and then, if it prevails, to throw one's lot with it. Rather, Jesus challenges his hearers to risk everything in the knowledge that one's present life has reached its end, and that a new life and new world await on the other side of the door; one simply must leave that old life behind.

One can understand Jesus fully identifying himself here with the Human Being. But it is also possible that Jesus sees the emergence of the Human Being as one of the significant new events in his ministry. As the Human Being's bearer and revealer, he can identify with it, but not exclusively. As we have seen, the disciples too are a part of this disclosure. Hence—as Adela Yabro Collins points out—in the verses that immediately follow, the formulations "*something* greater than Solomon" and "*something* greater than Jonah" are somewhat surprising. We expect "someone greater" than Solomon and Jonah, namely, Jesus, the son of man.⁵⁵ But Jesus does not point to himself. That is why he refuses to do a "sign." He is only the bearer of Sophia's Child. And yet he also cannot deny that he incarnates that new reality, so much so that he can virtually use it as a nickname for himself, in a way similar to Yahweh's use of the phrase for Ezekiel. Jesus thus identifies himself as a prophet like Ezekiel and like Jonah, divinely authorized, needing no external qualifications or credentials, no ordination or diplomas. But what a difference between Jesus declaring that he *himself* is greater than Solomon or Jonah, and declaring that what he bears and embodies—the Human Being—is greater.

G. The Human Being Serves:

Mark 10:35-45 // Matt. 20:20-28 // Luke 22:24-27

⁴³ [W]hoever wishes to become great among you must be your servant, ⁴⁴ and whoever wishes to be first among you must be slave of all. ⁴⁵ For the Human Being came not to be served but to serve, and to give his life to liberate [or "ransom"] many. (Mark 10:43-45)

The sayings about the first becoming the last and on service are among the most frequent in the Jesus tradition.

The context of the son-of-man saying here is the power play of James and John, who want top billing when Jesus assumes kingly power. He rejects their appeal, reminding them that the seating plan is the province of the Host, not him. Perhaps as we read this text today we should employ poetic license and imagine that in the Realm of God, everyone will be sitting around with no head table and no assigned seating whatever!

What gives pause is the miscomprehension of Jesus' ministry that these disciples' request betrays. The outrage of the other disciples when they hear of it shows that they harbored the same ambitions.⁵⁶ (Matthew is so alarmed at the obtuseness of James and John that he makes their mother the source of the request; but his failure to edit out the plural "you" in 20:22 reveals that the disciples themselves are the culprits.)

Tödt believes that the reference to the son of man's giving his life to liberate many (Mark 10:45b) is secondary, though early, Palestinian tradition, because it is inharmonious with the context. Jesus is calling the disciples to reverse the customary power relations of society. In this, they are to imitate his behavior. But they cannot give their lives as ransoms for many, as the son of the man does. That has been accomplished in the cross, once for all. The ransom reference, Tödt believes, has thus probably been introduced by the church under the influence of Isaiah 53.[57]

Tödt's argument presupposes a blood theory of atonement, a Christology in which the son of the man is identical with Jesus, and the belief that "ransom" refers to Jesus' crucifixion. But his study questions precisely those assumptions. "Ransom" draws its metaphorical power, not from crucifixion, but from slave manumission. The idea is that of liberating people from bondage to the Powers That Be. That is a behavior that Jesus' disciples imitate. Insofar as the disciples did carry forward Jesus' struggle to liberate people from the Domination System, they too could participate in the Human Being as a corporate entity.

The word "ransom" (*lutron*) is used only in this passage and in the passage's Matthean parallel in the Synoptic Gospels, but its background is the biblical hope that God would redeem the people. Jesus' disciples had been grasped by that hope, says Hooker; that hope was one with the inbreaking of God's reign into the world, with the restoration of Israel, with the new era visualized by Daniel 7, and with the "good news" that Mark proclaimed at the beginning of his Gospel. "It is, in fact, the message of the whole ministry of Jesus," who restores the sick to wholeness and casts out demons by the finger of God.[58]

It is not enough that people should be liberated from the Powers. They must also be made whole in order that they might help others become whole. We are not just liberated *from* something, insists Chris Rice, but also *to* something: the Beloved Community, which embraces freed oppressed and redeemed oppressors.[59] Unfortunately, liberation alone can lead to group empowerment as its own end: black power that excludes white allies, women-only churches and classrooms, reverse racism, ethnic cleansing and international fratricide. Much as some of these empowerment efforts have helped to liberate oppressed people, their failure to liberate *from*, without liberating *to*, has created new separatisms and even genocide. Liberation from, alone, is an idol. Full liberation involves exorcism of the internalized values and presuppositions of the Domination System, and healing from the wounds inflicted by the crushing of self. Liberation *to* requires becoming part of a sustaining community that welcomes even the former enemy. We are liberated in order to liberate. The ultimate service, then, is to give one's life for others. "Far from introducing a foreign concept into the verse, therefore, the word *lutron* expresses the supreme example of the 'service' that is spoken of in vv. 43-5."[60]

Later, as the archetype of the Human constellated around the life, death, and resurrection of Jesus, "service" became invested with increased profundity. What may have begun as Jesus' own reflection on his vocation became a new criterion for humanness and a cornerstone in the emerging myth *about* Jesus. The Human Being who had no place to lay his head, and who changed the definition of greatness, had become a universal standard of human values. In the process this saying may have attracted to itself the Suffering Servant of Isaiah 53, adding depth to what it means to serve.

Whether or not Jesus articulated the earliest form of this saying, it reveals an understanding of existence consistent with what Jesus expresses elsewhere. As to the historicity of the reversal formulas (first/last) and the service sayings, they have often been treated as pertaining only to the church or, at the earliest, to the disciples. But Richard Horsley points out that the governance of society generally is at stake ("kings," "those who rule over the Gentiles," "their great men," "those in authority over them"). Jesus commands his followers to repudiate the patriarchal social-economic-political hierarchy that constituted institutionalized injustice. One who would be "great" or "first" would have to be a servant—"which meant in effect there could be no great kings and high officials at all in the renewed Israel."[61]

In this passage, Jesus is depicted as dealing gently with the disciples' projection of worldly power onto him. He challenges them to take up the cup and baptism of suffering, and to leave the outcome to God. He points beyond himself to the Source, as if to say: Instead of centering your devotion on me, can you be devoted to what I am devoted to? They sense power in him, far greater than any they have experienced, and they want to share in that power, not by finding it deep within them, but by riding Jesus' coattails into office.

Jesus' death at the hand of the Powers would serve to expose the Domination System for what it is: a massive engine of greed and covetousness fueled by the sweat of unjustly treated workers and the blood of innocent victims. The death of Jesus and some of his disciples would "ransom many" by unmasking the Powers and revealing their defection from their divine vocations. The redemptive suffering of the few would show others a new world of power relations in which "success" is measured by the capacity to help liberate others, not out of emptiness, but out of the fullness of the Human Being. Thus, against the drift of later Christology, the book of Revelation depicts Satan's expulsion from heaven as the work, not of Jesus, but of Jesus' followers, who, in heavenly collaboration with Michael and his angels, "have conquered him [the Dragon, Satan] by the blood of the Lamb and by the word of their testimony" (12:11).

How easy it is to turn the *experience* of dying to the Powers (symbolized by the cup and baptism, Mark 10:38-39) into sacraments, in which we repetitiously remember Jesus' dying for us without necessarily dying to the Powers ourselves.

(The churches' liturgies of baptism and Eucharist could easily be rewritten to make explicit this liberating element.) People do not give up their dreams of power lightly; James and John show us that. And yet power is itself not the problem, but how we relate to power, what kind of power, and to what ends we put power. Community organizer Greg Galluzo remarks that power is a sign of God's presence, and where power is absent, evil will be perpetrated. Hence, the more people who have power the better.[62] Power can mean the capacity to dominate (Mark 10:42), or the power to prevent domination (10:43-45). Christians have projected so much power onto God that there is little left for themselves. We have rightly understood that an unredeemed ego cannot be trusted to exercise power responsibly, that the ego must be mortified so that the power of the Holy Spirit can act safely through us. But many have heard that formulation as avoidance of power altogether, fulfilling Feuerbach's objection by emptying themselves of their own most integral powers.

The gospel comes with power: "For the kingdom of God depends not on talk but on power" (1 Cor. 4:20). Christians are taught not to be ambitious, but to be self-effacing servants of the Lord. But, asks Elizabeth Howes, was Jesus not ambitious? Did he not aspire to end oppression and to replace it with the kingdom of God? Did he not want to open people to true living in the fullest sense, to unite them with his heavenly Abba, to reveal to people that they are infinitely beloved of God? Was it not his ambition to actualize the Human Being in himself and others fully, to embody his vocation, to use himself completely for God?[63]

Howes continues: Does Jesus serve in order to *find* life, or does he serve because he *has found* life? Is serving a way *to* life, or is service the overflow from having *discovered* life? Christians have too often performed acts of service in order to "earn" eternal life. They attempt to obey Christ, who said they should serve. But Jesus served not in order to get somewhere but because he had gotten somewhere. For him, you do not lose life to serve people, but the reverse: you serve people because you have lost and found your life. You serve out of joy, not obligation. Service is not the way, but a consequence of having found the way.[64]

Ambition can be positive or negative. In his vision of the new order of God, Jesus offers us a way to pour ourselves into an ambition worthy of our lives. And in his critique of domination, he shows us how to avoid the pitfalls of egocentric ambition.

There is a downside to this saying about service. It has been used to keep slaves docile, all in the name of serving God by serving one's master. Many women find the sayings about the great reversal (the first shall be last, and the last first) to be good news, but not the business about being slaves to all. They too long have been forced into the servant role by patriarchal families, churches, and an oppressive economic system. (Perhaps it is significant, then, that Jesus' advice was issued to *men* who aspired to greatness and dominion.) The reversal of first to last and last to first has nurtured fantasies of revenge rather than promoting all as *equal*.

What then is the son of the man in Mark 10:45 ("For the Human Being came not to be served but to serve, and to give his life as a ransom for many")? What we receive is a new image of human beings, ransomed from what possesses, oppresses, or depresses us. We are delivered from ladder climbing and from getting ahead, liberated to be responsive to the needs of each other. In this epochal reversal, power itself is cleansed of its association with might, the elite, sovereignty, ranking, and stratification. A new human order is established in which the ambition to excel, to transcend our limitations, and to develop our full potential is purified of the desire to be on top.

Jesus' saying about serving and giving also preserves the individual/collective complementarity that we often see in reference to the Human Being. As Morna Hooker writes:

> In this pattern [of service and suffering for others] Jesus and his followers are inextricably bound together: the necessity which is laid upon the Son of man is laid also upon the disciple. We must conclude that "the Son of man" is either a corporate term (as in Daniel) or a designation for one who is closely linked with his followers (as in Enoch).[65]

We saw earlier how that same archetypal image, at about the same time as the New Testament was being written, burst into the world in the Similitudes of Enoch. The image describes the great reversal that would thrust the marginalized into the center, when "that son of man" would destroy the Domination System and put in its place—domination by the elect! We find the same lust to counterdominate in Daniel which promises that the "one like a human being" would receive "dominion and glory and kingship, that all peoples, nations, and languages should serve him"—everlastingly (Dan. 7:14). Too often the valid critique of domination leads to new forms of domination. That is why the great reversal must be held in tension with the sayings on service. Unless our orientation toward power itself is altered, our schemes for ending domination will usher in new blood-drenched nightmares of righteous revolution. Jesus both maintains solidarity with the oppressed and refuses to endorse their visions of revenge. In his gospel, the nonviolent God seeks to overcome domination without creating new forms of domination. What Jesus or the early church comprehended in the expression "the son of the man" in this passage was a self-rectifying movement that implies a whole new politics. The faltering development of democracy today remains the battered yet promising prospect of fulfilling the front edge of that dream: a remote but nevertheless significant premonition of the Beloved Community.

H. THE HUMAN BEING SEEKS AND SAVES THE LOST: LUKE 19:10

^{10} For the Human Being came to seek out and to save the lost.

There is no reason to regard this saying as apocalyptic or inauthentic. Jesus could have said something like this in his encounter with Zacchaeus or elsewhere. Similar words are said in Luke 5:32 and 7:34; see also the variant in Luke 9:56—"For the son of the *anthrōpou* has not come to destroy the lives of *anthrōpon* but to save them." We find similar statements in Matt. 18:11—"For the child of the Human One came to save the lost," and Mark 10:45—"For the Child of the Human One came . . . to give up his life as a ransom for many." (Compare Ezek. 34:16—God "will seek the lost.") These parallels, of course, do nothing to prove that Jesus uttered these words. They are consistent, however, with the original impulse of Jesus, and deserve to be included in the data bank that comprises the myth of the human Jesus.

This text provokes the question: why did Christianity become such a powerful missionary religion? Judaism was not. A Jew was born a Jew, and while provision was made for proselytes (converts) and God-fearers (supporters who did not convert), Jews were largely content to maintain the ancestral religion. So why did Christianity develop such a passion and urgency about converting the world? There is little evidence in the New Testament that the delay of the second coming was a major problem for the church. The notion of saving as many souls as possible before the end of the world presupposes a vivid fear of hellfire for unbelievers. But while there was plenty of fire-fear in the New Testament, the focus is on saving oneself, not total strangers. The Zacchaeus story helps us understand at least something of that missionary impulse.

Jesus himself seems to have been the source of the gospel's urgency. According to the account of his baptism, Jesus received a powerful call to preach the reign of God. His calling, to judge from the teachings ascribed to him, included a revelation of the nature of the Domination System and the antidote for it. Compassion for the victims of domination—of poverty, inequality, illness, and possession by the mentality of domination—drove him to keep moving throughout the land and to abandon the normal conveniences of living ("the Human Being has nowhere to lay its head"—Luke 9:58). Love drove him, not fear or the end of time or the last judgment. The Spirit of God drove him, and through it the power that flowed from the future, the inbreaking communion of God (Matt. 12:28 // Luke 11:20).

Zacchaeus caught sight of what someone called "the God-possible response." He grasped the incompatibility between his greed and his desire to become a Human Being. Jesus declares, "Today, salvation has come to this house, because he too is a son of Abraham. For Wisdom's child came to seek out and to find the lost." This conclusion places the particularity of "the practice of Jesus" in the universal context of the arrival of God's new order. The Human Being may be a wanderer (Luke 9:58), but it is not lost; rather, it seeks what is lost. To see this, and not want to share it, was unthinkable.

I. The Human Being Must Suffer . . .

Thirteen prophecies of Jesus' death in the Synoptic Gospels include the expression "the son of the man," none of them in Q. In four sayings in the Fourth Gospel, Jesus speaks of the Human Being's glorification by being "lifted up" onto the cross. These Johannine sayings scotch any attempt to ascribe this class of sayings to the inventiveness of Mark. Seven of the Synoptic sayings reproduce the phrase "the son of the man will be delivered" or "betrayed" (using the same Greek word, *paradidōmi*) with execution the final outcome. The other six predict that "the son of the man must suffer many things and be rejected" (three times), be "treated with contempt" (Mark 9:12), or simply "suffer" (Matt. 16:21; 17:12). Most of the references to being "delivered" appear in mini-passion narratives, which has led scholars to regard these as predictions created by the church after the crucifixion. Such thumbnail sketches of the outcome of Jesus' ministry would have been ideal for the early preachers, who could detail aspects of the Jesus story and then wind up with brief summaries like this one from Mark 10:33-34—"The son of the man will be handed over to the chief priests and the scribes, and they will condemn him to death; then they will hand him over to the Gentiles; they will mock him, and spit upon him, and flog him, and kill him; and after three days he will rise again." These predictions seem too full of details from the passion narrative to be actual prophecies of Jesus (who apparently suspected, even close to the end, that he might be stoned rather than crucified). Surely we can conjecture that Jesus anticipated being executed without having to affirm the historicity of these full-blown "mini-passion narratives."

However, Catchpole and Hare argue that either Mark 8:31 or something like it must already have been in Mark 8:27-33, for it is inconceivable that any Christian community would have called Peter "Satan" or rejected the messianic title so vehemently. The frequency of son-of-the-man sayings related to suffering opens the possibility that the connection is early. It would have been more natural for the Christian creator of a passion prediction to have attributed first-person language to Jesus rather than this awkward third-person idiom.[66]

Perhaps the "suffer many things" predictions derive from one or more authentic sayings in which Jesus anticipated his death without providing the details (which he could not have known since it had not yet happened). A number of passages make no reference to Jesus' execution, resurrection, or the agents of his death. They simply observe that the son of the man "is to go through many sufferings and be treated with contempt" or "must suffer many things and be rejected by this generation." If we deduct from Mark 8:31 the details of Jesus' execution and resurrection, we have a similar saying: "The Human Being must undergo great suffering, and be rejected." One might also make the case that the *paradidōmi* sayings referred originally to Jesus being "betrayed" or "handed over" to the authorities for execution. That Judas's treachery is implied gives this speculation added weight, since the church was not likely to have created a betrayer in its inner circle when the blame could have been laid at the door of the religious leaders and Roman occupiers.

I assume that once Jesus made the decision to go to Jerusalem, he would have regarded his death there at the hands of the authorities to have been virtually inevitable. That he would have expressed this expectation to his disciples is also likely. Numerous troublers of a false peace have anticipated the death that the Powers eagerly visited upon them. There is nothing supernatural about such foreknowledge. Luke 13:31-33 provides a good example of the kind of prediction Jesus must have made: "It is impossible for a prophet to be killed outside of Jerusalem." Hare's conclusion is judicious: "While some of these [suffering-son-of-the-man sayings] are probably redactional, Mark derived his model for speaking of Jesus' passion in this way from earlier tradition. For our purposes it is immaterial which of the sayings corresponds most closely to the model Mark followed. All the sayings equally reflect the tradition (authentic or inauthentic) that Jesus spoke to his disciples about his impending passion in third-person statements employing 'the Son of man.'"[67]

Thus these sayings should be regarded as both authentic and inauthentic: an authentic prediction later elaborated in light of the actual event. That "the son of the man" appears in all seventeen passion predictions is striking. The tradition's insistence on using "the son of the man" instead of the fully sufficient "I" requires explanation. Why is the Human Being in these predictions at all?

Wisdom's Child, the son of the man, seeks to incarnate God in the human species. That Human Being lures people to the fuller humanity that is God, the Human One, and is exemplified by the life of Jesus. But this process is not one to which human beings respond with uniform enthusiasm. Few want to take on the sufferings of God. It is much easier to let someone else carry this dynamic and demanding supernova of the soul than to open ourselves to its birth within us. Like a baby bird pecking the inside of its shell, the Child of the Human wants to be hatched in us. But our world finds the Humanchild an intolerable threat. The Domination System is able to survive only as long as it can delude people into believing that it is in their best interests to abandon their best interests. Domination is taught from the start, in the home ("domination" is from the Latin *domina,* the one pertaining to a house, or the subduing one). It seduces its devotees into competing for a limited amount of prestige, wealth, and honor in an economy of scarcity, and it reserves the right to pronounce acceptance and rejection. The Domination System is calculated to crush the spirit and to produce predictable and pliant people to staff its economy and armies. The Human Being cracks open the shell of something new. But human beings are terrified by the sound of that scratching deep inside. The sound reminds them of their deprived humanity, which they know instinctively cannot be recovered without painful inner resistance and a massive reaction from the Powers. Drug addicts, multibillionaires, dictators, or perhaps simply bad teachers and domineering bosses—such people are seldom interested in changing, and they know how to deal with anyone who challenges them. To take on those who have power over our lives inevitably will require that one "suffer and be treated with contempt" and "be rejected by this generation."

The normal reaction to the threat of the new is resistance. Jesus' ministry stirred resistance at every turn. Yet he persevered, because resistance can mean, not just rejection, but a last-ditch attempt to quash the new. The vehemence of the resistance may betray an unwanted fascination with the new. (Think of Paul persecuting Christians up to the moment of his transformative vision of Jesus in Acts 9.) Resistance can be the final convulsion of the old order and a harbinger of change. The intent of the regressive pull (the "satanic") is to prevent consciousness; but when the regressive pull encounters consciousness, the resistance can hone consciousness and enable movement forward. So Jesus continued to sow the word, though most of it fell on unreceptive soil, because the few who faced resistance and overcame it provided a miraculous harvest (Mark 4:1-9 par.).

To be in touch with the Human Being, then, is to be vulnerable to suffering at the hands of the collective. Jesus warns people to expect suffering. This reading is buttressed by another saying about the Human Being that also anticipates suffering: "Blessed are you when people hate you, and when they exclude you, revile you and defame you on account of the son of the man" (Luke 6:22). But here it is disciples generally, and not just Jesus, who are the objects of rejection. Historically, the Human Being in this beatitude has been identified with Jesus. Perhaps we can see it instead as Divine Wisdom pressing for actualization in Jesus and in his disciples. For what is emerging is a new human being who no longer lives from the enticements, blandishments, and threats of the prevailing order. Rather, the new Human Being offers immediate relationship with the truly Human One, who alone holds the secret of our true nature and the society that could be.

I believe that Jesus himself articulated the necessity that the Human Being must suffer at the hands of the powers. (And if it was not Jesus, then it was someone else who understood the inevitability of resistance by the Powers equally well, so the saying is true regardless.) Scholars have long pondered what might be the Scripture to which Jesus was referring when he asks in Mark 9:12, "How then is it written about the son of the man that he is to go through many sufferings and be treated with contempt?" The consensus has been that no such passage exists. But it is in Scripture, wide as a house, in the fountainhead of son-of-man traditions: Ezek. 2:1—3:11. There we hear that the son of man must speak to a nation that has rebelled against God, a people who are like briers and thorns and scorpions who will not listen to what the son of man brings. The people, the text says, have foreheads of flint and stubborn hearts, and they hate the son of man for telling them a truth they cannot bear. Thus the son of man is rejected and treated with contempt. The whole Book of Ezekiel is an account of the son of man's sufferings and endurance of contempt. So Jesus, as the heir or "son" of that "son of man," Ezekiel, can scarcely escape a similar fate, since he is doing similar things.

True humanity, then, is not defined by the values of the Domination System, in which strength, power, and wealth prevail, and the "beautiful people" rise to the top. A real human being is an accusation against the counterfeit personalities that clutter magazine racks of our grocery checkout lines, and a challenge to the Powers That Be.

How curious that the Gospels nowhere describe Jesus as possessing exemplary qualities of character and action. No doubt he had such qualities, but the Gospel writers' interest lay elsewhere: in Jesus' attempts to establish a beachhead for a new reality. He is not an exemplar of perfection. He is, instead, a broken figure. Only those alienated by "this world" find him attractive, compelling, and magnetic. From the perspective of the "beautiful people"—the powerful, the successful, the achievers, the self-made-Jesus is a loser.

This insight casts a different light on the frequently used expression "it was necessary" in reference to the Human Being's execution. "It was necessary (*dei*)," in the sense of "inevitable," that "the Human Being *must* be lifted up" on the cross (John 12:34), "that the Human Being *must* be handed over to sinners, and be crucified" (Luke 24:7), that the Human Being "*must* endure great suffering and be rejected" (Mark 8:31 par.).

What creates the inevitability of crucifixions (and lynchings, disappearances, torture, assassinations, massacres, executions, and rape as state policy) are the requirements of power. Something coldly calculating exists in these forms of state and vigilante terrorism. The actions seldom are carried out in the hot flush of anger, but are usually bureaucratically conceived and executed. The death of Jesus was not "necessary" because God needed Jesus killed in order to save the world. Rather, Jesus was killed because the Powers are in rebellion against God and are determined to silence anyone who slips through their barbed-wire perimeter with a message from the sovereign of the universe. "For the Human Being is going as it has been determined, but woe to that one by who he is betrayed!" (Luke 22:22). God and Scripture could anticipate Jesus' death, but the Powers themselves are the perpetrators.

The early Christians made the necessity of suffering and rejection a virtue, and celebrated their marginalization by the dominant society. As Ignatius of Antioch (second century) thundered, "The greatness of Christianity lies in its being hated by the Domination System (*kosmos*), not in its being convincing to it."[68] In their experience of the Human Being, Christians had learned what it means to be treated with contempt and to be rejected. They were able to ascribe meaning to that suffering by seeing Jesus as their forerunner in the faith. In turn, they were living out the suffering of the Human Being in their own history. This provides us an insight into Jesus' choice of "marginal" people: they are those who the dominant and dominating culture has failed to "decompose." That term comes out of Central Europe and the Balkans, where the communist dictators did not employ murder on a wide scale, but aimed rather at what the Stasi, the East German secret police, called the "decomposition" of people. As Roger Cohen describes it, "Decomposition meant blocking people from acting.

It meant paralyzing them as citizen by convincing them that everything was controlled. It meant the relentless application of a quiet coercion leading to compliance." For the East German state, it was better to have no activity than an activity out of the Stasi's control. Hence, says Cohen, many Germans in the old East Germany are unable today to act on their own free will. This has left them incapable of taking risks or of acting on their personal initiative.[69] The "New Man" that communism was supposed to produce was systematically decomposed in people's souls. This is only one example out of many in which the Human Being is made to suffer and is treated with contempt.

It is exciting to wallow in the numinosity of the archetypal world, to let one's brain spin with Ezekiel's wheels, or to be caught up, with Daniel, in visions of human possibilities. It is another thing altogether to incarnate this numinous power in the humdrum of everyday life in the home, at work, in relationships, in the struggle against institutional evil, or with the homeless on the streets. Individuation is, in Jung's terms, the progressive unification of unconscious and conscious, inner and outer, spirituality and social transformation. It is a long and arduous process, and people often mistake the vision of a fuller life (which we are given to entice us onto the path) with its achievement. Wholeness as image and wholeness as reality are two different things. The self actualized is never the same as the self hoped for.

It might be appropriate, then, to end this section on a more personal note by meditating on the ways we reject the Human Being and treat it with contempt. Why, if God is trying to incarnate in me through Wisdom's Child, do I resist it? What would it mean for the way I live if I were in touch with this suffering and rejected aspect of the Human Being? Do I care enough about the integrity of God's new order that I am willing to take on the Powers, even if it means loss of a job, public disgrace, rejection by friends and family, threats, and even death? Why am I reluctant to be "treated with contempt"? What in the Domination System has the power to silence me, or to keep me in compliance? Can I repudiate the current world order and experience what Paul called "the glorious liberty of the children of God" (Rom. 8:21 RSV)?

For there is a more terrible dimension of resistance: betrayal. Much as it would have liked to, the early church could not forget that the betrayer who handed Jesus to the authorities had come from the inner circle of Jesus' most trusted disciples, "one who is dipping bread into the bowl with me" (Mark 14:20). How was it possible to be with Jesus and then to repudiate everything he stood for? Judas turned his back on everything God had so evidently been doing through Jesus. How was that possible? And why the *kiss?* "Judas, would you betray the son of the man with a kiss?" (Luke 22:48). The horror of that kiss is beyond comprehension. All Judas needed to do was point. Why a kiss?—and no peck this, but a kiss of intense emotion (*kataphileo*)?

"For the Human Being goes as it is written of him, but woe to that one by whom the Human Being is betrayed! It would have been better for that one not to have been born" (Mark 14:21). There is another kind of resistance: one that longs for the fullness of another's being but that despairs of achieving it oneself. For such persons, Jesus represents a living censure and condemnation. Desire draws them to Jesus, but envy poisons their relationship, because they know they can never find such plenitude within themselves. So love turns into antipathy, and the disciple gives Jesus the Judas kiss. The church eagerly spun tales of retribution in which Judas got what was coming to him (Matt. 27:3-10; Luke 22:3; Acts 1:16-20; John 12:4-6). Those at table on the night before Jesus' execution were wiser. They asked, "Is it I?" Well might I—could I—betray my own highest value? To save my skin, to prevent discovery, or simply for the sake of money, would I betray the Human Being with a kiss? Could I—have I—played Judas to my own destiny?

J. . . . And Be Killed (Mark 8:31)

I find it odd when scholars claim that we have no idea why Jesus was killed, that it might have been an accident, a mistake, or a tragic misunderstanding (Jesus was not really a political messiah, he did not really present a threat to the empire, he was just a sage or teacher refining his own tradition and was at the wrong place at the wrong time, and so forth.) None of those "reasons" explains why Jesus was executed. What we do know is that Jesus was perceived as a threat by the Powers That Be. And indeed he was a threat. Building on the words of the prophets, Jesus hammered out the first consistent critique of domination that we know of since the world began. Virtually everything Jesus did or said involved unmasking the Domination System.[70]

Jesus was setting the captives free, and the captors were not pleased. Thus his death was consistent with his life. He shows us not just the liberating God, but the consequences of following such a God in a world organized for exploitation and greed: "If any want to become my followers, let them deny themselves and take up their cross and follow me" (Mark 8:34). This means that the earliest theological explanation of the death of Jesus—the "Christus Victor" theory—was *historically correct*. Christ was the "victor" who overcame the Powers by exposing them for what they were, trumping their final sanction, which is death. The Powers wanted him dead. He was not a "sacrifice," but rather the victim of judicial murder. The Gospels are, in their essence, merely a theological elaboration of that historical fact.

What then do we make of the fact that Jesus was tried and executed as an insurrectionist? Traditional Christologies begin by assuming Christ's divinity, and then speak realistically of his coming "down" from heaven to earth as God incarnate to die on our behalf. Then they speculate about how Christ's blood washes us from all our sins. Sometimes this is seen as a transaction between Christ and God, in which God's honor is offended by our sins, which are so heinous that not even our own deaths can atone for them. Therefore God sends "his" only begotten son to die in our place. Others speak of Christ ransoming us from the power of Satan by his death. Still others speak of God sending the Son to reveal to us the unfathomable love of God, who sacrifices the one most precious to him in order to convince us that his love is absolute and our forgiveness certain. Or Christ is seen as identifying with our suffering and as our representative before God. All of these approaches begin from on high and depict God either as a cruel tyrant and dysfunctional father (Anselm), or as a more benign father who still treats his son as property at his disposal, whom he can freely offer up to death to win our love. All these views share the presupposition that God had Jesus killed in order to redeem the world. None of them makes realistic sense of the fact that the religious and political establishment executed Jesus. Let us recapitulate these positions in greater detail.

1. The Satisfaction Theory of the Atonement

This theory, developed by the medieval theologian Anselm (d. 1109), is usually called the blood-atonement theory. As Richard McBrian puts it:

> Anselm's theory is to be understood against the background of the Germanic and early medieval feudal system. There is a bond of honor between the feudal lord and vassal. Infringement of the lord's honor is tantamount to an assault upon the whole feudal system. A demand for satisfaction, therefore, is not for the sake of appeasing the lord's personal sense of honor but for the sake of restoring order to the "universe" (feudal system) in which, and therefore against which, the "sin" was committed. The feudal lord cannot simply overlook the offense, because the order of his whole economic and social world is at stake. So, too, with God.[71]

Sometimes called the penal or punishment theory of the atonement, the point of this theory is that God chooses to intervene so that sinners can avoid punishment even though they are guilty.72 In pagan cults, the gods were propitiated by those who offered gifts in order to avert the gods' anger or to gain their favor. But Paul declares us incapable of doing anything that can save us. Hence, according to Rom. 3:25, by an act of pure grace, God presents Christ in death as a means of expiation. Believers are saved from God's wrath, then, and reconciled to God not by their own efforts, but by God's own action in and through the death of Christ. But "no effort" translates into human passivity, which emphasizes even more that it is God who does the killing. This atonement theory turns the crucifixion into a voluntary sacrifice, as if it had been God's idea all along. As Thelma Megill-Cobbler notes, even the softer notion that God allows, but does not desire or inflict the punishment of the child, fits the pattern of abusive family systems (as when a parent passively observes his or her spouse beating their child). God thus becomes the model abuser.

At their most extreme, penal theories threaten to divide the Trinity, depicting the Father as a vindictive judge, and the Son as the loving savior who is willing that humanity be saved, meekly enduring an undeserved death. Perhaps the Son is for us, but the Father appears to be against both us and the Son.73

Anselm's younger contemporary Abelard (d. 1144) rightly protested, "Indeed, how cruel and wicked it seems that anyone should demand the blood of an innocent person as the price for anything, or that it should in any way please him that an innocent man should be slain—still less that God should consider the death of his Son so agreeable that by it he should be reconciled to the whole world!"74 The problem with the penal theory is that it pictures God as a cruel and unforgiving patriarch, unable to love as a decent parent should, trapped in his own rules that force him to commit a ghastly crime. In that view it is God who needs forgiveness, not us!

In addition, this theory introduces sacral violence back into the heart of Christianity. Jesus is the scapegoat on whom the sins of the world are laden. He is driven out and killed in a charade of justice that means regression to the sacrificial mentality from which Jesus had sought to free people. Why then have many Christians favored Anselm's theory, especially when there were less vindictive alternatives? Emile Durkheim, I think, put his finger on the reason. He observed that primitive peoples punish for the sake of punishing, seeking neither to strike back justly nor usefully, but merely to strike back. This passion for punishment of offenders subsides only when exhausted by excessive punishment. "A simple restitution of the troubled order would not suffice for us; we must have a more violent satisfaction." The force that the crime encounters is too intense to react with much moderation. Surely a force so powerful must come from a transcendent authority or god.

> [A]t the bottom of the notion of expiation there is the idea of a satisfaction accorded to some power, real or ideal, which is superior to us. When we desire the repression of crime, it is not that we desire to avenge personally, but to avenge something sacred which we feel, more or less confusedly, above us. . . . That is why penal law . . . always retains a certain religious stamp. It is because the acts that it punishes appear to be attacks upon something transcendent. . . .

Now comes the revelatory insight: "Assuredly, this representation is illusory. It is ourselves that we . . . avenge, ourselves that we satisfy, since it is within us and in us alone that the offended sentiments are found."[75]

According to Durkheim, the appeal of the penal theory of atonement lies in the human desire for revenge masquerading behind a concern for the honor of deity. The penal theory of the atonement seeks to satisfy, not God, but our own need to avenge *on behalf of God*, a need projected as God's own need when it is ours. Hence Christians have preferred a God of cruelty to a God of love. Durkheim's theory also casts light on why Americans cherish the death penalty.

There is also a contradiction, often noted, that both Jesus and those who killed him must have acted according to the will of God, and therefore Jesus' executioners were guilt-free, having only acted on behalf of God.

2. The Love Theory of the Atonement

Abelard had championed an earlier version of this view, which we might call the love theory, or perhaps the revelatory theory of the atonement, or even the sacrificial theory: God reveals God's love for us by sending God's Son to identify with us and to offer his life as proof of the depth of God's love. This is the milieu of John 3:16—"God so loved the world that God gave God's only Son, so that everyone who believes in him may not perish but may have eternal life." The theory is reflected in 2 Cor. 5:14-21, especially 19—"In Christ God was reconciling the world to Godself, not counting their trespasses." We find the most elaborate version of this theory in the Epistle to the Hebrews. But this theory still treats God as the initiator of Jesus' death, and still depicts Jesus as the divine Son in heaven who comes "down" on our behalf to demonstrate God's love by his death. However, this wonderfully reassuring theory can be restated in the terms of a Christology from below. As Ernst Bloch puts it: "By the hubris of complete surrender, a person has transcended every past idea of God; Jesus becomes a divine love such as had not been conceived in any deity."[76]

3. THE REPRESENTATIONAL THEORY OF THE ATONEMENT

Dissatisfied with the views above, others promulgated the representational theory. In this view, Jesus becomes one of us so completely that he takes on all our sin and becomes the greatest sinner of all sinners. In Luther's typically pungent phrase, "Christ was to become the greatest thief, murderer, adulterer, robber, desecrator, blasphemer, etc., there has ever been anywhere in the world . . . not in the sense that He has committed them, but in the sense that he took these sins, committed by us upon his own body."[77] God and Jesus concur in willing that the Son assume the flesh and blood of those who were immersed in sin. Now Christ is "wrapped up" and "clothed" in our sins. Reckoning him with sinners, the law puts him to death. "In this duel . . . it is necessary for sin to be conquered. . . . In Christ all sin is conquered, killed and buried; and righteousness remains the victor and ruler eternally."[78]

It is as if the judge renders the impartial verdict, whose punishment is death. But to the sinners' amazement, the judge steps over the bench, comes to our side, and takes the judgment on himself. The charge cannot be dropped because our sin is real; the punishment must be undergone, but God in Christ undergoes it for us. Having fully satisfied the demands of the law, Christ frees us from the charge and presents us to God cleansed from all our sins. "For our sake he [God] made him to be sin who knew no sin, so that in him we might become the righteousness of God" (2 Cor. 5:21). "God proves his love for us in that while we still were sinners Christ died for us" (Rom. 5:8). "Since all have sinned and fall short of the glory of God, they are now justified by his grace as a gift" (Rom. 3:23-24).

This view of atonement is an improvement on Anselm, but it is still a Christology "from above," in which God is still responsible for the death of Jesus, however willing Jesus might have been to die. The Gospel evidence is that Jesus was not executed by God, but by the Powers That Be, specifically, the religious authorities and the Romans. God may have been able to work out redemption *despite* the Powers, and even through the blind operation of the Powers, but God did not kill Jesus or have him killed or even allow him to be killed, and every view to the contrary depicts God as committing an unconscionable sin.

4. The Liberation Theory of Atonement

A Christology from below repudiates the notion that God killed Jesus. This position is sometimes called the "Christus Victor" (Christ the Victor) theory of atonement, but that expression is itself drenched with the assumptions about power that Jesus repudiates. So I will dub it the "liberation theory" of atonement, for that is what the term "ransom" in Mark 10:45 means. ("For the Human Being came not to be served but to serve, and to give his life to *ransom/liberate* many"). It was an absurd literalization that led Origen and Augustine to speak of this "ransom" as a payment Jesus made to the devil in order to win us free. When we speak of someone dying for their country, we do not envision another to whom their life is paid. When someone is liberated from a concentration camp, no payment is made. People are simply set free. Thus Isa. 35:10—"And the ransomed of the Lord shall return." Again, no payment.

This theory sees that people are both sinners and sinned against. They may be guilty of letting themselves be used to further the interests of the Powers, in exchange for financial and social benefits. They may be guilty of collusion in the repression of other races, classes, and genders. They may be guilty of despoiling the planet and raping its resources. They may exploit workers, abuse family members, violate the trust of loved ones, or harm and even kill others. People do sin, and the popular aversion to that word reveals our reluctance to admit our involvement in evil.

But people are also sinned against. Blacks, Hispanics, gays and lesbians, the homeless, the unemployed suffer discrimination. Those who find life unendurable in this System may turn to addictions to ease the pain, further inflicting damage on themselves. Young boys and girls seduced by their priests or clergy, or women who are sexually abused or raped, are made to feel guilt and shame for a sin they did not commit. For all these, the sinners and the sinned against, Jesus comes as liberator. There must be radical transformation both for people and for their systems: a new heaven and a new earth, on *earth*.

Jesus is more than a revealer. By his suffering and death, Jesus identifies with all who sin and are sinned against. Jesus spells liberation for those who suffer at the hands of the Domination System, and by his resurrection Jesus shatters the delusion that keeps people complicit with the Powers, and frees them to free others from bondage. Jesus exposes the scapegoating mechanism by which many innocents have been destroyed, exposing it by knowingly, voluntarily, deliberately taking it on himself—as the text always said! He died, not to satisfy the demands of an unforgiving God, but to break the spiral of violence.

In this view from below, Jesus does not come down from heaven and undergo birth from a virgin's womb. Rather, he experienced rebirth through the baptism of John. Of him we can say, not that God incarnated in him, but that Jesus incarnated God. He did so the same way that we must: by trial and error, by sinning, by learning, by listening, by going one's own path, by risking everything, even one's life. "He learned obedience through what he suffered" (Heb. 5:8). In this view, says Ernst Bloch, "the lowly were to be raised up; the cross was to be *smashed,* not to be borne."[79]

Jack Nelson-Pallmeyer suggests an additional atonement theory: what I call "The No-Atonement Theory."

5. THE NO-ATONEMENT THEORY

In this encounter with the paralytic, Jesus simply declared him forgiven. No divine transaction was needed. The son of the man already had the power on earth to forgive sins, and that included *anyone* who knew their sins to be forgiven and who could thus communicate that forgiveness to others (Matt. 9:8). In this view, says Nelson-Pallmeyer, a compassionate God is incompatible with *all* atonement theories. "Atonement theories grow out of the viler and violent portraits of God. They should be placed on the scrap heap of distorted history and theology."[80]

Jesus was not sent by God to die in order to appease a violent deity, nor did he defeat the powers by dying on the cross. His death was not an atoning sacrifice or a way of bringing a scapegoat mechanism to light. It was a political murder meant to sow terror and to undermine hope. His violent death exposes the domination system as oppressive and violent. His resurrection challenges the ultimate power of the system and invites us to be people of God here and now where oppressive systems remain powerful and must be challenged. Jesus teaches us how to live and shows us the risks of living God's compassion in an unjust world.[81]

There is truth in most of these atonement theories. Anselm's is the exception. His blood-atonement theory is beyond being salvaged. Likewise, I find the notion of God causing Jesus' death repulsive, and the thought of a divine being coming to earth anachronistic. But other views of the atonement may have a different effect for different kinds of people, or be of relevance for the same persons at different stages of their lives.

The point is that no religious experience can be made normative for all people. God reaches out to us in love wherever we are and instigates what leads us to wholeness. Each response is divinely tailored to meet our situation.[82] Perhaps a convict who has committed a serious crime that has caused irreversible harm can only come to believe his sins forgiven through the image of God as the judge who died in his place. Some women may need to be released from shame more than guilt, and delivered from a system that demeans them.[83] They may need the embrace of a womanly God who loves unconditionally and identifies with those on the margins.

The virtue of the multiple images of the atonement in the New Testament is that each communicates some aspect of forgiveness and new life without a single model being elevated as exclusively correct. Atonement theories are need-specific remedies for the spiritual afflictions that assail us. There can be, in principle, no "correct" or "true" atonement theories, in the exclusive sense, but only the necessary or right atonement theory in the current phase of our lives.

The real issue behind atonement is whether our anthropology is commensurate with our Christology. If we have a high Christology in which Jesus is divine, but a low anthropology in which we see ourselves as weak, sinful, and incorrigible, we will deny ourselves the powers that we see in Jesus. But if we have a high Christology and a high anthropology, as in the Orthodox tradition, we will be inspired, by our image of Jesus, to develop our God-given powers. Similarly, if we have a low Christology in which Jesus is fully human, and a matching anthropology that acknowledges the possibility of our becoming more fully human as well, then that low Christology is also valid. But a low Christology and a high anthropology will lead to arrogance and inflation and the unreflective assertion that we are gods. The inescapable relativity of Christologies, their number and variety, are eloquent witnesses to the high degree of subjectivity involved. You get the Jesus you need. Our needs change over our lifespan. Our developmental stage will predispose us to the appropriate Christological type. The Holy Spirit will be our guide.

K. Conclusion

This concludes the review of son-of-the-man sayings attributed to the pre-Easter Jesus. I am acutely aware that some of my colleagues will remain unconvinced that the texts above go back, even in part, to Jesus himself. However, as I mentioned at the beginning of this chapter, even if the church did create all the son-of-the-man sayings, they would still represent the church's earliest Christology. Thus the Human Being could still serve as the basis for a new Christology from below.

But at such a loss! For the myth of the human Jesus is a *historical myth*. That is the cross, as it were, on which the study of Jesus is nailed, the paradox from which there is no escape. The myth of the human Jesus can have no credibility unless grounded on data that appear to be both factual and true. Otherwise, what authority does the story of Jesus possess? Why should we preoccupy ourselves with Jesus at all? Unless we are gripped by something compelling that we see in him, why waste the time? Two centuries of painstaking effort have not been in vain. True, the quest for the historical Jesus has not presented "Jesus as he really was." Rather, that quest has all along been the largely unconscious search for a Jesus who can bring us to life.

As the Lakota Sioux, Black Elk, commented about his own rich tradition, "This they tell, and whether it happened so or not I do not know; but if you think about it, you can see that it is true."[84]

Notes

1. The discussion is handily summarized by Frederick Houk Borsch, *The Son of Man in Myth and History* (Philadelphia: Westminster Press, 1967).

2. Elizabeth Boyden Howes, *Intersection and Beyond* (San Francisco: Guild for Psychological Studies, 1971); idem, *Jesus' Answer to God* (San Francisco: Guild for Psychological Studies, 1984).

3. D. E. Nineham, *St. Mark* (Baltimore: Penguin Books, 1964), 107. See also Eduard Schweizer, *The Good News according to Mark,* trans. D. H. Madrig (Richmond: John Knox Press, 1970), ad loc.

4. Marcus Borg, *Jesus: Conflict, Holiness, and Politics in the Teaching of Jesus,* Studies in the Bible and Early Christianity 5 (Lewiston, N.Y.: Edwin Mellen Press, 1984), 153.

5. Phillip Sigal, *The Halakah of Jesus of Nazareth according to the Gospel of Matthew* (Lanham, Md.: University Press of America, 1986), 232 n. 59.

6. See the superb article by Maurice Casey, "Culture and Historicity: The Plucking of the Grain (Mark 2.23-28)," *NTS* 34 (1988): 1–23.

7. Oscar Cullmann, The *Christology of the New Testament,* trans. S. C. Guthrie and C. A. M. Hall (Philadelphia: Westminster Press, 1959), 152.

8. Gerd Theissen, *Sociology of Early Palestinian Christianity,* trans. J. Bowden (Philadelphia: Fortress Press, 1978), 26.

9. Hal Childs, "Son of Man: A Principle of Incarnation" (M.Div. thesis, Union Theological Seminary, New York, 1975), 107–10.

10. Ernst Hammel, "The Cambridge Pericope: The Addition to Luke 6.4 in Codex Bezae," *NTS* 32 (1986): 408, 421.

11. Ibid., 422.

12. Mark Twain, *The Adventures of Huckleberry Finn* (1884; New York: Grosset & Dunlap, 1918), 270–72.

13. Elizabeth Boyden Howes, "The Son of Man—Expression of the Self," in *Intersection and Beyond* (San Francisco: Guild for Psychological Studies Press, 1971), 177.

14. Nicolas Berdyaev, *The Destiny of Man,* trans. N. Duddington, 4th ed. (1937; London: Geoffrey Bles, 1954), 134.

15. José Cárdenas Pallares, *A Poor Man Called Jesus: Reflections on the Gospel of Mark,* trans. R. R. Barr (Maryknoll, N.Y.: Orbis Books, 1985), 22.

16. Howes, "Son of Man—Expression of the Self," 174.

17. See Vincent Taylor, *The Gospel according to St. Mark* (London: Macmillan, 1957), 192–95.

18. Ched Myers et al., *Say to This Mountain: Mark's Story of Discipleship* (Maryknoll, N.Y.: Orbis Books, 1996), 18.

19. C. C. Caragounis, *The Son of Man* (Tübingen: Mohr/Siebeck, 1986), 187.

20. For example, Bultmann, *History of the Synoptic Tradition*, 14–16.

21. Robert Tomson Fortna, *The Fourth Gospel and Its Predecessor: From Narrative Source to Present Gospel* (Philadelphia: Fortress Press, 1988), 113–17.

22. Caragounis, *The Son of Man*, 32

23. Neither Mark nor Luke develops the collective sense of the son of the man in this story. But the fact that Jesus sends out his disciples preaching repentance (Mark 6:7–13 par.), which implies a response of forgiveness, indicates that he has authorized them to forgive. Even if my defense of the historicity of the paralytic story fails to convince, Matthew's collective interpretation in 9:8 still gives us an open window into his understanding of the son of the man.

24. T. W. Manson, *The Teaching of Jesus*, 2d ed. (1931; Cambridge: Cambridge University Press, 1959), 227.

25. Ibid., 231.

26. Manson, "Mark ii.27f." *Coniectanea Neotestamentica* II (1947): 146.

27. Ibid., 235.

28. Ibid., 214.

29. E. A. Abbott, *The Son of Man, or Contributions to the Study of the Thoughts of Jesus* (Cambridge: Cambridge University Press, 1910), 161–62.

30. Smith, "No Place for a Son of Man," *Forum* 4 (1988): 99–100.

31. Ibid., 100.

32. Herman C. Waetjen, *The Origin and Destiny of Humanness: An Interpretation of the Gospel of Matthew* (Corte Madera, Calif.: Omega Books, 1976), 120.

33. Luke 10:4; 9:3; Matt. 10:10. Mark has them taking a staff and wearing sandals (6:9). See Richard A. Horsley, *Sociology and the Jesus Movement* (New York: Crossroad, 1989), 117.

34. Cited by R. Bracht Branham and Marie-Odile Coulet-Caze, eds., *The Cynics* (Berkeley: University of California Press, 1996), 27.

35. Ibid., 44.

36. Ibid., *passim*.

37. F. Gerald Downing, *Cynics and Christian Origins* (Edinburgh: T. & T. Clark, 1992), 134–35.

38. Derek Krueger, "The Bawdy and Society: The Shamelessness of Diogenes in Roman Imperial Culture," in Branham and Coulet-Caze, *The Cynics*, 229.

39. Howes "Son of Man—Expression of the Self," 181.

40. Carl Jung, *The Development of Personality*, CW 17, 174.

41. James D. G. Dunn, *The Christ and the Spirit*, vol. 2: *Pneumatology* (Grand Rapids: Eerdmans, 1998), 165.

42. Hans Dieter Betz, *The Greek Magical Papyri in Translation* (Chicago: University of Chicago Press, 1986), 4–6 (*PGM* 142–195).

43. Matt. 12:28 // Luke 11:20.

44. Douglas R. A. Hare, *The Son of Man Tradition* (Minneapolis: Fortress Press, 1990), 149.

45. Howes, *Jesus' Answer to God*, 72–74.

46. Contra Richard Horsley, *Jesus and the Spiral of Violence: Popular Jewish Resistance in Roman Palaestine* (San Francisco: Harper & Row, 1987), 212.

47. Jeremias, *New Testament Theology* (New York: Charles Scribner's Sons, 1971), 26.

48. Patrick J. Hartin, "'Yet Wisdom Is Justified by Her Children' (Q 7:35)," in *Conflict and Invention: Literary, Rhetorical, and Social Studies on the Sayings Gospel Q*, ed. John S. Kloppenborg (Valley Forge, Pa.: Trinity Press International, 1995), 155.

49. Bultmann, *History of the Synoptic Tradition*, 153.

50. Jeremias, *New Testament Theology*, 83.

51. Robert W. Funk, *The Five Gospels: The Search for the Authentic Words of Jesus. New Translation and Commentary* (New York: Macmillan, 1993), 42, 180

52. Frederick W. Danker, "Luke 16, 16—An Opposition Logion," *JBL* 77 (1958): 231–43.

53. Goodhue, "Jesus as Wino, God as Woman." (New Testament 340, Union Theological Seminary, 1974)

54. A. J. B Higgins, *Jesus and the Son of Man* (Philadelphia: Fortress Press, 1964), 138.

55. Adela Yarbro Collins, "The Son of Man Sayings in Q," paper delivered at the Society of Biblical Literature Annual Meeting, Orlando, Florida, 1998, p. 7.

56. Fernando Belo, *A Materialist Reading of the Gospel of Mark*, trans. M. J. O'Connell (Maryknoll, N.Y.: Orbis Books, 1981), 176.

57. H. E. Tödt, *Son of Man in the Synoptic Tradition*, trans. D. M. Barton (Philadelphia: Westminster Press, 1965), 132).

58. Morna Hooker, *Son of Man in Mark* (London: SPCK, 1967), 144–45.

59. Chris Rice, "Separate *and* Equal?" *Sojourners* (January/February 2000): 43.

60. Hooker, *Son of Man in Mark*, 144–45.

61. Horsley, *Jesus and the Spiral of Violence*, 244.

62. Cited by Stephen Hart, "How Grassroots Christians and Congregations Connect Faith to Local Social and Political Issues," in *SBLSP* (1992), 6.

63. Howes, "Son of Man—Expression of the Self," 182.

64. Ibid.

65. Hooker, *Son of Man in Mark*, 140.

66. Hare, *Son of Man Tradition*, 193, 275; David R. Catchpole, "The 'Triumphal' Entry" in *Jesus and the Politics of His Day*, ed. Ernst Bammel and C. F D. Moule (Cambridge: Cambridge University Press, 1984), 326–28.

67. Ibid., 227.

68. Ignatius, *To the Romans* 3:3.

69. Roger Cohen, "Big Brother Is Still Haunting Society in German's East," *New York Times*, 29 November 1999 (Internet edition).

70. Riane Eisler woke me to this insight in her pathbreaking *The Chalice and the Blade* (San Francisco: Harper & Row, 1987), 120–24.

71. Richard McBrien, *Catholicism*(Minneapolis: Winston Press, 1980), 1:462.

72. Thelma Megill-Cobbler, "A Feminist Rethinking of Punishment Imagery in Atonement," *Dialog* 35 (Winter 1996): 16.

73. Ibid. 17.

74. Peter Abelard, "Exposition of the Epistle to the Romans," quoted in ibid., 18.

75. Emile Durkheim, *The Division of Labor in Society* (New York: Macmillan, 1933), 85–86,99–100.

76. Ernst Bloch, *Man on His Own: Essays in the Philosophy of Religion*, trans. E. B. Ashton (New York: Herder and Herder, 1970), 192.

77. Martin Luther, *Commentary on the Galatians* (1535), ed. Jaroslav Pelikan and W. A. Hansen (St. Louis: Concordia, 1963), 26:277.

78. Ibid., 278, 281; cited by Megill-Cobbler, "Feminist Rethinking," 19.

79. Bloch, *Man on His Own*, 198. J. Denny Weaver calls the Christus Victor theory *The Nonviolent Atonement Theory* (Grand Rapids: Eerdmans, 2001).

80. Jack Nelson-Pallmeyer, *Jesus against Christianity* (Harrisburg, Pa.: Trinity Press International, 2001), 221–25.

81. Ibid., 225

82. James Killen, *Meeting the Savior* (Macon, Ga.: Smyth and Helwys, 2001), helpfully correlates existential need and atonement imagery.

83. See also Leanne Van Dyk, "Do Theories of Atonement Foster Abuse?" *Dialog* 35 (Winter 1996): 25.

84. John C. Neihardt, *Black Elk Speaks* (New York: Washington Square Press, 1932), 4.

16

The Human Being

Walter Wink completes his study of The Human Being *by highlighting Nicolas Berdyaev's notion of the "anthropological revelation"—the revelation of humanity's "christological consciousness." The implications of humanity's christological nature are that we must not look for guidance from "above," nor can we be overly dependent upon Scripture and tradition for guidance. Rather, we must look within and become conscious of that numinous reality that human beings incarnate—God. Jesus reveals both God's desire to "incarnate in humanity" and humanity's call to become human, "as God is human." Wink concludes that what Christianity has to give to the world is not institutionalized religious structures—they are all too often co-opted by the Powers That Be and provide religious sanction for the Domination System. Rather, what Christianity has to give to the world is the "myth of the human Jesus . . . the revealer and catalyst of our true humanity."*

Source: Wink 2002: Part 6, 257–260

> Lo, I tell you a mystery:
> God is human,
> And we are to become
> Like God.

Our spiraling itinerary brings us back to Nicolas Berdyaev, one of the true prophets of the twentieth century and the herald of the anthropological revelation. He believed that the future coming of the Human Being "with great power and glory" (Mark 13:26) will reveal humanity's christological nature. "The Coming Christ will come only to a humanity which courageously accomplishes a christological self-revelation, that is, reveals in its own nature, divine power and glory." Berdyaev bemoaned the false humility and passivity of much Christianity, which withers the people's creative capacities and renders them merely obedient. Christ, he said, will never come in power and glory to people who are not active creatively; for it is the creative act that reveals human nature.[1] But Christianity has often crushed the creative spirit. Believers are made to feel guilty of hubris for reaching too high or risking too much. Authorities punish people for failure, so they learn to defend themselves against possibilities too lofty. Against this tendency, Berdyaev announces the anthropic revelation, which John's Gospel had already declared: "The one who believes in me will also do the works that I do and, in fact, will do greater works than these, because I am going to the Father" (14:12). The same sentiment is expressed in an apocryphal saying about the Human Being: "When you make the two one, you will become Truly Human Beings ['sons of men'], and when you say, 'Mountain, move away,' it will move away" (*Gos. Thom.* 106).

The task of humanity's religious consciousness, Berdyaev thought, is to reveal its christological consciousness. Only the mystics, transcending all times and seasons, have glimpsed the Christology of humanity. Only the Christology of humanity, the reverse side of the anthropology of Christ, will reveal in the humanity of Christians the genuine image and likeness of God.[2] The great insight of Joachim de Fiore (d. 1202), an insight trivialized if treated literally, was that the era of the Father and the era of the Son were soon to inaugurate the era of the Holy Spirit. For us today that means that, for some situations, there is no explicit guidance from Scripture or tradition. In cases dealing with modern science, politics, technology, genetics, abortion, sexual orientation, and even situations in which the injunctions of Scripture are unambiguous, we must still, according to a saying ascribed to Jesus, "judge for yourselves what is right" (Luke 12:57). (And we must even decide whether *that saying* is right. Apparently most Christians have decided that it is not, since they do not live that way.) Our attempts to find guidance by prooftexting are born of religious anxiety bordering on despair. Our purpose can no longer be revealed from above. We are left without external authority, forced to find it within ourselves, like Jesus' disciples in the story of plucking on the Sabbath. The God who commands, withdraws. That absence of aid from on high shows the great wisdom of God. The attempt to limit our purpose to keeping the commandments turns creativity into submission, which is to say that there is no creativity. Only human beings in touch with the Human Being can reveal the truth about the daring now required of us. There can be no divine revelation of this secret, Berdyaev insists. God does not wish to know what the anthropological revelation will be, since to do so would violate the freedom God has given us. More fundamentally, God *cannot* know, because our creative responses, in principle, cannot be known in advance, even by God.[3]

So humanity is called to create a new and hitherto unknown world through creativity. The psychic bearer of that Christology of humanity is the Human Being, the son of the man. For two thousand years this powerful image has languished, unused and ignored, though individuals and movements have kept this archetype very much alive. Many have risked everything, persisting against incredible odds, because something was at work within them—the same archetype that gave birth to the image of the son of the man. Can it be that God within us, hungering to become human, prompts our quest to become human? Theologians have exploited to the limit every conceivable title of Jesus, while ignoring the Human Being. I believe that the time for the anthropological revelation has come, and that the stone the builders rejected will become the head of the corner.

The christological revelation, centered in Jesus, was that God desired to become incarnate in humanity. The anthropological revelation, not yet consummated, is that God has destined humanity, or at least has called it, to become human, as God is Human. We can redefine divinity, not as superhuman, posthuman, or godlike, but more fully as what we already are: human beings. As I said earlier, we are not called to become what we are not—divine—but to become what we are: human. Accomplishing these tasks—God incarnating in human beings and human beings incarnating God—will require great maturity, even heroism. Some will, like Feuerbach, decide that we create God by the powers of imagination, rather than the imagination enabling us to experience God. It is true that the God-archetype evolves in interaction with us, but it is nevertheless transcendent and Other, as all who have encountered the living God attest.

The gist of this book is, simply, that Jesus as the son of the man is enough. What a lean and pared-back Christianity has to give to the world is not its creeds, dogmas, doctrines, liturgies, and devotions, though some of these traditions still hold great validity for many. It offers, simply—Jesus. And the Jesus it has to give is not the Jesus of the two names, or the second person of the Trinity, or the one who is of one being (*homoousios*) with the Father, though people within certain belief traditions may value all these concepts. If the Human Being archetype is to carry out its transformative task, we will need to develop new theologies, liturgies, prayer forms, and devotional practices that can help people tap that numinosity. But I want to worship the God Jesus worshiped, not worship Jesus as God.

All Christianity has to give, and all it needs to give, is the myth of the human Jesus. It is the story of Jesus the Jew, a human being, the incarnate son of the man: imperfect but still exemplary, a victim of the Powers yet still victorious, crushed only to rise again, in solidarity with all who are ground to dust under the jackboots of the mighty, healer of those under the power of death, lover of all who are rejected and marginalized, forgiver, liberator, exposer of the regnant cancer called "civilization"—that Jesus, the one the Powers killed and whom death could not vanquish. Jesus' is the simple story of a person who gambled his last drop of devotion on the reality of God and the coming of God's new world. In the process, he lived out, in his flesh and blood, the archetype of the son of the man, the Child of the Human One, Sophia's Child, the New Being, the Sisterchild—call it what you will—as the intimation of what that new humanity might entail. In so doing, he not only incarnated God, he changed the way people *experienced* God. In short, the gift of Christianity to the world, as the Hindu Gandhi saw with such lucidity, is not Christianity, but Jesus, revealer and catalyst of our true humanity.

Notes

1. Nicolas Berdyaev, *The Meaning of the Creative Act,* trans. D. A. Lowrie (New York: Harper & Brothers, 1954), 336–37.
2. Ibid., 80–81.
3. Ibid., 94–101.

Bibliography

BOOKS BY WALTER WINK (LISTED CHRONOLOGICALLY)

John the Baptist in the Gospel Tradition. Cambridge Univ. Press, 1968.

The Bible in Human Transformation: Toward a New Paradigm for Biblical Study. Philadelphia: Fortress Press, 1973.

Transforming Bible Study: A Leader's Guide. Nashville: Abingdon, 1980.

Naming the Powers: The Language of Power in the New Testament. Philadelphia: Fortress Press, 1984.

Unmasking the Powers: The Invisible Forces That Determine Human Existence. Philadelphia: Fortress Press, 1986.

Violence and Nonviolence in South Africa. Philadelphia: New Society Publishers, 1987.

Engaging the Powers: Discernment and Resistance in a World of Domination. Minneapolis: Fortress Press, 1992.

Proclamation 5: Holy Week, Year B. Minneapolis: Fortress Press, 1993.

Cracking the Gnostic Code: The Powers in Gnosticism. Society of Biblical Literature Monograph Series 46. Atlanta: Scholars Press, 1993.

When the Powers Fall: Reconciliation in the Healing of Nations. Minneapolis: Fortress Press, 1998.

The Powers That Be: Theology for a New Millennium. New York: Doubleday, 1999.

The Third Way: Reclaiming Jesus' Nonviolent Alternative. Alkmaar, The Netherlands: International Fellowship of Reconciliation, 1999.

Editor. *Homosexuality and Christian Faith: Questions of Conscience for the Churches.* Minneapolis: Fortress Press, 1999.

Editor. *Peace Is The Way: Writings on Nonviolence from the Fellowship of Reconciliation.* Maryknoll, NY: Orbis Books, 2000.

The Human Being: Jesus and the Enigma of the Son of the Man. Minneapolis: Fortress Press, 2002.

Jesus and Nonviolence: A Third Way. Facet Series. Minneapolis: Fortress Press, 2003.

Index

Abelard, 291–92
adversary, the, 74–75, 77, 82, 100
Albigensians, 101
analogy, xxvi
angels, 36–37, 44, 49, 64, 67–68, 75, 86, 108, 117, 119, 135, 180
Anselm, 290–91, 296
anthropological or anthropic revelation, 301–3
anthropology: high, 296; low, 296
anti-structure, 185
Aphrodite, 121–23
archaeology of the subject, 15–16, 25
archetypes, 43, 52, 116–18, 126
atonement: the blood theory of, 278; Christus Victor theory of, 289, 294; the liberation theory of, 294; the love theory of, 292; the no-atonement theory, 295; the representational theory of, 293; the revelatory theory of, 292; the satisfaction theory of, 290
Awad, Murabak, 210

Babylonian religion, 146, 157
Bakan, David, 14, 96
Barbé, Domingos, 177
Bennett, Curtis, 119–20, 122
Berdyaev, Nikolai, 181, 301–2
Berrigan, Daniel, 192
Berry, Thomas, 138
biblical criticism, 4–5, 8–9, 14–15, 24
Blau, Peter, 184
Bloch, Ernst, 293
Brown, Norman O., 96
Bultmann, Rudolf, 7, 27, 273

Catharii, the, 101

charismatic movement, xxiv, xxvi, 123
Chavez, Cesar, 48, 208
Childs, Hal, 240, 245
Chilton, Bruce, 246
Christ: and the angels, 45; and archetype, 242; and atonement, 289–94; and creativity, 302; and the humanizing purposes of God, 143; and Jesus, 100; and the Powers, 36, 168–70, 185–87
Christianity: and conversion, 282; and creativity, 302; and Gnosticism, 64; and the gods, 108, 115; and heaven, 52–54; and Jesus, 245, 304; and Martin Luther King Jr., 57; and materialism 69; and the myth of redemptive violence, 161, 163; and nonviolence, 216; and other religions, 124; and Satan, 96, 100–102; and sex, 63
christological nature, humanity's, 301–3
christological self-revelation, 301
Christology: from below, 237, 293–94, 296; high, 296; low, 296
Cobb, John B., Jr., 82
Cohen, Roger, 288
collective unconscious, 43, 114, 138
Collins, Adela Yabro, 276
combat myth, 149, 151, 156, 163–64
communion, 12, 15, 25–27, 27n1
community of accountability, xxviii, 9
Conybeare, F. C., 113
Corbin, Henry, 33, 54
cosmology, 68–69
Cullmann, Oscar, 39, 253

daimones, 111–12
Danker, Frederick, 275

de Chardin, Teilhard, 54, 66, 138, 247
de Fiore, Joachim, 302
decomposition, 102, 288
deconstruction, 14–15
Deming, Barbara, 211
demonic, the, 32–34, 38–39, 59, 112, 116, 140, 142, 175, 180, 269
demons, 37–39, 49–50, 67, 74, 87, 99–102, 107, 111–13, 116, 140–41, 169, 175
demythologizing, 15, 36
devil, the, 66, 72–103, 269, 294
Dewey, Arthur, 267
dialectic, 12, 14, 27, 27n1, 41, 97
distance, 10–15, 20–21, 25, 27n1
Domination System, 144, 149, 155, 160, 168, 173, 283, 285–89, 294–95
Douglass, James W., 203
dualism, 39, 52, 95, 100
Dunn, James D. G., 268
Durkheim, Emile, 291–92

Eliot, T. S., 70, 104–5
Elliott, Willis, 151
Ellul, Jacques, 187
Elwood, Douglas J., 227
Enlightenment, 37, 222
Esquivel, Adolpho Pérez, 207
evangelism, 47–48, 177, 188, 228
evil, 36, 46, 48, 57–59, 70, 71–104, 134, 136, 147–49, 168, 172–73, 175, 178, 180, 204, 224, 280

Fall, the, 124, 171–72, 174–76, 179–80
false consciousness, 6–7, 13
Falwell, Jerry, 161, 217
fetishism, 40
Flowers, Betty Sue, 246
Fox, Matthew, 138
Freud, Sigmund, 14–15, 91, 104, 247
Funk, Robert, xxvii
fusion, 12–13, 15, 25, 27n1

Galluzo, Greg, 280

Gandhi, Mohandas K., 194, 205, 207–11, 247, 304
gestalt, 37, 126, 141
Gnosticism, 43, 63–64, 101, 136, 237
Gnostics, 43, 101
gods, 36–37, 102, 107–28, 141, 146–49, 158–59, 291
Gospel of Thomas, 50, 201, 165, 268, 302
Goss-Mayr, Jean, 227, 229
Guild for Psychological Studies, xxviii, 16, 240

Harris, Sidney, 85
Havel, Václav, 177
heaven, 49–59, 134–38
Heisenberg principle, xxxi, 240
Heitler, Walter, 92
henotheism, 109–10, 124–25
hermeneutic, 6, 8–9, 11, 15–16, 26, 124, 248
Higgins, A. J. B., 276
Hinkelammert, Franz, 40–42
historical biblical criticism, xxix, 3
historical criticism, 4–6, 9, 13, 240, 243, 245
Holy Spirit, 268–71, 280, 302
Hooker, Morna, 278, 281
Horsley, Richard A., 201, 266, 279
Howard, George, 204
Howes, Elizabeth Boyden, xxviii, 16, 252, 256–58, 271, 280
Human, the, 45–46, 285
Human Being, the. See Part V in its entirety
Human One, the, 281, 285–86, 304
humanization, 285

idolatry, 34, 37, 44, 47, 51, 108, 110, 115, 125–26, 168, 186
Ignatius of Antioch, 167, 287
incarnation, 267, 295
individuation, 65, 103, 121, 226, 288
inner aspect, 33, 36–39, 59, 135, 138–39

Jesus: and apologetics, xxxi–xxxii; as Christ, 100, 112, 169; and the criticisms, 13–14; and the Domination System, 185; as Lord, 45; and love of enemies, *see* Chapter 12 in its entirety; myth of the human, 237, 242–48, 271, 282, 296, 304; and the myths of Pagans, 124; and nonviolence, *see* Chapter 11 in its entirety; original impulse of, 236, 246, 248, 282; pre-Christological reading of, 20–24; and the reign of heaven/God, 50, 185; and Satan, 77–99; and transformation, 27
Jesus Seminar, xxxi, xxxii
John the Baptist, 219, 271, 174–75
Josephus, 197, 199, 203
Jung, Carl, 100, 108, 117–18, 123, 126, 138, 172, 240, 268, 288
Justin Martyr, 100

Käsemann, Ernst, 168
Kaufmann, Yehezkel, 110
Kelsey, Morton, 70n2, 72, 138
Khodr, Georges, 159
King, Martin Luther, Jr., 48, 57, 86, 207
Kleinknecht, Hermann, 115
Kluger, Rivkah Scharf, 82
Krueger, Derek, 267
Kundera, Milan, 179

Laszlo, Ervin, 183
LaVey, Anton, 102
Lerner, Michael, 174
liberation theology, 217
libido, 104, 118
Ling, Trevor, 83

Malina, Bruce, 243
Manichaeism, 136
Mannheim, Karl, 6
Manson, T. W., 263–64
Marx, Karl, 14–15, 41, 143, 178, 247
materialism, 32, 34, 54, 64–70, 119, 137
Mattingly, Harold, 184
McBrian, Richard, 290
Megill-Cobbler, Thelma, 291
Messiah, 81, 237
monotheism, 108, 120, 124
mono-Yahwist, 110, 124
Moses, 55, 74, 80, 84, 258
Mottu, Henry, 228
Myers, Ched, 260
myth: definition of, 15, 70n1; and evil, 180; and the Fall, 172; and the gods, 124; of history, 245; of the human Jesus, 237, 242–43, 245, 248, 271, 282, 298, 304; and individuation, 65; of materialism, 32, 65; and the Powers, 35–59; of the Primal Man, 252; of redemptive violence, 146–64, 206–7, 217, 224; of Satan, 5, 86, 103, 170; without redemption, 157

narcissism, malignant, 88
Nelson-Pallmeyer, Jack, 295
Neoplatonism, 51, 136
New Jerusalem, 41, 187–88
Niebuhr, Reinhold, 173, 186
Nietzsche, Friedrich, 6, 15, 118
nonviolence, xxx–xxxi, 171. *See* Chapter 11 in its entirety, 217–19, 229–30, 247
nonviolent revolutions, 217

O'Collins, Gerald, 244
objectivism, 6–9, 14, 24–26, 240, 244
objectivity, 5, 8, 13, 26–27, 241, 248
ontology, 5, 7, 112, 178, 245
Origen, 98, 160, 294
outer aspect, 33, 38, 135

paganism, 100, 108, 113–14
paradigm, 24
paradox, 55–56, 186–87, 296

Paul, 36, 38, 46, 52–53, 78–79, 83, 87, 112–13, 169, 216, 227, 272, 285, 288, 291
Peck, M. Scott, 88
Peretti, Frank, 142
personification, 36–37, 40, 88, 119, 139, 158
Philo, 111, 203
polytheism, 108, 112, 115, 124, 183
positivism, 240
Powers, the. *See* Chapter 4 in its entirety
Primal Man, 243, 252
principalities and powers, 32–33, 37, 67
process theology, 49
projection, 13, 16, 43, 51, 67, 77, 98, 114, 119–20, 139–40, 142, 223–26, 241–42, 279
prophetic tradition, 207
Protestantism, 9, 108, 187, 222
psyche, 81, 97, 101, 114–21, 183, 221, 223
Puritanism, 136

quest for the historical Jesus, xxxii, 241, 243, 297

racism, 57–58, 142, 278
ransom, 277–79, 281–82, 290, 294
redemption, 81, 124, 169, 173, 179, 186–87
reign of God, 54, 103, 173, 179, 185, 201, 209, 223, 246, 267, 269, 276
Rice, Chris, 278
Ricoeur, Paul, 15–16, 70n2, 124, 147, 149
Rilke, Rainer Maria, 122
Robertson, Pat, 161
Rohr, Richard, 244
Russell, Bertrand, 93

Sanders, James A., 217
Sanford, Agnes, xxvi

Satan: as the evil one, 85–94; as servant of God in the Old Testament, 74–77; as servant of God in the New Testament, 77–85; worship of, 101–2
satanic function, 97
Satanism, 102
satyagraha, 209
Schweitzer, Albert, 235, 241, 248
Self, the, 252, 257–58, 270
sexuality, 83, 101–2, 122–23, 136
Slotkin, Richard, 163
Smith, Mahlon, 266
social action, 47–48
socialization, 47, 65, 174–78, 246
Solzhenitsyn, Aleksandr, 94
Son of Man, 18–24, 242, 249n6, 252, 258–59, 262–64, 268, 271, 273, 276–77, 281, 285–86
Son of the Man, 236–37, 243, 249n6, 252, 296, 303–4
South Africa, xxx, 140, 160, 209, 217, 230
spiritual aspect, 34, 37, 136, 139
spiritual blindness, xxix
Stein, Murray, 126
Stevenson, W. Taylor, 245
Stock, Brian, 240
Stoner, John, 216
structural evil, 142, 169
subjectivism, 13, 25–26
subjectivity, 12, 27, 39, 241, 296
Sumner, William Graham, 224
syncretism, 108, 113, 124

technologism, 8–9
Theissen, Gerd, 218
Tillich, Paul, 224
Tödt, H. E., 277–78
totalitarianism, 179
transcendence, 27, 51, 64, 138, 173, 200
transformation: and the Bible, xxxi, 4, 24–25, 27, 245; creative, 82, 94, 99; by the divine, 59; of the economic

system, 170; and individuation, 288; of the oppressor, 205; of Satan, 86, 104; social and personal, xxxi, 4, 24, 27, 48, 56, 173, 177, 188, 207, 216, 244, 294; and the Son of the Man, 236, 252, 269; and the subject-object dichotomy, 25–26

Valliere, Paul, 206
violence: and Christianity, 291; and the Domination System 235, 246; institutional, 57–59, 64; and Jesus, 246–47, 294; mob, 143; myth of redemptive, 146–50; and the national security state, 158–63; one's own, 206–8; and popular culture, 150–58; responses to, 192, 203–6, 320

von Rad, Gerhard, 169

White, Victor, 43
Whitehead, Alfred North, 49, 93, 169
Wink, June Keener, xi, xiii, xxix, xxx, xxxi, 225
witchcraft, 101–2
women, subordination of, 149
World Council of Churches, 217
worldview: ancient, 135; integral, 138; materialistic, 136–37; spiritualistic, 136

Xirinacs, Llius Mario, 227

Yahweh, 51, 74–75, 95, 99–100, 109–11, 123, 127, 161
Yevtushenko, Yevgeny, 184

www.ingramcontent.com/pod-product-compliance
Lightning Source LLC
Chambersburg PA
CBHW051934290426
44110CB00015B/1978